*The Age of*
*Strict Construction*

# The Age of
# Strict Construction

A HISTORY OF THE GROWTH OF
FEDERAL POWER, 1789–1861

Peter Zavodnyik

THE CATHOLIC UNIVERSITY
of AMERICA PRESS
Washington, D.C.

The paper used in this publication meets the minimum requirements of
American National Standards for Information Science—Permanence of Paper
for Printed Library Materials, ANSI z39.48-1984.
∞
Library of Congress Cataloging-in-Publication Data
Zavodnyik, Peter, 1969–
The Age of strict construction : a history of the growth of federal power,
1789–1861 / Peter Zavodnyik.
p. cm.
Includes bibliographical references and index.
ISBN 978-0-8132-1504-4 (cloth : alk. paper)
1. United States—Politics and government—1783–1865.   2. Constitutional
history—United States.   I. Title.
JK171.Z39 2007
320.473'04909034—dc22
2007004674

*Special thanks to Merrill Peterson for*
*his advice and encouragement*

# *Contents*

# The Age of
# Strict Construction

# Introduction

The phrase *strict construction* has been defined as the "narrow construction of a statute, confining its operation to matters . . . specifically pointed out by its terms, and to cases which fall fairly within its letter."[1] In the context of the Constitution, strict construction provides that the powers of the federal government listed in Article I should be "narrowly construed."[2] The vagueness of the charter's terms made a narrow reading of them difficult.[3] What was included in the power to regulate commerce among the states? What was not? Strict constructionists, eager to ensure that federal authority remain within the lines marked out when the states approved the Constitution (1787–88), turned to the ratification debates. They insisted that the understanding of the Constitution possessed by those who wrote and ratified it should control its interpretation. The 1833 Report on Nullification for the Joint Committee of the New York legislature embraced strict construction. It explained that an "inflexible observance of [the Constitution's] specifications and restrictions, by which it was defined . . . by the Convention, and as understood by the people in the adoption of [it], are . . . indispensably necessary to its preservation."[4] Thus strict construction, although a textual method of interpretation in theory, constituted more of a hybrid approach in practice. Its practitioners cited discussions of constitutional clauses that occurred during ratification in support of their own narrow constructions of those clauses.

Americans embraced strict construction in order to ensure that Con-

1. *Ballentine's Law Dictionary*, ed. William S. Anderson, 3d ed. (Rochester, N.Y.: Lawyer's Cooperative Publishing Company, 1969), 1223.

2. *Encyclopedia of the American Constitution*, ed. Leonard W. Levy, 4 vols. (New York: Macmillan, 1986), 4:1787–88. See, for example, Jefferson's argument denying the constitutionality of the United States Bank in *Writings of Thomas Jefferson*, ed. Paul Leicester Ford, 10 vols. (New York: G. P. Putnam's Sons, 1892–1899) (hereafter *Writings of Jefferson*), 5:285–89.

3. As Leonard Levy wrote, "ambiguity cannot be strictly construed." Levy, *Original Intent and the Framers Constitution: The Debate over Original Intent* (New York: Macmillan, 1988), 342.

4. Report of the Legislature of New York (February 23, 1833), in *State Papers on Nullification* (Boston, 1834; reprint, New York: Da Capo Press, 1970), 136.

gress would exercise only those powers that had been granted to it with the ratification of the Constitution—the remaining prerogatives of government were to remain with the states.[5] As St. George Tucker explained in 1804, since each state possesses unlimited sovereign power, "every grant of jurisdiction to the confederacy . . . is to be considered as special, inasmuch as it derogates from the antecedent rights and jurisdiction of the state making the concession, and therefore ought to be strictly construed."[6] In 1854 Senator Isaac Toucey of Connecticut declared that "the role of strict construction is founded upon an essential element of public liberty—the right of each state to govern itself, and to regulate its own internal affairs, without the external control of thirty other states." The alternative would be "mere tyranny without responsibility." Thus the admonition: "the alienation of the power of a state to govern itself must be clearly shown, or the power is not granted."[7] Strict construction is associated with Jeffersonian Republicans and antebellum Democrats, who embraced it during the nineteenth century in order to keep power from accumulating in the hands of the federal government.[8] Under the standard view of American history, they were successful—the federal government remained a feckless creature without influence during the period before 1861.[9] It is the purpose of this book to demonstrate that this view is incorrect. Rather than lacking in power, the federal government quickly acquired a great deal of it, contributing to the sectional crisis that led to secession and the Civil War.

Centralization continued in the years following that conflagration. Even as public authority has continued to accumulate in Washington, strict construction has survived as a method of constitutional interpretation, albeit un-

---

5. Ibid. See also *Blackstone's Commentaries,* ed. St. George Tucker, (Union, N.J.: Lawbook Exchange Union, 1996), 1:98, Appendix, note D ("View of the Constitution of the United States," 1803): "The Constitution itself suggests that it should be strictly and not liberally construed. The Tenth Amendment provides that 'the powers not delegated to the United States, nor prohibited by it to the States, are reserved to the States respectively, or to the people.'" See also 150–55.

6. Tucker, *Blackstone's Commentaries,* Appendix, note D, 152.

7. U.S. Congress, *Congressional Globe,* 46 vols. (Washington, D.C.: Blair & Rives, 1834–73), 33d Cong., 1st sess., June 21, 1854, Appendix, 23.2:990.

8. See *The Oxford Companion to American History,* ed. Thomas H. Johnson (Oxford: Oxford University Press, 1966), 758.

9. "The decline of the powers of the federal government from the constructive centralism of George Washington's administration to the feeble vacillation of James Buchanan's is so familiar as to require no repetition." David Donald, *An Excess of Democracy: The American Civil War and the Social Process* (Oxford: Clarendon Press, 1960), 16, quoted in *The Causes of the Civil War,* ed. Kenneth Stampp, 3d ed. (New York: Simon & Schuster, 1991), 129.

der a different name: original intent. Practical considerations have reduced the utility of this approach, if not its appeal. As critics pointed out during the debate over Robert Bork's Supreme Court nomination in 1987, no one believes that we should interpret the whole of the Constitution according to the intent of those who wrote and ratified it. Judge Bork conceded as much when he acknowledged that the commerce clause was "framed by men who did not foresee the scope, technologies and intricate interdependence of today's economy."[10] The Constitution was a product of the classical theory of republican government, which embraced a minimalist, even negative approach to public power. Created for a world in which the chief threat to liberty was government itself, this ideology saw a virtuous citizenry of landowners as the chief bulwark against tyranny. Such a system might have been appropriate for the eighteenth century, when the electorate of the United States consisted largely of self-sufficient farmers. Citizens of the modern urban state operate in a world that is far more interdependent, leaving them more susceptible to economic dislocation. Nations regulate economic activity and provide a safety net in order to prevent the political extremism that can otherwise result. And so it is with the federal government—the demands made upon it over the last two centuries have grown, and it has responded accordingly. In the process, it has assumed powers that were not granted to it by either the Constitutional Convention or subsequent amendments. While ideologues decry this state of affairs, the fact remains that only by exceeding its designated sphere has the government of the United States been able to maintain a large middle class and the political stability that comes with it.

And yet, as the struggle over the Bork nomination demonstrated, original intent continues to have a certain appeal—thus the difficulties faced by the numerous scholars who have attacked it.[11] In theory it *is* undemocratic and abusive for federal judges—or presidents or members of Congress for that matter—to substitute their own interpretations of constitutional clauses for the intent of the persons who wrote and ratified them. Popular consent—what an Antifederalist once called the "spring" of republican government—was given to those clauses as they were originally presented, not as

10. Robert Bork, *The Tempting of America: The Political Seduction of the Law* (New York: Free Press, 1990), 168.

11. See, for example, Levy, *Original Intent and the Framers' Constitution;* see also Jack Rakove, *Interpreting the Constitution: The Debate over Original Intent* (Boston: Northeastern University Press, 1990).

they were later misinterpreted.[12] Thus James Madison's embrace of original intent. "I entirely concur," he wrote ". . . in the propriety of resorting to the sense in which the Constitution was accepted and ratified by the nation." After all, Madison warned, "if that be not the guide in expounding it, there can be no security for a . . . faithful exercise of its powers." The words alone provided an inadequate guide, in his view, as under such an approach, "the shape and attributes of the government must partake of the changes to which the words and phrases of all living languages are constantly subject."[13] Its widespread use demonstrates the utility and perhaps the necessity of original intent. Contracts are interpreted according to the intentions of their makers. When construing statutes, judges and lawyers focus upon the intent of the legislators who wrote them.[14]

In one form or another, original intent has been embraced by Americans throughout the nation's history. The popularity of this doctrine has not prevented the accumulation of public power in the hands of the national government. By the end of twentieth century, federal omnipotence was complete. While time has demonstrated the necessity of a national government armed with broad regulatory and spending powers, the utility of federal intervention in virtually every area of American life has been less apparent. In support of this state of affairs, advocates of centralization offer a rather idealistic account of the role played by the federal government in the nation's past. This view identifies federal authority with civil rights, protection against industrial abuses, and other positive legacies. It holds, in effect, that the history of the United States has been driven by a successful experiment in which central authority has been expanded with extraordinarily beneficial results. Only the decision to discard the restraining approach to the Constitution that prevailed in the nation's early years has made this experiment—and the blessings it has bestowed—possible.

This account is inaccurate, or at least incomplete. Centralization has hampered progress as often as it has aided it. It is true that only expansions of

---

12. "John DeWitt," no. 3, quoted in Ralph Ketcham, ed., *The Antifederalist Papers and the Constitutional Convention Debates* (New York: Penguin Books, 1986), 312.

13. James Madison to Henry Lee, June 25, 1824, in *The Writings of James Madison*, ed. Gaillard Hunt, 9 vols. (New York: G. P. Putnam's Sons/Knickerbocker Press, 1908) (hereafter *Writings of Madison*), 9:191.

14. "The primary object in construing a contract is to give effect to the intention of the parties involved." *Scheck v. Chicago Transit Authority*, 42 Ill.2d 362, 364, 247 N.E.2d 886, 888 (1969). "The cardinal rule of statutory construction is to determine and give effect to the legislature's intent." *Stewart v. Illinois Industrial Commission*, 115 Ill.2d 337, 341, 504 N.E.2d 84, 86 (1987).

national authority enabled the country to meet its two greatest challenges—abolishing slavery and limiting the excesses of the Industrial Revolution. Yet centralization worsened the strife produced by those great challenges for years and even decades before it enabled the nation to meet them. Before the national government turned out the slaveholder, it long did his bidding. Before federal intervention saved the country from class war in the 1930s, the Supreme Court struck down scores of state laws merely because they conflicted with the prevailing economic theories of the time. Centralization has empowered destructive factions as often as it has served the cause of progress.

During the ratification debates, the federal government's proponents insisted that it would limit the influence of factions.[15] Despite such assurances, antebellum America saw a proslavery minority use the expanding powers of the federal government to impose its views upon an unwilling nation. The excesses of this faction led directly to the watershed election of 1860, secession, and war—and in turn the abolition of slavery. Yet the fortunate consequences of the fall of the antebellum Union do not lessen the significance of its demise. It failed largely because of a breakdown in the federal system that centralized power in Washington and in turn spawned fears among southerners that the federal government posed a threat to slavery. Only by acknowledging and examining this process can we gain a full understanding of the role that the national government has played in American history.

This work is a survey of the growth of federal power in antebellum America and the contribution of that process to the sectional crisis of the 1840s and '50s. It focuses largely upon a series of disputes over the meaning of various clauses of the Constitution. Yet the text is not a legal treatise. Many developments within the realm of constitutional history are left unexamined because they did not concentrate power in the hands of the federal government. Other trends that do not qualify as legal in nature are explored because they played a critical role in the process of centralization. The text begins with a review of the ratification struggle. This crisis reveals that the key feature of the Constitution—the one that made ratification possible—was its enumeration of a handful of limited federal powers. In the years that followed, Americans held fast to the belief that Congress should exercise these powers in a manner consistent with the way in which they were described at the time the Constitution was ratified.

15. James Madison, *The Federalist*, No. 10, in Clinton Rossiter, ed., *The Federalist Papers* (New York: Penguin Books, 1961), 77.

Centralization nevertheless moved forward, particularly after 1815. This trend arose out of a variety of factors, one of which was the increasing popularity of a second method of constitutional interpretation that focused on the words of the charter at the expense of historical context. Liberated from their original meaning, the clauses of the Constitution authorized expenditures for projects formerly left to the states, and subjects once thought beyond the realm of Congress came within its reach. At the same time, an abundance of offices enabled executive branch officials to exercise a degree of influence over state political parties that was wholly out of line with the federative nature of American government. This proved disastrous as industrialization created a large urban populace dependent upon those same parties for protection from exploitation at the hands of employers, banks, and other powerful interests. This dependency combined with federal patronage to vest control over the votes of thousands of impoverished Americans in the federal executive branch. The federal judiciary meanwhile converted itself into a sort of American privy council, expanding the scope of various clauses of the Constitution and thereby bringing them into conflict with scores of state laws, which were held void as a result. In sum, a period associated with a miserly approach to federal authority saw power accumulate in Washington, D.C., at a startling pace. By the time of the sectional crisis at midcentury, the federal government enjoyed virtually unlimited influence. Proslavery elements initially benefited from this state of affairs; they exploited it in creating a national political machine during the 1840s and '50s. With the election of 1860, their work backfired, as southern politicians had to turn over to their enemies the beast they had created. It was no accident that secession followed a change in control of the executive branch. By that point it had become—along with the rest of the federal apparatus—too dangerous to trust to the opposition.

# CHAPTER I

# Ratification, 1787–1788

## THE ARTICLES OF CONFEDERATION

A survey of American Federalism must begin by answering a difficult question: when did federative government arrive in America? Its formal introduction occurred in 1774, when the first Continental Congress took control of foreign affairs while leaving other areas of governmental activity to the colonial assemblies. As a practical matter, federative government had been a fact of life in the American corner of the British Empire from the time the first settlers arrived in 1607.[1] *Webster's* defines an empire as a "state uniting many territories and peoples under a single sovereign power." A federation, on the other hand, comprises "a league of states in which each member agrees to subordinate its governmental power to that of the central authority in common affairs."[2]

Creatures of royal charters or acts of Parliament, the colonies were never in a position to delegate authority to the government that created them. Yet they shared public authority with British officials in a system that allowed them to largely govern themselves. The colonial governments attended to domestic matters, while Parliament regulated commercial activity and determined foreign policy. The Americans enjoyed almost complete freedom from taxation by the home government, as Parliament effectively delegated its power to tax to the colonial assemblies. As the authority to tax forms the most critical of governmental prerogatives, its delegation to the Americans effected a noticeable if quiet transfer of power. This devolution resulted in a colonial system that was federative in practice if not in law. British offi-

1. John C. Miller, *Origins of the American Revolution* (New York: Little, Brown, 1943), 29–30.
2. *Webster's New World Dictionary of American English,* ed. David B. Guralnik, 3d college ed. (New York: Prentice-Hall, 1994), 445, 496.

cials attached no significance to their failure to impose taxes upon the colonies. The home government had merely refrained from exercising its right to raise revenue in America. For the colonists, this omission made all the difference. As they saw it, their rights as Englishmen would be violated if they submitted to direct taxes levied by the home government. The House of Commons gained its monopoly over the tax power on the grounds that the people of England should be taxed only by their elected representatives. The same principle seemed to apply to the colonists. If the Crown could not tax the English people without their consent, how could Parliament tax the Americans when they were not represented in that body?

Following the French and Indian War (1754–63), Parliament asserted its long dormant authority to tax the colonies. Americans insisted on maintaining the federative status quo, in which they alone exercised the power to tax themselves. The inability to resolve this disagreement over the authority to tax constitutes the main cause of the American Revolution. Independence did not remove the need for a central government. On the contrary, fighting the Revolutionary War required centralization on a scale theretofore unseen in North America. Yet hostility to the notion of a central power continued and almost proved disastrous. Americans refused to grant their own national government authority to impose taxes, and it defaulted on its debts in 1780. The Continental Congress succeeded in raising funds for the war only because it borrowed heavily; it still had to issue $241 million in paper currency.[3] That amount proved inadequate, and the Continental army suffered horrific deprivations as a result.

Even after a new constitution, the Articles of Confederation, went into effect in 1781, national power continued to erode, largely because the new government remained dependent upon the states for revenue.[4] In addition to the lack of a tax power, the Articles impaired the fund-raising ability of Congress by linking the amount it could request from each state to the value of its lands. The states took issue with the Confederation's estimates of the value of their real estate in order to avoid payment. No wonder many regarded the Confederation as little more than an organization of sovereign states. (Article III described the Confederation as a "firm league of friend-

---

3. Richard B. Morris, *The Forging of the Union, 1787–1789* (New York: Harper & Row, 1987), 34.

4. Gordon S. Wood, *The Creation of the American Republic, 1776–1787* (Chapel Hill: University of North Carolina Press, 1969), 359.

ship.") As one might expect from an international organization, each state had one vote in the Confederation Congress. The delegates were chosen annually by the legislatures, thus further tightening the grip of the states over the national government. There was only a shadow of an executive (no veto power; elected by Congress) and no real judiciary (Congress doubled as a court of appeal for disputes between states). Article IX specified the powers of Congress. This decision to grant only certain powers—as opposed to a general grant of authority like that enjoyed by the legislatures—arose out of state jealousy. Several legislatures instructed their delegates to the Continental Congress to reserve the general mass of legislation, i.e., control over their "internal police," to the states themselves.[5] The enumeration of the powers of a legislature was something of a novelty. Although the English Bill of Rights (1689) reserved certain popular rights, it limited royal authority only. Parliament remained omnipotent. It was one thing for a watchful Parliament to tell the Crown what it *could not* do; it was quite another for the states to tell a national assembly what it *could* do and then leave nothing but the next election as a means of assuring that it exercised only those powers that had been granted to it. A variety of powers were included in Article IX. It authorized Congress to determine "peace and war" and to enter into "treaties and alliances." It also empowered Congress to appoint civil officers, borrow money, build a navy, and ask the states for assistance in raising an army. Lesser powers included fixing the standard of weights and measures and the establishment of post offices. The lack of an authority to tax rendered all these grants somewhat hollow, yet the Articles of Confederation still burdened Congress with additional limitations. Article IX required the vote of nine states, instead of a simple majority of seven, before Congress could carry out its most critical functions, such as borrowing or spending money. Article XI provided that the states retained all powers not "expressly delegated" to the Confederation Congress. Article XIII required the consent of every state before the Articles of Confederation could be amended.

From the day it first stood, a lack of funds left the new government a decrepit and decaying structure, waiting to be blown down by the first sustained winds. In early 1781 Congress asked the states for authority to collect a 5 percent impost, or tax on imported goods. Eleven states consented to the idea, but Rhode Island voted against it. The state was heavily dependent on

5. Merrill Jensen, *The Articles of Confederation: An Interpretation of the Social-Constitutional History of the American Revolution, 1774–81* (Madison: University of Wisconsin Press, 1970), 119.

its own impost for revenue.[6] Matters did not improve in subsequent years. A depression that set in during 1784 dried up state coffers and reduced contributions to the Confederation. Trade wars broke out between the states; New York levied burdensome taxes upon goods arriving from either New Jersey or Connecticut.[7] In 1785 the Confederation Congress defaulted again on the debt owed to France. The economic downturn worsened as specie (gold and silver) drained out of the country to Britain, whose merchants were unwilling to take the paper money being churned out indiscriminately by the legislatures.

By 1786 the depression had reduced the Confederation's income to a mere trickle; it paid only a third of the interest due on the national debt that year.[8] The record of the states in complying with Confederation requisitions was atrocious—of the $15.6 million requested between 1781 and 1786, the states provided only $2.4 million, less than one-sixth of the amount asked. As if eager to demonstrate the futility of the Confederation, when New York in 1786 became the final state to approve Congress's second request for a power to tax imports, it did so on the condition that it be allowed to pay in paper money. The Confederation Congress rejected the deal (it could not pay its creditors with paper notes) and continued to starve. As the national government floundered, the worsening depression produced widespread unrest. Reduced commodity prices led many farmers to default on loans they had taken out during the short-lived boom of the early 1780s. As imprisonment was the usual consequence of the failure to pay debts at that time, the jails filled with farmers. Angry citizens demanded that the state governments protect them from creditors. Legislatures responded by passing stay laws extending terms for the payments of debts. They also flooded the country with paper money. Seven states enacted such measures during the 1780s.[9] Rhode Island subjected those who refused to accept the state's paper notes to criminal sanctions and denied them jury trials. In other states the legislatures refused to bow to the debtor element and lawlessness resulted; New Hampshire residents angry over the lack of relief marched on the state capitol at Exeter in September 1786.[10]

6. Jackson Turner Main, *The Antifederalists: Critics of the Constitution, 1781–1788* (Chapel Hill: University of North Carolina Press, 1961), 76.

7. Henry Steele Commager and Samuel Eliot Morison, *The Growth of the American Republic*, 5th ed. (New York: Oxford University Press, 1962), 274.

8. Rossiter, *Seventeen Eighty-Seven: The Grand Convention* (New York: Macmillan, 1966), 49.

9. Ibid., 44.                    10. Ibid.

In Massachusetts discontent threatened to boil over into a general uprising. During the mid-1780s commercial interests in the legislature increased taxes on land in the hope of quickly paying off the state's war debts. By 1786, with the depression in full swing, no fewer than sixty towns had failed to pay their taxes; debtors made up more than 80 percent of the population of one county's jail.[11] That fall, armed mobs menaced western Massachusetts, forcibly closing courts in order to prevent foreclosures. (Eight states saw debtor riots during the 1780s.)[12] In early 1787 one Daniel Shays led an attack on a federal armory. Amid fears of an assault upon the state government in Boston, Massachusetts officials asked the Confederation Congress for assistance. The Confederation gave limited aid but generally proved itself incapable of constructive activity.

Although the conflagration in Massachusetts usually receives most of the credit, the Confederation's impotence had moved Americans to consider remedies as early as 1785. James Madison introduced resolutions in the Virginia general assembly suggesting that Congress be given authority to regulate trade. In support of the idea he cited the partial and punitive taxes imposed by some states on the goods of others. Madison also suggested that only uniformity in their commercial regulations would enable the states to obtain reciprocal trading privileges from foreign nations. Maryland and Virginia, each fearful that the other would attempt to tax traffic along the Potomac River or Chesapeake Bay, appointed delegates to discuss the idea of jointly regulating commerce on those waterways. They met at Mt. Vernon and produced resolutions endorsing uniform commercial regulations and a national currency. In August 1786 Charles Pinckney of South Carolina proposed amendments granting Congress the power to regulate commerce and the authority to penalize states that did not comply with requests for money. That same year Virginia invited the other states to send commissioners to a convention that would "take into consideration the trade of the states."[13] In September 1786 a commercial convention met at Annapolis, Maryland. As only five states sent representatives, the delegates called for another gathering the following May that would address the question of how "to render the Constitution of the federal government adequate to the exigencies

---

11. Morris, *Forging of the Union*, 260.

12. Main, *Antifederalists*, 6–7.

13. Jonathon Elliot, ed., *The Debates in the Several State Conventions on the Adoption of the Federal Constitution*, 5 vols. (New York, 1836; reprint, New York: Burt Franklin, 1968), 1:114–15.

of the Union."[14] In early 1787 Congress invited the state legislatures to send delegates to a convention that would meet in Philadelphia that summer. By May twelve states—all but Rhode Island—had appointed delegations.

The Constitutional Convention convened in May 1787, with each state delegation enjoying a single vote to be decided by a majority of its delegates. Measures passed once they were approved by a majority of states. Convention proceedings remained secret until adjournment. This may have been wise, as the delegates began their work under the impression that they would be merely amending the Articles of Confederation; they retired in September having moved far beyond their original assignment.[15]

## THE CONSTITUTIONAL CONVENTION

The delegates had barely assembled when they were asked to consider proposals to establish an entirely new government endowed with more authority than the Confederation enjoyed. The "Virginia Plan" authorized Congress to legislate "in all cases in which the states are incompetent" or when "the harmony of the United States may be interrupted by the exercise of individual [state] legislation."[16] On May 31, the Convention voted in favor of the Virginia Plan's provision for a broad power of legislation, nine states to zero, with one tie. The delegates then turned to the framework of Congress. In the Confederation Congress more populous states had more delegates (up to seven), but each state was still limited to a single vote, to be decided by a majority of its delegates. Under the Virginia Plan, the vote of each delegate counted in the final tally, thus giving the larger states more influence. Representatives of small states foresaw a future in which their delegations would be powerless. Nor did they buy the claim that abuses would be prevented by the Virginia Plan's provisions for an upper house. As its members would be elected by the lower house, they would be unlikely to turn on those to whom they owed their positions. Few gave the Virginia Plan much of a chance, as several delegations had been instructed by their legislatures to retain state equality in Congress at all costs.[17]

14. Quoted in Richard B. Morris, ed., *Encyclopedia of American History* (New York: Harper & Brothers, 1953), 115.

15. Morris, *Forging of the Union*, 256–57.

16. Max Farrand, ed., *The Records of the Federal Convention of 1787*, 4 vols. (New Haven: Yale University Press, 1966), 1:21.

17. Ibid., 1:54; 3:173.

Small-state delegates struck back with the New Jersey Plan on June 15. It preserved a unicameral Congress in which each state possessed a single vote. It also retained the Articles of Confederation's enumeration of powers, with the additional authority to tax imports. In support of the plan William Paterson of New Jersey pointed out that a British offer of representation in Parliament had been rejected because Americans would have been a permanent minority. The same situation faced the small states under the Virginia Plan. The New Jersey Plan's life as a viable alternative was a short one; the Convention voted it down, seven states to three, on June 19. Delegates from larger states pressed hard once more for population-based apportionment. One claimed that the Continental Congress had embraced state equality as a basis for representation only because it lacked the time or means to determine the population of each state. Another delegate warned that unless the Virginia Plan was accepted, "the Union itself must be dissolved." With large-state delegations continuing to resist compromise, their opponents made ominous noises over what they perceived as a scheme to dragoon them into a federation that would swallow the small states whole. Gunning Bedford of Delaware told his colleagues that he simply did not buy their assurances. "I do not, gentlemen, trust you. If you possess the power, the abuse of it could not be checked, and what then will prevent you from exercising it to our destruction?" An accommodation was gaining support among the delegates. Known as the Connecticut Compromise, it provided for state-based representation in the upper house, or Senate (two senators for each state) and a population-based lower house, in which measures passed upon approval by a majority of representatives (and not states). Senators would be elected by the legislatures, while representatives would be chosen by the voters of each state. The Convention approved the measure on July 16.[18]

The theatrics of June and early July obscured the fact that a more difficult task lay ahead: determining what powers should be augmented. Many delegates planned to do little more than grant the Confederation government a tax power; would they really concede authority to legislate in all cases in which the states were "incompetent?" Pierce Butler of South Carolina called "for some explanation of the extent of this power; particularly of the word incompetent. The vagueness of the terms render it impossible for any precise judgment to be formed." With little fanfare the Virginia Plan's grant of a broad legislative power was scrapped. Instead, a Committee of

18. Ibid., 1:246, 247, 184–85, 313, 200; 2:7; 1:500; 2:215.

Detail was appointed to prepare a list of the powers to be bestowed upon the new government. The Convention then adjourned until August 6. The draft submitted upon its return included eighteen enumerated powers, beginning with the authority to tax: "The legislature of the United States shall have the power to lay and collect taxes, duties, imposts and excises." It also granted Congress authority to regulate commerce. The draft went on to list other powers, almost all of which appeared in the Articles of Confederation.[19] Hence the comment of one observer that the proposed Constitution did not constitute an expansion of the national government's authority; it merely enhanced its ability to achieve ends already assigned to it.[20]

With the arrival of the August 6 draft, discussion focused on the powers thereby granted to Congress. Both the tax clause and the commerce power survived examination, despite the attempts of southerners to add an amendment that would have required the approval of two-thirds of each house for tariffs.[21] The Convention also contemplated adding additional powers. On August 18 a delegate suggested authorizing Congress to (1) grant charters of incorporation and copyrights, (2) establish a university, (3) award premiums to encourage "the advancement of useful knowledge and discoveries," and (4) establish schools for the promotion of the arts and sciences, as well as "agriculture, commerce, trades and manufactures." Of these proposals, only the protection of copyrights was added to the Constitution. Suggested powers were often linked to others that had already been accepted, in the hope that the association would increase the odds of approval. On September 14 Benjamin Franklin proposed to supplement the power to establish post roads with the authority to cut canals. The idea was rejected, eight states to three. On September 14 the Convention again considered adding a power to incorporate. The proposal was defeated, perhaps because delegates agreed with Rufus King of Massachusetts when he warned that it would "be referred to the establishment of a bank" or "mercantile monopolies." The Convention also rejected a clause that would have empowered Congress to establish a university.[22]

19. Ibid., 2:17, 181, 182.

20. James Madison expressed this view at the Virginia ratifying convention in June 1788. Elliot, *Debates in the Several State Conventions,* 3:259.

21. See Farrand, *Records of the Federal Convention,* 2:369–75, 415–17, 449–53. Southerners feared that because their region was the country's leading importer, it would pay more than its fair share of impost taxes. The two sections eventually agreed to authorize Congress to ban the importation of slaves, but not until 1808. Export taxes were prohibited, while tariffs required approval of only majorities in each house.

22. Ibid., 2:321–22, 615–16, 620.

Toward the end of September the Convention approved the draft Constitution and sent it to the Confederation Congress, which referred it to the states for ratification. The proposed charter differed from the Articles of Confederation in several respects. It bestowed new powers, the most important of which was the authority to tax. It included a supremacy clause: Article VI stated that the Constitution, laws, and treaties of the United States "shall be the supreme law of the land." The Constitution also established three independent branches of government. Each was empowered to perform its duties relatively free of interference from the other branches—a novel arrangement. The president enjoyed executive power, command of the armed forces, the right to veto bills (subject to override), and the power of appointment for all government personnel, with the approval of the Senate required for high-level positions. The judiciary possessed at least theoretical jurisdiction over all cases arising under the Constitution, laws, or treaties of the United States.

There were numerous objections to the proposed charter; ratification appeared to be very much in doubt during the fall of 1787. Many Americans viewed the Constitution as a betrayal of the Revolution.[23] As Congress would exercise more power than the Crown and Parliament ever had, Americans would be giving away what they had fought so hard for—the right of self-government.[24] Nor was this concern limited to those outside the Convention. Throughout the summer, delegates concerned with what they saw as overreaching either voiced their concerns or simply left Philadelphia. Others refused to endorse the Constitution. On August 31 George Mason of Virginia declared that he would rather "chop off his right hand" than sign it.[25] Elbridge Gerry of Massachusetts and Governor Edmund Randolph of Virginia also refused to sign it—the latter despite having presented the even more centralizing Virginia Plan to the Convention in May.

### RATIFICATION, FALL 1787

The Confederation Congress referred the Constitution to the states on September 28, 1787. Within a month the charter dominated public discussion in towns large and small. While little more than a soft and steady drumbeat

23. Rossiter, *Grand Convention,* 279.
24. Wood, *Creation of the American Republic,* 521–22.
25. Farrand, *Records of the Federal Convention,* 2:479.

at first, the criticisms of those who opposed ratification (Antifederalists) eventually rose to a deafening roar. Luther Martin of Maryland predicted that the presidency, with its monopoly over the selection of lower-level federal employees, would place too much power in the hands of a single person.[26] The judiciary did not escape criticism, either; writers such as "Brutus" pointed to the royal courts in Britain, which had expanded their jurisdiction through disingenuous constructions of the law, and claimed that federal judges would do the same.[27] Antifederalists directed most of their fire at the powers of Congress and in particular that of taxation. Burdensome taxes and tyrannical methods of collection would inevitably follow ratification, Americans were told. Closely tied to the issue of taxation was that of representation; in a country used to having an elected representative for every three or four thousand persons, a single congressional seat for thirty thousand people seemed a fraud on the idea of representative government.

Other factors exacerbated the negative reaction to the proposed Constitution. Class friction—already worsened by the depression—greatly affected its reception. While the proposed charter received much support from merchants and creditors, groups that fought for debtor-friendly legislation took an instant dislike to it. (One clause barred the states from impairing contracts; another prohibited them from issuing paper money.) Farmers tended to predominate among those opposed to the Constitution.[28] The debtor element appeared particularly strong in Pennsylvania, site of the opening battle in the ratification struggle. The Federalist (pro-ratification) legislature supported the Constitution and feared that a long debate would undermine its prospects. It set the state's ratification convention for late November 1787, thus allowing the opposition only two months to mobilize.[29] Other states followed suit; all but Rhode Island scheduled conventions that would meet before the end of 1788. A fierce debate in the nation's eighty or so newspa-

26. "From his having the appointment of all the variety of officers in every part of the civil department, who will be numerous—in them and their connections, relations, friends and dependents—he will have a formidable host devoted to his interest, and ready to support his ambitious views." Luther Martin, "Genuine Information to the General Assembly of the State of Maryland," in Herbert Storing, ed., *The Complete Anti-Federalist*, 9 vols. (Chicago: University of Chicago Press, 1981), 2:67.

27. "Brutus," no. 11, *New York Journal*, January 31, 1788, in Bernard Bailyn, ed., *The Debate on the Constitution: Federalist and Antifederalist Speeches, Articles, and Letters during the Struggle over Ratification*, 2 vols. (New York: Literary Classics of the United States, 1993), 2:134–35.

28. Robert A. Rutland, *Ordeal of the Constitution: The Antifederalists and the Ratification Struggle of 1787–88* (Norman: University of Oklahoma Press, 1966), 115.

29. Main, *Antifederalists*, 189.

pers ensued.[30] The overwhelming majority of these sheets were Federalist—only about twelve opposed ratification.[31]

If there was an overriding concern behind Antifederalist complaints, it was that the proposed Constitution would spawn a single omnipotent government and thereby destroy the states. This was a problem because Americans viewed themselves as citizens of their states first and of the Confederation second. Many regarded their states as fundamentally unique; they did not take lightly the idea of a centralized government that might allow officials from one state to impose their values on the people of another. Some of this jealousy stemmed from religious differences. The American colonies of the late eighteenth century formed a varied sample of the Christian denominations that dominated northern Europe during the eighteenth century. Congregationalists occupied New England; Anglicans ruled in much of the South. The Dutch Reformed Church dominated the area around New York City, while Presbyterians and Quakers reigned in large parts of the mid-Atlantic States. Pennsylvania was home to a variety of sects, from Mennonites to Moravians, German Calvinists, and Lutherans. Neighboring Maryland possessed many Catholics. Methodists and Baptists had appeared in the South and West. Americans were also divided along lines of national origin; those of English descent predominated, but Pennsylvania counted many German immigrants among its inhabitants, and New York City still revealed its Dutch origins. Farmers of Scottish, Welsh, and Irish descent occupied the hinterlands from Pennsylvania to Georgia. Sectional rivalries were already apparent; New England Puritans and southern planters viewed each other with suspicion. Political differences also divided Americans; hardscrabble farmers in the interior fought endless battles with the coastal elites who dominated the legislatures. These conflicts occasionally became violent; uprisings occurred in Pennsylvania in 1764 and in North Carolina in 1768. The states argued over borders and imposed confiscatory tariffs on each other's goods. Americans in the late eighteenth century remained divided in a multitude of ways. No less a nationalist than John Adams acknowledged this diversity when, many years later, he suggested that the ability of the colonies to work together despite their great differences was one of the signal accomplishments of the revolutionary generation.[32]

30. Rossiter, *Grand Convention*, 35.

31. Rutland, *Ordeal of the Constitution*, 135.

32. John Adams, *The Works of John Adams*, ed. Charles Francis Adams, 10 vols. (Boston, 1850–56), 10:283.

Adams did not exaggerate. Regionalism dominated. Americans therefore readily embraced the belief, common among political theorists, that "only a small homogeneous society whose interests were essentially similar could properly sustain a republican government."[33] America did not qualify. Thus the query of John Mason: "Is it to be supposed that one national government will suit so extensive a country, embracing so many climates, and containing inhabitants [of] so very different manners, habits and customs?"[34] Self-government would inevitably disappear under such an arrangement, as a single government for the whole of the nation would subject local communities to the whims of indifferent national majorities. As one critic wrote in the Boston *Massachusetts Gazette:* "It is impossible for one code of laws to suit Georgia and Massachusetts. They must, therefore, legislate for themselves. Yet there is not one point of legislation that is not surrendered in the proposed plan."[35]

Antifederalists feared such horrors not so much because of any of the powers found in the Constitution but because of those that might be inferred from it. As Thomas B. Wait warned in January 1788, "There is a certain darkness, duplicity and studied ambiguity of expression running through the whole Constitution. . . . As it now stands but very few individuals do or ever will understand it, consequently Congress will be its own interpreter."[36] Critics focused on those clauses whose vagueness left them particularly susceptible to manipulation. Chief among these were the necessary and proper and general welfare clauses. The first had been added to the end of the enumerated powers. Critics attacked it out of fear that it might be used to justify any act that advanced, even indirectly, the powers listed in Article I.[37] The general welfare clause also gave critics cause for concern. Some feared that it would be used to justify "any extravagant expense which [Congress] shall be pleased to incur," as the clause "includes every other power afterwards mentioned."[38] Richard Henry Lee complained that the right to "judge of what

33. Wood, *Creation of the American Republic,* 356.

34. Quoted in Elliot, *Debates in the Several State Conventions,* 3:330.

35. "Agrippa" [James Winthrop], "The Despotism and Misery of a Uniform National State," *Massachusetts Gazette,* December 4, 1787, in Bailyn, *Debate on the Constitution,* 1:449.

36. Quoted in Samuel Bannister Harding, *The Contest over the Ratification of the Federal Constitution in the State of Massachusetts* (New York: Longmans, Green, 1896), 39.

37. See, for example, "Brutus," no. 1, *New York Journal,* October 18, 1787, in Storing, *Complete Anti-Federalist,* 1:164.

38. "A Review of the Constitution Proposed by the Late Convention by a Federal Republican," quoted in ibid., 3:75.

may be for the general welfare" amounted to a power "coextensive with every possible object of human legislation."[39] "Timoleon" claimed that the clause authorized Congress to impair the freedom of the press: "if preachers and printers are troublesome to the new government, and in the opinion of its rulers, it shall be for the general welfare to restrain or suppress both the one and the other, it may be done consistently with the Constitution."[40]

The general welfare clause was a familiar phrase; similar language had been used twice in the Articles of Confederation without incident. In the preamble it formed part of a sentence declaring the purposes of the Articles and thus served as little more than ornamentation—no powers were derived from it. It also appeared in Article VIII, which obligated the states to pay the debts incurred by Congress for the "common defence and general welfare." The Confederation Congress did not act under the view that it possessed authority to spend money on any subject conducive to those great ends. Rather, the phrase broadly defined the debts for which the states would be liable in order to assure that they did not avoid payment on the grounds that Congress had exceeded its authority. The phrase also appeared in both the preamble and the body of the Constitution (Article I, Section 8). The circumstances of its inclusion in the latter remain something of a mystery. James Madison included the phrase in the Virginia Plan as part of its preamble. It was not included in the draft Constitution of August 6. On August 21 a committee recommended a clause that would have empowered Congress to pay the debts of the states incurred during the Revolution for the "common defence and general welfare." The Convention tabled the measure, apparently out of fear that such a broad power might negatively affect the Constitution's prospects for ratification. Those states that kept their debts under control would, it was thought, be reluctant to assume responsibility for their more free-spending brethren. A revised tax clause suggested on August 23 provided that "the Legislature shall fulfill the engagements and discharge the debts of the United States, and shall have the power to lay and collect taxes, duties, imposts and excises." It was approved. Two days later, on August 25, the Convention considered a clause that would have empowered Congress to tax "for the payment of said debts and for the defraying of expences that shall be incurred for the common defence and general welfare." The proposal was voted down, ten states to one.[41]

39. *Virginia Gazette*, December 6, 1787, in Bailyn, *Debate on the Constitution*, 1:467.
40. *New York Journal*, November 1, 1787, quoted in Main, *Antifederalists*, 155.
41. Farrand, *Records of the Federal Convention*, 2:352, 382, 414.

At that point it appeared that the phrase "general welfare and common defense" would appear only in the preamble. On August 31 the Convention agreed to submit all the spare clauses that had been proposed and ignored to a committee that would consider them one last time. It would then advise the delegates of any clauses it thought worthy of one last vote by the Convention. Among these spare parts was the proposal to assume the debts incurred by the states during the Revolution for the "common defence and general welfare." On September 4 the committee submitted its revisions. The list did not include anything concerning state debts. Oddly, it did contain a revised version of the tax clause: "The Legislature shall have power to lay and collect taxes, duties, imposts and excises, to pay the debts, and provide for the common defence and general welfare of the United States." "Provide for the common defence and general welfare?" What did that mean? No one had proposed such a clause—it was not among the spare parts the committee had been appointed to consider. Nevertheless, the delegates agreed to add the revised tax clause to the draft Constitution on September 4. Some immediately saw great possibilities; others had to be led. Maryland delegate James McHenry expressed concern that Congress might not be able to erect lighthouses or dredge harbors. Pennsylvania delegate Gouverneur Morris assured McHenry that such activities qualified as providing for "the general welfare." McHenry was pleased to hear it—such an interpretation would, he believed, also authorize the establishment of trading companies.[42]

Gouverneur Morris could answer the question with some authority, as he played a larger role than any other delegate in drafting the Constitution. (He wrote much of the August 6 draft.) On the other hand, the idea that the clause bestowed so broad an authority would have come as a shock to most delegates. They had just spent six weeks debating the enumerated powers of Congress; the general welfare clause, at least in the eyes of Mr. Morris, would serve to resuscitate powers they had rejected, some of them repeatedly.[43] Nor did the clause appear on its face to grant such broad powers. Its vagueness made it difficult to assign the phrase any meaning at all. Delegates may well have viewed the clause as merely an introductory flourish, coming as it did at the head of the enumerated powers. Yet McHenry and Morris were not alone in their ambitions for the general welfare clause. Toward the end of September, two delegates from Connecticut, Roger Sher-

42. Ibid., 2:493, 504, 529–30.
43. See ibid., 2:321, 325, 615, 616.

man and Oliver Ellsworth, informed the governor of their state that "the objects, for which congress may apply monies, are the same mentioned in the eighth article of the Confederation, for the common defence and general welfare, and for the payment of the debts incurred for those purposes."[44] Sherman could also speak with some authority on the subject, as he sat on the committee that added the general welfare clause to the Constitution. Yet his claim would also have come as news to other delegates, as the Convention considered and rejected a broad spending power on August 25.[45]

Federalists responded to concerns over the general welfare clause and the rest of the Constitution with the assurance that Congress could exercise only those powers granted to it. In embracing this tack, Federalists borrowed from the Articles of Confederation (Article II), which provided that Congress could exercise only those powers "expressly delegated" to it. James Wilson, a Philadelphia lawyer and a delegate to the Constitutional Convention, provided the first and most famous example of this approach in an address he gave in Philadelphia on October 6, 1787. Known as the Stateyard speech, it constituted one of the first attempts by Federalists to dispel concern over the lack of a bill of rights—next to the issues of taxation and representation, the leading complaint of those who opposed ratification. Critics asked what was to keep the proposed government from abridging the freedom of the press? Or religion? In response, Mr. Wilson pointed to the scheme of legislative power with which most citizens were familiar—that of the states. "When the people established the powers of legislation under the separate governments, they invested their representatives with every right and authority which they did not in explicit terms reserve." Therefore, "upon every question, respecting the jurisdiction of the house of assembly, if the frame of government [the state constitution] is silent, the jurisdiction is efficient and complete." He contrasted that arrangement with the proposed Constitution: "in delegating federal powers, another criterion was necessarily introduced, and the congressional authority is to be collected, not from tacit implication,

---

44. Ibid., 3:99. In 1782 a committee of the Confederation Congress asserted that the Articles of Confederation's general welfare clause "comprehends an indefinite power of prescribing money to be raised, and of appropriating it when raised." Alexander Hamilton, *The Papers of Alexander Hamilton*, ed. Harold C. Syrett and Jacob E. Cooke, 27 vols. (New York: Columbia University Press, 1961) (hereafter *Papers of Hamilton*), 3:213–23.

45. On August 25 the Convention voted down—ten states to one—a proposal authorizing Congress to incur debts "for the payment of said debts and for the defraying of the expences that shall be incurred for the common defence and general welfare." Farrand, *Records of the Federal Convention*, 2:414.

but from the positive grant expressed in the instrument of union." Thus "it is evident, that in the former case [state legislatures] every thing which is not reserved is given, but in the latter [Congress] the reverse of the proposition prevails, and every thing which is not given, is reserved." A bill of rights was therefore unnecessary. "It would have been superfluous and absurd to have stipulated with a federal body of our own creation, that we should enjoy those privileges, of which we are not divested, either by the intention or the act, that has brought that body into existence."[46]

It would be an understatement to say that Federalists embraced Wilson's argument. It served as the standard reply to complaints over the lack of a bill of rights.[47] In time it became the most important speech of the ratification debates. George Washington arranged for it to be printed and distributed in Virginia in an effort to counter the influence of Antifederalists George Mason and Patrick Henry. By the end of 1787, excerpts of the speech had appeared in thirty-four newspapers in twelve states.[48] A copy of it reached Thomas Jefferson in Paris. James Madison echoed Wilson's approach in a November 30, 1787, article in the *New York Packet* (*The Federalist*, No. 14). The federal government's jurisdiction, he announced, "is limited to certain enumerated objects, which concern all members of the republic, but which are not to be obtained by the separate provisions of any." He made the point more emphatically in a January 1788 article (*The Federalist*, No. 39), when he suggested that in the extent of its powers, the proposed government was merely "federal" (as opposed to "national") because "its jurisdiction extends to certain enumerated objects only, and leaves to the several states a residuary and inviolable sovereignty over all other objects."[49] Other commentators made the same point. In a November 1787 essay, Rufus King and Nathaniel Gorham insisted that the powers of Congress were "explicitly defined" both as to the "quantity & the manner of their exercise." Roger Sherman also asserted that the powers of the national government were "particularly defined." Therefore each state retained the "right to exercise every power of a sovereign state not delegated to the United States."[50]

46. John Bach McMaster and Frederick D. Stone, eds., *Pennsylvania and the Federal Constitution, 1787–1788* (Philadelphia: Historical Society of Pennsylvania, 1888), 143–44.

47. Wood, *Creation of the American Republic*, 539–40.

48. Bailyn, *Debate on the Constitution*, 1:1142, 1159.

49. Rossiter, *Federalist Papers*, 99, 102, 245.

50. James H. Hutson, ed., *Supplement to Max Farrand's The Records of the Federal Convention of 1787* (New Haven: Yale University Press, 1987), 284, 287.

As winter approached, all eyes turned toward Philadelphia. Although Delaware ratified first, in early December, it was the vote in Pennsylvania—the second-largest state in the Confederation—that served as the first major test for the Constitution. The rural West, which had supported the democratic state constitution of 1776, opposed ratification. The East, with its political establishment dominated by the creditors and merchants of Philadelphia, supported it. The state convention proved to be anticlimactic. Speaking to the other delegates, James Wilson insisted that the proposed government's powers were fixed and that it need not be feared.[51] Approval followed on December 12, in a 46–23 vote. Pennsylvania Antifederalists refused to let the loss discourage them. On the contrary, they understood a truth that would haunt their opponents throughout the struggle: rejection of the draft Constitution by any of the large states would make another convention likely and thereby stop ratification in its tracks. As large and vocal Antifederalist forces existed in the three other large states (Virginia, Massachusetts, and New York), the battle had only just begun. With this fact in mind, Antifederalist delegates to the Pennsylvania state constitutional convention issued their famous "Dissent" on December 18, 1787, in the Philadelphia *Pennsylvania Packet.* The essay was subsequently reprinted in thirteen newspapers throughout the country, an impressive tally for an Antifederalist piece. It offered a substantial if familiar criticism: the country was too large to be governed as a single republic, yet that was exactly what would happen if the Constitution was ratified. Why? Because the powers granted to Congress would enable it to "annihilate and absorb the legislative, executive, and judicial powers of the several states." Pennsylvania Antifederalists also feared that Congress would monopolize the tax base. It would achieve that end "by construing every purpose for which the state legislatures now lay taxes, to be for the general welfare, and therefore as of their jurisdiction."[52]

By mid-January, Georgia, New Jersey, and Connecticut had also ratified the Constitution, bringing to five the number of states that had approved it. The nation's eyes turned toward Massachusetts, cradle of the Revolution and the third-largest state in the Confederation. Federalists were alarmed by developments there with good reason. The Constitution's most damaging setback of the fall occurred when Elbridge Gerry—a well-known advocate of

51. Elliot, *Debates in the Several State Conventions,* 2:425.

52. "Dissent," *Pennsylvania Packet,* December 18, 1788, in Bailyn, *Debate on the Constitution* 1:526–552, 1168, 536–38.

a stronger central government—announced his opposition to it. A series of letters he addressed to the Massachusetts General Court in late 1787 had a particularly devastating effect.[53] Nor were matters helped by the sectional proclivities of the state; many delegates to the state's ratifying convention carried a somewhat impolitic view of southerners as idle slaveholders. Bay State Puritans failed to see the advantages of union with such people. Many shared Nathaniel Gorham's view that "the eastern states had no motive for union but a commercial one."[54]

The Constitution's prospects also suffered because of the turmoil of the previous year, which had culminated in Shays' Rebellion. Since that time voters had elected a populist legislature, thus empowering the elements that were unlikely to embrace a charter identified with merchants and creditors. The Massachusetts General Court came very close to dispensing with a ratifying convention altogether—it flirted with the idea of submitting the Constitution directly to the voters. Had it done so, the electorate probably would have rejected it (voters in neighboring Rhode Island voted against ratification the following spring).[55] For a time it appeared that the decision to call a state ratifying convention had only postponed the inevitable, as Antifederalists won a majority of delegates.[56] When the convention itself met in Boston during the second week of January 1788, approval appeared most unlikely. The fears of Massachusetts Antifederalists revolved around the suspicion that with Congress able to impose taxes, the federal government would prove to be beyond anyone's control. William Symmes warned that Congress would not confine itself to a "rigid economy" in its spending, as the term "general welfare" might be "applied to any expenditure whatever." The fear that the clause constituted a power of appropriation had clearly not abated. Significantly, Mr. Symmes went on to say that he did not know what the clause meant. What he really wanted was to hear those "who so ably advocate this instrument . . . enlarge upon this formidable clause."[57]

The most significant obstacle for Federalists in Massachusetts was not the general welfare clause but Samuel Adams. One of the earliest proponents of independence and the living embodiment of the Revolution, Mr. Adams enjoyed wide influence in eastern Massachusetts, especially among the me-

53. See Storing, *Complete Anti-Federalist,* 2:6–8.
54. Rutland, *Ordeal of the Constitution,* 90, 13.
55. Harding, *Contest over Ratification in Massachusetts,* 46–47.
56. Rossiter, *Grand Convention,* 287.
57. Elliot, *Debates in the Several State Conventions,* 2:57–107, 74–75.

chanics and tradesmen who had spearheaded early resistance to the British. On January 3 he announced his opposition to ratification at a caucus in Boston. Adams's decision stamped the Constitution with a most unwelcome seal, as the Bay State—only a year removed from Shays' Rebellion—was still more than discontented enough to follow its own mind. Why did Adams oppose ratification? In a letter of December 3, 1787, to Richard Henry Lee, he confessed that "I stumble at the threshold. . . . I meet with a national government, instead of a federal union of sovereign states." In his view, the people of the United States were too varied to live under a single government.[58]

The state ratifying convention met in Boston on January 9, 1788. The Antifederalist cause sustained an immediate blow with the news that Elbridge Gerry had decided against attending. Other absences also helped the cause of ratification. Because of the economic difficulties that plagued the state, forty-six towns could not afford to send delegates, thus weakening Antifederalist ranks.[59] Samuel Adams alone provided the Antifederalists with a figure of stature. The Federalist delegation, on the other hand, included Rufus King, Caleb Strong, Theodore Sedgwick, and Fisher Ames—all formidable advocates. The Constitution would have lost had a vote been held when the convention first met. Antifederalists consequently tried to move matters along; Federalists were in no hurry and sought to address each and every objection. In the process, they repeated the assurance already used by their brethren elsewhere: the Constitution granted only those powers enumerated within it. As one delegate put it, could "a better rule of yielding power be shown than in the Constitution? . . . For what we do not give . . . we retain."[60]

In short order Federalists won two important victories. On January 24 the convention rejected a proposal to hold an immediate vote.[61] Shortly thereafter Federalists organized a huge rally of Boston mechanics in an attempt to counter the influence of Samuel Adams. The meeting—with four hundred persons in attendance—adopted resolutions in favor of ratification.[62] Federalist merchants were said to have won over the caulkers by promising to build more ships.[63] The dam broke on January 31. In proposing that the conven-

---

58. Quoted in Bailyn, *Debate on the Constitution*, 1:446.
59. Harding, *Contest over Ratification in Massachusetts*, 99.
60. Elliot, *Debates in the Several State Conventions*, 2:61.
61. Bailyn, *Debate on the Constitution*, 1:1095.
62. Harding, *Contest over Ratification in Massachusetts*, 97.
63. Commager and Morison, *Growth of the American Republic*, 291.

tion accept the Constitution, Governor John Hancock recommended several amendments to the rest of the states, to be added to the document at a later date. Up until that time the Federalists had bitterly opposed the idea of amendments; realizing it would cost them nothing to go along with Hancock's demand, they acquiesced. Sam Adams soon dropped his opposition to ratification. When the vote on the proposed Constitution was held on February 6, 1788, the Massachusetts ratifying convention approved it, 186 to 168.

As in Pennsylvania and most of the other states, the Massachusetts convention did not stop at voting—it passed nine amendments it thought should be added to the charter at a later time.[64] The first provided that "all powers, not expressly delegated by the aforesaid constitution, are reserved to the several states."[65] A similar phrase had appeared in the Articles of Confederation; its adoption by Massachusetts and other states also had much to do with the promise issued in Wilson's Stateyard speech. In a sense these state resolutions proposed to codify Wilson's proviso and thereby issue a joint declaration of the terms upon which ratification been obtained—all powers not granted were reserved to the states.

### RATIFICATION, SPRING 1788

Antifederalist criticisms of 1788 did not differ from those of 1787: a highly centralized government, higher taxes, and all manner of abuses were promised as the inevitable consequences of ratification. Federalists in turn pointed to the enumerated and limited nature of the powers granted to the proposed government. In response, Antifederalists emphasized those portions of the Constitution that would enable the government, despite the charter's apparent constraints, to assume by construction whatever powers it chose to exercise. They pointed to the vague wording of the general welfare clause in particular and claimed, as one critic put it, that "restrictive constructions" of the Constitution would be "unavailing."[66]

Antifederalist notions of the meaning of the general welfare clause continued to vary wildly. One observer complained that it would give Con-

64. Bailyn, *Debate on the Constitution*, 1:1097.

65. Elliot, *Debates in the Several State Conventions*, 1:322.

66. "Address by Sydney," *New York Journal*, June 13, 1788, in Storing, *Complete Anti-Federalist* 6:113.

gress the power "to lay taxes at pleasure for the general welfare; and if they mis-judge of the general welfare, and lay unnecessary oppressive taxes, the Constitution will provide ... no remedy for the people of the states."[67] Silas Lee feared that Congress might cite the clause as authority for silencing the opposition.[68] "Deliberator" went so far as to suggest that "Congress may, if they shall think it for the 'general welfare,' establish a uniformity in religion throughout the United States."[69] Another critic warned that the clause was so broad that it would bestow a power "to ring and yoke all the hogs in the country."[70] "Brutus" declared explicitly what many others implied—that the phrase granted a general legislative power. It would authorize "Congress to do anything which in their judgment will tend to provide for the general welfare, and this amounts to the same thing as general and unlimited powers of legislation in all cases."[71] One skeptic warned that the central government would arrogate "to itself the right of interfering in the most trifling domestic concerns of every state, by possessing a power of passing laws 'to provide for the general welfare of the U.S.' which may affect life, liberty, and property in every modification that they may think expedient."[72]

Federalists initially refused to define the clause in a manner that would ease these concerns. Instead they held fast to the approach that had proved so successful in the fall—emphasizing the limited and enumerated nature of the national government's authority and the fact that all powers not granted were retained by the states.[73] Of course this argument did not answer the Antifederalist warning that the proposed Constitution was too vague. Even if the federal government could exercise only those powers that had been explicitly granted, it remained to be seen what those powers were. It was perhaps inevitable that Federalists would move beyond James Wilson's approach. They would have to spell out the meaning of those clauses that troubled their critics. Did the general welfare constitute an enumerated power,

67. "Federal Farmer," no. 9, January 4, 1788, ibid., 2:280.

68. Main, *Antifederalists*, 154.

69. "Essay by Deliberator," *Philadelphia Freeman's Journal*, February 20, 1788, in Storing, *Complete Anti-Federalist*, 3:179.

70. "Letters from a Countryman," *Albany Gazette*, January 17, 1788, ibid., 6:86.

71. "Brutus," no. 12, *New York Journal*, February 7 and 14, 1788, in Bailyn, *Debate on the Constitution*, 2:175.

72. "Address by Sydney," *New York Journal*, June 13 and 14, 1788, in Storing, *Complete Anti-Federalist*, 6:120.

73. See, for example, *Norfolk and Portsmouth (New Hampshire) Journal*, February 20, 1788, in Bailyn, *Debate on the Constitution*, 1:364; *Newport (Rhode Island) Herald*, March 20, 1788, ibid., 2:369; *The Federalist*, No. 45, in Rossiter, *Federalist Papers*, 288.

or did it merely serve as an introductory flourish? James Madison answered this question in a January 19, 1788, article in the *New York Packet* (*The Federalist*, No. 41). It served as the major Federalist response to complaints that the clause would be the Constitution's Trojan horse. Madison pointed out that the very existence of the enumerated powers that followed it undermined the idea that the general welfare clause constituted a broad power of legislation. "For what purpose could the enumeration of particular powers be inserted, if these and all others were meant to be included in the preceding general power?" The phrase instead served as a sort of preamble to the enumerated powers. "Nothing is more natural or common than first to use a general phrase, and then to explain and qualify it with particulars." Objections to the clause seemed particularly misplaced to Madison in light of the fact that the same words had been used without incident in the Articles of Confederation. What would have been thought of members of the Confederation Congress "if attaching themselves to these general expressions, and disregarding the specifications, which ascertain and limit their import, they had exercised an unlimited power of providing for the common defence and general welfare?"[74] Although the effect of the articles that came to be known as *The Federalist* has long been debated, they clearly had some influence, particularly in New York. James Madison arranged for hundreds of copies to be sent to Virginia. In addition, supporters of the Constitution throughout the nation read New York City newspapers in which the *Federalist* articles were printed, as they contained the most comprehensive debates over the proposed Constitution. They naturally repeated the arguments first offered by Madison, Alexander Hamilton, and John Jay. One may therefore infer that Madison's explanation of the general welfare clause—that it meant, in effect, nothing—put many minds at ease.

Maryland approved the Constitution in April, 63 to 11, despite the strenuous efforts of Luther Martin. South Carolina ratified in May, 149 to 73. Its convention passed a series of proposed amendments that included the now obligatory proviso—all powers not expressly delegated to the new government were retained by the states.[75] The success of the Federalists was muted by the fact that their prospects for victory remained tenuous throughout the spring. They would have been reasonable to presume, and no doubt many did, that with each state's ratification, Antifederalist hopes would dim

74. *The Federalist*, No. 41, in Rossiter, *Federalist Papers*, 262–64.
75. Elliot, *Debates in the Several State Conventions*, 1:325.

and their energies would diminish. On the contrary, opponents of the Constitution focused on New York and Virginia with confidence. If either state failed to ratify, another national convention would be held and the Constitution would fail. For the Federalists this must have been particularly galling; with each step closer to victory (the approval of nine states was needed for the Constitution to take effect), the possibility of defeat became more apparent.

The pressure on Federalists continued to increase in the spring of 1788 as it became evident that the Constitution would have an even harder time in Virginia and New York than it had in Massachusetts. Antifederalist prospects also appeared good in North Carolina, New Hampshire, and Rhode Island. North Carolina in particular looked bad. It was split between western farmers irritated with their tax burden and easterners who supported the state government. Many observers had already written off the state as a lost cause. The first defeat for the Constitution occurred in the North. On March 24, 1788, Rhode Island voters rejected it, 2711–239 (Federalists boycotted the vote). Things did not go much better in New Hampshire. The state ratifying convention met in February 1788. Realizing that many delegates had been instructed by their towns to reject the Constitution, Federalists had to settle for adjournment until June. Events there were said to be of particular concern to the Federalists; many took them as an indication that the opposition's belief in low taxes and weak government had taken hold.[76]

The main test of the spring took place in Virginia—the largest and most influential state in the Union. It was generally agreed that her opposition alone would sink the Constitution.[77] Federalists had reason to be fearful, as a majority of Virginians—three-quarters by one estimate—opposed ratification.[78] Antifederalists dominated in the central and western portions of the state, while Federalists held the Tidewater region and several northern counties.[79] The opposition began with Governor Edmund Randolph. After introducing the Virginia Plan in Philadelphia, he turned on the Constitution and refused to sign it. Although he explained that he had not decided whether he would support ratification, Randolph's refusal to endorse the

76. Rutland, *Ordeal of the Constitution*, 199, 123.

77. Ibid., 171.

78. Albert J. Beveridge, *The Life of John Marshall*, 4 vols. (New York: Houghton Mifflin, 1919), 1:321.

79. Charles Henry Ambler, *Sectionalism in Virginia from 1776 to 1861* (Chicago: University of Chicago Press, 1910), 58–59.

charter constituted a blow. An even more formidable opponent loomed in the figure of Patrick Henry, a former governor and a hero of the Revolution. George Mason and Richard Henry Lee—both of whom had been elected to the Constitutional Convention and then declared its work unacceptable— filled out the roster of leading Antifederalists in Virginia.

The battle in the Old Dominion began in the fall of 1787 over an issue unseen in the North: the power to impose tariffs. George Mason warned that by requiring only a simple majority in Congress to pass "commercial and navigation laws," the Constitution would subject the southern states to high taxes on imports. The North would face enormous temptation to push through such measures, as they would enable the section's merchants to "monopolize the purchase of commodities, at their own prices, for many years."[80] Another concern was the treaty power, largely because of John Jay's proposed treaty with Spain. It would have ceded American navigation rights on the Mississippi River in exchange for commercial favors. In the South, where access to the Mississippi River was viewed as critical to the region's economic future, disgust with Jay ran high and the Constitution's vesting of the treaty power in the president and Senate alone appeared an invitation to disaster.

Given the strength and quality of the opposition in Virginia, Federalists took heart when elections for the state ratifying convention resulted in a draw. Within the convention, Patrick Henry, George Mason, and James Monroe led an Antifederalist group that focused on the same fears that had alarmed skeptics across the country. Mason warned the delegates that the tax power would enable the federal government to starve the state governments to death, as it would monopolize the tax base. This would leave Americans with a single government—something that could never work for a country so large and diverse. Federalists responded with their usual assurances—the proposed government's powers were too modest for it to threaten the states. What came through most was James Wilson's proviso. Henry Lee had obviously read the script. "When a question arises with respect to the legality of any power, exercised or assumed by Congress, it is plain on the side of the governed: *Is it enumerated in the Constitution?* If it be, it is legal and just. It is otherwise arbitrary and unconstitutional." Lee compared the proposed charter with the "familiar manner" of "a man [who has] delegated certain pow-

---

80. "Objections of the Honorable George Mason," in Elliot, *Debates in the Several State Conventions*, 1:495.

ers to an agent." It would, he claimed, "be an insult upon common sense to suppose that the agent could legally transact any business for his principal which was not contained in the commission whereby the powers [of the agent] were delegated."[81]

Inevitably, Virginia Federalists felt compelled to define those clauses that appeared particularly vague. Governor Randolph—who declared his support for the Constitution on June 4—spoke of the general welfare clause on June 10. "The plain and obvious meaning of this is, that no more duties, taxes, imposts and excises, shall be laid, than are sufficient to pay the debts and provide for the common defence and general welfare, of the United States." If Congress could raise all the funds necessary for those great objects, did it also have authority to spend money on any matter related to them? Randolph did not say. Wilson Nicholas was even more ambiguous. "Is it not," he asked, "necessary to provide for the general welfare? It has been fully proved that this power could not be given to another body. Congress must then possess it." No harm would result, for the "amounts to be raised are confined to these purposes" (general welfare and the common defense).[82] Nicholas too failed to say whether the funds raised for those ends could also be devoted to them in the form of appropriations.

As the hour of decision approached, Virginia Antifederalists mounted a furious assault upon the Constitution. James Monroe called for its rejection on the grounds that the tax power would be exercised in an oppressive manner. Speaking on June 11, George Mason warned that Congress would impose heavy burdens, such as a poll tax that would fall mainly on the poor.[83] The efforts of Antifederalists were in vain. On June 25 the Virginia convention ratified the Constitution with all of four votes to spare (89–79). Before the convention adjourned, Governor Randolph received a letter from George Clinton, governor of New York. Clinton proposed that the two states jointly call for a second constitutional convention. Randolph did not disclose its contents. If he had, the Constitution would probably have met its demise.[84] Before it adjourned, the convention issued a list of twenty amendments it thought should be added to the charter. The first repeated the key Federalist promise that induced consent to the constitutional contract: "That each state

81. Ibid., 3:29–30, 186.                    82. Ibid., 3:207, 244–45.
83. Ibid., 3:217–18, 263–64.
84. Charles Grove Haines, *The Role of the Supreme Court in American Government and Politics, 1789–1835* (Berkeley and Los Angeles: University of California Press, 1944; reprint, New York: Da Capo Press, 1973), 70.

in the Union shall respectively retain every power, jurisdiction, and right, which is not by this Constitution delegated to the Congress of the United States, or to the departments of the federal government."[85]

With Virginia, ten states had ratified the Constitution (New Hampshire did so on June 21, 57–47). A new government would come into being, at least temporarily, whether New York ratified or not. Yet the debate in the Empire State still proved important—if it rejected the charter, another convention would probably have followed and the Constitution would have died in its infancy. Prospects for ratification were poor in part because of the unusual nature of the opposition. While Antifederalist elements in most states were disorganized and lacked money or power, in New York they formed much of the political elite. Antifederalists dominated a patronage-based political machine that feared a loss of influence if the national government was strengthened and the state lost its ability to collect tariffs.[86] (The Constitution both gave Congress the power to impose tariffs and barred the states from doing so.) This faction was led by Governor George Clinton, a skilled operator who recognized in the Constitution an attack on the power of his party. Although Clinton did not participate in the state's ratification debates, his public opposition to the charter strengthened the Antifederalist cause.[87]

Two of New York's delegates to the Constitutional Convention, Robert Yates and John Lansing, left Philadelphia before the proceedings concluded. In a letter addressed to Governor Clinton, they attacked the proposed charter as a recipe for consolidation. Ratification would lead to the immersion of the states within a vast republic, they warned, despite the fact that the country was far too large to be ruled by a single government.[88] New York Antifederalists also complained of the high ratio of voters to representatives, the use of slaves in apportioning congressional seats, and the Constitution's lack of protection for freedom of the press and the free exercise of religion.[89] Fear of higher taxes—state as well as federal—was the chief concern of New Yorkers; they knew that other state taxes would have to be raised in order to replace lost tariff revenues.[90]

85. Elliot, *Debates in the Several State Conventions*, 3:659.

86. Rutland, *Ordeal of the Constitution*, 202.

87. Linda Grant DePauw, *The Eleventh Pillar: New York State and the Federal Constitution* (Ithaca: Cornell University Press, 1966), 83.

88. Ibid., 86–87, 172–73.

89. Clarence E. Miner, "The Ratification of the Federal Constitution by the State of New York," *Studies in History, Economics and Public Law* 94, no. 3 (1921): 92–93.

90. DePauw, *Eleventh Pillar*, 174.

Because New York's convention met almost a year after the Constitution was submitted to the states, its residents witnessed an exhaustive debate in the local press. Although the Federalists held a crucial advantage in that almost all of the newspapers in the state were on their side, Antifederalist writers such as "Brutus" and "Federal Farmer" proved the equal of any in the whole of the Confederation in the quality of their arguments. In the elections for the ratifying convention held at the end of April, Antifederalists won an overwhelming majority of seats (46 out of 65).[91] The convention convened on June 17 at a courthouse in Poughkeepsie, a small town on the Hudson River. The most prominent Antifederalist in attendance was Governor Clinton; on the floor they were led by Melancton Smith. Federalist ranks contained skilled advocates as well, including Alexander Hamilton, New York chief justice Richard Morris, state chancellor Robert Livingston, and John Jay.

By the time the state convention met, ratification by other states had already begun to convert popular sentiment in New York to the side of the Constitution. The prospect of New York City seceding from the rest of the state if it did not approve the proposed government also had a chastening effect. Melancton Smith and the other Antifederalist leaders compounded their difficulties with an error that had doomed their cause in other states—they agreed to a Federalist proposal to debate the Constitution clause by clause, thereby postponing a vote until at least July. Word of New Hampshire's ratification arrived on June 26; a week later the delegates received news of Virginia's approval. For a time Antifederalists remained firm, but starting around July 4 the debate turned to what sort of amendments the convention ought to propose—a sure sign that New York would accept the Constitution.

In late June, before its decision became a foregone conclusion, the convention turned the proposed charter inside out. The tax clause underwent a particularly thorough examination; for a week the convention discussed nothing else.[92] Melancton Smith held out little hope that the enumeration of powers would effectively limit the proposed government. He warned that Congress would raise all the money it could spend.[93] The general welfare clause also alarmed delegates. Antifederalists described it as an inde-

91. Main, *Antifederalists*, 237.
92. Elliot, *Debates in the Several State Conventions*, 2:330–81.
93. See, for example, Smith's speech of June 27, 1788, ibid., 2:333.

pendent legislative power; in so doing they demonstrated that even as late as the summer of 1788, James Madison's description of it in *The Federalist*, No. 45 had not reached everyone. On June 27 John Williams warned that if Congress "should judge it a proper provision for the common defence and general welfare," it could destroy the state governments, as the terms of the clause were "indefinite" and "undefinable." Federalists focused on fears that the proposed government would prove a costly burden. Alexander Hamilton insisted that the federal government's "leading objects, where the revenue is concerned, are to maintain domestic peace, and provide for the common defense." That was it. "In these are comprehended the regulation of commerce—the support of armies and navies, and of the civil administration."[94]

Antifederalist lines began to crack in early July. With their main weakness—no alternative to offer—more glaring than ever, delegates who had opposed the Constitution began to fall to the opposition. On July 23 Governor Clinton agreed to a change of the ratification resolution so that it no longer rested upon the condition that the convention's list of proposed amendments be added to the Constitution.[95] The Antifederalist majority was so large that ratification in New York remained in doubt until the very end. When it finally came on July 26, Federalists prevailed with no votes to spare (30–29). The convention thereafter passed a series of resolutions. These included thirty-two proposed amendments, a declaration of rights, and a letter to the other states calling for a second constitutional convention.[96] North Carolina's convention met later that summer. After initially rejecting it, the state ratified the Constitution in 1789, several months after George Washington took the oath of office as president. Rhode Island did not accede to the new government until May 1790.

George Washington greatly influenced the ratification debates despite the fact that he did not campaign for the Constitution. Americans knew he supported the charter, and many accepted it for that reason alone. They also believed that if the proposed government came into being, Washington would probably serve as its first president.[97] The Constitution also profited from the fact that the Antifederalists never bothered to devise an alternative. Their chief battle cry—the demand for a bill of rights—itself held the seeds of their de-

94. Ibid., 2:338, 350.
95. Rutland, *Ordeal of the Constitution*, 262.
96. Elliot, *Debates in the Several State Conventions*, 1:327–33; 4:243–44.
97. Rutland, *Ordeal of the Constitution*, 253.

struction. The Federalists simply embraced the idea and promised to enact one after ratification, and the closest thing the Antifederalists had to an alternative was lost. Yet the subsequent adoption of a bill of rights constituted an Antifederalist victory of sorts. Concerns over the Constitution's more obscure clauses and their possible misuse led several states to issue versions of Wilson's proviso at the time they ratified, either as proposed amendments or as resolutions indicating the understanding upon which ratification had turned.[98] The phrase was subsequently included in the Constitution as the Tenth Amendment. Whether the Federalists liked it or not, Americans intended to hold them to the representations they had made during the struggle of 1787–88.

98. Bailyn, *Debate on the Constitution,* 2:536–76.

# CHAPTER 2

# The Federalists,

# 1789–1801

## ALEXANDER HAMILTON AND CONGRESS

With New York's ratification of the Constitution, the country moved into an uneasy phase during which one government lapsed while another came to life. Many Americans continued to fear that the nation was too large and diverse to be ruled by a single entity. Fearful that the new government would exercise too much power, Virginia called for another constitutional convention, as did New York—the latter in February 1789, less than a month before the new regime came into existence. Fear of federal power proved so great that almost as soon as the first Congress met, legislators offered amendments designed to further limit the authority of the new government. Much of the work had been completed during the ratification process—nine states issued more than eighty amendments along with their ratification resolutions. Almost all proposed further limitations of federal authority. Only three ideas appeared in the proposals of each state. The first two limited congressional authority in the areas of taxation and elections. The third, echoing Wilson's Stateyard speech, provided that the federal government could exercise only those powers granted to it.[1]

When the House of Representatives met in the spring of 1789, the task of boiling the proposed amendments down to a more manageable figure fell to James Madison. He reduced them to twelve, the last being James Wilson's proviso regarding the limitation of federal authority to those areas list-

---

1. Forrest McDonald, *The Presidency of George Washington* (Lawrence: University Press of Kansas, 1973), 35. For the resolutions of Virginia, North Carolina, and Massachusetts declaring that Congress could exercise only those powers granted to it, see Elliot, *Debates in the Several State Conventions*, 3:56, 4:249, and 2:177.

ed in the Constitution. Madison tried to extend some of the rights protected by the proposed amendments—freedom of the press and worship as well
as jury trials in criminal cases—to the state governments.[2] The Senate rejected the idea and Congress sent the amendments to the states for ratification.
Ten—the "Bill of Rights"—became law in late 1791 when Virginia became
the tenth state to ratify them.[3]

James Madison had to agree to work for passage of a bill of rights before his fellow Virginians would send him to Congress. Alexander Hamilton did not have to trim his sails in order to secure a place in the new regime. Throughout the struggle of 1787–88, Hamilton held fast to his own
unique vision for American government. At the Constitutional Convention,
he proposed a highly ambitious plan that all but called for the abolition
of the states.[4] The Convention ignored the proposal and Hamilton—infuriated—almost went home. Although he decided to remain until the end
and became the lone delegate from New York to sign the Constitution, it
still struck him as inadequate—it left too much power in the hands of the
states.[5] Contempt did not stop Hamilton from becoming one of the charter's leading advocates during the ratification struggle. He realized that if
the states rejected the Constitution and devised a new government, it would
be weaker than the one devised in Philadelphia. Hamilton wrote over half
of the newspaper articles that later became known as *The Federalist*, thus securing his place in history as one of the chief advocates of a framework of
government he originally dismissed.

Alexander Hamilton would have enjoyed a prominent place in American history had he never involved himself with the events of 1787 and '88.
During the Revolutionary War he served as George Washington's aide-
de-camp; at Yorktown he led a crucial assault on British positions. The loy-
alty and limitations of his former commander ensured that Hamilton would

2. See U.S. Congress, *Annals of the Congress of the United States, 1789–1824*, 42 vols. (Washington, D.C.: Gales & Seaton, 1834–56) (hereafter *Annals of Congress*), 1st Cong., 1st sess., August 17, 1789, 1:783–84.

3. Article V required that proposed amendments be ratified by three-quarters of the states
in order to become part of the Constitution. All twelve of the amendments submitted to the
states in September 1789 are contained in *Statutes at Large of the United States of America, 1789–
1873*, 17 vols. (Boston: Little, Brown, 1845–74) (hereafter *Stats at Large*), vol. 1, 97–98.

4. Farrand, *Records of the Federal Convention*, 1:287.

5. Hamilton to Gouverneur Morris, February 1802: "Mine is an odd destiny. Perhaps no
man in the United States has sacrificed or done more for the present Constitution than my-
self—and contrary to all my anticipations of its fate, as you know from the very beginning I am
still laboring to prop the frail and worthless fabric." *Papers of Hamilton*, 25:544–45.

remain near the center of American political life during most of the 1790s. George Washington was not a politician by training or temperament; he knew little but the life of a planter and soldier. He presided at the Constitutional Convention but said little during it. Washington was also old enough to have served in the British army during the French and Indian War, now three decades past. Fifty-seven years old when he was inaugurated as president in April 1789, he was by the standards of his time an old man. It was perhaps inevitable that Washington would rely heavily upon the assistance of his former chief of staff. Hamilton had practiced law, served in the Confederation Congress, and helped organize the Bank of New York. Where to put him? Congress established three departments in 1789, all of which would operate under the president's command: state, war and treasury. Perhaps owing to the financial difficulties faced by the country and Hamilton's experience with the Bank of New York, Washington nominated him for secretary of the treasury. The Senate confirmed the nomination in September 1789.

Given the government's fiscal difficulties, the Treasury Department would have played a critical role under any circumstances. Alexander Hamilton brought to it a dynamism that enabled him to become the national government's primary actor during its first five years. Almost total dominance of the first Congress by supporters of the administration (soon to be known as Federalists) further enhanced Hamilton's power. Federalists held forty-nine of fifty-nine places in the House and almost every seat in the Senate.[6] Hamilton exploited the opportunity afforded him and pushed the national government to the very limits of its jurisdiction, and occasionally beyond them.

In Congress, lawmakers explored the extent of their jurisdiction whenever novel legislation was proposed; hence the questions surrounding a 1790 naturalization bill. Although the Constitution authorized federal legislation on the subject, the question arose whether Congress could limit the rights of persons after they were naturalized. The bill provided for naturalization after one year's residence; it also required that another year pass before the newly arrived could hold federal or state office and imposed limitations on the right to own land during the same period.[7] Protests were heard immediately. As John Lawrence of New York put it, while Congress was authorized to establish a uniform rule of naturalization, "the effects resulting from the

6. David Currie, *The Constitution in Congress: The Federalist Period, 1789–1801* (Chicago: University of Chicago Press, 1997), 112.

7. *Annals of Congress*, 1st Cong., 2d sess., February 3, 1790, 1:1147.

admission of persons to citizenship is another concern and depends upon the constitutions and laws of the states now in operation."[8] When a bill was approved in early March, it did not limit the rights of naturalized citizens.[9] Congress next considered the limits of its powers in June 1790, when the House took up a proposal to lend money to a glass factory. Representative John Vining of Delaware suggested that Congress had the power to encourage arts and manufactures and that the loan constituted "one mode of affording this encouragement."[10] In fact, the Constitution mentioned neither subject. Critics quickly declared the measure beyond the pale, and it died without a struggle.[11]

The national government faced significant problems in its early years, few of which had anything to do with the attempts of Congress to determine the outer limits of its jurisdiction. On the contrary, the problems of 1790, like those that had proved so embarrassing in 1786, stemmed from a lack of revenue. Unlike the Confederation, the new government possessed the means to alleviate the situation. This was fortunate, because the national debt—$50 million by 1789—threatened to ruin the country.[12] Particularly troublesome was the $11 million in foreign debt (owed mostly to France and Spain), as the failure to pay the interest on it made new loans impossible.[13] Congress addressed the situation quickly. First it enacted a tariff and imposed tonnage duties, thereby ensuring that the national government would have the means to carry out its day-to-day operations without having to obtain additional loans.[14] The national debt was so large that a formal plan for payment had to be devised if the government was to regain access to European credit. The House of Representatives, as it so often did during this period, called on the Treasury Department for guidance. Alexander Hamilton made the most of his opportunity.

In early 1790 the secretary of the treasury presented his famous "Report on the Public Credit" to Congress. He recommended pledging a portion of federal revenues irrevocably to a "sinking fund," the proceeds of which would pay off not only the federal government's debts but also those of the states

---

8. Ibid., 1:1154.

9. 1 *Stats at Large* 103 (March 26, 1790).

10. *Annals of Congress*, 1st Cong., 2d sess., June 3, 1790, 2:1686.

11. Ibid., 2:1688.

12. John C. Miller, *The Federalist Era* (New York: Harper & Row, 1960), 38.

13. Ibid.

14. 1 *Stats at Large* 24 (July 4, 1789); ibid., 63 (September 1, 1789).

that had been incurred in waging the Revolutionary War.[15] He recommended paying the debt at par in order to assure Europeans that America was
creditworthy. As the revenue derived from tonnage duties and tariffs could
not fund this ambitious program, Hamilton urged Congress to impose a variety of new taxes. The plan immediately ran into objections. Much of the
debt consisted of bonds that had fallen into the hands of speculators, among
whom they had recently passed for as little as a quarter of their face value.
James Madison and others questioned why they should be funded at par. As
they saw it, the proposal would give speculators a windfall, while Continental army veterans, who were given the notes as payment for wartime service, would receive nothing. (Poverty led many of them to sell the bonds at
less than face value.) Madison suggested that some of the money go to the
original recipients of the bonds instead of the current holders.[16] Federalists
pointed to Article VI's provision obligating the government to pay the debts
of its predecessor and argued that Congress must pay off the government's
debt in full—to the current bondholders.[17]

The proposal to assume state debts proved even more controversial than
the funding scheme. The bulk of the opposition came from the southern
states, most of which had already paid off their Revolutionary War loans.[18]
Why should they be forced to subsidize states that had not been fiscally
prudent? Critics asked whether Congress had authority to assume the debts
of the states. On April 22, 1790, James Madison addressed the issue directly
and answered it in the negative, recalling that the Constitutional Convention had considered and rejected the idea.[19] Hamilton's supporters thought
otherwise. Representative Theodore Sedgwick of Massachusetts insisted that
the general welfare clause authorized Congress "to levy money in all instances where, in their opinion, the expenditure shall be for the 'general welfare.'"[20]

Largely because of southern opposition, the House passed a funding bill
alone in June 1790. Assumption floundered until a deal was struck between

15. For the text of the Report on the Public Credit, see *Annals of Congress*, 1st Cong., 2d
sess., 2:1992–2022.
16. Ibid., February 11, 1790, 2:1236.
17. Ibid., February 9, 1790, 1:1190.
18. James Roger Sharp, *American Politics in the Early Republic: The New Nation in Crisis*
(New Haven: Yale University Press, 1993), 36.
19. *Annals of Congress*, 1st Cong., 2d sess., April 22, 1790, 2:1591–92; see Farrand, *Records of
the Federal Convention*, 2:327–28.
20. *Annals of Congress*, 1st Cong., 2d sess., February 24, 1790, 2:1382.

Madison, Thomas Jefferson, and Hamilton at a June 20 dinner. The two Virginians agreed to persuade Virginia representatives to support assumption; in exchange, Hamilton promised the support of his House allies for a bill to move the national capital to a site on the Potomac River. Compromise failed to end to the controversy. In December 1790 the Virginia House of Delegates issued a resolution holding that because a power to assume state debts did not appear in the Constitution, Congress lacked authority to enact such a program. It pointed to James Wilson's promise and made clear that word of it had reached Richmond. "During the whole discussion of the federal Constitution by the convention of Virginia, your memorialists were taught to believe 'every power not granted was retained.'" It was "under this impression and upon this positive condition, declared in the instrument of ratification, the said government was adopted by the people of this commonwealth; but your memorialists can find no clause in the Constitution authorizing Congress to assume the debts of the states!"[21]

Despite doubts over its legality, history has been kind to the Assumption Act. In a sense it fulfilled the promise of the Constitution by proving that the new nation could—and would—meet its obligations. The United States began to pay off the balance of its foreign debt in 1790, much earlier than anyone on either side of the Atlantic expected.[22] At the same time, the national debt soared to more than $80 million—one-fourth of which stemmed from the assumption of state liabilities.[23] Burdensome excise taxes on everything from whiskey to windows followed. This development represented a major and significant departure; during the ratification debates, Federalists had promised that tariffs alone would provide ample revenue for the federal government.[24] The new taxes and the funding/assumption programs became inextricably linked in the popular mind. To critics, the measures constituted a single monstrosity of artificially increased expenses and taxes that brought to mind the bloated public establishment of Great Britain.[25] They also in-

21. "Virginia Resolutions on the Assumption of State Debts," issued on behalf of the General Assembly of the Commonwealth of Virginia, December 16, 1790, in Henry Steele Commager, ed., *Documents of American History*, 5th ed. (New York: Appleton-Century-Crofts, 1949), 155.

22. Stanley Elkins and Eric McKitrick, *The Age of Federalism* (New York: Oxford University Press, 1993), 334.

23. Miller, *Federalist Era*, 53.

24. See Alexander Hamilton, *The Federalist*, No. 12 and No. 22, in Rossiter, *Federalist Papers*, 93 and 143, respectively.

25. See, for example, letter of John Steele, January 27, 1791, in Noble E. Cunningham Jr.,

dicated that despite Federalist assurances, the state governments would not serve as sentinels of the Constitution. Virginia was a perfect example. While it complained that the Assumption Act was unauthorized, its legislature embraced the opportunity to unload a sizeable portion of the state's debts. In 1788 Virginia asked for $500,000 in compensation from the Confederation Congress for expenses incurred in connection with the Revolution; following the Assumption Act, its costs somehow doubled. Nevertheless, the Old Dominion obtained compensation in full.[26] Other states also unloaded debts that were not incurred in fighting the Revolution.[27]

Four months later, and after a suitable period of recovery, Hamilton set Congress to work on his next project. In December 1790 he sent two reports to the House of Representatives. In the first he proposed a schedule for the excise taxes on spirits he had recommended earlier that year. In the second he called for the establishment of a national bank.[28] Congress enacted the tax measure without incident. The idea of a bank raised the problem of authority once again. Did Congress have it? Although he avoided answering the question directly, Hamilton offered a multitude of arguments for the utility of a bank. It would serve as a depository for federal funds, as a fiscal agent for the treasury, and as a conservative influence over the state banks. Its notes, backed by specie, would function as the country's circulating medium.[29] The elements in the House that had opposed assumption quickly took up arms against the plan. Their hostility arose in part from an agrarian dislike for creditors and in part from fears that a national financial institution would, like the Bank of England, corrupt the political system that created it.

While the fears of the administration's opponents could be dismissed, their constitutional objections proved a more formidable obstacle. James Madison expressed his concerns on the floor of the House on February 2, 1791. Some thought the general welfare clause authorized a bank; Madison disagreed. The phrase, he insisted, merely stated the purposes for which Congress could impose taxes. It had been copied from the Articles of Confederation, where it served the same purpose.[30] As for the bank established by

---

ed., *Circular Letters of Congressmen to Their Constituents, 1789–1829* (Chapel Hill: University of North Carolina Press, 1978), 1:4.

26. McDonald, *Presidency of George Washington,* 75.

27. Elkins and McKitrick, *Age of Federalism,* 160.

28. *Annals of Congress,* 1st Cong., 3d sess., Appendix, 2:2082.

29. Hamilton, "Report on the Bank," December 13, 1790, *Papers of Hamilton,* 7:305–42.

30. *Annals of Congress,* 1st Cong., 3d sess., February 2, 1791, 2:1944–46.

the Confederation Congress, Madison continued, it "was known . . . to have been the child of necessity. It never could be justified by the regular powers of the Articles of Confederation." Some believed the necessary and proper clause authorized formation of a bank because such an institution would help Congress carry out its enumerated powers. In Madison's view, the text of the clause itself "condemn[s] the exercise of any power, particularly a great and important power, which is not evidently and necessarily involved in an express power." The bank failed this test—it "could not even be called necessary to the government; at most it could be but convenient." State banks could conduct as much business as a federally chartered one. In perhaps his strongest argument, Madison suggested that ratification occurred only because Federalists embraced an approach to the Constitution wholly at odds with the one implicit in the bill before Congress. "The defence against the charge founded on the want of a bill of rights pre-supposed that the powers not given were retained; and that those given were not to be extended by remote implications. On any other supposition, the power of Congress to abridge the freedom of the press, or the rights of conscience could not have been disproved." Thus, Madison concluded, the "explanations in the state conventions all turned on the same fundamental principle, and on the principle that the terms necessary and proper gave no additional powers to those enumerated."

Fisher Ames of Massachusetts thought the bill presented two questions, the first being whether Congress could exercise powers "not expressly given in the Constitution, but which may be deduced by a reasonable construction of that instrument?" For Ames, the answer was yes. Thus the second question: did "such a construction warrant the establishment of a bank?" He thought so. Congress had "scarcely made a law in which we have not exercised our discretion with regard to the true intent of the Constitution."[31] Under the commerce power it had already "taxed ships, erected light-houses, made laws to govern seamen, etc., because we say that they are the incidents to that power."[32] Turning to the bank, Ames held that the government ought to be able to transport money quickly and that only banks could enable it to

31. Ibid., 2:1944–54.
32. Ibid., 2:1956. An act of August 7, 1789, included appropriations for aids to navigation (1 *Stats at Large* 53); an act of July 20, 1790, provided for the protection of members of the merchant marine (1 *Stats at Large* 131). It required written contracts and prompt payment of wages. See Currie, *Constitution in Congress: Federalist Period*, 65.

perform that task. State banks would not be able to fill the void—ten states had no banks at all.[33]

On February 8, 1791, the measure passed the House with ease, 39 to 20.[34] It then went to the president's desk, where it sat. Attorney General Edmund Randolph, Secretary of State Thomas Jefferson, and James Madison all submitted essays to the president arguing against the constitutionality of a bank. Jefferson's paper carried the indignation of a plaintiff in a breach-of-contract action. He began by reminding the president of the language of the Tenth Amendment—the "foundation of the Constitution." As Congress could exercise only those powers granted to it, the legality of the bank depended on whether it bore a necessary relationship to one of those powers. Jefferson thought not. The power to borrow did not authorize the bill, as it neither borrowed money "nor ensures the borrowing of it." The tax power did not fit, as the bill did not pay a debt or impose a tax. Nor did the commerce power, as the establishment of a bank did not constitute a regulation of "buying and selling." At best it created, in the bills to be issued by the bank, a "subject of commerce." The general welfare clause merely stated the purposes for which taxes could be imposed. Jefferson then turned to the attempts of some to erode the restrictive qualities of the necessary and proper clause: "the Constitution allows only the means which are 'necessary,' not those which are merely 'convenient' for effecting the enumerated powers." There are no governmental powers, Jefferson continued, "which ingenuity may not torture into *convenience,* in some way or other to some one of so long a list of enumerated powers." The embrace of this approach would, he warned, "swallow up all the delegated powers." Thus the conclusion that the Constitution restrained Congress to those means truly necessary to carry out its authorized ends, i.e., those without which the enumerated powers could not be exercised at all.[35]

Hamilton issued his own opinion regarding the legality of the bank on February 23, 1791. He embraced precisely the approach Jefferson had attacked—that while the national government was limited in its powers, its discretion as to the means by which it exercised those powers was unlimited and in fact absolute: "every power vested in government is in its nature sovereign, and includes by force of the term, a right to employ all means req-

33. *Annals of Congress,* 1st Cong., 3d sess., February 2, 1791, 2:1947–49.
34. Ibid., February 9, 1971, 2:2012.
35. *Writings of Jefferson,* 5:285–87.

uisite and fairly applicable to the attainment of the ends of such power"[36] "There are implied, as well as express powers," he continued, "and . . . the former are as effectually delegated as the latter." The power to incorporate qualified as constitutional whenever it helped the federal government achieve any of the ends listed in the enumerated powers. Thus "the only question must be, in this, as in every other case, whether the means to be employed, or in this instance the corporation to be erected, has a natural relation to any of the acknowledged objects or lawful ends of the government." A corporation, in Hamilton's view, "may not be erected by Congress for superintending the police of the city of Philadelphia, because [it is] not authorized to regulate the police of that city." However, corporations might be formed "in relation to the collection of taxes, or to the trade between the states, or with the Indian tribes; because it is the province of the federal government to regulate those objects and because it is incident to a general sovereign or legislative power to regulate a thing, to employ all means which relate to its regulation to the best and greatest advantage." Hamilton next turned to the word "necessary" and gutted it of any restrictive connotations: "necessary often means no more than needful, requisite, useful or conducive to." As he saw it, the "whole turn of the clause . . . indicates that it was the intent of the Convention . . . to give a liberal latitude to the exercise of specified powers." Hamilton then made a rather startling assertion. As he saw it, the question of necessity should not decide a proposed measure's constitutionality anyway. All that the Constitution required was that a "relationship" exist between the proposed act and one of the enumerated powers.[37]

Hamilton believed that Congress had already acted under the view that it possessed broad discretion in exercising its powers. He pointed to appropriations for navigational aids such as lighthouses, beacons, and piers, and claimed that these measures confirmed the difficulties that would result from a narrow construction of the Constitution. Such expenditures "must be referred to the power of regulating trade, and [are] fairly relative to it." Yet, he continued, "it cannot be affirmed, that the exercise of that power, in this instance, was strictly necessary; or that the power itself would be nugatory without that of regulating establishments of this nature."[38] Hamilton had a point. During the ratification process, parties on all sides viewed the commerce power as encompassing little more than the authority to impose tar-

36. *Papers of Hamilton*, 8:98–99.    37. Ibid., 100–104.
38. Ibid., 104.

iffs. There is no evidence that anyone viewed it as authorizing expenditures for aids to navigation. On the other hand, it was not clear that Congress had the commerce clause in mind when it appropriated funds for that purpose— the first such act described its purpose as rendering the navigation of coastal areas "easy and safe."[39] These appropriations arguably constituted an exercise of the power to raise a navy. Buoys and lighthouses thus seemed necessary to the exercise of to at least one of the enumerated powers; it remained to be seen whether banks were as well. Hamilton thought so. He pointed out that a bank would be necessary if the country had to wage war on short notice. The only taxes in existence at that time were based on consumption (tariffs and excises), and the national government would therefore be unable to raise a great deal of money quickly. The consequences of this defect received ample demonstration during the American Revolution; who could say whether European bankers would be available at the time of the next war?[40]

The doctrine of implied powers was born. While all sides conceded that Congress could exercise powers not specifically mentioned in the Constitution if they qualified as necessary and proper to the execution of powers listed in it, not everyone embraced Hamilton's approach, and many found it breathtaking. A requirement that all acts be necessary to the exercise of one of the enumerated powers qualified as much more restrictive than a mere caution that some relationship exist. Federally operated gold and silver mines might bear a relationship to the enumerated power of coining money, but that did not mean they qualified as necessary and proper exercises of that authority. No wonder Madison complained that Hamilton's approach to constitutional interpretation would, if accepted, "strike at the very essence of a government . . . composed of limited and enumerated powers."[41] Flawed as they were, Hamilton's arguments took root in the body politic, where they were often inert but always available.

For the president, Hamilton's logic was probably unnecessary. Washington had never embraced the narrow constructions of national power embraced by opponents of the bank. He was in fact as fervent an advocate of federal power as any Federalist, owing in part to his witnessing the deprivations visited upon the Continental army during the Revolution. In his view, the nation's economic resources would never be fully developed if left to the caprices of the

39. 1 *Stats at Large* 53–54 (August 7, 1789).
40. *Papers of Hamilton*, 8:124.
41. Quoted in Haines, *Role of the Supreme Court*, 212.

penurious and squabbling state governments. To no one's surprise, the president signed the bank bill on February 25, 1791. He probably made the right decision. As James Madison would learn to his regret, money is the raw material from which wars are made. In addition, the Bank of the United States proved such a valuable asset that even the most narrow-minded had to concede its value. Its notes became a stable circulating medium. The bank served as a restraining influence upon state banks with which it did business by forcing them to back their notes with specie (gold or silver).[42]

Having twice driven Congress before him, Hamilton pressed his advantage. In his Report on Manufactures (December 5, 1791), the secretary of the treasury unveiled a program of financial aid for manufacturers. It included protective tariffs, the elimination of duties for certain raw materials, and bounties or subsidies designed to encourage the nation's fledgling manufacturing sector. The proposals did not surprise anyone, though assorted southerners complained that the tariff power was being abused. (Their fears had already received confirmation when legislators crammed the bill that would become the tariff of 1789 with steep duties designed to protect various industries.)[43] No one went so far as to claim that protective tariffs were unconstitutional. Bounties were another matter—which of the enumerated powers authorized them? Hamilton met the expected objections at the end of the Report on Manufactures. Unlike his paper on the bank, in which he argued for broad discretion with respect to the means used to exercise the enumerated powers, Hamilton gave a broad reading of what he at least viewed as one of those powers: the general welfare clause. In so doing he confirmed that despite Federalist assurances, the clause would serve as the Trojan horse of the Constitution: "The power to raise money is plenary, and indefinite; and the objects to which it may be appropriated are no less comprehensive, than the payment of the public debts and the providing for the common defence and general welfare." He explained that "the terms 'general welfare' were . . . doubtless intended to signify more than was expressed or imported in those [powers] which [they] preceded; otherwise numerous exigencies incident to the affairs of the nation would have been left without a provision." After casting his line so far out, Hamilton found it easy to conclude that giving money to manufacturers fell within the reach of Congress. There is,

42. Miller, *Federalist Era*, 60.
43. Elkins and McKitrick, *Age of Federalism*, 65. Tariffs were levied on a variety of items, including nails, boots, shoes, soap, salt, sugar, and coffee. 1 *Stats at Large* 24 (July 4, 1789).

he insisted, no room for doubt that "whatever concerns the general interests of learning of agriculture and manufactures and of commerce are within the sphere of the national councils as far as regards an application of money." In fact, Hamilton argued, the spending power of Congress had no limits at all, save one: "the object to which the appropriation of money is to be made [must] be general and not local; its operation extending in fact, or by possibility; throughout the Union, and not being confined to a particular spot."[44]

Congress reacted to the Report on Manufactures with something less than unanimous approval. The bill's cause was not helped by the fact that legislators were already considering a measure to expand a subsidy for the New England fishing industry. The tariff of 1789 provided for the payment of cash bounties to fishing interests in order to ease the burden of high tariffs on imported salt, which was used in large quantities to cure fish. In effect, the measure constituted a rebate. As these went only to merchants, New England fishing interests sought an expansion of the program in 1791. The Senate approved a bill to pay a bounty of $2.50 for every ton and a half of fish. Members of the House had trouble convincing themselves that the measure did not constitute a subsidy, and debate quickly focused upon the power of appropriation. At least one legislator, Robert Barnwell of South Carolina, echoed Hamilton's sentiments and claimed that the general welfare clause authorized bounties. New England members scrambled to find higher ground. Benjamin Goodhue of Massachusetts defended the bill on the grounds that it required no bounty, but only "the usual drawback for the salt used on the fish." Elbridge Gerry of Massachusetts also defended the payments. They could not be described as bounties, he insisted, as bounties are grants for which there is no consideration.[45]

Hugh Williamson of North Carolina feared the precedent that might be set—every imaginable interest would line up for subsidies, and unequal taxes would result. In fact, he continued, they already had—the assumption of state debts had effectively transferred $2 million from the South to the North. A broad spending power via the general welfare clause would hasten the day when northern representatives would have yet another excuse (large expenditures) to impose high taxes on southerners. James Madison opposed the bill on constitutional grounds. In so doing he repeated the interpretation of the general welfare clause he had first offered during ratification (*The*

44. *Annals of Congress*, 2d Cong., 2d sess., 3:1011-12.
45. Ibid., 2d Cong., 1st sess., February 1792, 3:375, 366, 376.

*Federalist*, No. 41). The clause, he explained, was not a power at all: "after giving Congress power to raise money and apply it to all purposes which they may pronounce necessary to the general welfare," it would be absurd "to add a power to raise armies, to provide fleets, etc." In Madison's view, the "meaning of the general terms in question must either be sought in the subsequent enumeration which limits and details them, or they convert the government from one limited, as hitherto supposed, to the enumerated powers, into a government without any limits at all." Madison then turned to the history of the phrase. "The terms 'common defense and general welfare,' . . . are . . . found in the Articles of Confederation, where . . . they are susceptible of as great latitude . . . as is now assigned to them." Yet, he continued, "it was always considered as clear and certain, that the old Congress was limited to the enumerated powers, and that the enumeration limited and explained the general terms." Did anyone remember otherwise? "I ask the gentlemen themselves, whether it was ever supposed that the old Congress could give away the moneys of the states in bounties, to encourage agriculture, or for any other purpose they pleased?" He went on to spell out the consequences that would occur if the interpretation of his opponents gained acceptance. "If Congress can apply money indefinitely to the general welfare, and are the sole and supreme judges of the general welfare, they may take the care of religion into their own hands; they may establish teachers in every state, county, and parish, and pay them out of the public treasury; they may take into their hands the education of children, establishing in like manner schools throughout the Union; they may undertake the regulation of all roads, other than post roads." Hence the conclusion: if the powers of Congress were "established in the latitude contended for, it would subvert the very foundation, and transmute the very nature of the limited government established by the people of America."[46] Nothing so traumatic occurred. Instead, Madison devised a solution acceptable to all sides. He proposed an amendment altering the fisheries bill so that while the cod industry received payments, they would be issued in the form of a drawback or allowance on the amounts paid in salt tariffs. The deal went through; it had the ancillary effect of killing the manufactures subsidy.[47] Unlike the fishing industry, which used huge quantities of imported salt to cure fish and thus paid steep tariffs, manufacturers did not depend heavily on imported raw materials, so there

46. Ibid., 3:378–80, 386–89.
47. Elkins and McKitrick, *Age of Federalism*, 277.

was no way to disguise payments to them as anything other than subsidies.

While the fisheries debate killed any hopes for a large-scale program of aid to manufacturers (or anyone else), Congress still occasionally spent money on ends whose relation to the enumerated powers was not easily discernible. The debates surrounding those measures made clear that at least some legislators took seriously Hamilton's claims regarding the general welfare clause. In early 1794 Elias Boudinot of New Jersey cited it to justify a bill to aid hurricane victims in Santo Domingo (the Dominican Republic). Samuel Dexter of Massachusetts refused to accept the general welfare clause as authority for the appropriation but nonetheless asked for a delay—he did not want to vote against the bill and so desired "leisure [so that he might] find proper reasons for voting in its favor."[48] James Madison could not believe what he was hearing. After conceding that Congress ought to help, he expressed hope that it would do so without "establishing a dangerous precedent, which might hereafter be perverted to the countenance of purposes very different from those of charity." He persuaded the House to alter the bill so that the money would be deducted from the government's debt to France, as Santo Domingo was a French colony at that time.[49]

Congress addressed the spending power question for the last time during the Washington administration in late 1796, after a fire destroyed much of Savannah, Georgia. Proponents of a bill to aid the victims wasted no time in pointing out that Congress had provided aid to other disaster victims and in appealing to the chauvinism of their peers: "Shall we … treat the citizens of Savannah with more disrespect than the people of Santo Domingo?" Andrew Moore of Virginia recalled that claims of "distressed veterans" had been approved even though they were not filed within the period provided by statute. "If [Congress] were to act from generosity … generosity ought to be extended universally." Robert Goodloe Harper of South Carolina declared that "the present case might justly be included under the head of promoting the general welfare of the country." Abraham Baldwin of Georgia believed that appropriations for navigational aids demonstrated "that though the Constitution was very useful in giving general directions, yet it was not capable of being administered under so rigorous and mechanical a construction as had been sometimes contended for." Besides, he concluded, what if an entire state was stricken by a natural disaster, such as an earthquake?[50]

48. *Annals of Congress*, 3d Cong., 1st sess., January 10, 1794, 4:172–73.
49. See Currie, *Constitution in Congress: Federalist Period*, 188–89.
50. *Annals of Congress*, 4th Cong., 2d sess., December 28, 1796, 6:1714, 1720–22.

The opposition would have none of it. Nathaniel Macon of North Carolina allowed that "the sufferings of the people of Savannah were doubtless very great; no one could help feeling for them." Yet he "wished gentlemen to put their finger on that portion of the Constitution which gave the House power to afford them relief." Aaron Kitchell of New Jersey warned that passage of the bill would tempt state governments to withhold aid from citizens on the pretense that they could expect help from Congress. Virginia's John Nicholas also objected to the bill. "If the general welfare was to be extended to objects of charity, it was undefined indeed. Charity was not a proper subject for them to legislate upon; and, if this resolution were to pass, all the powers of which they were possessed would not be adequate to raise funds to answer the demands which would be brought against the treasury." William Smith of South Carolina thought the measure constitutional and pointed to the relief provided to the victims of Indian atrocities as precedent for it. Thomas Claiborne of Virginia reminded the House that funds had been spent upon "trading-houses" on the western frontier and suggested that they had been appropriated for the "general welfare; for the support of trade, and the increase of the revenue."[51] The Savannah aid bill did not come close to passing. Yet advocates of a broad spending power were clearly becoming adept at finding precedents in support of their position—though almost all of the acts cited in connection with the Savannah bill could be tied to one of the enumerated powers. Trading posts constituted an exercise of the commerce power (which itself referred to trade with the Indians). Compensation for veterans bore a necessary relation to the government's war powers. Aid for Santo Domingo constituted nothing more than repayment of the government's debts.

With the defeat of the Savannah aid bill, the first phase of the struggle over the congressional power of appropriation came to an end. There were some ancillary scuffles; the president twice mentioned the possibility of establishing a national university (in his first and last annual messages), but Washington cited none of the enumerated powers in support of the idea, and his recommendations were not given serious consideration. A 1796 proposal to establish an agricultural board that would disburse information advanced only a bit further.[52] (A House committee endorsed the idea but it never reached the floor.)[53] What mattered in the end were those ideas that

51. Ibid., December 1796, 6:1717, 1719, 1723, 1724, 1726.
52. James D. Richardson, ed., *A Compilation of the Messages and Papers of the Presidents, 1789–1897*, 10 vols. (Washington, D.C.: U.S. Government Printing Office, 1896–99), 1:58, 193–94.
53. *Annals of Congress*, 4th Cong., 2d sess., January 1797, 6:1835.

actually became law. Despite Hamilton's creativeness, Congress did not embrace the view that it possessed a broad spending power. The assumption of state debts constituted the only really substantial usurpation by Congress in the area of appropriations during the 1790s.

There was also the practical question: what harm could possibly arise from the adoption of a broad spending power? The consequences had already been amply demonstrated: more spending required more taxes, and by the end of Washington's first term some of these had proved burdensome enough to create grave difficulties for thousands of Americans. The most notorious tax was the excise on whiskey, which had been levied in order to pay for the assumption of state debts. Americans found the tax difficult to pay and it quickly became very unpopular. The law required payment of the excise in gold or silver, of which there was very little in the country and almost none in the West. (Whiskey itself often served as a form of currency on the frontier.)[54] Those to whom the tax posed the greatest burden—the rural poor—had largely escaped taxation thus far. Revenues were instead obtained from tariffs or, in the case of the states, land taxes. Whenever excises were introduced—in 1643 in Britain and 1783 in Pennsylvania—resistance among poor farmers was overwhelming.[55] The federal government's abject failure put an end to Indian attacks in the West, even as it sought to impose heavy taxes upon settlers, infuriated many as well. The act's passage at a time when government spending appeared excessive also caused widespread consternation.[56]

The harsh terms of the statute establishing the whiskey tax did not help matters. It authorized revenue agents to enter any building that might contain a still even if they did not suspect wrongdoing.[57] The law also required that taxpayers maintain voluminous and complex records to justify their estimates of their tax liabilities.[58] Even worse was the decision of Congress to base the tax rate upon each still's capacity.[59] This arrangement proved an egregious and unfair burden for most farmers; they might leave their stills

54. Sharp, *American Politics in the Early Republic*, 94.

55. Thomas P. Slaughter, *The Whiskey Rebellion: Frontier Epilogue to the American Revolution* (New York: Oxford University Press, 1986), 14–18, 73–74.

56. Elkins and McKitrick, *Age of Federalism*, 473. See also Slaughter, *Whiskey Rebellion*, 112, 207.

57. 1 *Stats at Large* 206, section 29 (March 2, 1791); see Currie, *Constitution in Congress: Federalist Period*, 61.

58. Slaughter, *Whiskey Rebellion*, 202.

59. 1 *Stats at Large* 204, sections 21, 24.

alone for months. While they could avoid this provision by paying an alternative minimum tax on whiskey actually distilled, the tax forced them to increase the prices of their product and left them unable to complete with the larger distilleries that sold whiskey at a discount.[60]

Reaction to the tax came quickly. The legislatures of Maryland, Virginia, North Carolina, Georgia, and Pennsylvania passed resolutions critical of it. Resistance broke out along the frontier. Western Pennsylvania proved particularly hostile, as its inhabitants, struggling farmers in good years, saw their incomes almost disappear during the 1780s.[61] Their hatred of the tax was worsened considerably by the fact that persons charged with failing to pay it had to cross the Appalachians and appear in Philadelphia for trial, thus depriving their families of their services for weeks. As tempers heated up, farmers assembled at a large meeting in Pittsburgh, where they drafted resolutions that called on residents to refrain from aiding revenue officials.[62] Federal officials found themselves unable to collect the tax in much of Pennsylvania, Kentucky, Virginia, the Carolinas, and Georgia.[63] In July 1794 five hundred Pennsylvanians surrounded the house of a Treasury Department official; their quarry, one John Neville, barely escaped with his life. A few weeks later seven thousand men converged at Braddock's Field outside Pittsburgh. An antitax mob destroyed property and abused those whom it suspected of paying the tax. In response, the president called out the state militias. Units from eastern Pennsylvania, Maryland, Virginia, and New Jersey, as well as a portion of the U.S. Army, arrived in Pittsburgh by the end of October, by which time most of the malcontents had dispersed.[64] Some two hundred Pennsylvanians were arrested. Federal prosecutors succeeded in having two of the accused convicted of treason despite the Constitution's requirement that a person make war on the United States or aid her enemies to be guilty of that crime. A handful of assaults upon civilians and federal officials did not seem to qualify.

In the view of Federalists, the successful dispersal of armed mobs in Pennsylvania constituted a ringing affirmation of the supremacy of the national government. For others, the Whiskey Rebellion and its aftermath raised questions about the prospects for freedom under the new Consti-

60. Slaughter, *Whiskey Rebellion*, 148.
61. Ibid., 99, 65–70.
62. Elkins and McKitrick, *Age of Federalism*, 462.
63. Slaughter, *Whiskey Rebellion*, 117–18, 151, 169.
64. Elkins and McKitrick, *Age of Federalism*, 462–63.

tution. Had its intricate system of checks and balances failed at the critical hour to protect individual Americans from overbearing public officials?
Within five years of its birth, leaders of the new government arrested scores
of citizens over little more than opposing their policies. They also imposed
burdensome, even confiscatory taxes on Americans, well within memory of
Antifederalist warnings that such acts would follow ratification. That the
tax had been made necessary by what many viewed as an unconstitutional appropriation—assumption—seemed to confirm the belief that Congress
would spend money on ends beyond its jurisdiction and then usurp the tax
base of the states to pay for its excesses. Was there no middle ground between stillborn government and tyranny?

### EXECUTIVE BRANCH INFLUENCE
### AND THE RISE OF PARTIES

During the early 1790s, critics began to express dismay over Alexander
Hamilton's domination of Congress. Thomas Jefferson complained to the
president that the secretary of the treasury exercised undue influence over
members of the House of Representatives through favors doled out by the
Bank of the United States.[65] Hamilton did not bother to reply. If interro-
gated, he undoubtedly would have denied the charges; on the other hand, he
made no secret of his admiration for the British system, in which successive
ministers secured majorities in the House of Commons through a careful
distribution of government offices.

Fears of legislative corruption likely had more to do with events in Britain than with anything occurring in the United States. The increasingly ve-
nal politics of the mother country had long served as an object of grim fas-
cination for Americans. During the revolutionary period they read of how
the key to British liberty, an independent Parliament, had been brought low
by the enticements of the Crown.[66] The monarchy steadily increased its influence during the eighteenth century, mainly through the use of royal offices to buy support in the House of Commons. By the time of the American Revolution, the monarchy enjoyed more power than it had possessed
in more than a century. Thus the ponderous indictment of Edmund Burke:

65. *Writings of Jefferson*, 6:1–5.
66. Bernard Bailyn, *The Ideological Origins of the American Revolution* (Cambridge: Harvard
University Press, 1967), 86.

"the power of the crown, almost dead and rotten ... has grown up anew, with much more strength, far less odium, under the name of influence."[67] The numbers confirmed Burke's assessment: out of roughly 550 MPs, 190 held government jobs in 1770. Americans knew of this situation and it was a factor in their dismissal of the idea of representation in Parliament. They realized that their representatives might well end up in the pocket of the ministry and sacrifice American interests. Many recalled the example of Scotland, which had been granted representation in Parliament by the 1707 Act of Union, only to see their MPs develop a reputation as the most corrupt legislators in the House of Commons.[68]

At the time of the Revolution, Americans viewed uncorrupted or independent legislatures as a critical ingredient of free government. Belief in the need to insulate lawmakers from executive influence would eventually give birth to the doctrine of separation of powers.[69] In an effort to preserve legislative independence, Americans added clauses to their state and national constitutions barring lawmakers from accepting jobs in the executive branch. Article V of the Articles of Confederation (1777) prohibited members of the Confederation Congress from holding federal office. At the Constitutional Convention Roger Sherman suggested banning members of Congress from the executive branch for life.[70] The delegates would not go that far; instead they prohibited the appointment of representatives and senators to offices created during the terms for which they had been elected (Article I, Section 6). Many delegates to the state ratifying conventions feared that the Constitution's lack of a complete ban on the appointment of lawmakers to office would lead to the corruption of legislators on a scale similar to that which existed in Britain.[71]

Widespread concern also arose out of the Constitutional Convention's decision to vest the appointive power in the president alone (subject to senate approval for high-level posts). Some thought it should be divided between the legislature and the executive, as it was in some states. Others favored a solution embraced by many legislatures: making lower-level ex-

67. Edmund Burke, *Thoughts on the Cause of the Present Discontents* (London, 1770).

68. George Stead Veitch, *The Genesis of Parliamentary Reform* (1913; reprint, Hamden, Conn.: Archon Books, 1965), 21, 18.

69. Wood, *Creation of the American Republic*, 157.

70. Farrand, *Records of the Federal Convention*, 2:490.

71. See James Monroe's speech at the Virginia ratifying convention, in Storing, *Complete Anti-Federalist*, 5:295. See also Farrand, *Records of the Federal Convention*, 2:490–92.

ecutive positions elective.[72] Critics also expressed dismay over the president's power to remove officers. When the first Congress met in the spring of 1789, several legislators expressed the view that since the Constitution required Senate consent for cabinet-level appointments, the Senate's approval was also needed for the removal of senior officials.[73] This approach promised to greatly reduce the president's ability to use executive branch offices for political purposes. A rather furious debate ensued, as the need for an effective executive collided with a determination to prevent the powers of patronage from accumulating in a single branch of the federal government. In the end, the House of Representatives passed a bill organizing the State Department with a clause recognizing the president's removal power.[74] The House probably made the right decision. As James Madison pointed out, presidents could not be expected to execute the laws if they did not have control over their underlings, and they would not have that control without the threat of termination.[75]

Along with acceptance of the removal power, the rise of political parties vested enormous influence in the hands of the president. He would need it, as the ranks of the opposition grew by the day in the early 1790s. Between scandals in the Treasury Department, unfavorable reaction to the excise taxes, and hostility toward the United States Bank, the administration made a variety of enemies by 1793. Most of its opponents were former Antifederalists. Political parties formed in part along sectional lines, with the supporters of Hamilton's policies (Federalists) dominating in the North, and their critics (Republicans) holding sway in the southern states. Both sides did what they could to cut into the other's base; as early as 1791 Madison and Jefferson ventured to New York, where they met with Governor George Clinton. Federalists, on the other hand, enjoyed some success in Virginia and South Carolina.

Over what did Americans disagree that led them to support one of the two competing parties? To a large extent, they fought over the same issues that had created divisions during the ratification struggle. Both Antifederalists and Republicans subscribed to a minimalist view of government, which

72. See Farrand, *Records of the Federal Convention,* 2:537; Leonard D. White, *The Federalists: A Study in Administrative History* (New York: Macmillan, 1956), 255.

73. See U.S. Constitution, Article II, Section 2.

74. *Annals of Congress,* 1st Cong., 1st sess., June 1789, 1:473–608, 592; 1 *Stats at Large* 28, 29, section 2, (July 27, 1789). For further discussion, see Currie, *Constitution in Congress: Federalist Period,* 36–41.

75. *Annals of Congress,* 1st Cong., 1st sess., June 1789, 1:480–81.

was itself rooted in the Whig ideology that served as the driving force behind the American Revolution. They both viewed national power as subject to abuse, much as it had been in Britain. Federalists, by contrast, took a more aggressive and optimistic approach to public authority. The Federalist/Republican conflict also grew out of differing reactions to the convulsion under way in Europe. The seminal political event of the eighteenth century, and perhaps of the millennium, had just occurred, and it had very little to do with the United States. Republicans embraced the French Revolution, while Federalists recoiled in horror. Both sides made of it what they wished. What it actually represented—the beginning of a seismic shift in Europe from monarchical to republican government—was lost in the mix. Republicans initially perceived the significance of the House of Bourbon's fall more accurately than their foes did. Beginning around 1795, they suffered from the unfortunate fact that the French Revolution had given way to a revenge-driven bloodbath. Scores of families within the nobility were herded out into the open and summarily shot. The September 1792 massacres saw more than a thousand people executed, and by the end of the Terror, more than a hundred thousand had been put to death. The Republicans worsened their plight by turning a blind eye to these excesses—they simply could not move beyond the notion that the American and French Revolutions were of the same species. For them, the overthrow of Louis XVI appeared to be a signal achievement in the liberation of mankind from tyranny. The French people, whose aid had proved so critical during the American fight for independence, had embraced the cause of liberty for themselves. How, Republicans asked, could Americans fail to support the heroic efforts of their former allies?

Federalists were appalled. As they saw it, monarchy had not given way to freedom; rather, the stability that came with ancient forms of government had been replaced by the tyranny of the demagogue and the violence of the mob. They contemplated the murder of thousands in France and wondered if such a thing could happen in the United States. The Whiskey Rebellion led many Federalists to believe that it could; they feared that resistance to the collection of a tax might well be followed by wholesale insurrection and even civil war. From this perspective, bringing treason charges against those who had counseled resistance was more than understandable; it was necessary if order was to be preserved. That American farmers lived under much better conditions than the peasants of France and had no motive for revolution was overlooked.

It was in this atmosphere of mistrust and fear that the American two-party system was born in the early 1790s. From the outset, the Federalists were hobbled by a weakness that ultimately brought about their downfall: an unmitigated hostility to the idea of broad-based republican government, even in the starched form it took in 1790s. Federalists all too often betrayed an elitist hostility to the idea of sharing power with their fellow citizens. When they wrote off opposition to their policies as the protests of the ignorant, their Republican opponents were only too glad to quote such sentiments for the voters. Federalists also paid a price, at least in the short term, for their hostility to the French Revolution, for few Americans realized the extent of its excesses until the mid-1790s. Republicans profited from Federalist hostility to an event that appeared to be born of the same spirit as the American Revolution. When "republican societies" supportive of the French Revolution brought new elements of the population, such as immigrants and urban laborers, into politics, these groups invariably supported the Republicans. The party consequently developed a populist base that the Federalists were never able to match.

The lone Federalist advantage in the battle for political supremacy during this period (apart from George Washington) was the party's control of federal patronage. Federal civil servants operated in a bewildering array of departments, offices, and bureaus, including customhouses, trading posts, the Internal Revenue Service, nine hundred post offices, and even marine hospitals. The customhouses provided the richest source of jobs; by 1800 the offices in Baltimore, New York, and Philadelphia all counted more than fifty employees, and the one in Charleston, South Carolina, had forty-seven.[76] Once party lines began to develop, Federalists wasted little time in pressing their advantage. As early as 1792 one partisan warned Hamilton that because each of the collectorships "possesses vast influence," they "ought not to be given away lightly." The president's approach to appointments furthered the cause of partisanship, as he frowned upon the idea of bringing into the civil service those who had opposed ratification.[77] As most Antifederalists (though not all) ended up in the Republican camp, this policy constituted something of a party test for those seeking appointments. The civil service thus came to resemble an arm of the Federalist Party during the 1790s. Between 1791

76. White, *Federalists*, 303.

77. Carl Prince, *The Federalists and the Origins of the U.S. Civil Service* (New York: New York University Press, 1977), 15, 4-7.

and 1794, Postmaster General Timothy Pickering thoroughly politicized his department. He used the available positions to employ Federalists and supported their efforts to gain influence within their communities. A competitive advantage was not enough for Pickering; during his term the post office received numerous complaints that opposition newspapers were not reaching their subscribers. Bureaus that owed their existence to Alexander Hamilton's financial policies also gained a reputation for partisan behavior. The Internal Revenue Service, which had been set up to collect excise taxes and employed 450 people by 1800, became so heavy-handed that it helped trigger the Whiskey Rebellion. Revenue workers engaged in widespread voter intimidation during the election of 1800.[78]

Although critics initially feared executive branch patronage out of concern for the independence of Congress, the growth of the federal civil list actually had a much greater effect on the nascent political parties—it allowed the chief executive and his cohorts to exercise enormous influence over them. Parties, after all, were made of men, and men, particularly in that age of scarcity, were always short of funds and seeking positions that paid in cash. The simultaneous arrival of a civil service rich with jobs and political parties that could exploit it concentrated power in the hands of the federal executive branch to a remarkable degree. In New Hampshire, Jeremiah Olney's appointment as collector at Portsmouth made him the key political figure in the state. In Massachusetts the federal customhouses played a central role in the state's Federalist organization. Executive branch patronage enabled Federalists to remain competitive in democratic Rhode Island even when their policies became unpopular. Places in the customhouse helped James Simons dominate the Federalist Party in Charleston, South Carolina. In small towns, postal contracts and jobs enabled made the postmasters leading political figures overnight.[79] The situation contrasted sharply with the assurances made during ratification, when James Madison predicted that the state governments would provide more "offices and emoluments" and therefore carry more influence.[80]

As political parties increased in importance, officials placed more emphasis on party affiliation when filling places in the executive branch. John Adams, who succeeded Washington as president in 1797, recalled that his

---

78. Ibid., 185, 187, 136, 140.
79. Ibid., 64, 22–26, 57–64, 129, 192.
80. James Madison, *The Federalist*, No. 46, in Rossiter, *Federalist Papers*, 294.

predecessor had "appointed a multitude of democrats and Jacobins of the deepest die." He was pleased to report that he had "been more cautious in this respect." Adams became the first president to terminate an officehold-er for partisan reasons when he removed Republican Tench Coxe from his post as commissioner of revenue in December 1797. He also went beyond his predecessor in making political affiliation a consideration when staffing even the lowest ranks of the federal bureaucracy. The Adams administration con-sidered the political loyalties of U.S. marshals, and even the organization of the provisional army in 1798 was hobbled by partisan considerations.[81]

The use of federal jobs and printing contracts to obtain the support of newspapers constituted the most invidious form of executive patronage dur-ing the 1790s. The system had two components. Postmaster General Picker-ing began the first when he appointed scores of printers to postmasterships. As every decent-sized town needed a post office, publicly supported Feder-alist sheets could be found throughout the country. Stonington, Connecti-cut's Samuel Trumbull served as both postmaster and editor of the *Journal of the Times*. The Pennsylvania towns of Reading, Harrisburg, and Pittsburgh also had Federalist postmasters who happened to publish newspapers. Some newspaper editors held other federal jobs; John Dorrance of Rhode Island of the *United States Chronicle* served as a land tax commissioner.[82] A 1799 law that empowered the secretary of state to pick at least one newspaper in each state to publish federal statutes served as the second component of the executive branch's court press.[83] A government expected to be seen and not heard had, within ten years of its founding, secured the power to influence what Americans read, wrote, and thought. Federalists benefited enormously from this situation; by 1800 they enjoyed, through their control of the feder-al executive branch, influence over political parties and newspapers in every state of the Union. With the trophies of incumbent power so formidable, it is a wonder the Federalists ever lost their place.

81. Quoted in White, *Federalists*, 273, 289, 276, 274.

82. Prince, *Federalists and the U.S. Civil Service*, 208–9, 219, 220, 174.

83. 1 Stat 724 (March 2, 1799). See also Culver H. Smith, *The Press, Politics, and Patronage: The American Government's Use of Newspapers, 1789–1875* (Athens: University of Georgia Press, 1977), 41.

## THE FEDERAL JUDICIARY

The early subservience of Congress came as a surprise to many, as they expected it to dominate the other branches just as the legislatures monopolized power within the state governments. Perhaps the relative strength of the executive and the judiciary should have been anticipated, as the Constitutional Convention vested in them a degree of strength beyond that seen in governors and state judges. The president could veto bills, and federal judges could invalidate laws that violated the Constitution (judicial review). Alexander Hamilton promoted a federal judiciary on these grounds—it would, he promised, help keep Congress within the confines of its enumerated powers.[84]

At the state level, the power of judicial review had been invoked on only a handful of occasions. Assurances that the judiciary would stand guard over the prerogatives of the states therefore fell on deaf ears. Many Antifederalists viewed the judicial branch as dangerous. These concerns stemmed in part from colonial experience, when judges did the king's bidding. Judges in America continued to serve at the "pleasure of the Crown" long after the monarchy lost the power to remove them at home.[85] Antifederalist fears also stemmed from familiarity with the judiciary in Britain, where the royal courts had used tortured interpretations of the law to expand their sphere.[86] Federal judges faced a similar conflict of interest in determining the constitutionality of acts of Congress. As "Brutus" put it, "every extension of the power of the general legislature [Congress] will increase the powers of the courts; and the dignity and importance of judges, will be in proportion to the extent and magnitude of the powers they exercise."[87]

Antifederalists found the judiciary threatening because the new government lacked a means for the correction of judicial abuses. The House of Lords had always been able to reverse the decisions of British courts; in America, most of the legislatures retained the power to reverse decisions of state courts. Yet neither Congress nor any other body would be able to correct errant rulings issued by the federal judiciary.[88] Nor could federal judges be removed

84. Alexander Hamilton, *The Federalist*, No. 78, in Rossiter, *Federalist Papers*, 466–67.
85. Wood, *Creation of the American Republic*, 160.
86. "Centinel I" [Samuel Bryan], *Philadelphia Independent Gazetteer*, October 5, 1787, in Bailyn, *Debate on the Constitution*, 1:58.
87. "Brutus," no. 11, January 31, 1788, in Ketcham, *Antifederalist Papers*, 297.
88. "Brutus," no. 15, March 20, 1788, ibid., 305; see also speech of Mr. Grayson at Vir-

easily, as the Constitution provided them with lifetime tenure. Only the powers of impeachment and amendment limited the third branch. Many viewed these safeguards as inadequate; hence the conclusion that the decisions of the federal judiciary, "whatever they may be, will have the force of law; because there is no power provided in the Constitution, that can correct their errors, or control their adjudications. From this court there is no appeal."[89]

While the Founders protected individual judges from attack, they left the judicial branch as an institution extraordinarily susceptible to Congress, which under Article III had the task of establishing the federal courts. The Judiciary Act of 1789 vested in the Supreme Court the power to review decisions of state courts involving questions of federal and constitutional law as well as treaties.[90] The need for federal supremacy required this broad grant of power, yet the very fact that the judiciary's framework had to be devised by Congress indicated that the two branches were far from equal. Nor did Congress help matters with its attempts to manage the affairs of the Supreme Court. It assigned the justices to what became known as "circuit duty": traveling through the judicial circuits into which the country had been divided, hearing cases in towns large and small. At a time when roads were largely nonexistent, this policy forced members of the high court into the role of trailblazers. While it was true that lawyers of the time also had to "ride circuit," they did not have to travel from state to state. The justices repeatedly asked Congress to end the practice, but their pleas were in vain.

Circuit riding cast doubt upon the claim that judges would serve as vigilant guards around the congressional pen. How could they be expected to stand up to the legislative branch when they had to beg it for relief? Not surprisingly, few men cared to serve on the high court under these circumstances. While only one of the first six men nominated for the Supreme Court turned down the offer (Hanson Harrison), the others served only short periods before resigning.[91] In 1791 two Federalist lawyers, Charles C. Pinckney and Edward Rutledge, both declined Supreme Court nominations.[92] In 1795 Chief Justice Jay resigned—more than a year after he left for Great Britain

ginia ratifying convention of June 21, 1788, in Elliot, *Debates in the Several State Conventions*, 3:563–64.

89. "Brutus," no. 11, January 31, 1788, in Ketcham, *Antifederalist Papers*, 295.

90. Section 25 of the Judiciary Act of 1789 may be found at 1 *Stats at Large* 73, 85 (September 24, 1789).

91. Haines, *Role of the Supreme Court*, 121.

92. White, *Federalists*, 265.

to negotiate a treaty. To replace Jay, the president tried to nominate Alexander Hamilton, but the former treasury secretary wanted no part of it. Washington turned to John Rutledge, but his nomination was rejected by the Senate. The president then tried to nominate Patrick Henry—now a hardbitten Federalist—only to have him refuse the offer. At that point William Cushing was nominated and confirmed, but he refused to accept the appointment. Finally the office fell to Oliver Ellsworth, almost by default.[93]

Despite its feeble position, the Supreme Court mustered the will to stand up to Congress on at least one occasion during the 1790s. In *Hayburn's Case* (1792), it refused to order federal judges to enforce a statute that assigned them the rather thankless task of deciding the appropriate compensation for Revolutionary War veterans.[94] A number of judges had refused to accept the assignment on the grounds that the statute violated the Constitution by assigning them nonjudicial functions. The case gave the Supreme Court a perfect opportunity to assert itself: by merely refusing to carry out the law, it could demonstrate its power to invalidate a statute *and* enforce its ruling. If the Court, on the other hand, held unconstitutional a law that depended on the executive branch for enforcement, its ability to enforce its judgment would have depended on the acquiescence of officers over whom it had no real control. Although the justices did not explain their reasoning with precision, the Supreme Court probably invalidated the law for the same reason that lower-level judges refused to carry it out: the pension claims did not present a justiciable case or controversy, as required by Article III of the Constitution.[95] Congress responded with another statute aimed at the same end. It was a transparent attempt to evade the ruling. Instead of charging the federal courts with the duty to review veterans' cases, the law assigned the task to individual judges.[96]

Unlike its relationship with Congress, the federal judiciary operated from a position of strength when it came to the states. It was perhaps inevitable that federal judges would prove more willing to invalidate state legislation. In 1791 Supreme Court justices on circuit held void a Connecticut statute that violated the Treaty of Paris.[97] In 1792 a federal circuit court ruled

93. Haines, *Role of the Supreme Court*, 146–47.

94. 2 U.S. 408 (1792).

95. David P. Currie, *The Constitution in the Supreme Court: The First Hundred Years, 1789–1888* (Chicago: University of Chicago Press, 1985), 6–9.

96. 1 *Stats at Large* 324–25 (February 28, 1793).

97. The official reports do not contain a written opinion explaining the ruling. For dis-

unconstitutional a state law that extended the deadline for debt payments on the grounds that it violated the contract clause.[98] In 1795 two Supreme Court justices on circuit held void a Pennsylvania statute on the same grounds.[99] In 1796 the Supreme Court invalidated a Virginia statute that discharged a resident's debt to a British merchant, because it violated the Treaty of Paris.[100] From the beginning, there were occasional acts of resistance. Litigants in a North Carolina case tried to have it removed to federal court, only to have a state judge refuse to obey the federal court's writ of certiorari. The legislature passed a resolution approving the judge's conduct.[101]

A more serious dispute arose in Georgia. Article III, Section 2 of the Constitution gave federal courts jurisdiction over suits "between a state and citizens of other states." Antifederalists feared that states would be dragged into federal court against their will. Despite the Constitution's clear wording, Federalists promised they would not.[102] When the executor of a Tory merchant's estate sued Georgia in federal court, the state refused to contest the suit, claiming sovereign immunity. Justice James Wilson ruled for the plaintiff by default; he pointed out that Georgia's interpretation of the Constitution would strip the federal government of its ability to impose its will on the states.[103] In early 1794 Justice Wilson issued a writ of inquiry for the purpose of carrying out the decision. The lower house of the Georgia legislature responded by passing a bill imposing death on anyone who attempted to enforce the ruling.[104] Federal officials, perhaps thinking prudence the better part of valor, never executed the writ. Discontent over the case was widespread. Newspapers pointed to Federalist promises of state immunity that had been made during ratification, and several legislatures demanded action. Massachusetts called for an amendment barring suits against states

cussion, see Haines, *Role of the Supreme Court*, 125, and Charles Warren, *The Supreme Court in United States History*, 2 vols. (Boston: Little, Brown, 1926), 1:66.

98. The opinion is not contained in the official reports. It is discussed in Warren, *Supreme Court in United States History*, 1:67.

99. *Van Horne's Lessee v. Dorrance*, in *The Federal Cases: Comprising Cases in the Circuit and District Courts of the United States*, 30 vols. (St. Paul, Minn.: West Publishing Co.) (hereafter Federal Cases), 28:1012 (1795).

100. *Ware v. Hylton*, 3 U.S. 199 (1796).

101. Haines, *Role of the Supreme Court*, 124–25.

102. Elliot, *Debates in the Several State Conventions*, 3:533 (Madison), 3:555 (Marshall); Alexander Hamilton, *The Federalist*, No. 81, in Rossiter, *Federalist Papers*, 487–88. See also Currie, *Constitution in Congress: Federalist Period*, 195–98, for discussion.

103. *Chisholm v. United States*, 2 U.S. 419 (1793).

104. Warren, *Supreme Court in United States History*, 1:100.

by citizens of other states from the federal courts.[105] An indignant congress-man had already proposed a constitutional amendment to achieve that end; it passed both houses easily and the states approved what became the Eleventh Amendment with startling dispatch.

It would be easy to conclude that the Supreme Court inadvertently triggered an overreaction on the part of the states, and in so doing weakened the federal judiciary. Nothing could be further from the truth. President Washington took the same approach to federal judges that he embraced with other senior-level civil servants—he wanted only men who supported the Constitution during ratification.[106] This policy ensured that the judiciary would be staffed by judges who embraced the idea of a strong, vigorous central government. Some jurists overreached; they exhibited a willingness to hold invalid not only those state laws that violated constitutional provisions but also those that merely appeared unwise. In substituting their own values for the text of the Constitution as the test for the legality of state legislation, these judges initiated the long process of converting the federal judiciary into a sort of American privy council, such as that which supervised the colonies during the colonial period. Operating under the Board of Trade, it invalidated statutes passed by colonial assemblies that conflicted with acts of Parliament or simply appeared to be unwise. This development qualified as particularly obnoxious in light of the fact that the Constitutional Convention rejected the idea of giving the federal government veto power over the acts of the legislatures precisely because it would have destroyed the sovereignty of the states.[107]

The first hint that certain federal judges were ready to convert their branch into an American privy council occurred in 1798. In *Calder v. Bull*, the Supreme Court refused to hold void a Connecticut law that set aside a state court's invalidation of a will. Some thought the law violated the Constitution's ex post facto clause; the justices held that the clause applied only to criminal matters. Justice Samuel Chase made an extraordinary claim. In a concurring opinion, he insisted that the Supreme Court could void state laws even if they did not violate the Constitution: "An act of the legislature (for I cannot call it a law), contrary to the great first principles of the social

105. Peter W. Low and John C. Jeffries, *Federal Courts and the Law of Federal-State Relations*, 3d ed. (Westbury, N.Y.: Foundation Press, 1994), 876.
106. Haines, *Role of the Supreme Court*, 117.
107. Farrand, *Records of the Federal Convention*, 1:164–68.

compact, cannot be considered a rightful exercise of legislative authority." What sort of acts did Justice Chase have in mind? Those that punish the innocent, destroy contracts, make citizens judges in their own cause, or take the property of one and give it to another. "It is," he wrote, "against all reason and justice, for a people to entrust a legislature with such powers; and, therefore, it cannot be presumed that they have done it." Justice James Iredell disagreed. If Congress or a legislature "shall pass a law, within the general scope of their constitutional power, the Court cannot pronounce it to be void, merely because it is, in their judgment, contrary to the principles of natural justice." Why? Because "the ideas of natural justice are regulated by no fixed standards; the ablest and purest men have differed upon the subject; and all that the Court could properly say, in such an event, would be, that the legislature, possessed of an equal right of opinion, had passed an act which, in the opinion of the judges, was inconsistent with the abstract principles of natural justice."[108]

In the short run the Supreme Court did not assume the right to invalidate state laws merely because they were unjust or unwise. Yet judicial abuses occurred during the 1790s, and they proved far more immediate in their consequences than abstract debates over the appropriate role of the federal judiciary. All of the states had adopted at least portions of British common law—the body of written opinions handed down by English judges over the centuries. State courts applied useful precedents in every area of the law, from criminal cases to property disputes. A handful of federal judges claimed that the federal courts enjoyed jurisdiction over certain common law crimes that threatened the national government. There was not a shred of evidence from the ratification debates to support this assertion; on the contrary, Federalists emphasized that the courts, like Congress, were limited in their jurisdiction to those subjects enumerated in the Constitution.[109] Nonetheless, certain judges pressed on, determined to stamp out those common law crimes they felt threatened the national government. Seditious speech was the main focus of this witch hunt. Federal judges and attorneys rarely stuck to the legal definition of sedition (incitement to resistance against lawful authority); instead they sought to imprison editors who attacked the policies of George Washington and his successor, John Adams. These prosecutions took place in the wake of two war scares that marked the last decade of the century.

108. 3 U.S. 386, 391–92, 388, 399 (1798).
109. See Hamilton, *The Federalist*, No. 80, in Rossiter, *Federalist Papers*, 475.

The first, in which the United States went to the brink with Great Britain, occurred in 1794; the second, involving France, took place in 1798–99. Federal prosecutors secured the indictments of three printers for common law sedition during the decade.[110] A New York City editor was convicted of libel in federal court.[111] Benjamin Franklin Bache provided Federalists with their biggest prize. Printer of the Philadelphia *Aurora*—the most prominent Republican newspaper in the country—he regularly engaged in defamatory attacks upon leading Federalists. Following his conviction for common law sedition, Bache spent several months in jail.

Federal judges also tried defendants under the related theory that the federal government derived powers from international law. The practice began with President Washington's 1793 Neutrality Proclamation, in which he instructed federal attorneys to prosecute all persons who violated the "law of nations" by aiding or taking up arms against those countries then at war in Europe.[112] Federal prosecutors thereafter secured the indictment of one Ravara after he sent threatening, extortionist letters to British officials. In *United States v. Ravara* (1793), the Supreme Court held that the federal judiciary had jurisdiction over Ravara's offense via the common law, which itself included the law of nations.[113] Also occurring in 1793 was the matter of Gideon Henfield. Federal attorneys charged Henfield with violating the law of nations after he served aboard a French privateer that captured a ship belonging to Great Britain. He was indicted in July 1793. His attorneys argued that no statute made Henfield's act a crime. Nevertheless Justice James Wilson instructed the jury of the possibility of an offense against the United States under its common law jurisdiction. The jury acquitted Mr. Henfield.[114] The president reacted with anger; for a time he considered calling a special session of Congress. Yet the public proved supportive, as it was unclear why Henfield had been indicted. As Virginia Federalist John Mar-

110. Richard Hofstadter, *The Idea of a Party System: The Rise of a Legitimate Opposition in the U.S., 1780–1840* (Berkeley and Los Angeles: University of California Press, 1969), 108. Colonial legislatures did not shy away from prosecuting troublesome printers. Benjamin Franklin's brother was imprisoned for a month in the 1720s after writing an article critical of the Pennsylvania assembly. Franklin, *The Autobiography of Benjamin Franklin,* ed. Leonard Labaree (New Haven: Yale University Press, 1964), 69.

111. Stephen B. Presser, *The Original Misunderstanding: The English, the Americans and the Dialectic of Federalist Jurisprudence* (Charlotte, N.C.: Academic Press, 1991), 76.

112. Richardson, *Messages and Papers of the Presidents,* 1:56.

113. 2 U.S. 297 (1793).

114. Henfield's Case, 11 Federal Cases 1099 (1793).

shall wrote, "It was universally asked, what law had been offended, and under what statute was the indictment supported?"[115]

In a 1798 case Judge Richard Peters affirmed the view that the federal judiciary had jurisdiction over common law crimes. He explained that the federal courts necessarily enjoyed a power to punish offences "aimed at the subversion of any federal institution, or at the corruption of its public officers." In fact, any "offence against the well-being of the United States; from its very nature, it is cognizable under their authority; and consequently it is within the jurisdiction of this Court." Justice Chase disagreed: "the United States, as a federal government, have no common law; and consequently, no indictment can be maintained in their courts, for offences merely at the common law." After all, he continued "the Constitution of the Union is the source of all jurisdiction of the national government." Thus, "departments of the government can never assume any power, that is not expressly granted by that instrument, nor exercise a power in any other manner than is prescribed." He conceded that in the exercise of its enumerated powers, Congress might have occasion to outlaw particular types of conduct. It remained, however, "essential, that Congress should define the offences to be tried, and apportion the punishments to be inflicted." As for the idea that the national government had somehow "inherited" English common law, Chase pointed out that even the states had adopted only portions of it, usually by statute. Nothing similar had occurred in Congress.[116]

Of the twelve men who sat on the Supreme Court during the 1790s, seven held that there was a federal common law of crimes.[117] The significance of this can hardly be overstated. Viewed as perhaps the weakest branch in a government of limited powers, the federal courts had assumed for themselves jurisdiction over any behavior that could be tagged as a crime against the state under English common law. Republicans could hardly believe their eyes. As Thomas Jefferson wrote in August 1799, earlier Federalist excesses were "solitary, inconsequential, timid things in comparison with the audacious, barefaced and sweeping pretension to a system of law for the U.S. without the adoption of their legislature [Congress], and so infinitely beyond [its] power to adopt."[118]

115. Quoted in Presser, *Original Misunderstanding*, 73.
116. *United States v. Worrall*, 2 U.S. 384, 395, 394 (1798).
117. Presser, *Original Misunderstanding*, 68.
118. *Writings of Jefferson*, 7:384.

1798

Just before John Adams succeeded George Washington as president in March 1797, elements unfriendly to the United States (the Directory) gained power in France. The new French leadership believed the Americans were behaving like ungrateful children; having obtained their independence with French money, they were now unwilling to aid France when it was under attack by the leading powers of Europe. Even worse was the fact that American trade with Britain—then at war with France—had gone through the roof. The French government therefore declared in early 1797 that any neutral ship carrying even a single item belonging to one of France's enemies would be subject to capture. By June, the French navy had taken more than three hundred American ships.[119]

The new administration did not respond immediately, in part because on the day Adams was inaugurated, the national government had at its disposal an army of fewer than two thousand men and no navy whatsoever. A single unarmed boat used by customs officials belonged to the Treasury Department. The new administration and the Federalist majority in Congress hurried to put the country on a war footing. As they saw it, the contagion of revolution appeared ready to swallow Europe whole, and America would be next. They had good reason to take this view. France was not exactly under siege; in fact, it was waging an offensive war upon other countries, and one that was ideologically motivated to boot. Its leaders wished to export their scorched-earth, anti-Christian brand of centralized government to the rest of the continent. Americans feared for their own future as well as that of Europe when word arrived in early 1798 that Austria had fallen and Britain stood alone.

Republicans in the fifth Congress resisted Federalist demands for increased defense expenditures. A logjam developed; it did not break until the spring of 1798, when they committed a tactical error, thereby uniting the country behind the administration. When the president blamed French intransigence for the failure of peace negotiations, Republicans demanded that he turn over the correspondence sent to him by American diplomats in Paris. The President provided the material, albeit with the names of the French officials deleted in favor of the letters X, Y, and Z. The correspon-

119. Henry Steele Commager, William Leuchtenberg, and Samuel Eliot Morison, *The Growth of the American Republic*, 6th ed. (New York: Oxford University Press, 1968), 318.

dence revealed that the three Americans sent to France had been pressured by their hosts to disavow their own government's policies. The public reacted with outrage and the president finally won support for a massive buildup of the armed forces. Republicans, on the other hand, suffered, owing to their support for the French; the party's leading newspaper went bankrupt almost overnight. With the opposition weakened, Federalists in Congress pushed through laws establishing the Department of the Navy and the Marine Corps. They also expanded the army, provided money for coastal fortifications, and cut off trade with France. In order to fund the increase in defense expenditures, Congress devised a variety of new taxes, including levies on stamps, houses, land, and slaves. In an indication of the gravity of the situation, George Washington came out of retirement to accept appointment as lieutenant general in command of the provisional army.

Congress addressed other perceived threats as well. The Naturalization Act of June 18, 1798, extended from five to fourteen years the period of residency required before immigrants were naturalized. Federalists pushed the law through with the hope of disenfranchising immigrant voters. It proved wholly ineffective, as the states determined who was eligible to vote. Many allowed immigrants to vote even before they were naturalized. The original draft would have posed a much more serious problem, as it proposed to establish classes of citizenship, with naturalized immigrants unable to hold office. The Alien Act authorized the president to deport any alien deemed "dangerous to the peace and safety of the United States."[120] While a power to expel aliens did not appear in the Constitution, lack of authority to expel foreigners seemed an invitation to folly—surely the government could remove agents or soldiers of hostile governments from American territory in the exercise of its war powers.[121]

Whatever their defects, the Alien and Naturalization Acts fell within the pale. The same could not be said for the Sedition Act. Enacted on July 14, 1798, the law made it a crime to utter or publish "any false, scandalous, and malicious writing or writings against the government of the United States, or either House of the Congress of the United States, with intent to defame ... or to bring them ... into contempt or disrepute."[122] While the federal government possessed the right to prohibit persons from inciting resis-

---

120. 1 *Stats at Large* 570–71 (June 25, 1798).

121. See speech of Harrison Gray Otis, *Annals of Congress*, 5th Cong., 2d sess., June 1798, 7:1986–87, for the argument that the war powers included the right to expel aliens.

122. 1 *Stats at Large* 596 (July 14, 1798).

tance to lawful authority, the Sedition Act went far beyond this standard. It subjected all persons who criticized the federal government to criminal sanctions. Several factors combined to produce the measure, the most immediate of which was the conviction that federal officials should have statutory authority to prosecute individuals who preached resistance to federal law. It also arose out of the inability of Federalists to accept the idea that Americans had a right to engage in endless, often scurrilous attacks on the administration and the national government. George Washington became deeply embittered over the rise of an organized opposition party.[123] The failure of many in the Federalist Party to recognize the right of Americans to criticize the national government's policies stemmed in part from the fear that such actions would aid the enemy in wartime; it also arose out of the fact that political parties had not yet gained wide acceptance. They were viewed as factious, disruptive forces that prospered only in malfunctioning political systems. Federalists therefore found it easy to view Republican opposition to the government's policies as beyond the acceptable limits of debate. Given Republican sympathies for France, their objections to administration attempts to meet the danger appeared partisan at best and disloyal at worst.

While some Federalists confessed to having trouble with the Sedition Act (it passed the House by a single vote), the congressional debates that preceded its passage revealed an alarming indifference to the First and Tenth Amendments. Federalist Representative John Allen of Connecticut detected sedition in a Philadelphia *Aurora* essay that accused the administration of pushing the country into war even as peace negotiations continued. Allen also lambasted Representative Edward Livingston of New York for suggesting that the House pass a resolution asking the president to reach an accommodation with France. As Allen saw it, the comments of the *Aurora* and Congressman Livingston provided evidence of "what I call a combination against the government [and] attempts to persuade the people of certain facts, which a majority of this House, at least, and of the people at large, I believe, know to be unfounded." Allen also cited a recent article from the *New York Time-Piece*. Complaining that it called the president "a person without patriotism, without philosophy, and a mock monarch," he spelled out the obvious conclusion: "if this be not a conspiracy against government and people, I know not what to understand from the 'threats of tears, exe-

---

123. See, for example, Washington's farewell address, in Richardson, *Messages and Papers of the Presidents*, 1:210–12; see also Hofstadter, *Idea of a Party System*, 90–102.

crations, derision, and contempt' of these opposition newspapers." Allen did not buy the notion that the First Amendment protected such remarks. "Because the Constitution guaranties the right of expressing our opinions, and the freedom of the press, am I at liberty to falsely call you a thief, a murderer, an atheist?" He thought not. "The freedom of the press and opinions was never understood to give the right of publishing falsehoods and slanders, nor of exciting sedition, insurrection and slaughter, with impunity. A man was always answerable for the malicious publication of falsehood; and what more does this bill require?"[124]

Most Republicans opposed the sedition bill. They were motivated in part by the knowledge that a sedition law recently enacted by Parliament had muzzled the opposition in Great Britain.[125] Nathaniel Macon of North Carolina thought the bill was in "direct opposition to the Constitution." If the law passed, he warned, "Congress would have the same right to pass a law making an establishment of religion, or to prohibit its free exercise, as all are contained in the same clause of the Constitution." The question was not even a close one. "Several laws had been passed which violated the spirit, but none before this which directly violated the letter of the Constitution; and, if this bill was passed, I should think it hardly worth while in the future to allege against any measure that it is in direct contradiction to the Constitution." Samuel Dana of Massachusetts disagreed. What, he asked, did people understand as the meaning of the First Amendment? "Is it a license to injure others or the government, by calumnies, with impunity? Let it be remembered that the uttering of malicious falsehoods, to the injury of the government, is the offence which it is now intended to restrain; for if what is uttered can be proved true, it will not, according to this bill, be punished as libelous." Albert Gallatin illustrated the absurdity of the sedition bill when he noted that Federalists labeled as seditious assertions that not only were truthful but that they themselves had made. "Was it criminal to say that the executive is supported by a party when gentlemen declare that it must be supported by a party? When the doctrine has been avowed on this floor that men of a certain political opinion, alone ought to be appointed to offices; and when the executive had now adopted and carried into practice that doctrine in its fullest extent?"[126]

124. *Annals of Congress*, 5th Cong., 2d sess., June 1798, 7:2094, 2097.
125. Presser, *Original Misunderstanding*, 93.
126. *Annals of Congress*, 5th Cong., 2d sess., June 1798, 7:2105, 2112, 2108–9.

On July 10, John Nicholas of Virginia turned the focus back to what he saw as the threshold issue—whether Congress had authority to prohibit seditious speech. Nicholas had "looked in vain," he said, "amongst the enumerated powers given to Congress in the Constitution, for an authority to pass a law like the present"; but he found what he considered an "express prohibition against passing it." After acknowledging Federalist claims that "licentiousness" and not the liberty of the press was at issue, he asked the bill's supporters to inform him "where they drew the line between this liberty and licentiousness of which they speak." Federalists insisted that the national government necessarily enjoyed certain inherent powers, as it must if it was to preserve itself. As Harrison Gray Otis of Massachusetts put it, "every independent government has a right to preserve and defend itself against injuries and outrages which endanger its existence." Seditious speech fell under this description—the government therefore enjoyed an inherent power to eradicate it. Besides, the common law (which encompassed the crime of sedition) had been adopted by all states and was familiar to the Framers; therefore "a safe recourse may be had to it in all cases that would otherwise be doubtful." As for demands that Federalists draw a line between acceptable and licentious speech, Otis declared that he would be more than happy to leave that task to an "honest jury." Albert Gallatin was unmoved. He reminded the House that the Constitution enumerated those crimes the federal government had authority to punish: piracies, counterfeiting, treason, all crimes within the capital district, forts and other military installations, as well as resistance to the enforcement of the laws of the United States. It did not mention sedition.[127]

Following passage of the Sedition Act, events took a turn that, had it been predicted during the ratification struggle, would not have been believed. Secretary of State Pickering took to reading opposition newspapers, looking for "seditious utterances."[128] The president did the same, at one point writing of his desire to put the Republican *Aurora* out of business and to expel its editor, William Duane (an alien) from the country.[129] Even as the president spoke, proceedings against Duane had begun. Authorities arrested Benjamin Franklin Bache, publisher of the *Aurora*, and charged him with violating the Sedition Act. Over the next two years, federal district attorneys brought sedition charges against Republican newspapers throughout the country. The

127. Ibid., 7:2139, 2146, 2149, 2158.     128. Quoted in White, *Federalists*, 407.
129. Adams, *Works of John Adams*, 9:5.

victims included the editors of the *New York Time-Piece,* the *Boston Independent,* the *Bennington Gazette,* the *New London Bee,* the Mount Pleasant (New York) *Register,* and the *New York Argus.*[130] By the time the witch hunt came to an end, Republican printers in every state but New Hampshire and Rhode Island had been prosecuted for sedition. No wonder one historian described the Sedition Act as aimed principally at "silencing the Republican press."[131] Private citizens were also prosecuted. A resident of Dedham, Massachusetts, received a four-year prison sentence after he incited friends to install a liberty pole with a "provocative inscription" upon it in front of the house of Federalist Party leader Fisher Ames.[132]

Overall, federal authorities tried fourteen men under the Sedition Act. They obtained ten convictions.[133] Most of the trials did not take place until 1800, when the danger of war had long passed. Gross partisanship characterized the proceedings, as judges and marshals packed juries with Federalist partisans. Significantly, most of the prosecutions occurred in areas in which Federalist popularity was on the wane. Many concluded that the prosecutions had more to do with the election of 1800 than with national security concerns. Several prominent Republicans were among the victims. William Duane of the *Aurora* avoided being deported, but authorities arrested him in the spring of 1799 for inciting a seditious riot after he circulated a petition calling for repeal of the Alien Act. A federal grand jury thereafter indicted Duane for seditious speech. His trial was postponed twice and the charges were eventually dropped. Authorities also charged Thomas Cooper, a Pennsylvania Republican, with sedition. Cooper had warned that the president intended to establish a standing army; he also complained that the government had borrowed at exorbitant rates in a time of peace. These comments led U.S. attorney William Rawle to charge Cooper with attacking the president's character in order to render him contemptuous in the eyes of the American people. At Cooper's trial in April 1800 Justice Samuel Chase (who heard the case on circuit) informed the jury that the defendant must prove the truth of his attacks on the administration "to the marrow."[134] Cooper failed to convince the jury of the truth of his opinions; he received six months in jail and a $400 fine.

130. Sharp, *American Politics in the Early Republic,* 218.
131. Haines, *Role of the Supreme Court,* 160.
132. Commager, Leuchtenberg, and Morison, *Growth of the American Republic,* 325.
133. Bailyn, *Debate on the Constitution,* 2:1110.
134. *United States v. Cooper,* 25 Federal Cases 631, 643 (1800).

Philadelphia journalist James Callender also fell victim to the wrath of Justice Chase. Federal authorities prosecuted him for sedition after Callender labeled the president an aristocrat who sought to render America subservient to the British Empire. Following a May 1800 trial in which Chase instructed the marshal to keep Republicans off the jury, Callender was convicted of sedition. He served nine months in jail.[135] Justice Chase later tried to have the editors of Republican papers in Baltimore and Wilmington, Delaware, indicted as well.[136] He managed to rig the trial of a sitting member of the House of Representatives, Matthew Lyon (Vermont), who had been charged with violating the Sedition Act. In fact Lyon was guilty of nothing more than a series of longwinded attacks on the president's character and motives. In October 1799 the congressman received a four-month jail term and a $1,000 fine. Horrified members of the Philadelphia bar resolved to stop trying cases before Chase. Thousands of Vermont residents petitioned the president seeking the release of their lone representative, to no avail.[137] Nor was Lyon the only congressman caught up in the witch hunt. Inspired by Justice Iredell, a federal grand jury in Virginia issued a bill of presentment (similar to an indictment) for U.S. Representative Samuel Cabell after he wrote a circular letter critical of the Adams administration.[138]

The Federalist excesses that followed passage of the Sedition Act triggered a hostile reaction. Vice President Thomas Jefferson and James Madison—leaders of the Republican Party—sought to exploit the discord. In resolutions passed by the Kentucky House of Representatives in November 1798 (the identity of the author was kept secret), Jefferson claimed a right for the states that would eventually create more trouble than the Sedition Act itself. He began with an undisputed point regarding the Constitution: "to this compact each state acceded as a state, and is an integral party; its co-states forming, as to itself, the other party." Because the states were parties to the compact, Jefferson continued, they could judge the legality of federal acts for themselves. Someone had to do so; otherwise the federal government would be left in the odd position of deciding for itself the extent of its

135. *United States v. Callender*, 25 Federal Cases 239 (1800). See Dumas Malone, *Jefferson the President: First Term, 1801–1805* (Boston: Little, Brown, 1970), 35.

136. Haines, *Role of the Supreme Court*, 160.

137. *United States v. Lyon*, 15 Federal Cases 1183 (1800); Haines, *Role of the Supreme Court*, 162; William J. Watkins Jr., *Reclaiming the American Revolution: The Kentucky and Virginia Resolutions and Their Legacy* (New York: Palgrave Macmillan, 2004), 47.

138. See Cunningham, *Circular Letters of Congressmen*, 1:xxxvii–xxxviii.

authority. "As in all other cases of compact among parties having no common judge, each party has an equal right to judge for itself, as well of infractions as of the mode and measure of redress."[139] In one sense at least Jefferson was correct; the states held the power to amend the Constitution, and they could thereby correct infractions or excesses. Unfortunately, Jefferson did not stop at that point. He went on to declare that when "powers are assumed [by the federal government] which have not been delegated, a nullification of the act is the rightful remedy."[140] Because it was clearly unconstitutional, the Sedition Act was "void and of no force." The vice president closed by declaring that the First and Tenth Amendments made clear that the states intended to "retain to themselves the right of judging how far the licentiousness of speech and of the press may be abridged without lessening their useful freedom."[141]

In December 1798 the Virginia legislature passed resolutions that had been drafted by James Madison. The identity of the author remained a secret. After declaring Virginia's "warm attachment" to the Union, Madison made clear the state's expectation that the powers of the national government, "as resulting from the compact to which the states are parties," would be "limited by the plain sense and intention of the instrument constituting that compact." Acts of the national government were valid only so long as "they are authorized by the grants enumerated in that compact." What could the states do when the federal government exceeded its limits? "In case of deliberate, palpable, and dangerous exercise of other powers not granted by the said compact, the states . . . have the right and are in duty bound to interpose for arresting the progress of evil." "Interpose?" Did that mean nullify or void offensive laws? Madison did not say; instead, he declared the Sedition Act both unconstitutional and dangerous.[142] Although Jefferson and Madison stood on strong ground in attacking the constitutionality of the act, Jefferson at least overreached—nothing in the text of the Constitution or the ratification debates so much as hinted at a right of nullification or interposition. (John Breckinridge, the member of the Kentucky legislature who introduced Jefferson's resolutions in that body, deleted the word "nullification.") Federal laws in violation of the Constitution could be rendered void in only two ways: through amendment or invalidation by the federal courts. The Virginia and Kentucky resolutions received a hostile response from the

139. *Writings of Jefferson*, 7:291.
141. Ibid., 7:293–94.
140. Ibid., 7:301.
142. *Writings of Madison*, 6:326, 328.

other states. Seven legislatures passed resolutions denouncing the theories propounded by the two Virginians.[143] Undeterred, Madison again took up his pen and issued a second paper—the "Report on the Resolutions." In addressing the argument that the federal courts alone had the power to rule on the constitutionality of federal legislation, Madison pointed out that not all abuses would be litigated. In addition, the judges might sanction excesses instead of impeding them. The states therefore had the right to judge the constitutionality of federal acts. "On any other hypothesis, the delegation of judicial power would annul the authority delegating it; and the concurrence of this department with the others in usurped powers, might subvert forever, and beyond the possible reach of any rightful remedy, the very Constitution which all were intended to preserve."[144]

Despite the efforts of Madison and Jefferson, the country did not immediately fall into line behind the Republican cause. Fortunately for them, their opponents helped. The Federalist-dominated Congress enacted a steep property tax during the summer of 1798. It constituted a far more serious irritation for most Americans than the handful of sedition trials had. The Treasury Department foreclosed on thousands of farms when their owners could not pay the tax.[145] The Federalists did not help themselves by dismissing complaints as evidence of an unwillingness to accept the fact that the country must be placed on a war footing.[146] Discontent over the land tax quickly bubbled over into outright resistance. Pennsylvania again served as the focus of trouble. A band of farmers led by one John Fries expelled tax collectors and liberated prisoners in federal custody. Federal marshals reacted with exuberance, rounding up persons charged with resisting collection of the tax and hauling them to Philadelphia for trial. John Fries was tried for treason. It was no wonder that Americans began to associate Federalists with onerous taxes and an approach to law enforcement that bordered on the tyrannical.

Republicans selected Thomas Jefferson to be their presidential nominee in 1800, just as they had in 1796. Adams sought a second term. Although the treatment of Mr. Fries offended the country, neither it nor the Alien and Sedition Acts threatened the administration (though the Alien Act drove

143. Miller, *Federalist Era*, 241.
144. *Writings of Madison*, 6:351–52.
145. Charles G. Sellers, *The Market Revolution: Jacksonian America, 1815–1846* (New York: Oxford University Press, 1991), 73.
146. Elkins and McKitrick, *Age of Federalism*, 696.

thousands of Pennsylvania Germans into Republican ranks).[147] More than anything else, the onerous new property taxes turned voters against the president and his party.[148] The Federalists did what they could to stave off defeat. They painted Jefferson as a debauched Francophile; Americans heard that he had fathered mulatto children, prayed to the French goddess of reason, and even experimented on animals at Monticello, or "Dog's Misery," as some called it. Republicans emphasized themes that would help them (and their descendants, the Democrats) hold the executive branch for all but twelve of the next sixty years: "a government rigorously frugal and simple; the prompt liquidation of the public debt; a small army and navy, freedom of religion and of the press; commerce with all nations; political connections with none; and little or no diplomatic establishment."[149] Cheap government, it appeared, would be the dominant American political ethos in the new century just as it had been in the old. Neither strict construction nor the resolutions of Kentucky and Virginia played much of a role in the campaign, despite Martin Van Buren's subsequent claim that the latter served as "the flag under which the Republicans conquered."[150] Although Jefferson's general views on the subject of national power were known to the country, his authorship of the Kentucky resolutions remained secret.

The Republicans won, narrowly. In the process they triggered a serious if short-lived constitutional crisis. Republican electors cast seventy-three votes for both Jefferson and his running mate, Aaron Burr, in order to prevent the election of a Federalist vice president. (Adams received sixty-five votes.) Under the constitutional provisions in effect at the time, the candidate who received the second-highest number of electors became vice president. The deadlock was resolved in the House of Representatives. For a time the Federalist majority toyed with the idea of electing Burr to the presidency; as a result Jefferson could not obtain the support of more than eight states. (When deciding presidential elections, the House voted by states instead of representatives. With Vermont, Kentucky, and Tennessee having joined the Union since 1789, a candidate needed nine states to prevail.) After extensive lobbying, Republicans persuaded James Bayard, the lone Congressman from Delaware, to switch his vote from Burr to Jefferson. Bayard's vote carried a

147. Ibid., 695.
148. Hofstadter, *Idea of a Party System*, 110.
149. Quoted in Miller, *Federalist Era*, 265, 266.
150. Martin Van Buren, *Inquiry into the Origins of Political Parties in the United States* (New York: Hurd & Houghton, 1867), 267.

steep price. Jefferson had to agree to leave untouched both the Bank of the United States and incumbent civil servants. He also promised to maintain the army and navy at expanded levels and to remain neutral with respect to the conflict in Europe.[151] Needless to say, these conditions were unenforceable, but whatever the exchange that took place, it led Bayard to change his vote and thereby resolve the crisis. The Republican era was born. Strict construction would have a chance to succeed.

151. Miller, *Federalist Era*, 274.

CHAPTER 3

# *The Republicans,*
# *1801–1829*

## ECONOMY IN GOVERNMENT

Although John Adams almost won the presidential contest, Federalists sustained a drubbing in the 1800–1801 congressional elections. Republicans took over the Senate (18-14) and won almost two-thirds of the seats in the House (66-40). They did not take long to exploit their advantage. At Jefferson's urging, the seventh Congress abolished most internal taxes, including the excise on whiskey, soon after it met in December 1801. The Alien Act was repealed. The Sedition Act had expired the previous spring; the new president pardoned those who had been convicted under it. When Federalist judges sought the indictments of critical newspaper editors—this time for common law sedition—U.S. attorneys refused to cooperate.[1] Republicans found the task of deconstruction more complex in other areas. In some cases, such as the federal judiciary, the obstacles were constitutional and therefore immovable; in others, such as executive branch patronage, the difficulty was reality itself. The Republicans had talked of the need for a smaller federal establishment and in fact reduced the payroll considerably upon taking office. Yet the problem of the president's vast patronage powers remained, and no solution was apparent—nor was one pursued. On the contrary, Republican Party leaders pressured Jefferson to pack the civil list with party members, even if doing so required the removal of Federalists.[2]

Perhaps inevitably, Jefferson found his way around the promises that had

---

1. A decade later, the Supreme Court held that the federal judiciary had no jurisdiction over common law crimes. *United States v. Hudson,* 11 U.S. 32 (1812).

2. Leonard D. White, *The Jeffersonians: A Study in Administrative History, 1801–1829* (New York: Macmillan, 1956), 349n18.

been made when the outcome of the election was in doubt. He felt free to remove those officeholders who had been appointed during the waning hours of the Adams administration, when the outgoing president packed the federal bureaucracy with his supporters. Jefferson later extended the purge to all those who received places after December 12, 1800, on the grounds that Adams's defeat became certain on that date.[3] The new president found cause for still more removals after distributing a circular barring federal employees from using their positions to influence citizens exercising the franchise. He terminated those who nevertheless insisted on "electioneering."[4] Yet another excuse appeared when Jefferson realized that most of the offices were in the hands of Federalists. The president professed to be surprised by this state of affairs.[5] That the judiciary had been packed with Federalists provided justification for still more removals. The president reasoned that since the judges themselves could not be dispatched, other court officers—particularly U.S. attorneys and marshals—ought to be. The prominent role played by many of the victims in the execution of the Sedition Act provided additional grounds for terminations.[6]

Even after moderate culling had taken place, Republican state party leaders demanded more removals so their own supporters might be appointed.[7] Jefferson cooperated at least with the more important offices, such as the collectorships. He removed Federalists unfortunate enough to hold these positions, along with almost all of their staff members in New York City and Philadelphia.[8] Employees of the Portsmouth, New Hampshire, customhouse lost their places as well.[9] Five collectors received the ax in New Jersey, as did ten in Massachusetts.[10] In New England the administration removed Federalists until Republicans held two-thirds of the available offices.[11] Massachusetts alone was thought to have lost more executive branch employees than the entire South. Nor was it an accident that Connecticut politician Gideon Granger was appointed postmaster general—he exhibited great skill in iden-

3. Noble E. Cunningham Jr., *The Jeffersonian Republicans in Power: Party Operations, 1801–1809* (Chapel Hill: University of North Carolina Press, 1963), 14.

4. Malone, *Jefferson the President: First Term,* 81.

5. *Writings of Jefferson,* 8:70.

6. Malone, *Jefferson the President: First Term,* 74.

7. Cunningham, *Jeffersonian Republicans in Power,* 56–57.

8. Winfred Bernhard, *Political Parties in American History,* 3 vols. (New York: Putnam, 1974), 1:307.

9. Prince, *Federalists and the U.S. Civil Service,* 56.

10. Binkley, *Political Parties in American History,* 1:307.

11. Cunningham, *Jeffersonian Republicans in Power,* 21–22.

tifying political opponents so they could be removed from the post office payroll.[12]

Given their emphasis on economy, the Republicans might have been expected to dismantle the system of publicly fed newspapers that had been erected during the 1790s. They did not. Instead they simply cleaned house—Federalists printers lost their postmasterships, and those who held State Department printing contracts saw them revoked.[13] In their place, a network of publicly subsidized Republican newspapers appeared. Samuel Harrison Smith's *National Intelligencer* led the pack. Smith enjoyed a State Department contract; his newspaper had the somewhat dubious honor of being both the leading newspaper in the country and the administration's mouthpiece.[14] William Duane—now free from tyrannical federal judges—secured a position of command in the administration's fleet for his *Aurora*. He held the Senate's printing franchise.[15]

When the ninth Congress met in December 1805, Republicans held 114 of 142 seats in the House and 27 of 34 in the Senate.[16] Jefferson made the most of this state of affairs by exerting enormous influence over congressional Republicans. Representative John Randolph served both as the leader of administration forces and as chairman of the Committee on Ways and Means. Jefferson's influence was such that when Randolph turned on the president over the Yazoo affair and the administration's attempts to buy Florida, he lost his chairmanship. Executive hegemony was also secured by the leadership skills of the secretary of the treasury, Albert Gallatin. The Swiss-born Pennsylvanian proved Alexander Hamilton's equal in his ability to lead members of Congress down paths chosen by the administration. Party discipline was also maintained by the use of the caucus—meetings attended exclusively by Republican legislators (and sometimes by Gallatin) in which the verdict of a majority decided how all party members would vote in Congress. Perhaps the one figure in the administration more skilled than Gallatin in herding lawmakers was the president himself. Thomas Jefferson was a remarkably skillful backroom politician, and he devoted a great deal of energy

12. Allen Johnson, ed., *Dictionary of American Biography*, 20 vols. (New York: Scribner's Sons, 1931), 8:483.

13. Cunningham, *Jeffersonian Republicans in Power*, 248–49.

14. Smith, *Press, Politics, and Patronage*, 28.

15. Cunningham, *Jeffersonian Republicans in Power*, 270.

16. Kenneth C. Martis, *The Historical Atlas of Parties in the United States Congress, 1789–1989* (New York: Macmillan, 1989), 78.

to imposing his own vision of party orthodoxy upon Republican members of Congress. Echoing earlier complaints about Alexander Hamilton, Senator Timothy Pickering of Massachusetts charged that the president "secretly dictates every measure which is seriously proposed and supported" in Congress.[17]

The administration consolidated its influence over Congress through a variety of tactics. None proved more useful than the appointment of legislators to places in the executive branch. More than twenty members of Congress accepted appointment to federal office during Jefferson's tenure, and if the Constitution forced them to resign before doing so, the practice still eroded the independence of the legislative branch.[18] The appeal of executive offices stemmed in part from the generous compensation enjoyed by those who obtained higher-level posts. Postmasters and collectors could earn as much as $5,000 a year, while members of Congress received an annual salary of $200.[19] Hence the willingness of one U.S. senator to resign in order to become the New York City postmaster; a Virginia senator quit in order to accept appointment as the collector at Norfolk. While jobs were not given in exchange for votes, the capacity of the executive department to alleviate the hardships of public service was not lost on lawmakers. The administration had other tools at its disposal as well, such as executive branch contracts. During Jefferson's second term, when war with Britain was a constant threat, he chose to hand out gunboat building contracts—some of which went to members of Congress—rather than fund an oceangoing navy. The ranks of enterprising legislators included Matthew Lyon, who also did business with the State Department. Fearful of public reaction to the worsening problem, Congress enacted a measure in 1808 barring senators and representatives from doing business with the federal government.[20] The law was less than wholly effective; newspapers owned by lawmakers continued to obtain printing and postal delivery contracts. The influence of the president grew steadily during the early nineteenth century, as the number of jobs, contracts, and prizes grew with the nation itself. This development contributed to the growth of federal power because it eroded the ability of the legislative branch to check the executive. Thomas Jefferson was not disposed to use

17. Quoted in White, *Jeffersonians*, 35.
18. Carl Fish, *Civil Service and the Patronage* (New York: Russell & Russell, 1963), 56.
19. Robert A. Rutland, *The Presidency of James Madison* (Lawrence: University Press of Kansas, 1990), 34.
20. 2 *Stats at Large* 484 (April 21, 1808).

patronage for the purpose of obtaining congressional acquiescence in violations of the limits upon federal authority. Still, his use of federal offices and contracts for partisan ends contributed to the long process of centralizing national political life.

If characterized by an innate conservatism, Republicans on occasion wielded power with excessive fervor. In doing so, they inflicted damage on the constitutional framework they professed to cherish. The chief object of their exuberance was the federal judiciary. To some extent, a reaction was understandable. Federal judges, even more than Congress, led the way in violating the rights of Americans during the 1790s. As late as the summer of 1801 two judges in the capital ordered district attorneys to indict the editor of the *National Intelligencer* for common law sedition.[21] The last Federalist Congress did its best to worsen the partisanship of the third branch by overloading it with additional offices and sinecures via the Judiciary Act of 1801. (In its one redeeming feature, the law abolished circuit riding for members of the Supreme Court.)[22] Among the appointees was John Marshall, a forty-five-year-old Virginia Federalist who became chief justice.

When the seventh Congress met in late 1801, Republicans—still angry over the sedition trials—sought retribution. Some contemplated altering the Constitution in order to provide a more direct method of checking judicial excesses. A Virginia jurist suggested an amendment providing for the removal of federal judges through passage of a "joint address" by both houses of Congress.[23] Although nothing so extreme occurred, the ensuing reaction threatened for a time to inflict permanent damage upon the judiciary. The first assault came in the form of the Judiciary Act of 1802.[24] A partisan and injurious piece of legislation, the law was almost rejected by the Republican-controlled Senate. It abolished the new federal circuit courts that had been created by the Judiciary Act of 1801, under the pretense that they did not have enough cases to justify their existence. Republicans thereby secured the removal of sixteen newly appointed federal judges from the bench. To make up for their absence, the act required that members of the Supreme Court resume circuit duty.

The abolition of the circuit courts violated the Constitution's provision of

21. Warren, *Supreme Court in United States History*, 1:195.
22. 2 *Stats at Large* 89 (February 13, 1801).
23. Malone, *Jefferson the President: First Term*, 118.
24. 2 *Stats at Large* 156 (April 29, 1802).

lifetime tenure for judges.[25] Judges could be removed only through impeach-ment. Federalists in Congress were appalled. Representative James Bayard of Delaware flatly declared the measure unconstitutional, citing the Consti-tution's bar against the reduction of judicial salaries as well as the provision that defines the tenure of judges. The law, Bayard warned, would impair the independence of the judiciary. He reminded the Republican majority that eviscerating the federal bench would leave the Constitution at the mercy of Congress and render hollow the limits on federal power contained in that charter. "Of what importance," he asked, "is it to say, Congress is prohibited from doing certain acts, if no legitimate authority exists in the country to decide whether an act done is a prohibited act?" Pass this bill, he continued, and none will exist, as the judiciary will not be in a position to stand up to Congress. "Can any thing be more absurd than to admit, that the judges are a check upon the legislature, and yet to contend that they exist at the will of the legislature?" The two ideas "cannot exist together."[26]

It was left to the new chief justice to reestablish the third branch in the eyes of the public—the only sure way to protect it from congressional excess. In John Marshall the country had a man of the same mettle as Washington. The eldest of fifteen children, Marshall was born into modest circumstanc-es on a farm near the Blue Ridge Mountains in Virginia. He served in the Revolutionary War, taking part in action at Brandywine and Monmouth. Along with three thousand other hardy souls, Marshall survived the win-ter of 1777 at Valley Forge. He was later instrumental in convincing his fel-low Virginians to ratify the Constitution. A tall, broad-shouldered farmer who exuded decency, courage, and warmth, Marshall retained a degree of physical stamina that was unusual even for his day. During the summer of 1812—at age fifty-six—he led a survey across the Appalachians to search for appropriate routes from the James River to the Ohio River.[27] Before his ap-pointment to the Supreme Court, Marshall practiced law, fought for ratifi-cation in Virginia, raised six children (often alone after his wife was stricken by mental illness), and served with distinction in the Adams administration. John Marshall combined yeoman simplicity and strength with a firm devo-tion to the Union whose independence he helped secure. This dedication al-

25. See U.S. Constitution, Article III, Section 1. For the text of the Judiciary Act of 1802, see 2 *Stats at Large* 156 (April 29, 1802).

26. *Annals of Congress*, 7th Cong., 1st sess., February 27, 1802, 11:626–31, 645, 848.

27. Jean Edward Smith, *John Marshall: Definer of a Nation* (New York: Henry Holt & Co., 1996), 411.

lowed him to stand almost alone against the anticourt fervor that pervaded national politics almost continuously during his thirty-five years as chief justice.

When the members of the Supreme Court assembled for the 1803 term, Marshall faced the temptation to respond sharply to the recent excesses of Congress. He wisely chose to bide his time and dropped the idea of holding void the Judiciary Act of 1802 despite his own misgivings about it.[28] When a case that turned on the act's legality came before the high court in 1803 *(Stuart v. Laird),* the majority ignored the issue of removals and ruled circuit riding constitutional on the grounds that it had been the practice prior to 1801.[29] The justices were undoubtedly aware that an opinion holding abolition of judicial offices unconstitutional would not automatically produce their restoration. That would require cooperation from Congress in the form of appropriations for salaries, something the Republican majority was most unlikely to provide.

In the hands of other men, the Supreme Court and the federal judiciary might have receded into oblivion, a withered arm of the national government. John Marshall was equal to the challenge of the Republican regime that so dominated the other branches. Finding a case in which the constitutionality of a federal law was at issue and that bestowed upon the Supreme Court the means of enforcing its decision, the chief justice embraced the principle that the judicial branch possesses the right to hold acts of Congress unconstitutional. The case was *Marbury v. Madison* (1803).[30] Announced the same day as *Stuart v. Laird,* it resulted from President Adams's appointment, in early 1801, of twenty-three justices of the peace for the District of Columbia. After the Senate approved the nominations on March 3, commissions—documents officially recognizing the appointees as justices of the peace—were issued by the secretary of state. Some failed to reach the appointees by the time Adams's term expired at noon on March 4, 1801. The new president ordered State Department officials to retain the remaining commissions. One of the spurned appointees, William Marbury, brought an action in the Supreme Court against Secretary of State James Madison, in which he claimed a legal right to the appointment.

28. Haines, *Role of the Supreme Court,* 242.

29. *Stuart v. Laird,* 5 U.S. 299, 309 (1803). See also Malone, *Jefferson the President: First Term,* 134.

30. 5 U.S. 137 (1803).

The public and press anticipated the decision with great interest. Many expected the Supreme Court to order the secretary of state to deliver the commission to Marbury, at which point it would be ignored. The federal judiciary would lose prestige as a result. The chief justice solved the problem in a way that took Republicans by surprise. He held that the Supreme Court did not have jurisdiction to hear the case, as the provision of the 1789 Judiciary Act under which Marbury brought his suit in the Supreme Court violated the Constitution. As Marshall saw it, section 13 of the 1789 law purported to expand the Supreme Court's original jurisdiction beyond the areas prescribed by the Constitution. The Court thus found a federal statute unconstitutional and was able to enforce its judgment, merely by refusing to rule on Marbury's complaint. Marshall did not miss the opportunity to declare loudly that the Supreme Court had the power to declare void acts of Congress that violated the Constitution. "The particular phraseology of the Constitution of the United States confirms and strengthens the principle, supposed to be essential to all written constitutions, that a law repugnant to the Constitution is void; and that courts, as well as other departments, are bound by that instrument."[31] Certain aspects of the Court's decision came in for heavy criticism. Some observers, including the president, believed that everything the Court said after it declared a lack of jurisdiction was entirely dictum and not a binding interpretation of the law (Marshall strongly implied that Marbury had a right to his commission). Nevertheless, the Court's assertion of the power of judicial review passed without protest.[32]

The reaction to the judiciary that began with passage of the Judiciary Act of 1802 worsened in succeeding years. Like the other officers of the federal government, judges were subject to impeachment for "Treason, Bribery, or other high Crimes and Misdemeanors" (Article II, Section 4). In 1803 the House of Representatives impeached federal judge John Pickering for intemperance, and shortly thereafter the Senate removed him from the bench, though not before altering the impeachment resolution. It originally stated that he was guilty of high crimes and misdemeanors; as amended it simply provided for his removal.[33] As the alteration of the resolution indicated, many did not believe Pickering's conduct met the constitutional requirement for impeachment, as drunkenness was not a crime. Critics also

---

31. Ibid., at 174, 180.
32. Warren, *Supreme Court in United States History*, 1:254–55.
33. *Annals of Congress*, 8th Cong., 1st sess., January 1804, 13:367.

took a jaundiced view of attempts to impeach Supreme Court Justice Samuel Chase. The jurist's partisan conduct of the sedition trials of James Callender and Thomas Cooper appalled citizens across the country. Perhaps the most serious allegations arose out of Chase's conduct during the Callender trial, in which he barred evidence and witnesses favorable to the defense and made prejudicial statements in front of the jury.[34] Chase had clearly prejudiced Callender's right to a fair trial; in doing so he arguably deserved impeachment. Surely his partisan conduct of a trial for the purpose of securing the incarceration of a political opponent warranted Chase's removal. The House passed an impeachment resolution, but the two-thirds vote required for the justice's removal could not be obtained in the Senate. A majority did approve three articles of impeachment, two of which concerned his conduct during the Callender trial.[35] The acquittal was probably fortunate; Chase's removal might well have been followed by the impeachment of the other justices, thus destroying what was left of the independence of the judicial branch.

Republicans, annoyed by the Senate's failure to remove Chase, as well as Chief Justice Marshall's conduct of the treason trial of former vice president Aaron Burr, contemplated the possibility of amending the Constitution to rein in the judiciary. (Burr was acquitted after Marshall determined that treason required taking up arms against the United States—a conspiracy did not qualify.)[36] Proposed amendments designed to reduce the power of the federal judiciary poured forth in 1807–8. John Randolph suggested one that would have allowed Congress to removed federal judges by a majority vote in each house.[37] Senator Edward Tiffin of Ohio proposed a constitutional amendment under which judges would be appointed for a period of years and subject to removal by two-thirds of both houses of Congress.[38]

34. The articles of impeachment alleged in part that Justice Chase had abused his powers in the Callender trial by (1) providing an opinion on the law that "prejudiced the minds of the jury"; (2) keeping a jury member on who wanted to recuse himself; (3) wrongly barring the testimony of a key witness; (4) treating the defendant's attorneys in a contemptuous manner; and (5) wrongly securing the indictment of Callender. Chase also harangued a grand jury in Baltimore after it refused to issue an indictment he wanted (*Annals of Congress*, 8th Cong., 2d sess., December 3, 1804, 14:728–30). Most legal scholars have concluded that Chase's actions did not warrant impeachment. See, for example, David Currie, *The Constitution in Congress: The Jeffersonians, 1801–1829* (Chicago: University of Chicago Press, 2001), 36–38.

35. *Annals of Congress*, 8th Cong., 2d sess., March 1, 1805, 14:665–69.

36. *United States v. Burr*, 25 Federal Cases 55 (1807).

37. Malone, *Jefferson the President: First Term*, 381.

38. U.S. Senate, *The Journal of the Senate: Thomas Jefferson Administration, 1801–1809*, 10 vols. (Wilmington, Del.: Michael Glazer, Inc.), 7:26–27.

The legislature of Massachusetts passed resolutions endorsing a similar measure.[39] Chief Justice Marshall feared for the judiciary enough to suggest that perhaps Congress should be given an "appellate jurisdiction" over Supreme Court decisions.[40] Unlike the uproar that led to the Eleventh Amendment, nothing came of these proposals. Yet the possibility of congressional sanction remained and in fact hovered over the high court like a dark cloud.

That the judiciary did not suffer a reduction of its powers stemmed largely from the fact that the Republican Party had other priorities. Above all else, Jefferson and his followers were determined that the federal apparatus must be reduced to its bare essentials. This devotion to "economy in government" served as the core of the Republican Party's governing philosophy.[41] Even strict construction served in part as a means to the end of keeping the cost of government—and in turn taxes—as low as possible. This attitude dated to the struggle with Britain and formed the basis of Antifederalist objections to the Constitution. It fueled the growth of an opposition party in the 1790s and helped Jefferson win the presidency in 1800. Thereafter, Republicans imposed this devotion to penury upon the national government. The civil list was slashed, the armed forces stripped bare, and taxes cut. If, as Jefferson put it in his inaugural address, Americans wanted nothing more from government than "to regulate their own pursuits of industry and improvement," they had made progress toward that goal by the end of 1802.[42]

And then the outside world intervened. Americans had long worried about their access to the Mississippi River. The lower portion of it flowed through foreign territory—Louisiana, which was under the control of Spain during the 1790s. Ratification nearly became a casualty of the issue when southerners feared that the proposed government might cede access to it in exchange for trading privileges. Under a 1795 agreement, Americans secured the right of deposit at New Orleans as well as the right of navigation on

39. Dumas Malone, *Jefferson the President: Second Term, 1805–1809* (Boston: Little, Brown, 1974), 367.

40. Beveridge, *Life of John Marshall*, 3:177.

41. In a letter to William Plumer of February 21, 1816, Jefferson described economy as "among the first and most important of republican virtues, and public debt as the greatest of the dangers to be feared." He pointed to the sufferings of the poor of Great Britain, owing to their onerous tax burden, as the inevitable consequence of an extensive governmental apparatus. Albert Ellery Bergh, ed., *The Writings of Thomas Jefferson*, 20 vols. (Washington, D.C.: Thomas Jefferson Memorial Association, 1905), 15:46–47.

42. Richardson, *Messages and Papers of the Presidents*, 1:311.

the Mississippi. The matter appeared to have been resolved until Napoleon forced Spain to relinquish control of Louisiana. In 1802 the territorial governor revoked the right of deposit of goods for export at New Orleans. Kentucky and Tennessee considered an armed seizure of the city—without passage through New Orleans, they were cut off from the outside world. Eager to find a peaceful solution, the administration considered purchasing New Orleans. Might the French be willing to sell it?

Such an inquiry was significant in and of itself. The purchase of New Orleans might be in the best interests of the United States, it might even be reconciled with Republican notions of minimalist government—but did it come within the scope of the federal government's enumerated powers? Fortunately, elements on all sides agreed that with the country's future at stake, an overly strict construction of the Constitution would be unwise. A $2 million appropriation was approved "to defray any expenses which may be incurred in relation to the intercourse between the United States and foreign nations."[43] Administration officials hoped the money might serve as a down payment for New Orleans and possibly the Florida panhandle. Upon arriving in France, American commissioners were offered the territory of Louisiana. New Orleans would be included, all for a total price of $12 million and the condition that all residents of the region become American citizens. The commissioners accepted the offer, with the understanding that their acceptance would have to be ratified by the president and the Senate in the form of a treaty.

Jefferson embraced the deal and called Congress into session in October 1803 (about a month ahead of schedule) in order to secure Senate approval before Napoleon changed his mind. Although it proved to be a strictly academic exercise, legislators insisted on reviewing the question of whether the national government had authority to enter into the agreement. Critics offered a number of constitutional objections to the treaty. It provided for the purchase of territory and promised the French and Spanish duty-free access to New Orleans for twelve years. Neither of these acts appeared to be authorized by the enumerated powers, and the second provision was thought to violate the ban on giving preference to certain ports over others (Article I, Section 9). There was also the prospect of new states being carved out of the annexed territory. From where did Congress obtain authority to do that?

43. See 2 *Stats at Large* 202 (February 26, 1803).

Chief among the critics was the president himself. His strict constructionist tendencies had not lessened upon his election—every proposed measure had to have as its end one of the enumerated powers. Already this approach had led to interpretations that were a bit forced; when Jefferson suggested in January 1803 that the government fund an expedition to the mouth of the Columbia River, he felt obligated to say that "the interests of commerce" placed the expedition "within the constitutional powers and care of Congress."[44] The president and members of his cabinet discussed the constitutionality of purchasing land before they sent commissioners to France. The attorney general suggested that the legal obstacles could be surmounted through an extension of the boundaries of the Mississippi Territory and Georgia. Treasury Secretary Albert Gallatin replied that if it was unconstitutional for the national government to acquire territory, it was also illegal for a state to do so. Gallatin believed that the national government had an inherent right to acquire territory.[45]

The president was ambivalent. At first he accepted the claim that the treaty power authorized the federal government to purchase territory. As events unfolded, he confessed to having doubts. In an August 9, 1803, letter to John Dickinson, he wrote of his concerns. "The general government has no powers but such as the Constitution has given it; and it has not given it a power of holding foreign territory, & still less of incorporating it into the Union. An amendment of the Constitution seems necessary for this." The opportunity, however, would not be missed. "In the meantime we must ratify & pay our money, as we have treated, for a thing beyond the Constitution, and rely on the nation to sanction an act done for its great good, without its previous authority." Jefferson was clearly troubled by the precedent he was setting, though not enough to seek an amendment before completing the purchase. The treaty provided for an exceedingly brief time during which the Senate could ratify (by the end of October 1803). Jefferson realized that he faced a situation in which the best interests of the nation could not be met within the parameters of the Constitution. Yet even if he had no intention of letting his scruples get the better of him, he did not ignore them altogether. The new states clause (Article IV, Section 3) had been relied upon by many as authorizing the purchase. Jefferson did not buy it. In a September

44. Richardson, *Messages and Papers of the Presidents*, 1:342.
45. Henry Adams, *History of the United States during the Administrations of Thomas Jefferson* (Boston, 1889–91; reprint, New York: Literary Classics of the United States, 1986), 354–55.

7, 1803, letter to Wilson Cary Nicholas of Virginia (who placed his faith in the clause), the president explained that he thought it applied solely to lands under the control of the United States in 1783. As "the Constitution expressly declares itself to be made for the United States," he could not avoid the conclusion that the intent of the Framers was "to permit Congress to admit into the union new states, which should be formed out of territory for which & under whose authority alone they were then acting." Otherwise, even the nations of Europe could seek admission to the Union. "I do not believe it was meant that they might receive England, Ireland, Holland, etc. into it, which would be the case on your construction."[46] Nor did Jefferson see the treaty power as an option, despite its broad language. Reliance on it by some only demonstrated to him the danger of forcing novel acts into the guise of one of the enumerated powers—doing so bred the sort of forced constructions that would surely render toothless the Constitution's limits on federal authority. "I had rather ask an enlargement of power from the nation, where it is found necessary, than to assume it by a construction which would make our powers boundless. Our peculiar security is in possession of a written Constitution. Let us not make it a blank paper by construction." Thus his dismissal of an unlimited treaty power: "if it is, then we have no Constitution. If it has bounds, they can be no others than the definitions of the powers which that instrument gives." He closed by pointing out that perhaps the country ought to accustom itself to the practice of amending the Constitution if the integrity of that charter was to be maintained. "Nothing is more likely than that [the] enumeration of powers is defective. This is the ordinary case of all human works. Let us go on then perfecting it, by adding, by way of amendment to the Constitution, those powers which time & trial show are wanting."[47]

Some Federalists failed see any reason for all the anguish. Speaking in the House in October 1803, James Elliot of Vermont pointed to the "law of nations" in support of the legality of the purchase, as well as the idea that colonies are national property. They could be bought and sold by nations just as individuals buy and sell property. Caesar Rodney of Delaware thought the general welfare clause and the treaty power provided the necessary authority.[48] Other Federalists found the purchase more difficult to swallow. Gou-

46. *Writings of Jefferson*, 8:241n1, 262, 247.

47. Ibid., 8:247–48. Scholars have concluded that the treaty power provided ample authority for the purchase. See, for example, Currie, *Constitution in Congress: Jeffersonians*, 101–5.

48. *Annals of Congress*, 8th Cong., 1st sess., 13:447–48, 472–73.

veneur Morris declared flatly that Congress lacked the authority to either acquire territory or admit new states from it. The very assertion of such a power, Morris continued, would have increased the difficulty of ratification.[49] Senator Timothy Pickering of Massachusetts detected another obstacle. In his view, "the assent of each individual state . . . [is] necessary for the admission of a foreign country as an associate in the Union: in like manner as in a commercial house, the consent of each member would be necessary to admit a new partner into the company." Although he acknowledged a right to obtain territory "either by purchase or by conquest," Pickering insisted that such a region could be governed only as a "dependent province" until all states consented to its admission to the Union.[50] Many New England Federalists, already irritated by the dominance of the southern-led Republican Party, shared Pickering's concerns. They feared that annexation of an area so large would further worsen the region's minority status. New England would not, they warned, "tamely . . . shrink into a state of insignificance."[51] Even disunion loomed as a possibility.

Many Republicans who had once taken a narrow approach to federal power now embraced a more generous view. Senator John Taylor of Virginia, who in 1798 introduced Madison's resolutions in the Virginia legislature, thought the purchase of foreign lands was authorized by the territories clause. He claimed that because the powers of war and compact (treaty-making) were expressly ceded to the federal government and the states had been expressly denied those powers, the authority to acquire land also "merged from the separate states to the United States, as indispensably annexed to the treaty-making power, and the power of making war." Taylor pointed out that the treaty did not require the creation of states out of the Louisiana Territory, but only provided that the "inhabitants of the ceded territory shall be incorporated in the Union of the United States." This requirement, he concluded, could be satisfied by the organization of Louisiana as a territory.[52]

Senator Uriah Tracy of Connecticut disagreed. He would, he announced, vote against the treaty as unconstitutional. Tracy insisted that the limited nature of the national government's authority necessarily applied to the treaty-

---

49. Farrand, *Records of the Federal Convention*, 3:404.
50. *Annals of Congress*, 8th Cong., 1st sess., November 1803, 13:44–45.
51. Quoted in Malone, *Jefferson the President: First Term*, 329.
52. *Annals of Congress*, 8th Cong., 1st sess., November 3, 1803, 13:50–51. See Article IV, Section 3.

making power—it could not, for example, cede Connecticut. In the case of such treaties, he continued, the other branches would not be obligated to execute them. Under any other interpretation, "we must submit to the most extraordinary condition, of seeing the parts of a government, when acting separately, possessing more power than the whole when acting together."[53] New Hampshire senator William Plumer objected to the Senate and the president alone addressing the matter of naturalization, when the Constitution listed that subject among the powers of Congress. Nor did Plumer believe that the national government could purchase land—all knew full well, he insisted, that the treaty of Paris "established the limits of the United States." At the very least, the federative nature of the Union required the consent of each of the old states before a new one could be admitted.[54]

In December 1803 Senator John Quincy Adams of Massachusetts proposed the formation of a committee for the purpose of devising an amendment that would ratify the purchase, as in his opinion the treaty was "in direct violation of the Constitution."[55] No such amendment ever received serious consideration. It was because of this failure that the Louisiana Purchase created a gaping hole in the enumerated powers doctrine. With no amendment to recognize and limit the value of the purchase as a precedent for future acts, proponents of a broad construction of the powers of Congress received a gift from Thomas Jefferson that would have been beyond their wildest dreams in 1800. As John Quincy Adams put it, the purchase constituted "an assumption of implied powers greater in itself and more comprehensive in its consequences than all the assumptions of implied powers in the years of the Washington and Adams administrations put together."[56]

Mr. Adams was not the most objective critic with respect to Jefferson. Yet there was some truth to his comment—particularly when viewed from the state-based approach to the Union embraced by most Americans. From this perspective, the national government was essentially a partnership of states. None of the partners in 1787 anticipated a further dilution of their share of national sovereignty—or at least not beyond that which would result from the admission of states carved from those territories that lay between the original thirteen states and the Mississippi River (territory ceded

53. *Annals of Congress*, 8th Cong., 1st sess., November 3, 1803, 13:54–55.

54. William Plumer, *William Plumer's Memorandum of Proceedings in the United States Senate*, ed. Everett Somerville Brown (New York: Macmillan, 1923), 8, 12.

55. Ibid., 75.

56. Quoted in Malone, *Jefferson the President: First Term*, 331.

to the United States by the Treaty of Paris). Hence the reaction of a committee of the Massachusetts legislature to the admission of Louisiana into the Union (1813). Making states out of what had been foreign territory would, it warned, "divest the old United States of a proportion of their political sovereignty, in favor of such a foreigner. It is a power, which, in the opinion of your Committee, no wise people ever would have delegated, and which they are persuaded, the people of the United States, and certainly, the people of Massachusetts, never did delegate."[57] Federalist Josiah Quincy went so far as to call the admission of Louisiana "virtually a dissolution of the Union." He thought the New England states had a duty to prepare for "separation."[58]

In addition to serving as precedent for the liberal-minded and inviting Americans to alter their ideas about the nature of the Union, the Louisiana Purchase created a vast area in which the national government's powers were relatively unlimited. Congress governed those areas under the grants of authority contained in the broad language of the territories clause and the new states clause. Additional land purchases meant that by 1850 Congress effectively governed more than half of the nation under a general power of legislation.

### EMBARGO AND WAR

Thomas Jefferson faced two events as president that required a vigorous exercise of federal power. The first was Louisiana; the second was a blockade. Both grew out of events in Europe. On October 21, 1805, Lord Nelson led the Royal Navy to victory over the French and Spanish fleets at the Battle of Trafalgar, thereby ensuring British dominance of the Atlantic Ocean for the next century. Napoleon countered by barring British goods from Europe. Britain imposed its own blockade of the continent. American merchants, heavily dependent on European trade, demanded that their rights under the law of nations—to trade as citizens of a neutral country with continental Europe—be respected. The British turned a deaf ear to American protests. The Royal Navy thereafter searched American ships for contraband and removed sailors suspected of having deserted from the British fleet. (Desertions were common, as conditions in the Royal Navy were exceedingly bad.)

---

57. "Resolves of Massachusetts on Extension of Territorial Limits," June 16, 1813, in Herman V. Ames, ed., *State Documents on Federal Relations* (Philadelphia, 1900), 65.

58. Haines, *Role of the Supreme Court*, 301.

Known as impressment, the practice of forcibly removing sailors from their ships infuriated Americans.

In May 1806 HMS *Leander*, while lurking in the waters off New York City, fired a round at an American merchant ship, killing one sailor. In June 1807 the British frigate *Leopard* opened fire on the USS *Chesapeake* in waters off Virginia after its captain refused to allow it to be searched for deserters. When the volley ended, three sailors were dead and twenty injured. British officers boarded the *Chesapeake* and removed four sailors, three of whom were American citizens. The country was furious. The president would have been justified, albeit foolhardy, if he had sought a declaration of war. Instead, after calling the incident the worst insult to the country since Lexington, Jefferson ordered all British ships out of American waters. He also contemplated a suspension of trade. Exports had doubled between 1790 and 1807, largely because the British, cut off from Europe during the Napoleonic wars, had become dependent on American agricultural commodities.[59] At the same time, British manufacturers discovered new customers in the growing American marketplace. Even before the *Chesapeake* incident, Congress sought to take advantage of this increase in trade by prohibiting the importation of leather, silk, brass, woolens, and other items from the British Isles.[60] The terms of the act suspended its operation in the hopes that a diplomatic solution might be attained. The administration finally ran out of patience in late 1807. It sought a bill barring all exports in order to ensure that none reached Britain. After secret deliberations and an aggressive lobbying campaign, Congress enacted a law prohibiting ships bound for any foreign nation from leaving American ports.[61]

Serious difficulties in the enforcement of the embargo manifested themselves from the start. Commerce along a two-thousand-mile coast had to be brought to a halt by a government that possessed no oceangoing navy worthy of the name. It had not demonstrated a propensity to spend the necessary funds; at one point Congress put ships in dry dock to save money despite knowing they would rot. Lacking an adequate navy or even a decent collection of revenue cutters, Jefferson and his Republican allies in Congress attempted to make their embargo a reality by imposing a series of burdensome regulations upon coastal navigation. An act of January 1808 required

---

59. Commager, Leuchtenberg, and Morison, *Growth of the American Republic,* 352.
60. 2 *Stats at Large* 379 (April 18, 1806).
61. Ibid., 451 (December 22, 1807).

the posting of a bond worth four times the value of the ship and cargo prior to a vessel's departure.[62] (The bond would be forfeited if the vessel failed to deliver the goods to an American port.) An act of March 1808 prohibited the export of goods via land; it might just as well have prohibited agriculture.[63] A third act required coastal vessels to obtain clearance from customs officials before leaving port. This same law authorized Treasury Department officials to detain ships whose captains were suspected of intending to engage in foreign trade.[64] Enforcement proved a hugely difficult task. The main problem stemmed from American ships leaving port and then transferring their cargo to foreign vessels on the high seas. New England—with its shipping industry and numerous inlets and bays—had both the means and the motive to evade the embargo. Consequently the region became a hotbed of smuggling.[65] When grain prices in Canada went through the roof, land-based smuggling took on epidemic proportions as well, particularly in upstate New York. President Jefferson was not sympathetic to this outburst of commercial initiative; in April 1808 he declared the Lake Champlain region to be in a state of insurrection and called out the militia.[66] Shortly thereafter, a group of Vermont lumberjacks attempted to retrieve a raft of lumber that had been confiscated by authorities who feared it was on its way to Canada. When they were caught, the lumberjacks were charged with treason, even though they had not come any closer to committing that crime than John Fries or the leaders of the Whiskey Rebellion. Fortunately, they were acquitted.

The suspension of foreign trade dominated congressional debate throughout Jefferson's second term; its constitutionality was only rarely questioned. Administration supporters pointed to a 1794 embargo as precedent.[67] Representative John Smilie of Pennsylvania cited the power to a raise a navy as well as the commerce clause in support of the constitutionality of the measure.[68] Given the adverse impact of the embargo on so many important interests, it was perhaps inevitable that the federal judiciary would be asked to rule on it. In *United States v. The William* (1808), federal district judge John Davis found the embargo to be a valid exercise of the war and commerce

---

62. Ibid., 453 (January 9, 1808).
63. Ibid., 473 (March 12, 1808).
64. Ibid., 499 (March 25, 1808).
65. White, *Jeffersonians,* 444.
66. Richardson, *Messages and Papers of the Presidents,* 1:438–39.
67. See, for example, *Annals of Congress,* 10th Cong., 1st sess., April 8, 1808, 18:2226.
68. Ibid., 9th Cong., 1st sess., March 6, 1806, 15:584.

powers, as well as a necessary component of protecting the "inherent sovereignty" of the nation. ("Congress has power to declare war. It, of course, has power to prepare for war; and the time, the manner, and the measure, in the application of constitutional means, seems to be left to its wisdom and discretion.")[69] A handful of critics declared the law beyond the pale. Speaking in the House of Representatives in January 1809, James Sloan of New Jersey expressed doubt as to whether the commerce clause authorized Congress to prohibit foreign commerce in its entirety. He also pointed to the Constitution's prohibition of duties upon exports. "Congress therefore, have not the power of laying a duty of one cent upon articles exported, yet, by this bill, a right is assumed of prohibiting . . . exportation altogether." Nor did he buy the idea that the embargo derived its legality from the power to make "war and peace." As he saw it, "preventing the citizens from exporting their produce to nations in amity was never contemplated."[70] Sloan closed by distinguishing the 1794 embargo. It had been temporary, he pointed out, and was imposed only because privateers were at American shores.[71]

Discontent over the embargo increased as Jefferson's second term drew to a close. The man who ushered in the "Revolution of 1800" had imposed a policy upon the nation that was widely viewed as more egregious than anything devised by his predecessors. Certainly more Americans were affected. The loss of foreign markets caused wheat prices to drop by more than half. Thousands had their livelihoods destroyed. The president received hundreds of letters from citizens whose lives had been broken by the poverty that followed in the wake of his policies. Some contained threats; some told of people who could not feed their children.[72] In the Northeast, where trade played a critical role in the lives of thousands, years would pass before Jefferson's reputation recovered.

When the second session of the tenth Congress met in late 1808, Republican leaders prepared another enforcement measure, the most draconian yet. It banned the movement of commodities by ship along the coasts, even if the entire trip took place within the confines of a single state. It also empowered the president to call out the militia, navy, and army if necessary

69. *United States v. The William*, 28 Federal Cases 614, 622 (1808).

70. *Annals of Congress*, 10th Cong., 2d sess., January 5, 1809, 19:1005, 1009.

71. Ibid., 19:1010. The 1794 act authorized President Washington to impose an embargo whenever he thought the "public safety shall so require." 1 *Stats at Large* 372 (June 4, 1794).

72. Paul Johnson, *A History of the American People* (New York: HarperCollins, 1998), 257.

to enforce the embargo. Finally, the measure authorized collectors to refuse clearance or confiscate the cargo of any ship they suspected of having a foreign port as its destination—no warrants would be necessary. Objections on constitutional grounds quickly followed. Senator James Lloyd of Massachusetts complained of the bill's provisions for regulating the coastal trade. This commerce, he pointed out, often took place between ports in the same state. "If this be not trade with foreign nations, trade among the several states, or trade with the Indian tribes, then sir, whence arises your power even to regulate it, except from sufferance?"[73] Josiah Masters of New York complained of the discretion vested in customs officials over persons suspected of engaging in foreign trade. "Your collectors are to be armed with unlimited power to search from the closet of the farmer to his wagon or cart."[74] Despite the objections, the Force Act passed with ease in early January 1809.[75] The act nearly brought interstate commerce—highly dependent on the coastal trade—to a halt.

At that point the legislatures of New England, where an embargo-induced depression had set in, began making serious trouble. New Hampshire attorney Daniel Webster reasoned that since the embargo was not a regulation of commerce but a complete prohibition of it, the Constitution did not authorize it. The chief justice of Massachusetts, Theophilus Parsons, viewed an embargo as unconstitutional because the subject did not appear among the enumerated powers.[76] In January 1809 the Massachusetts assembly took a momentous step when it declared the enforcements acts "unjust, oppressive, and unconstitutional, and not legally binding on the citizens of this state."[77] The following month, Senator James Lloyd read the "memorial and remonstrance" of the Massachusetts legislature on the floor of the Senate. It too declared the enforcement acts beyond the authority of Congress—they vested too much discretion in customs officials, exposed individuals to pecuniary loss for actions that were legal when they occurred, required excessive bonds, and denied the right of trial by jury.[78] In Connecticut

73. *Annals of Congress*, 10th Cong., 2d sess., February 14, 1809, 19:251.

74. Ibid., December 1808, 19:935.

75. Ibid., 19:1024. For the provisions of the Force Act, see 1 *Stats at Large* 506 (January 9, 1809).

76. Marshall Smelser, *The Democratic Republic, 1801–1815* (New York: Harper & Row, 1968), 166.

77. Quoted in Haines, *Role of the Supreme Court*, 298.

78. *Annals of Congress*, 10th Cong., 2d sess., February 27, 1809, 19:444–47.

the governor refused to comply with the president's request to appoint officers of the state militia. He insisted that the states possessed a right to interpose when Congress exceeded its authority. The Connecticut general assembly ordered all state government employees to refrain from aiding in the enforcement of the embargo.[79] The legislature of Rhode Island passed resolutions only slightly less ominous; it affirmed the state government's duty to be vigilant in defending those rights that the people of the state had reserved to themselves.[80]

Just as the embargo reached its harshest phase, it disappeared. The Non-Intercourse Act of March 1, 1809, replaced the embargo with a ban on trade with belligerents. James Madison took the oath of office shortly thereafter; in May 1810 he signed what became known as Macon's Bill No. 2. It allowed the resumption of commerce with both France and Great Britain—subject to the goodwill of the Royal Navy, which continued to prevent American ships from reaching continental Europe. The law provided for the termination of trade with either of the main belligerents if the other promised to respect America's neutral rights. Napoleon responded by leading Madison to believe he accepted these terms. Madison promptly notified the British that they had three months to withdraw the orders in council (which imposed a blockade upon France). When London failed to comply, Congress imposed a second embargo in March 1811.

By the last year of Madison's first term (1812), the Royal Navy had removed almost four thousand sailors from American ships. (The Americans put the number at six thousand.)[81] Matters were moving toward war well enough on their own; an accelerant was provided by the twelfth Congress when it convened in late 1811. Present were two men who would play prominent roles in that body during the first half of the nineteenth century—Henry Clay of Kentucky and John C. Calhoun of South Carolina. There were other skilled newcomers as well, including Peter Porter of New York, Felix Grundy of Tennessee, and William Lowndes of South Carolina. Ostensibly Republicans, these men embraced a more aggressive view of national power than their forebears had. In the future their paths would vary widely, but for the present they shared a common goal—war, for the purpose of obtaining Canada. Many Americans viewed its annexation as inevitable, and

79. Malone, *Jefferson the President: Second Term*, 654.
80. Ames, *State Documents on Federal Relations*, 44.
81. Smelser, *Democratic Republic*, 206.

why not? The United States already vastly surpassed Canada in population, and if there were certain cultural differences, could the same not be said of Louisiana? In May 1812 President Madison asked Congress for a declaration of war. With the number of kidnapped American sailors growing by the month and the appearance of a new Indian confederation in the Northwest (it was thought to be receiving aid from Britain), the president concluded he had no choice. Congress was not so sure; the vote for war was only 79-49 in the House and 19-13 in the Senate.[82] The congressional debates that preceded the vote, which had been held in secret, might have secured peace had they been made public and thereby lengthened, as Parliament withdrew the orders in council a month after they ended. The Republican-controlled Congress refused to follow its declaration of war with the necessary appropriations. It decided against an oceangoing navy on the grounds that the war would involve little more than an invasion of Canada, which would probably conclude by the time the ships were built. Only through much labor did Congress bring itself to spend $600,000 on lumber, to be used for a future war which would be fought at sea. The United States thus proposed to fight the world's chief naval power with six frigates and three sloops of war.[83]

The events of the War of 1812 need not be recited in detail; suffice it to say that the ill-prepared government and people of the United States reaped what they had sown. The long-awaited invasion of Canada ground to a halt by the end of August 1812. That same month the British took Detroit, and Indians massacred the inhabitants of Fort Dearborn on Lake Michigan. By the following spring the Royal Navy had shut down the East Coast except for New England, which was allowed to continue trading as part of what the president called an attempt to "seduce and separate" one part of the Union from the rest of it.[84] In late 1813 the citizens of Buffalo, New York, were forced to watch a fire set by British troops engulf their city. The American effort had a few successes; in August 1812 the USS *Constitution* captured HMS *Guerriere;* in September 1813 the British were routed on Lake Erie. American privateers harassed shipping even within the Irish Channel, causing no little annoyance to the London press.

In the summer of 1814 British soldiers landed in Maryland; they entered Washington, D.C., almost unmolested and set fire to the Capitol and ex-

82. *Annals of Congress,* 12th Cong., 1st sess., June 1812, 23:1637 (House), 23:298 (Senate).
83. Commager, Leuchtenberg, and Morison, *Growth of the American Republic,* 366.
84. Quoted in Rutland, *Presidency of James Madison,* 122.

ecutive mansion as well as the Treasury, State, and War Department buildings. The government and army retreated in haste across the Potomac; after riding for hours in the dark of the Virginia countryside, the president
finally found respite when he stumbled upon a sympathetic innkeeper. The
invaders turned north and laid siege to Baltimore; naval bombardment of
Fort McHenry proved futile. In August 1814 the Americans narrowly defeated a British naval squadron on Lake Champlain, largely through the efforts of Captain Thomas McDonough and the men under his command. At
that point the British mercifully returned to the bargaining table, albeit with
the demands of a victor. They proposed to bar the U.S. Navy from the Great
Lakes, carve a new, more southerly border in the Northwest, ban American
fishing off the Grand Banks, and secure for His Majesty's subjects the right
of navigation on the Mississippi River. Fortunately the British did not hold
to these demands, and American and British diplomats meeting in Ghent
completed a rather harmless treaty by the end of 1814. Neither impressments
nor predations upon American shipping were addressed.

    In January 1815, before news of the peace treaty reached the New World,
American troops under General Andrew Jackson used long rifles and elevated positions to throw back an attacking British force at New Orleans. The
battle not only gave Americans an opportunity to proclaim victory, it also
provided the country with its most prominent military hero since Washington. Jackson's victory and the burst of patriotism it spawned came not a
moment too soon. A secessionist movement, long simmering among New
England Federalists, boiled over during the last year of the war. The realignment that followed the Republican triumph of 1800, the Louisiana Purchase, and the embargo combined to turn the region into a hotbed of anti-
government hysteria even before 1812. The war pushed many regional leaders
over the edge. Resistance began when President Madison summoned the
state militias for national service. The governors of Massachusetts, Rhode
Island, and Connecticut declared that he had usurped their authority and
refused to cooperate. The latter two states later relented; Massachusetts did
not. Governor Caleb Strong insisted that he alone had the power to call out
the state militia. Since the people of his state were under no apprehension
of invasion, to activate the militia would, he announced, lessen its usefulness. Strong eventually relented, though he still refused to allow the militia
to leave the state. The legislature compounded the insult when it requested
compensation from the federal government for costs incurred in the exer-

cise.[85] The episode proved all the more appalling because while U.S. forces experienced setbacks, the Massachusetts state government maintained a force of seventy thousand men—far larger than anything placed in the field by either side.[86]

Unable to muster adequate manpower, the Madison administration proposed a conscription bill. New England leaders responded with threats of resistance. Daniel Webster called the idea unconstitutional and warned that the states would be obligated to "interpose between their citizens and arbitrary power" if the government tried to enforce the law.[87] The governor of Massachusetts made inquiries to the British regarding their interest in an alliance with a New England severed from the rest of the Union.[88] In December 1814 twenty-six representatives from the New England states met in Hartford, Connecticut. The convention asserted the right of states "to interpose" when necessary to protect their citizens from federal excesses, but on the whole the delegates took a moderate approach. They recommended a series of amendments that provided (in part) for the following: no new states would be admitted without the concurrence of two-thirds of both the House and Senate; withdrawal of the power to impose embargoes beyond sixty days; a sitting president could not be reelected. The final plank provided for a second regional convention if the resolutions were not acted upon by Congress.[89] The convention sent agents to Washington to negotiate with Congress, but the news of General Jackson's victory at New Orleans arrived first, and its demands were lost in the euphoria that followed.

While New England Federalists seethed, Congress stumbled. With the Capitol gutted by fire, lawmakers met at a nearby inn (they would not return to the refurbished Capitol until 1819). Lawmakers tried desperately to alleviate the national government's financial difficulties, with only limited success. The suspension of trade quickly dried up the impost-dependent federal treasury. With no national bank (its charter had expired in 1811), the treasury had no source of credit from which to make up the shortfall quickly. Congress responded by authorizing the treasury to issue $5 million in paper

85. White, *Jeffersonians*, 540–42.

86. Rutland, *Presidency of James Madison*, 141.

87. Quoted in Merrill D. Peterson, *The Great Triumvirate: Webster, Clay and Calhoun* (New York: Oxford University Press, 1987), 44.

88. George Dangerfield, *The Era of Good Feelings* (New York: Harcourt, Brace & World, 1952), 87.

89. *Old South Leaflets* (Boston: Old South Association, 1910), 9:58, 60–65.

notes. Officials also sold bonds at excessive rates and even then had trouble moving them. When all else failed, Congress opened trade with Britain before the war was over, in the hope of obtaining tariff revenue. The plan succeeded only partially, and the government experienced a short period of bankruptcy in late 1814, as it was unable to transfer funds.[90]

It was not a bravura performance. James Madison's reputation for leadership proved a casualty of the war; so did the idea that the federal government should be kept in a state of perpetual deprivation. Even the Hartford Convention resolutions, although in part a response to perceived excesses like conscription, complained of the federal government's failure to act vigorously in defending in the nation.[91] The War of 1812 served as a painful lesson regarding the consequences of weakness. The burning of the Capitol and executive mansion, along with the fiscal impotence of Congress and the success of the British in shutting down the East Coast, demonstrated that a weak government could be just as dangerous as a strong one.

### JOHN MARSHALL AND THE SUPREME COURT

Federal power underwent a period of accelerated growth in the years after the War of 1812. Executive patronage expanded dramatically and novel interpretations of the Constitution eased the way for ambitious legislative programs in Congress. The federal judiciary also pushed outward the limits of federal jurisdiction. At the same time, it offered no sign that it intended to keep Congress within the confines of its enumerated powers. A few isolated incidents notwithstanding, the federal judiciary proved no more disposed to taming the other branches than the courts of England had been up to the task of checking the Stuarts. This predilection stemmed in part from the whipping the judges sustained at the hands of Congress during the first Jefferson administration. The fact that the Supreme Court's own jurisdiction met with the same limits as that of Congress may also have disposed the justices against a narrow reading of congressional power.

Even as it proved unwilling to check Congress, the federal judiciary enjoyed almost complete discretion in establishing the limits of its jurisdiction with respect to the states. For Chief Justice Marshall, the situation proved to be ideal. He was, after all, a Federalist with a Hamiltonian view of national

---

90. Dangerfield, *Era of Good Feelings*, 82.
91. See *Old South Leaflets*, 9:58–60.

power. He had no interest whatsoever in limiting Congress; on the contrary, his task as he saw it was to check irresponsible state legislatures. In opinions painted in broad strokes of simple language and logic, the chief justice described a national government supreme in its sphere and therefore necessarily possessed of broad and liberal powers. He succeeded Alexander Hamilton as the great counterweight to the strict construction of Jefferson, Madison, and the Republican Party. In perhaps his greatest accomplishment, Marshall imposed his centralizing views upon the rest of the Supreme Court despite the fact that Republicans held the executive branch throughout his tenure. Jefferson in particular had been careful in his selection of judicial nominees. He settled on his first, William Johnson, only after making sure of the candidate's strict constructionist credentials.[92] Johnson nevertheless proved to be a source of great disappointment, at least from a Republican perspective. In time he became as centralizing in his opinions as Marshall (he proved willing, as one historian put it, to "out-Herod Herod himself").[93] Jefferson took umbrage at Johnson's conversion; this frustration undoubtedly worsened when his next two appointees, Thomas Todd and Brockholst Livingston, also fell under the influence of Chief Justice Marshall.

Madison exercised less vigilance then Jefferson, and it was on his watch that another wolf entered the hen house. After Levi Lincoln and John Quincy Adams refused to accept appointment to the Supreme Court, and Alexander Wolcott, a Republican Party operative, was rejected by the Senate, Madison turned to Representative Joseph Story of Massachusetts. Thomas Jefferson suspected the young congressman's credentials. He therefore advised Madison against nominating Story, calling him a "pseudo-Republican and a Tory."[94] Jefferson's fears proved to be well founded—the new justice eventually surpassed both Johnson and Marshall in his centralizing tendencies. Madison fared no better with his second nominee, Gabriel Duvall (1811). The former comptroller of the treasury almost immediately came under the influence of the chief justice. Whether Marshall induced experienced jurists to change their views is doubtful, but he certainly instilled an esprit de corps. It was on Marshall's watch that the justices began the practice of issuing a single opinion containing the Court's ruling; dissent was rare. That all of the justices lodged together in the same inn during the one-month annual session of the

92. Malone, *Jefferson the President: Second Term*, 282.
93. Dangerfield, *Era of Good Feelings*, 169.
94. Quoted in Rutland, *Presidency of James Madison*, 57.

Court undoubtedly contributed to this unanimity. (Night conferences at their lodgings followed dinner each evening.) So did the fact that while members of Congress and presidents came and went with startling regularity, the justices of the Supreme Court remained in office year after year.

Like Alexander Hamilton, John Marshall viewed the Constitution as a mandate for the protection of property and the development of commerce. To give it anything other than a broad reading would impair the national government's ability to achieve those great ends. His influence with the other justices enabled Marshall to implement this approach in a series of landmark decisions between 1810 and 1825. The first was *Fletcher v. Peck* (1810).[95] In 1795 four land companies secured a grant from the Georgia legislature under which they acquired some 35 million acres at rock-bottom prices (less than two cents an acre). The governor vetoed the bill, only to be overridden. Every legislator but one owned stock in one of the four land companies. Word of the episode soon became public, and following the next election (which decimated the ranks of incumbent lawmakers), the state legislature passed a bill invalidating the sale. The four companies involved in the transaction were naturally horrified by this turn of events, but they continued to sell tracts to enthusiastic buyers. The Georgia legislature sold the lands to the federal government in 1802 with the understanding that innocent investors would be compensated by Congress. Virginia congressman John Randolph—peerless in his capacity to detect excess and usurpation in federal expenditures—single-handedly kept the House of Representatives from passing the requested appropriation for more than a decade.[96] With one option for relief blocked, investors turned to the federal courts and brought suit against the state of Georgia. They based their suit in part upon Article I, Section 10, which prohibited the states from impairing the obligations of contracts. Alexander Hamilton—in private practice as an attorney—assured the plaintiffs that the clause prohibited Georgia from rescinding the 1795 law.[97] When the case reached the Supreme Court, Chief Justice Marshall embraced Hamilton's view. As he saw it, grants were but a type of contract, and there was no reason to assume that contracts involving states were exempt from the requirements of the contract clause.[98] Marshall's anal-

95. 10 U.S. 87 (1810).

96. Haines, *Role of the Supreme Court*, 312, 322.

97. "Every grant, whether from a state or an individual, is virtually a contract." Quoted in ibid., 311.

98. 10 U.S. at 137.

ysis on this point was subject to question. A grant is a conveyance of real property through the transfer of a deed. A contract, on the other hand, involves a promise to perform an act given in exchange for something of value (consideration). A land grant often occurs as part of a contract, but only as a part, and it cannot properly be described as the equivalent of the whole, as it lacks consideration. In *Fletcher v. Peck* the grant was preceded by payment; thus, even if the grant alone did not qualify as a contract, the overall exchange could be described as one. Yet difficulties remained. During ratification the contract clause was understood as targeting stay laws.[99] These measures—which extended the period during which debts owed by one private citizen to another could be paid—plagued the states on the eve of the Constitutional Convention. These acts alone were the abuses the Founders wished to eradicate with the contract clause; there is no evidence that they intended to strip the states of the power to alter the terms of their own commercial relationships when necessary for the public good.

In making land grants irrevocable, *Fletcher v. Peck* created enormous temptation for speculators—no matter the means used to obtain these grants, the federal courts would see that the states lived up to their obligations. Thus the complaint of Congressman George M. Troup of Georgia: "it is proclaimed by the judges, and is now to be sanctioned by the legislature, that the representatives of a people, may corruptly betray the people, may corruptly barter their rights and those of their posterity, and the people are wholly without any kind of remonstrance whatsoever."[100] Speculators viewed the decision as a guarantee that the federal government would see they retained whatever they could extract. There were gifts to be had. The period after the War of 1812 saw the first of several great land booms that took place in America during the nineteenth century. Wild fluctuations in land prices made investors rich overnight. The state governments owned much real estate and greatly affected the value of land they did not own through the selection of routes for turnpikes, canals, and railroads. Real estate speculators thus had both the means and the motive to buy favors. *Fletcher v. Peck* ensured that their efforts—no matter how unsavory—would not be in vain. Thus one historian's conclusion that the decision "seemed to cast the protection of federal law over much that was dubious in the land business."[101]

99. See, for example, "Brutus," no. 14, *New York Journal,* February 28 and March 6, 1788, in Bailyn, *Debate on the Constitution,* 2:265.

100. *Annals of Congress,* 12th Cong., 2d sess., January 20, 1813, 25:858.

101. Dangerfield, *Era of Good Feelings,* 164.

While the exchange at issue in *Fletcher v. Peck* possessed the characteristics of a contract, the same could not be said for the laws invalidated by the Supreme Court in its next two major cases involving the contract clause. In *Terrett v. Taylor* (1815), the Court held unconstitutional a Virginia statute revoking the legislature's previous recognition of the Episcopal Church's ownership of a tract of real estate.[102] Although Justice Story did not refer to the contract clause in his opinion for the Court, scholars view it as the basis for the ruling. If the Court did act through the contract clause, the decision was deeply flawed. The Episcopal Church purchased the land from an individual in 1770 and paid no money to the state when the legislature passed a bill recognizing the church's right to the property (1776).[103] The statute did not qualify as a contract because the state received nothing in exchange for it. The Supreme Court appeared to have stuffed a round peg into a square hole. The state legislature's termination of the church's property rights undoubtedly constituted an abuse of power and a taking of private property. The Fifth Amendment might have prohibited the act had it been attempted by the federal government. Yet the U.S. Constitution banned only a handful of state acts, and the taking of private property without compensation was not among them. The Supreme Court was therefore faced with a legislative act that was clearly unjust; yet none of the clauses of the federal Constitution prohibited it. That the Court nevertheless invalidated it demonstrated that some justices viewed the federal judiciary as more than an entity charged with the duty to ensure federal supremacy in selected areas. They appeared intent on empowering it with a sort of general veto power over state legislation, at least when necessary to protect what they viewed as property rights.

Four years after *Terrett v. Taylor* the Supreme Court issued its most important contract clause decision, *Dartmouth College v. Woodward* (1819).[104] In a case viewed as the most important in the Court's history until well into the twentieth century, the justices extended the scope of the contract clause to charters. The suit that produced the decision arose out of political conflict in New Hampshire. In 1816 the Republican-controlled state legislature revoked the charter of Dartmouth College and replaced it with one that turned control of the institution over to a state-appointed board of overseers. School officials were understandably furious; they brought suit and won at trial. The

102. 13 U.S. 42, 55 (1815).
103. Currie, *Constitution in the Supreme Court*, 138–39.
104. 17 U.S. (4 Wheaton) 518 (1819).

decision was appealed to the New Hampshire Supreme Court, which reversed the trial court's decision and ruled against the college. In doing so, it refused to accept the claim that the law was void because it interfered with the property rights of the board of trustees. To hold otherwise, the justices insisted, would place the legislature in a straitjacket. "If we decide that these acts are not 'the law of the land' because they interfere with private rights, all other acts, interfering with private rights, may . . . fall within the same principle; and what statute does not either directly or indirectly interfere with private rights?" The Court insisted that the contract clause was not aimed at state control of public institutions or grants of power made by a state to individuals for public purposes, and that to hold otherwise would invite disaster. "It is a construction, in our view, repugnant to the very principles of all government because it places all the public institutions of all the states beyond legislative control."[105]

The college appealed to the U.S. Supreme Court, with attorney and alumnus Daniel Webster arguing on its behalf. In time Webster's reputation as a lawyer grew to the point that the room in the Capitol occupied by the Supreme Court slowly filled when he entered and emptied again upon his departure.[106] In 1819 true fame still awaited, but his talent had already made its presence known. Webster claimed that the state legislatures necessarily operated under certain restrictions that might or might not be included in written constitutions. "The legislature of New Hampshire would not have been competent to pass the acts in question . . . because these acts are not the exercise of a power properly legislative." Once rights vest, he explained, courts alone have the authority to remove them. Even in the absence of prohibitory constitutional provisions, the states could not, for example, take private property without compensation—justice itself prohibited it. In this case, the state could not assume possession of the college, as it belonged to the board of trustees. Almost as an afterthought, Webster asserted that the charter constituted a contract and thus came within the scope of the contract clause. The attorney for New Hampshire, John Holmes, disagreed. He insisted that the contract clause did not apply to grants of "political power" that concern the "internal government and police power of a sovereign state." Holmes claimed that the Constitutional Convention saw the contract clause as protecting the

105. *Dartmouth College v. Woodward*, 1 N.H. 111, 131, 134 (1817).

106. Harriet Martineau, *Retrospect of Western Travel*, 3 vols. (New York: Harper Brothers, 1838), 1:166.

"inviolability of private contracts and private rights." The charter at issue, however, concerned a public institution. Nor did it meet the legal definition of a contract, as school founder Eleazar Wheelock paid no money to the institution or the Crown when it gave him the school's charter.[107]

The Supreme Court ruled in favor of Dartmouth College and against the state of New Hampshire. Justice Duvall alone dissented. In a majority opinion handed down on February 2, 1819, Chief Justice Marshall explained why the law was beyond the pale—or at least he almost did. Marshall dispensed with the key issue in perhaps the most succinct analysis of a constitutional question yet to appear in a Supreme Court opinion. "It can," he wrote, "require no argument to prove that the circumstances of this case constitute a contract." Having passed the main problem, Marshall next addressed the question of whether the law fell within the scope of the contract clause, and at the same time made a startling admission: "It is more than possible that the preservation of rights of this description was not particularly in the view of the framers of the Constitution, when the clause under consideration was introduced into that instrument." He explained that "interferences of a more frequent recurrence [stay laws], to which the temptation was stronger, and of which the mischief was more extensive, constituted the great motive for imposing this restriction on the state legislatures." Having conceded that the Founders did not have charters in mind when they devised the contract clause, Marshall insisted that it nevertheless prohibited their impairment. "It is not enough to say, that this particular case was not in the minds of the Convention, when the article was framed, nor of the American people, when it was adopted." It is, he continued, "necessary to go further, and to say that, had this particular case been suggested, the language would have been so varied, as to exclude it, or it would have been made a special exemption." Such was not the case in the matter before the Court. "The case being within the words of the rule, must be within its operation likewise, unless there be something in the literal construction so obviously absurd, or mischievous, or repugnant to the general spirit of the instrument, as to justify those, who expound the Constitution in making it an exception."[108]

The chief justice did not explain how a charter came "within the words of the rule" of the contract clause—he merely cited *Fletcher v. Peck* for the

---

107. 17 U.S. 518, 558–88, 595–96, 600–601, 607, 609–10 (1819).
108. Ibid., at 627, 628, 644–45.

proposition that all grants are contracts.[109] The Dartmouth College charter did not meet the definition of a contract—no consideration changed hands at the time it was issued. The Crown received nothing when George III granted a charter authorizing the formation of a school for Indians (which later became Dartmouth College). While donors had given money at the time the charter was granted, those donations had gone to the school it-self (Moor's Charity School for Indians). They reacted with anger when the funds—and the charter itself—passed to Dartmouth College.[110] No one un-derstood the charter as irrevocable when it was issued in the 1760s; in effect it constituted a license or permit from the Crown, which could be abolished by Parliament at any time. In the end, the Supreme Court overreached in *Dartmouth College* in the same way that it had in *Fletcher v. Peck*—it altered the contract clause's meaning in order to prevent a state from taking prop-erty without compensation.[111]

The *Dartmouth College* ruling was followed by an explosion in the use of corporations for commercial purposes. (They had formerly been employed only for educational and religious purposes.) The owners of these new en-terprises sought relief in federal court whenever legislatures threatened their investments. In time *Dartmouth College* forced federal courts to sift through scores of state laws in order to invalidate not only those that revoked cor-porate charters but also those that merely impaired their value.[112] The deci-sion also increased corruption in the state legislatures.[113] Bribed by lobbyists, state legislatures found themselves handing out astonishing privileges and franchises. Justice Story anticipated this problem in his concurring opinion in *Dartmouth College* when he pointed out that states could add clauses to charters expressly reserving the right to amend or even revoke them.[114] Leg-islatures failed to embrace Story's remedy in part because the private inter-ests that extracted favorable grants and charters were able to prevent the in-clusion of language that would have reserved such rights to the legislatures.

---

109. Ibid., at 656.

110. Benjamin Fletcher Wright Jr., *The Contract Clause of the Constitution* (Cambridge: Harvard University Press, 1938; reprint, Westport, Conn.: Greenwood Press, 1982), 43–44. See also Levy, *Original Intent and the Framers' Constitution*, 314.

111. Currie, *Constitution in the Supreme Court*, 133, 142–45.

112. See, for example, *Charles River Bridge Company v. Warren Bridge*, 35 U.S. 420 (1837).

113. Haines, *Role of the Supreme Court*, 417. See also Warren, *Supreme Court in United States History*, 1:491–92.

114. 17 U.S. at 712.

Approximately a month before the *Dartmouth College* decision, the Supreme Court issued a ruling that also contained a rather controversial statement of federal power. *McCulloch v. Maryland* did not on its face appear to be terribly aggressive.[115] A second national bank had been incorporated in 1816, and although a handful of strict constructionists held that such an institution was beyond the authority of Congress, for most Americans the question was moot. When a Maryland branch of the Bank of the United States refused to pay state taxes, a state judge imposed fines upon it. Litigation ensued and the matter found its way to the U.S. Supreme Court. Counsel for Maryland insisted that the power to establish a bank was neither explicitly granted by the Constitution nor truly necessary to the exercise of one or more of the powers listed within it. While formation of a national bank might have been necessary to the exercise of the enumerated powers in 1791, numerous state banks existed in 1819, and they could provide the same services as a federally incorporated institution. The justices disagreed. In his opinion for the Court, Chief Justice Marshall cut a broad swath. "The government of the Union, though limited in its powers, is supreme within its sphere." In arriving at this conclusion, Marshall rejected the idea that the federal government was only the agent of sovereign states, and that its powers therefore ought to be narrowly construed. The federal government had been formed by the American people, who had delegated a portion of their sovereignty to it. Thus it was sovereign with respect to the powers committed to it. It could therefore exercise discretion in choosing how to carry out its enumerated duties. "The government which has a right to do an act, and has imposed on it the duty of performing that act, must according to the dictates of reason, be allowed to select the means." For those who doubted the propriety of this approach, Marshall pointed to the necessary and proper clause. The Founders added it to the Constitution, he insisted, in order to ensure that Congress would enjoy broad discretion in carrying out its enumerated powers. He specifically rejected the suggestion—offered by counsel for Maryland (and James Madison in *The Federalist*, No. 33) that it had been placed in the Constitution merely to confirm the power of Congress to pass laws necessary to the attainment of its enumerated ends. Such an approach would, Marshall wrote, withdraw from Congress "the choice of means," and instead allow it to choose only those means which are the "most direct and

115. 17 U.S. 316 (1819).

simple." Like Hamilton, Marshall stripped the word "necessary" of any restrictive connotations. It "frequently imports no more than that one thing is convenient, or useful, or essential to another." Thus, "to employ the means necessary to an end is generally understood as employing any means calculated to produce the end, and not as being confined to those single means, without which the end would be entirely unattainable." If, Marshall continued, the approach to the necessary and proper clause embraced by counsel for Maryland were applied to the postal power, it "might be said, with some plausibility, that the right to carry the mail, and to punish those who rob it, is not indispensably necessary to the establishment of a post-office and post-road." Hence the "absolute impracticality" of maintaining a restrictive approach to the necessary and proper clause.[116]

The chief justice's analysis proved enormously significant. In essence, Marshall raised Alexander Hamilton's indulgent approach to the Constitution from the dead. Almost three decades later, broadminded legislators could still be heard citing *McCulloch* for the proposition that the means employed by Congress to reach its enumerated ends need only be "useful for the purpose indicated."[117] Republicans warned that Marshall's sovereignty-based approach would, if adopted, expand the domain of Congress from a handful of limited authorities to a general legislative power. They saw the federal government as a mere agent, authorized to carry out certain powers by its principals, the states. Representative Peter Porter dismissed the sovereignty-based approach to federal power when it was offered in support of the constitutionality of a national bank in 1811. "The proposition that the government is sovereign is assumed to prove that it possesses the attributes of sovereignty." If, he continued, "the position that the powers of this government are sovereign as to all the objects of them, be proved, I will concede the consequence, to wit: that we have a right to establish corporations to attain these objects—but I deny the fact of sovereignty." As he saw it, because Congress served merely as an agent, it could never presume to have absolute discretion in performing those duties assigned to it. Its position bore close resemblance to that of a sheriff, who, when he puts a man to death, "executes an act of as high import and authority as human power can execute; and yet the sheriff of a county is not sovereign. His authority is a mere delegated au-

116. Ibid., at 332–33, 405–10, 413–14, 418.
117. See the March 14, 1846, speech of Representative Andrew Stewart of Pennsylvania, *Congressional Globe*, 29th Cong., 1st sess., Appendix, 15:497.

thority—his act is a mere ministerial, mechanical act." The same was "true for Congress, as it did not have unlimited discretion in carrying out its powers. Congress derives its powers from the people of the United States—and they are sovereign. Congress is not."[118] As for the question of how much discretion Congress should have in carrying out its powers, Porter offered his own test. "You must show that the plain, direct, ostensible, primary object and tendency of [the] law is to execute the power, and not that that it will [merely] tend to facilitate the execution of it."[119]

A severe reaction against the Bank of the United States occurred in the aftermath of *McCulloch v. Maryland.* Republican newspapers called for limiting the bank's operations to Washington, D.C. The Virginia legislature asked the state's congressional delegation to secure passage of an amendment barring Congress from establishing a bank.[120] The legislatures of Pennsylvania, Tennessee, Ohio, Indiana, and Illinois endorsed the idea.[121] While popular resentment subsided, the fury of Republican leaders did not. James Madison and Thomas Jefferson were familiar with Marshall's arguments; they had first responded to them almost thirty years before when they appeared in Hamilton's Report on the Public Credit. It did not require the mind of a legal scholar to detect the threat in the chief justice's approach. It would render the enumerated powers meaningless by giving Congress unfettered discretion as to the means by which those powers might be executed. As Virginia judge Spencer Roane wrote, there was little difference "between an unlimited grant of power and a grant of power limited in its terms, but accompanied with unlimited means of carrying it into execution." Thus the warning of Virginia editor Thomas Ritchie: acceptance of Marshall's interpretation meant that the federal government would not long remain one of limited powers.[122]

James Madison attacked the *McCulloch* decision in a September 2, 1819, letter to Roane. "Is there," he asked, "a legislative power . . . not expressly prohibited by the Constitution, which might not, according to the doctrine of the Court, be exercised as a means of carrying into effect some specified

118. *Annals of Congress,* 11th Cong., 3d sess., January 1811, 22:631. The modern view holds that the federal government is sovereign within its designated sphere. Commager and Morison, *Growth of the American Republic,* 283.

119. *Annals of Congress,* 11th Cong., 3d sess., January 18, 1811, 22:636.

120. Haines, *Role of the Supreme Court,* 366–67.

121. Dangerfield, *Era of Good Feelings,* 173–74.

122. Quoted in Haines, *Role of the Supreme Court,* 360, 364.

power?" The embrace of such an approach in 1787–88, Madison continued, would have made ratification of the Constitution far more difficult. Nor did he accept the argument that absolute discretion was necessary. "It may surely be remarked that a limited government may be limited in its sovereignty as well with respect to the means as to the objects of its powers; and that to give an extent to the former, superseding the limits of the latter, is in effect to convert a limited into an unlimited government." Madison thought there was "certainly a reasonable medium between expounding the Constitution with the strictness of a penal law, or other ordinary statute, and expounding it with a laxity which may vary its essential character, and encroach on the local sovereignties with which it was meant to be reconcilable."[123]

Gibbons v. Ogden (1824) is not normally viewed as a companion case to McCulloch v. Maryland, yet it too saw the Court proclaim broad legislative powers for Congress.[124] The state of New York granted a monopoly over the transportation of passengers in waters surrounding New York City to steamboat operator Robert Fulton. The growth of the metropolis made violations of the law inevitable. Among the interlopers was Thomas Gibbons, who ferried passengers between New Jersey and Manhattan. Fulton obtained an injunction barring Gibbons from local waters. Gibbons sought redress in federal court on the grounds that the New York law constituted an impermissible state regulation of interstate commerce. When the matter reached the Supreme Court, the justices had several options. They could invalidate the measure because it conflicted with the commerce clause, or because it conflicted with a 1793 federal coasting statute (under which Gibbons had obtained a license), or both.[125] The Court could also have allowed the law to remain in place. Daniel Webster, who represented Gibbons, once again offered the Court a Hamiltonian blueprint for its decision, yet he went further than Hamilton would have dared. As Webster saw it, the statute violated the Constitution because the commerce clause prohibited not only discriminatory legislation but all state laws affecting interstate commerce, whether or not they impeded trade. The Founders intended to remove the power to regulate interstate commerce from the states, he reasoned, as it could be exercised effectively only by a single authority.[126]

123. Writings of Madison, 8:449–452.
124. 22 U.S. 1 (1824).
125. 1 Stats at Large 305 (February 18, 1793).
126. 22 U.S. at 9, 13–14.

Chief Justice Marshall would not go that far. As he saw it, the 1793 federal licensing act had as its subject the transportation of passengers along the coast. He went on to hold the New York statute void, though he failed to say whether it conflicted with the federal statute, the commerce clause, or both. Justice Johnson accepted Webster's invitation. As he saw it, the Constitution vested the power to regulate commerce exclusively in Congress, and the New York statute therefore would have been unconstitutional even without a conflicting federal law. Although unwilling to follow Johnson's lead, the chief justice made clear that he too was sympathetic to Webster's argument. "As the word 'to regulate' implies in its nature, full power over the thing to be regulated, it excludes, necessarily, the action of all others that would perform the same operation on the same thing.... There is great force in this argument, and the court is not satisfied that it has been refuted." Marshall described the national government's powers under the commerce clause in the broadest possible terms, thus demonstrating that he would not relinquish his sovereignty-based approach to federal authority, despite Republican complaints. "This power, like all others vested in Congress, is complete in itself, may be exercised to its utmost extent, and acknowledges no limitations, other than are prescribed in the Constitution." Thus, as "the sovereignty of Congress, though limited to specific objects, is plenary to those objects, the power over commerce with foreign nations, and among the several states, is vested in Congress as absolutely as it would be in a single government." The chief justice went on to all but abdicate the power of judicial review with respect to federal legislation purportedly enacted under the commerce clause. "The wisdom and the discretion of Congress, their identity with the people, and the influence which their constituents possess at election, are, in this, as in many instances, as that, for example, of declaring war, the sole restraints on which they have relied to secure themselves from its abuse."[127]

Despite Marshall's failure to adopt the idea that the Constitution removed from the legislatures all power over interstate commerce, the idea quickly moved into the mainstream. Within a year of the decision William Rawle endorsed it in one of the earliest treatises on American constitutional law, *A View of the Constitution of the United States*.[128] In his monumental

127. Ibid., at 213–14, 226–29, 197.
128. William Rawle, *A View of the Constitution of the United States of America*, 2d ed. (Philadelphia: Philip H. Nicklin, 1829), 82–84.

work of 1833, *Commentaries on the Constitution of the United States,* Justice Joseph Story did so as well. Story conceded that the states retained the power to enact regulations of "police" such as "inspection laws, health laws [and] laws regulating turnpikes, roads, and ferries," as long as they did not conflict with federal legislation.[129] The idea that Congress possessed exclusive authority to regulate interstate commerce had no basis in the original understanding of the commerce clause. During the ratification contest, Federalists had not represented it as removing all power over commerce from the states. On the contrary, they treated it as doing little more than transferring the power to impose tariffs to the national government.[130] When the Constitutional Convention intended to grant an exclusive power of legislation, it explicitly did so, as in the case of the capital. When it sought to prohibit states from legislating in particular areas, it also did so in language that could not have been more clear.[131]

While Republican critics may have had reason to object to certain aspects of *Dartmouth College, McCulloch,* and *Gibbons,* they stood on weaker ground when they attacked two jurisdictional decisions handed down by the Supreme Court during the postwar period. In 1813 the Supreme Court invalidated a Virginia law that provided for the confiscation of lands belonging to a British subject; the justices held that it violated the Treaty of Paris.[132] The Court issued a writ of mandamus to enforce the ruling, only to have the Virginia Court of Appeals ignore it and issue a decision holding that the U.S. Supreme Court lacked appellate authority over state courts. In doing so it found section 25 of the Judiciary Act of 1789 unconstitutional. In *Martin v. Hunter's Lessee* (1816), the Supreme Court reversed the Virginia Court of Appeals' invalidation of the Judiciary Act of 1789.[133] Writing for the Court, Justice Story held that because Article III vested in the federal courts jurisdiction over all cases arising under the federal Constitution, laws, or treaties, they necessarily had the power of appellate review over state court cases involving federal questions. Uniformity required a central interpreter of U.S. laws, constitutional provisions, and treaties. Hence the need for the feder-

129. Joseph Story, *Commentaries on the Constitution of the United States,* 2 vols., 4th ed. (Boston: Little, Brown, 1873), 2:9–11 (sections 1067–70).

130. Alexander Hamilton, *The Federalist,* No. 22, in Rossiter, *Federalist Papers,* 144–45, and James Madison, *The Federalist,* No. 42, ibid., 267–68.

131. See U.S. Constitution, Article I, Section 10. See also Currie, *Constitution in the Supreme Court,* 173.

132. *Fairfax v. Hunter's Lessee,* 11 U.S. 603 (1813).

133. 14 U.S. 304 (1816).

al courts to enjoy at least appellate jurisdiction over all cases in which they were at issue.[134] In order to avoid being ignored by the Virginia Court of Appeals for a second time, the Supreme Court returned the case to the trial court, but that court, too, refused to implement the decision.[135] While the Supreme Court lost the battle, it won the war, as the claim that the federal judiciary lacked authority to accept appeals of federal questions from state courts eventually faded. The second important jurisdictional opinion of the period stemmed from Virginia's conviction of two Washington, D.C., men for selling lottery tickets in the state *(Cohens v. Virginia)*. Chief Justice Marshall affirmed the ruling first handed down in *Martin v. Hunter's Lessee:* the Supreme Court's appellate jurisdiction extends to cases in state court involving federal questions. Republicans feared that the Supreme Court might reverse Cohens's conviction on the grounds that the state could not ban the sale of lottery tickets issued under the authority of federal law (by the municipal government of Washington, D.C.). Marshall did not go that far; instead, he pointed out that Congress had not authorized the sale of lottery tickets in Virginia. Yet he implied that it could have—a claim that was both questionable and pointless.[136]

The most infamous jurisdictional decision of the period arose out of the reaction against the Bank of the United States that followed *McCulloch v. Maryland.* After Ohio imposed a $50,000 tax on local branches of the Bank of the United States, it sued the state. The Supreme Court ordered the state to return the money *(Osborne v. Bank of the United States* [1824]). In doing so, Chief Justice Marshall used a rather infamous evasion to overcome the argument that the Eleventh Amendment prohibited suits against states. As he saw it, the amendment prohibited only those suits in which the state was the party of record, and not those in which state officers were the defendants—as was the case in the matter before the Court.[137] The ruling all but gutted the Eleventh Amendment.[138] In dissent, Justice Johnson pointed out that the Supreme Court had previously held that a corporation was a party to a suit that had been brought against corporate officers.[139] Pleadings

134. Ibid., at 348.

135. Forrest McDonald, *States' Rights and the Union: Imperium in Imperio, 1776–1876* (Lawrence: University Press of Kansas, 2000), 77.

136. 19 U.S. 264, 440–48 (1821).

137. *Osborn v. Bank of the United States,* 22 U.S. 738, 858 (1824).

138. Currie, *Constitution in the Supreme Court,* 105.

139. 22 U.S. at 911–12, referring to *Bank of the United States v. Deveaux,* 9 U.S. 61 (1809).

against corporate institutions such as state governments regularly named officers, rather than the entity itself, as defendants.

The Supreme Court stood on strong ground in *Martin v. Hunter's Lessee* and *Cohens v. Virginia*. Nevertheless, those decisions, along with Marshall's emasculation of the Eleventh Amendment in *Osborne* and the needlessly provocative opinions in *McCulloch* and *Gibbons*, triggered the second reaction against the federal courts to occur during Marshall's tenure. As John Taylor of Virginia had already pointed out in his 1819 book, *Construction Construed and Constitutions Vindicated* (1819), the Court threatened, via novel interpretations of certain clauses, to completely undermine all constitutional limitations on federal power.[140] In a second work issued four years later *(New Views on the Constitution)*, Taylor warned that the high court was rapidly approaching the point at which it would enjoy a general veto power over the state legislatures, despite the fact that the Constitutional Convention explicitly rejected the idea of vesting such a power in the national government.[141]

A number of observers resuscitated the charge first made some thirty years before—that the Supreme Court could not be trusted to treat cases involving disputes between the federal and state governments in an unbiased manner.[142] Judge Spencer Roane wondered if the states had really intended to commit "an act of such egregious folly as to agree that their umpire should be altogether appointed and paid by the other party." In his view, the "Supreme Court may be a perfectly impartial tribunal to decide between two states, but [it] cannot be considered in that point of view when the contest lies between the United States and one of its members."[143] Critics, ready to exploit the breach, came forward with a bevy of ideas. Thomas Jefferson suggested an amendment limiting the terms of federal judges to six years, with reappointment by the president, subject to the approval of both houses of Congress. He noted that judges in Britain could be removed from office by Parliament.[144] *Niles' Weekly Register,* perhaps the nation's leading newspaper during the 1820s,

140. John Taylor, *Construction Construed and Constitutions Vindicated* (Richmond: Shepherd & Pollard, 1820), 169–72.

141. John Taylor, *New Views of the Constitution of the United States* (Washington, D.C., 1823), 233.

142. See "Brutus," no. 11, in Ketcham, *Antifederalist Papers,* 297.

143. Quoted in Haines, *Role of the Supreme Court,* 359.

144. Jefferson to James Pleasants, December 1821, *Writings of Jefferson,* 10:198. "A judiciary independent of a king or executive alone, is a good thing; but independence of the will of the nation is a solecism, at least in a republican government." Jefferson to Thomas Ritchie, December 25, 1820, ibid., 10:170–71.

endorsed the idea of appointing judges for a period of years.[145] In December 1821 Senator Richard M. Johnson of Kentucky proposed an amendment giving the Senate appellate jurisdiction over Supreme Court cases in which a state was party. Speaking in support of the amendment, Johnson cited *Dartmouth College* and *McCulloch* as cases in which the Supreme Court failed to heed the Constitution.[146] For a time in 1826 the Senate considered a bill that would have required seven votes (out of ten justices) to invalidate state laws.[147] In 1831 the Supreme Court's intervention in a dispute between the Cherokee Indians and Georgia led the House Judiciary Committee to recommend a bill to repeal section 25 of the Judiciary Act of 1789. A week later the full House rejected the measure by an overwhelming margin, 138-51.[148]

Judging from the House vote, it may be assumed that most of the country would have agreed with James Madison's response to the idea of withdrawing the power to resolve federal and state disputes from the central government. In a letter to Thomas Jefferson, he explained why he could not join the attack. "A paramount or even a definitive authority in the individual states would soon make the Constitution and laws different in different states, and thus destroy the equality and uniformity of rights and duties which form the essence of the compact." Chaos would follow. "To leave conflicting decisions to be settled between the judicial parties could not promise a happy result. The end must be a trial of strength between the posse headed by the marshal and the posse headed by the sheriff."[149] Perhaps the most interesting idea was proposed in 1830 by the secretary of the treasury, Louis MacLane. He suggested providing for the removal of federal judges upon the request of two-thirds of the state legislatures.[150] The idea's chief strength derived from the fact that it would give a check to the one element in the federal system—the states—that had lost ground at the expense of the judiciary. Congress did not consider MacLane's proposal, yet questions remained. Perhaps the most important of these had first been asked in 1787-88: were there adequate checks on the judiciary to prevent it from improperly extending its jurisdiction at the expense of the states?

145. Warren, *Supreme Court in United States History*, 1:656-57.

146. *Annals of Congress*, 17th Cong., 1st sess., December 1821-January 1822, 38:23, 85-86, 89.

147. For discussion, see U.S. Congress, *Register of Debates*, 14 vols. (Washington, D.C.: Gales & Seaton, 1825-37), 19th Cong., 1st sess., April 1826, 2:548-71.

148. Ibid., 21st Cong., 2d sess., January 29, 1831, 7:542; see also Warren, *Supreme Court in United States History*, 1:239.

149. *Writings of Madison*, 9:141.

150. Warren, *Supreme Court in United States History*, 1:721.

FEDERAL PATRONAGE AND THE REPUBLICAN PARTY

During the first quarter of the nineteenth century, the United States doubled in both population and land area. The country's terrific growth made a larger civil list necessary. From a total of 6,327 employees in 1816, the federal civil service more than tripled, to 19,800, by 1831.[151] Most of these places were in the nation's 8,450 post offices. Customhouses also employed thousands. Even in the underpopulated West, job seekers could find a land office nearby—the first opened in 1796; by 1824 there were thirty-nine.[152] The addition of so many executive branch employees vested enormous political power in the hands of the president. Three successive Republican admin-istrations proved more than willing to exploit the situation between 1801 and 1825. Jefferson allowed lower-ranking Federalist officeholders to remain, while only Republicans received appointments. Madison embraced this ap-proach as well upon his ascendancy in 1809. By the last year of James Mon-roe's presidency (1825), the executive branch was composed almost solely of Republicans.

Executive influence over members of Congress grew with the civil list. Lawmakers continued to accept appointments to executive branch offices. James Madison appointed twenty-nine lawmakers to the civil service.[153] The modest pay and short careers of most legislators made the relative security of appointive office little short of irresistible. Fearful of scandal, the House of Representatives in 1811 came within three votes of passing an amendment that would have prohibited members of Congress from accepting appoint-ment to civil office until the expiration of the current president's term.[154] Prospecting for jobs continued to serve as a pastime for lawmakers in the postwar years. In 1821 Secretary of State John Quincy Adams complained that at any given moment half of the members of Congress were seeking places for themselves, while the other half wanted jobs for relatives and friends.[155]

As the growth of the civil service expanded the influence of the presi-dent, members of Congress began to grow envious. The most tangible mani-

151. U.S. Department of Commerce, *Statistical Abstract of the United States, 1957* (Washing-ton, D.C.: U.S. Government Printing Office, 1957), 766.

152. White, *Jeffersonians*, 519–21.

153. Fish, *Civil Service and the Patronage*, 56.

154. *Annals of Congress*, 11th Cong., 3d sess., February 1811, 22:899.

155. White, *Jeffersonians*, 92.

festation of this jealousy was the Benton Report of 1826. This report was the brainchild of a Senate committee chaired by Thomas Hart Benton of Missouri. A partisan document, it nonetheless made clear that Congress was acutely aware of the potential for abuse of federal patronage. Because "power over a man's support, has always been held and admitted to be a power over his will," the president enjoyed great influence over persons employed in the executive branch. These civil servants in turn obtain "power over . . . the daily support of an immense number of individuals, professional, mechanical and day-laboring, to whom they can and will extend, or deny a valuable private as well as public patronage, according to the part which they shall act in state, as well as in federal elections." Hence the dire conclusion: the "power of patronage, unless checked by the vigorous interposition of Congress, must go on increasing until federal influence, in many parts of the Confederation, will predominate in elections, as completely as British influence predominates in the elections of Scotland and Ireland, in rotten borough towns, and in the great naval stations of Portsmouth and Plymouth." The predictions made in *The Federalist* (Nos. 45 and 46) regarding a modest federal establishment—that the officers of the national government would remain few in number and without influence—had proved incorrect. In no other respect, the report concluded, had the predictions of the Constitution's advocates during ratification been "more completely falsified."[156]

The centralizing effects of federal patronage received their most graphic demonstration in the continued growth of a publicly fed party press. During the presidency of James Madison (1809–17) approximately thirty newspapers obtained State Department printing contracts each year.[157] By 1827 the number had climbed to eighty-two.[158] That the press was corrupted by this state of affairs is indicated by the fact that editors wrote long letters to cabinet members pointing out how supportive their newspapers had been during recent elections.[159] The situation was all the more egregious because newspapers served as almost the only source from which citizens could obtain information about their government. And while the dependence of many sheets on federal largesse was well known, from a politician's point of view newspapers had no peer in their ability to shape public opinion. It was no acci-

---

156. *Report of the Select Committee on Reducing Executive Branch Patronage*, 19th Cong., 1st sess., May 4, 1826, S. Doc. 88, 7, 9.

157. Smith, *Press, Politics, and Patronage*, 45.

158. *Register of Debates*, 19th Cong., 2d sess., February 1, 1827, 3:898.

159. Smith, *Press, Politics, and Patronage*, 48.

dent that presidential candidates invariably began their campaigns by securing the support of one or more newspapers. The universal faith in the power
of press is perhaps best indicated by a comment made by Henry Clay when
he joined the already disliked administration of John Quincy Adams: "Give
us the patronage of the government and we shall make ourselves popular!"[160]
Clay embraced the opportunity presented to him; after taking over the State
Department in 1825, he immediately dropped unfriendly newspapers from
the payroll.[161] During the fall of 1827, with the president's prospects for re-
election in peril, Clay withdrew State Department contracts from six newspapers for their attacks on the administration; four others received the ax the
following year.[162] Clay's actions predictably elicited a sharp response from
Congress in the form of a "retrenchment" drive. During this first fishing
expedition, legislators cast the State Department's procedures—which they
could have revised at any time—in the darkest possible terms. Some dared
to accuse Clay of dropping newspapers for partisan reasons. Congressman
Romulus Saunders of North Carolina claimed that the State Department
had purchased the allegiance of scores of editors. The policy had been "much
more effectual and much more dangerous than the far-famed alien and sedition acts. They were open, and seen to all."[163]

Occasionally these retrenchment drives yielded new legislation. In 1820
congressional Republicans arrived at the conclusion that the principle of
rotation in office—term limits—ought to be applied to federal civil servants. The Tenure of Office Act changed the term of office for senior officials, such as collectors and district attorneys, from good behavior to four
years.[164] While officeholders were usually renominated (at least until 1829),
the law greatly increased those occasions on which the Senate had before it
a nomination for the civil service—thereby enhancing the ability of individual senators to find jobs for allies and supporters. The Tenure of Office Act
arose in part out of divisions within the Republican Party. Friction worsened
considerably during James Monroe's second term, leading to the appearance
of several factions. By the beginning of 1824 the party had split into five
camps, each supporting its own presidential candidate. The hopefuls included

160. Quoted in Peterson, *Great Triumvirate,* 145.

161. Smith, *Press, Politics, and Patronage,* 77.

162. Mary W. M. Hargreaves, *The Presidency of John Quincy Adams* (Lawrence: University
Press of Kansas, 1985), 267–68.

163. *Register of Debates,* 19th Cong., 2d sess., February 1, 1827, 3:897–98.

164. 3 *Stats at Large* 582 (May 15, 1820).

John C. Calhoun, William Crawford, John Quincy Adams, Andrew Jackson, and Henry Clay. The candidates who happened to be cabinet members—Adams, Crawford, and Calhoun—faced the temptation to use federal patronage to their advantage. The president frowned on the use of offices for partisan ends. Despite appointing only Republicans to office, Monroe had been adamant in his insistence that "no person at the head of the government has . . . any claim to the active, partisan exertions of those in office under him."[165] Secretary of the Treasury William Crawford did not take the hint. He pursued an aggressive approach toward patronage during Monroe's second term, seeking to undermine fellow southerner John C. Calhoun while bolstering his own position. The lower levels of the customhouses provided scores of places for Crawford's supporters.[166] War Department employees labored on behalf of Calhoun. Their efforts, though infuriating to the president, were in vain.[167] Secretary of State John Quincy Adams won the presidential election of 1824, albeit under difficult circumstances. General Andrew Jackson secured a plurality of the Electoral College vote, but as no one obtained a majority, the matter ended up in the House of Representatives. A deadlock prevailed for a time, but Adams obtained the necessary majority of states when a representative from New York changed his vote. Upon taking office, Adams appointed both Republicans and Federalists to the civil service. He also refused to dispatch incumbents in order to make way for his supporters, thereby reducing their numbers accordingly.[168] The raw material for an effective party system was there; it needed only a president willing to put it to use.

INTERNAL IMPROVEMENTS

Although federal power made advances on a number of fronts between 1815 and 1830, its most dramatic growth occurred in the area of congressional appropriations. Federal patronage may have been a more centralizing force at the local level, but for sheer drama nothing quite equaled the battles over internal improvement subsidies that took place during the postwar pe-

165. Quoted in Ralph Ketcham, *Presidents above Party: The First American Presidency, 1789–1829* (Chapel Hill: University of North Carolina Press, 1984), 127.

166. Hargreaves, *Presidency of John Quincy Adams*, 236.

167. Johnson, *History of the American People*, 326–27.

168. George Dangerfield, *The Awakening of American Nationalism* (New York: Harper & Row, 1965), 240.

riod. The fight lasted so long and cut so deep that it eventually broke down and recast the nation's political parties. For a time it threatened to alter the Constitution itself. While resistance to federally funded internal improvements may in retrospect seem incomprehensible, critics opposed these measures because of genuine legal concerns. In their view, because a power to construct roads and canals appeared nowhere in Article I, it was an issue to be addressed by the states.

The incursion began with an 1802 statute authorizing residents of the Ohio territory to form a state constitution and government. It provided for the application of 5 percent of the proceeds of land sales in Ohio to the construction of "public roads, leading from navigable waters emptying into the Atlantic, to the Ohio, to the said state, and through same."[169] Three years later, in March 1806, Congress appropriated $30,000 for the construction of a highway from Maryland to Steubenville, Ohio—the Cumberland Road.[170] By 1820 Congress had spent some $1.5 million on the project; it finally reached the Ohio River in 1824.[171] As it went through states, the road could not be justified under the territories clause. Was it a military necessity? A postal road? The latter seems unlikely, at least from Jefferson's perspective—in 1796 he had claimed that the power to establish postal roads bestowed nothing more than authority to designate the routes to be used.[172] Members of Congress did not discuss constitutional issues when they appropriated funds for the project. Later commentators justified it on the grounds that the appropriations formed part of a compact between the federal government and the state of Ohio.[173]

During his second term Jefferson spoke favorably of internal improvements, though he always included the proviso that Congress would first have to submit to the states an amendment authorizing the use of federal funds for these projects.[174] Legislators did not take the hint. Instead the Senate asked Secretary of the Treasury Albert Gallatin for a report on the appropriate locations for improvements. Gallatin responded with his famous "Report on Roads and Canals." He called for the construction of one set

169. 2 *Stats at Large* 173, 175 (April 30, 1802).

170. Ibid., 357 (March 29, 1806).

171. White, *Jeffersonians*, 485.

172. *Writings of Jefferson*, 7:64.

173. See James Monroe's May 1822 "Message on Internal Improvements," in Richardson, *Messages and Papers of the Presidents*, 2:739.

174. See Jefferson's second inaugural message, as well as his annual message of 1806, ibid. 1:367, 397–98.

of canals parallel to the Atlantic coast, another around the falls that impeded passage on several coastal rivers, and still more at key points on the Great Lakes—all at a projected cost of $20 million.[175] Gallatin avoided constitutional concerns in his report; his proposals nonetheless died quickly. The major obstacles were Republicans in Congress and the president, who insisted that an amendment authorizing such projects had to be passed before any funds could be appropriated.

While James Madison stayed the course of Republican orthodoxy, the country began to look at the issue in a different light in the years that followed the War of 1812. The inability to move troops quickly owing to a lack of adequate roads left a lasting impression. The war also instilled within the American people a more nationalistic outlook than they had theretofore embraced. They formed a willing audience for those who advocated developing the nation's resources. This change in attitude manifested itself in Congress just as that body began to assert itself at the expense of the executive branch. Shortly after James Madison succeeded Thomas Jefferson, the Senate rejected his nominee for secretary of state (Albert Gallatin). In the House of Representatives, party leaders appropriated to themselves the party machinery that had been carefully constructed in that body by the Jefferson administration and its allies. The pace of change accelerated with the rise to power of a new generation of talented and independent-minded legislators, including Henry Clay, John C. Calhoun, Peter Porter, and Richard M. Johnson. They embraced a more positive approach to national power than either Jefferson or Madison, and one that was less encumbered by constitutional scruples. The election of 1812 furthered weakened the president's influence with Congress, as Madison barely won a second term. Even the demise of the Federalists weakened the cause of strict construction, as the defection of so many of that school to the party of Jefferson inevitably modified its ideological tilt. The war slowed the pace at which power accumulated in Congress, but it picked up again in 1815 as legislators contemplated an increase in military spending, a bank, protective tariffs, and a program of internal improvements. The president endorsed all these measures in his famous seventh annual message, of December 1815—with the proviso that federally funded internal improvements required passage of a constitutional amendment.[176]

175. *American State Papers: Miscellaneous*, 1:724.
176. Richardson, *Messages and Papers of the Presidents*, 1:562.

The popularity of internal improvements increased all the time. From New Hampshire to Louisiana, farmers demanded transportation improvements that would bring them within reach of the national marketplace. Thus the conclusion of Henry Adams: if Americans of the early nineteenth century "agreed in any opinion, they were united in wishing for roads." Unfortunately, as Adams noted, they were almost as unanimous in their hostility to the idea of paying for them.[177] The rise of a world market stimulated the demand for roads. Rapid population growth, crop shortages, and war left Europe dependent on imported foodstuffs, and American farmers discovered they could profitably export grain. A prosperous wheat belt formed in an area extending from Connecticut to Virginia during the first years of the new century, but the new prosperity benefited only those farmers within reach of waterborne transportation networks. For those a hundred miles or more from the nearest river, getting crops to market remained too expensive to be worth the bother.[178]

Politicians at the federal as well as the state level catered to the mania for transportation improvements by promising assistance for roads, coastal improvements, navigational aids, and the dredging of interior rivers. They received an enthusiastic response. It seemed only natural to farmers that the same government to which they paid taxes ought to help them bring their crops to market. Unfortunately for them, the Virginia planter who occupied the executive mansion did not quite see it that way. In his eighth annual message, of December 3, 1816, Madison acknowledged the need for federally funded internal improvements but insisted once again that a constitutional amendment had to be enacted first.[179] The Republican-dominated House of Representatives ignored Madison's suggestion. Thirty-four-year-old John Caldwell Calhoun of South Carolina led the mutiny. Like Henry Clay and Daniel Webster, Calhoun stood head and shoulders above his peers. Born in 1782 of Scotch-Irish farmers who had settled in the Carolina backwoods (Indians killed his paternal grandmother and uncle in the area on the same day), Calhoun nonetheless received a thorough education. After attending Yale, he practiced law, won a seat in the House of Representatives, and served as chairman of the Foreign Relations Committee before reaching thirty. Although in time he would gain a reputation as an opponent of

177. Adams, *History of the United States during the Administrations of Jefferson*, 46–47.
178. Sellers, *Market Revolution*, 16, 22.
179. Richardson, *Messages and Papers of the Presidents*, 2:552–53.

centralization, in the years after the War of 1812 Calhoun embraced a vigorous approach to federal power. The South Carolina congressman supported the Republican Party's postwar program; he could not see the need for constitutional revisions. On December 16, 1816, Calhoun rose in the House to recommend the formation of a committee to consider the creation of a permanent internal improvements fund. It would be derived from those moneys paid to the federal government by the stockholders of the new Bank of the United States in exchange for its charter. The House formed a committee for that purpose and appointed Calhoun chairman. A week later, on December 23, 1816, the committee recommended a bill to the House. The measure did not appropriate any money. Instead, it stated the purpose for which the bank charter proceeds were to be used: internal improvements.[180]

In a speech of February 4, 1817, Calhoun spoke to the country's growing sense of nationalism. "Distances," he announced, tend "to break the sympathies of human nature. . . . Let us . . . bind the Republic together with a perfect system of roads and canals. Let us conquer space." How to do this within the constraints of the Constitution? Calhoun met that difficulty by claiming for the national government a power that had not been asserted by anyone in more than a decade: authority to make appropriations for any purpose within the scope of the general welfare clause. As he saw it, if the delegates to the Constitutional Convention intended the clause to be limited and defined by the enumerated powers that followed it, they would have said so. Besides, Calhoun continued, there was also precedent: Congress had provided funds for disaster victims in Santo Domingo. Nor was that all. "If we are restricted in the use of our money to the enumerated powers, on what principle . . . can the [Louisiana] purchase be justified?" More recently, funds had been appropriated for the Cumberland Road. Calhoun concluded with a lure for strict constructionists. A broad spending power via the general welfare clause would, he promised, ease the pressure to give generous readings to other clauses. Speaker of the House Henry Clay placed his considerable influence on the side of Calhoun's proposal. While avoiding Calhoun's provocative argument, Clay assured lawmakers that the use of the bank "bonus" for internal improvements would not "interfere with the jurisdiction of the several states." The House of Representatives passed the bonus bill by a razor-thin majority (86-84) on February 9, 1817. Representatives from New

180. *Annals of Congress,* 14th Cong., 2d sess., December 1816, 30:296, 361, 923.

England and the Deep South opposed the measure, while those from New York, Pennsylvania, and the West approved it.[181] The Senate passed the bill (20-15) and it reached President Madison's desk on March 3, 1817, his last full day in office.

Most observers expected the president to sign the measure. Madison dispelled these illusions when he pulled John C. Calhoun aside at a reception and told the mortified congressman that he could not sign the bill.[182] In a message issued with his veto, the president reintroduced the country to the Tenth Amendment. "It does not appear that the power proposed to be exercised by the bill is among the enumerated powers, or that it falls by any just interpretation within the power to make laws necessary and proper for carrying into execution those or other powers vested by the Constitution in the government of the United States." The commerce clause could not justify such a program in light of "the known inconveniences [interstate tariff wars] which doubtless led to the grant of this remedial power to Congress." Nor did the general welfare clause authorize the measure. A broad power of appropriation, he pointed out, would "leave within the legislative powers of Congress all the great and most important measures of the government, money being the ordinary and necessary means of carrying them into execution." Madison concluded by pointing out that the "permanent success" of the Constitution "depends on a definite partition of powers between the general and state governments, and . . . no adequate landmarks would be left by the constructive extension of the powers of Congress as proposed in this bill."[183]

Members of Congress were stunned by the veto. "Not even an earthquake," said Henry Clay, "could have excited more surprise, than when it was first communicated to this House."[184] He promptly organized an effort to override the veto. He cast the first vote himself—an extraordinary step, as the speakership in that era was viewed as a nonpartisan position and its occupant did not, as a custom, vote.[185] Strict constructionists applauded the veto. Thomas Jefferson agreed with the president's argument—the "strained constructions" that had been offered by the bill's proponents would "loose

181. Ibid., 854–57, 867, 933–34.
182. Dangerfield, *Awakening of American Nationalism*, 19.
183. Richardson, *Messages and Papers of the Presidents*, 2:569–70.
184. Quoted in *American Heritage History of Congress* (New York: McGraw Hill, 1975), 157.
185. *Annals of Congress*, 14th Cong., 2d sess., March 1817, 30:1062.

all the bands of the Constitution."[186] In a June 1817 letter to Albert Gallatin, Jefferson expressed hope that the veto might lead to a constitutional amendment that would both grant Congress the power to effect internal improvements and abolish that "mere grammatical quibble" (the general welfare clause) that threatened to endow the national government with a "claim of universal power." Jefferson also rejoiced in the veto's political ramifications. It would strengthen party identity, as the spending power issue was "almost the only landmark which divides the Federalists from the Republicans."[187] Unfortunately for Jefferson, the issue also divided Republicans themselves—as the party continued to win large majorities in each house of Congress, the bill would never have reached the president's desk without Republican votes. (A majority of the House voted to override the veto.)[188]

Henry Clay posed a particularly formidable challenge for party elders. Although he was a Virginia-born planter (he studied law under George Wythe, who also taught Jefferson), his similarities with the old guard went no further. Born in 1777, Clay found early in his career that the Old Dominion had too many lawyers; he went west to Kentucky.[189] Charm and wit as well as skill elevated him to the top of the legal profession in that state. Before he was thirty-five he had won election to Congress, served as Speaker of the House, and converted what had been a ceremonial post into a position of enormous influence. In 1814 Clay served as a member of the delegation that negotiated the Treaty of Ghent, ending the War of 1812. The country was full of successful men; Clay's particular distinction stemmed from the fact that he was America's first modern politician. He realized that the increased interdependence of people in a developing economy required a more active role for government—including the federal government. This is not to say that he embraced the idea of an activist state in the modern sense, but he was among the earliest American politicians to sense the changes that were coming with the market revolution. Possessed of a deep sense of patriotism, and aware that the era would be characterized by economic competition between nations, Clay wanted Americans to accept the challenge and move forward aggressively. Like other nationalists, Clay believed that the United States should make the

186. Quoted in David N. Mayer, *The Constitutional Thought of Thomas Jefferson* (Charlotte: University Press of Virginia, 1994), 219.

187. Jefferson to Albert Gallatin, June 16, 1817, *Writings of Jefferson*, 10:91.

188. *Annals of Congress*, 14th Cong., 2d sess., March 3, 1817, 30:1061–62.

189. Johnson, *History of the American People*, 321.

most of its vast resources; thus his support for canal and road-building programs. From his point of view America had no choice if it wished to compete with the great nations of Europe. Nor was he troubled by the fact that an expansion of public authority promised to enrich the well connected. On the contrary, it was the task of government to help citizens make the most of the resources available to them; that some people exploited new opportunities evinced to him not corruption but success. "Prince Hal" enjoyed wealth himself, yet his deepest hope was for the presidency. This wish consumed him all his life, and he was hobbled by it. Clay was no martyr, though. He was a vibrant, optimistic figure who invited Americans to see the potential of their country and act accordingly.

The Republican Party establishment, still led by Thomas Jefferson and James Madison as well as the new president, stood astride the path of Clay's ambition. All three Virginians remained formidable figures on the American scene. Although his reputation suffered with the embargo, Jefferson's place in the hearts of the American people was cemented in the years leading up to and following his death in 1826. The widespread appeal of Jefferson's ideas— economy in government, fee simple lands available to all, equality before the law, religious tolerance, and the primacy of the states—enabled the Virginian to leave a larger imprint upon American political life than any other person during the first half of the nineteenth century. The third president's appeal was so pervasive that when two new parties arose during the 1830s, both claimed to be the true heirs of his Republican Party.[190] In time the Democratic Party succeeded in claiming him as its founder.[191] It is not too much to say that Jefferson's principles formed the ideological background against which the drama of American history unfolded during the nineteenth century, even as they were repeatedly dismissed as outdated. While Jefferson was the high priest of American republicanism, James Madison was its most prominent cardinal—though he too contributed to the impression of a party led by ancient men with ancient ideas.[192] His knee britches and wig gave the

190. Merrill D. Peterson, *The Jefferson Image in the American Mind* (New York: Oxford University Press, 1960), 70–76.

191. Said L. D. Evans of Texas on the House floor in 1856, "Jefferson is fairly entitled to the praise of being the genuine parent and chief apostle of the Democratic Party—that party which was based on the idea of equal sovereignty distributed among all the citizens of the Union without distinction." *Congressional Globe*, 34th Cong., 1st sess., May 13, 1856, Appendix, 25:599.

192. Senator Elijah Hunt Mills of Massachusetts: "He has more the appearance of what I have imagined a Roman cardinal to be." Quoted in Henry Adams, *History of the United States during the Administrations of Thomas Jefferson*, 128.

diminutive planter a look that was already two decades out of fashion in 1817, and his views on the Constitution were equally outdated, at least in the eyes of his critics. President-elect James Monroe, who served as a colonel in the Continental army before leading the fight against ratification in Virginia, also had an air of antiquity about him.

If the past accomplishments of these three men elicited the admiration of Americans, Henry Clay opened their eyes to the broad vistas before them, and he did it with a degree of enthusiasm that was palpable and contagious. While other politicians resigned themselves to the necessity of distributing whiskey to their neighbors, Clay relished the prospect of raising a toast with his fellow citizens. Where others avoided stump speaking, Clay embraced it.[193] Bold and effusive, whether on the floor of the House of Representatives or in the parlor of a neighbor, Clay charmed men and women alike with his warmth, wit, and vision. His combination of western background and epic talent seemed itself to confirm the country's vast potential. Americans could point to him, as one admirer did, and assert that while the intellectual powers of men such as Jefferson and Madison arose out of privilege, Clay's greatness "is all his own."[194]

Yet Clay's powers were greatest not with the voters themselves—laborers and immigrants came to distrust both him and his party—but with other politicians. This influence stemmed largely from his aggressive approach to public power, to which Jefferson's notion of economy in government paled in comparison. It also arose out of his sense of humor—he was perhaps the sharpest wit of his time. When a congressman rose to his feet during the Missouri Compromise debates for what everyone feared would be yet another longwinded speech and announced that he spoke for posterity, Clay expressed concern that the gentleman would still be speaking when his audience arrived.[195] During a short-lived bout of strict construction early in his career, Clay spoke of the "vagrant power to erect a bank" that had "wandered throughout the whole Constitution in quest of some congenial spot on which to fasten."[196] When James Buchanan of Pennsylvania told the Senate that he had marched on Baltimore during the War of 1812 only to arrive af-

193. For descriptions of some of Clay's more amusing exploits, see Dangerfield, *Era of Good Feelings*, 10–13, and Johnson, *History of the American People*, 320–24.

194. Gaillard Hunt, ed., *The First Forty Years of Washington Society Portrayed in the Family Letters of Mrs. Samuel Harrison Smith* (New York: Scribner's Sons, 1906), 285.

195. Dangerfield, *Era of Good Feelings*, 222.

196. *Annals of Congress*, 11th Cong., 3d sess., February 15, 1811, 22:211.

ter the British left, Clay asked "whether the British retreated in consequence of his valiantly marching to the relief of Baltimore, or whether he marched to the relief of Baltimore in consequence of the British having already retreated?"[197] Clay's humanity also manifested itself in other ways. John Quincy Adams recalled seeing men trickle out of the dwelling of his more genial colleague following all-night card games on more than one occasion.[198] In an 1826 duel, Clay put a bullet through John Randolph's coat and then shook hands with his longtime opponent.[199] The doctrinaire Randolph, who long viewed the Kentuckian as a dangerous advocate of centralizing policies, once described him as "brilliant, yet so corrupt, that like a rotten mackerel by moonlight, he shined and stunk."[200] Perhaps more than any other politician of the period, Henry Clay expressed the good humor, imperfections, and optimism that symbolized what later became known as the Era of Good Feelings, and his countrymen seemed to know it. In taking on this man, Jeffersonian Republicans opposed more than a faction of the House, or even the greatest party leader in American history. Owing in no small part to Clay's ability to define the terms of the debate, they often seemed to oppose the nineteenth century itself.

Fortunately for them, strict constructionists still had the executive branch. In his March 1817 inaugural address, James Monroe announced that while he supported federally funded internal improvements, he acknowledged the necessity of "proceeding always with a constitutional sanction." Monroe reiterated his orthodoxy in his first annual message, of December 2, 1817, when he expressed his belief that the federal government lacked authority to establish a system of internal improvements.[201] When Congress convened, John C. Calhoun and his allies insisted on pushing ahead without an amendment. On December 15, 1817, Representative Starling Tucker of South Carolina read aloud the report of a committee that had been appointed to consider President Monroe's annual message. It disagreed with the new president's approach. The committee's report proclaimed that "it would be difficult to reconcile either the generality of the expression or the course of administration

197. Quoted in Robert V. Remini, *Henry Clay: Statesman for the Union* (New York: W. W. Norton, 1991), 477.

198. Dangerfield, *Era of Good Feelings*, 11.

199. See Thomas Hart Benton, *Thirty Years' View: A History of the American Government for Thirty Years, from 1820 to 1850*, 2 vols. (New York: Appleton & Co., 1864), 1:70–77.

200. Quoted in Henry Adams, *John Randolph* (Boston: Houghton Mifflin, 1896), 289.

201. Richardson, *Messages and Papers of the Presidents*, 2:577, 587.

under it, with the idea that Congress has not a discretionary power over its expenditures, limited by their application 'to the common defence and general welfare.'" In support of its assertion of a broad spending power, the committee cited appropriations for the Cumberland Road, congressional largesse (paintings, a library, and a chaplain), aid for disaster victims, the Lewis and Clark expedition, Indian trading houses, and the original sin of congressional expenditures: bounties for the New England fisheries.[202]

A hundred miles away in Virginia, the fathers of strict construction might have winced if they had read the transcripts of the congressional debates that spring. James Madison received inquiries from the president as to the various precedents cited by Tucker. In responding, he acknowledged that at the time of the first Cumberland Road Act, "the question of constitutionality was but slightly if at all examined." Thereafter, "additional appropriations took place, of course under the same administration . . . with less critical investigation perhaps than was due to the case." Madison insisted that the Cumberland Road appropriations derived authority from the territorial, postal, and military powers of Congress. ("The post cannot travel, nor troops march without a road. If the necessary roads cannot be found, they must of course be provided.") He warned Monroe not to be swayed by references to past acts of Congress, as they had not received due consideration at the time of their passage.[203]

If Madison was frustrated by the citing of past legislation, he surely found it difficult to stomach what became known as the internal improvements debate of 1818. During the winter and spring of that year, the House of Representatives examined the report of the Tucker committee, the federal government's authority to effect internal improvements, and the spending power of Congress. Precedent played a prominent role in the proceedings. A handful of legislators dominated the debate, for reasons having very little to do with the issues at hand. Turnover in Congress reached astonishing levels during the nineteenth century, and the 1816–17 elections marked a high tide in public impatience. Members of the fourteenth Congress raised their own pay substantially and voters reacted with anger—only a third of the representatives won re-election. A collection of novices had not been in Washington for three months before they found themselves in the midst of one of the great congressional debates of American history.

202. *Annals of Congress*, 15th Cong., 1st sess., December 15, 1817, 31:458–59.
203. *Writings of Madison*, 8:404–7.

On March 6 Starling Tucker pointed out that various projects around the country, such as the Cumberland Road and the Erie Canal, might not be completed if Congress failed to provide funds—a particularly unfortunate development in light of the poor condition of the nation's roads. The worst thing the House could do, he warned, would be to submit an amendment to the states. If an amendment was "recommended, and should not be obtained, we should have surrendered a power, which we are bound to maintain if we think we possess it." Ballard Smith of Virginia allowed that Congress could build canals as well as roads, but he insisted they must be for military purposes, the "expeditious and certain transportation of the mails," or to give "life and activity to . . . internal commerce." Alexander Smythe of Virginia expressed concern over the idea that Congress could do anything that enhanced commerce. If that was the case, Congress could take upon itself "the sole administration of justice, so far it related to contracts, under the pretence of giving security to internal commerce." Nor did the power to designate post roads authorize a road-building program such as the one proponents of the bill had in mind. ("Are they really post roads, and post roads only, that you propose to make?") Smythe did not accept the Tucker committee's assertion that novel appropriations in the past meant that Congress could embrace a broad spending power. "If they were violations of the Constitution, they will not sanction a violation of the Constitution by us; and, if they are consistent with the Constitution, they are too dissimilar to that which it is now proposed to pass, to furnish a precedent."[204]

Perhaps fearful of the influence precedent would have with new members, Smythe turned to the appropriations cited by the Tucker committee. The purchase of a library and furniture by Congress qualified as necessary to its ability to legislate. Lighthouses and bounties for the New England fisheries received authorization from the commerce clause. The federal government's power to regulate trade with the Indians authorized the construction of trading houses in the territories. Smythe allowed that some excesses had occurred; aid for disaster victims was, he admitted, unconstitutional. The Cumberland Road appropriations were also beyond the pale. Yet, as no discussion of the legal issues had occurred when they were passed, no precedent could be derived from those acts. Smythe reminded the House that while the powers of Congress had been combed over repeatedly during ratifica-

204. *Annals of Congress,* 15th Cong., 1st sess., March 1818, 31:1118, 1120, 1132, 1140.

tion, so far as he knew, no one detected a broad spending power. "In construing the Constitution, it is material to inquire, how did the framers understand it? How did those who adopted the Constitution understand it?
How did the people understand it? It may be confidently asserted, that they
all understood the power to make and to take care of the roads would be left
to the states."[205]

Representative Philip Barbour of Virginia dismissed ambitious claims
for the general welfare clause. In his view it merely defined the ends "to be
attained—the enumerated powers which followed, were the means of at-
taining them; and . . . money was the instrument, as far as it was necessary,
by which those powers were to be executed." Barbour asked the same question that Madison posed during ratification: "for what purpose could the
enumeration of particular powers be inserted, if these, and all others, were
meant to be included in the preceding general powers?" He dismissed claims
that the Louisiana Purchase proved the existence of a broad spending authority; in his view it constituted an exercise of the treaty power. Barbour
closed by pointing out that past acts cannot carry the same precedent in a
government "based upon a written charter which delineates our powers and
defines their boundaries" as they did in Britain, where Parliament's authority
was not limited by any document.[206]

The Speaker of the House took the floor. At first Mr. Clay seemed to
agree with everyone. He applauded strict constructionists for stating their positions with such skill; he even complimented James Madison for his authorship of the Virginia resolutions. The Speaker then turned to the issue of constitutional interpretation. Embracing a Hamiltonian approach, he declared
that if a particular act proves to be "in all its effects and consequences, benefi-
cent; if it were free from the danger of abuse; if it promoted and advanced all
the great objects which led to the confederacy; if it materially tended to effect that greatest of all those objects—the cementing of the Union, the construction was recommended by the most favorable considerations." Clay went
on to declare that while he subscribed to the idea that "power in the general
government was deducible only from express grant, or as fairly incident to
express grant," he would nonetheless give the Constitution, "in all that relates
essentially to the preservation of the Union, a liberal construction."[207]

Clay then moved on to the main issue—"how the revenue, when raised,

205. Ibid., 1148–249.　　　　　　206. Ibid., 1161–63.
207. Ibid., 1166.

is to be expended [and] the places where it is to be disbursed, and on what objects"—and managed to both address and avoid the question. Revenues were on the rise, he pointed out, and they would soon reach $60 million annually. Were funds to be expended only "on the margin of the ocean for naval depots?" (The implication was that naval fortifications would be the only improvements that the national government would be able to fund under the president's approach.) Clay hinted at the purposes for which he thought internal improvements could be effected when he suggested that the facilitation of commerce, the transportation of military "force and means," and the "circulation of intelligence" all promoted the Union—the "first and dearest object of the Constitution."[208]

On March 11, Edward Colston, a Virginia Federalist, attacked the notion that a broad spending authority rendered the enumerated powers pointless by noting that the opposite was also true. If the enumerated powers alone granted authority, the general welfare clause was meaningless. Such an interpretation violated the principle of construction that held that all parts of a document ought to be given effect. Colston then returned, as broad constructionists invariably did, to precedent. The national government had performed acts conducive to the common defense or general welfare—such as the establishment of a military academy—that could not be fairly linked to any of the enumerated powers. On March 12, Charles F. Mercer, also a Virginia Federalist, claimed that the Articles of Confederation both enumerated the powers of Congress and granted a broad spending power via Article VIII. Mercer quoted the 1782 report of a committee of the Confederation Congress regarding Article VIII: "this provision of the Confederation comprehends an indefinite power of prescribing money to be raised, and of appropriating it when raised."[209] The Framers' decision to use similar language in the Constitution must have resulted from a decision to grant a broad spending power. Besides, he continued, the power to spend had to be conferred somewhere, and the general welfare clause, in light of its use in the Articles of Confederation, was the most appropriate place. Mercer then returned to the claim that a broad spending authority would render the enumerated powers meaningless. Exercise of the enumerated powers, he pointed out, did not always require appropriations.[210]

208. Ibid., 1176–79.
209. Ibid., 1280, 1311. See *Papers of Hamilton*, 3:219.
210. *Annals of Congress*, 15th Cong., 1st sess., March 1818, 31:1311.

Mercer's argument did not withstand examination. Despite the 1782 report, the Confederation Congress never acted under the impression that it possessed a broad spending power. In addition, the Framers did not use the language of the Articles of Confederation's "appropriating clause" in the Constitution. They did not declare that "all charges of war, and all other expenses incurred for the common defence and general welfare, and allowed by Congress, shall be defrayed out of a common treasury." Instead, the Constitution states that Congress shall "pay the debts, and provide for the common defense and general welfare." This language—to "provide for the general welfare"—was much more obscure than that used in the Articles of Confederation. The clause did not appear to grant a broad spending power. Rather, it bore great similarity to the preamble, which used a similar phrase: "promote the general welfare."

Claims of a power to effect internal improvements left James Pindall of Virginia incredulous. "I trust it will not be contended, by any of the honorable gentlemen opposed to me, that, if the framers of the Constitution, upon a proposition to insert any specific additional power, rejected that proposition, still that power might be inferred."[211] Yet, he continued, "by construction, we are to derive a power [to effect internal improvements], not granted, but expressly withheld, . . . and which, from extraneous evidence of facts which transpired in the body that framed our Constitution, it is most apparent, was never intended to be given." The gall of his peers amazed Pindall. "Sir, it is singular, that a lapse of thirty years should have made it to appear, that the men, in whose wisdom the nation put great confidence, were really ignorant of what they had done, and that powers then clearly and expressly withheld are not, as clearly conferred by the Constitution, by implication."[212]

As the debate came to a close, Representative William Lowndes of South Carolina (a Calhoun ally) secured passage of a resolution providing that "Congress has power, under the Constitution, to appropriate money for the construction of post-roads, military and other roads, and of canals, and for the improvement of water courses."[213] Shortly thereafter, President Monroe came under pressure to modify his opposition to internal improve-

---

211. Ibid., March 1818, 32:1353. Pindall was probably referring to the refusal of the Constitutional Convention to adopt a clause authorizing Congress to cut canals. See Farrand, *Records of the Federal Convention*, 2:616.

212. *Annals of Congress*, 15th Cong., 1st sess., 1353.

213. Ibid., 1385.

ments. The cabinet was composed of men who were not disposed to help him resist the onslaught. Although the views of John Quincy Adams on the subject of federal power had yet to become famous for the lack of proportion that made even Calhoun's appear moderate, there is no reason to think that Monroe's secretary of state was ever a strict constructionist. (His split with the Federalists in 1806 stemmed solely from his support for the embargo.) The latitudinarian ideas of Secretary of War John C. Calhoun were well known. Even the secretary of the treasury, William Crawford, a strict constructionist Georgian who fancied himself a worthy successor to the Virginia presidents, betrayed no interest in firming up Monroe's resolve. Crawford had resigned himself to the inevitability of an internal improvements program without benefit of a constitutional amendment. The matter had, in his view, been "easily settled by precedent." As Crawford saw it, a "system will be introduced gradually, if not directly at once."[214]

Monroe broke down under the onslaught and prepared a message during the summer of 1819 in which he recognized a broad spending power via the general welfare clause. The president's conversion did not become public until three years later, when Congress passed a bill establishing tollgates on the Cumberland Road for the purpose of funding repairs. To everyone's surprise, the president vetoed the bill in May 1822, suggesting that if Congress wished to exercise powers such as those contemplated by the bill, it should submit a constitutional amendment authorizing federal supervision of internal improvements to the states. Monroe then issued a second message—the one drafted in 1819. It was in this statement that he acknowledged his conversion. He began by explaining why each of the enumerated powers usually cited in support of federal funds for roads did not authorize the bill. The power to establish postal roads bestowed nothing more than the authority to designate them. The war powers, which were listed individually, did not include road construction. Nor did the commerce clause bestow the necessary authority: "A power ... to impose such duties and imposts in regard to foreign nations and to prevent any on the trade between the states was the only power granted." Monroe then turned to the general welfare clause and stated flatly that it "gives a right to appropriate the public money." And so it must, he insisted, for the power of appropriation is mentioned nowhere else in the Constitution. The former Antifederalist refused to limit this authority to appropriations made for the exercise of the enumerated powers,

214. Quoted in Dangerfield, *Era of Good Feelings*, 444n25.

as the Constitutional Convention could have said so if it intended to delineate the spending power in that way. A broad approach to the clause would, Monroe promised, mean less pressure to expand the scope of other powers. As for the idea that the spending power was limitless, the president insisted that Congress could appropriate funds only for "great national purposes." He closed by suggesting that Congress ought to submit an amendment to the states if it wished to exercise jurisdiction over internal improvements, as opposed to merely appropriating money for them.[215]

To the surprise of many, Henry Clay dismissed Monroe's argument. In January 1824 he pronounced himself in agreement with Virginia congressman Philip Barbour's claim that the general welfare clause provided no authority of any kind, including that of appropriation.[216] "The truth is that there is no specific grant, in the Constitution, of the power of appropriation; nor was any such requisite. It is a resulting power." The Constitution, Clay explained, "vests in Congress the power of taxation, but with few limitations, to raise a public revenue. It then enumerates the powers of Congress. And it follows, of necessity, that Congress has the right to apply money so raised to the execution of the powers so granted." The president's interpretation of the general welfare clause would, he warned, "overturn, or render useless and nugatory, the careful enumeration of our powers; and . . . convert a cautiously limited government into one without limitation." If the president's approach prevailed, he continued, "what human restraint is there on it? . . . If we have a right, indefinitely, to apply the money of the government to internal improvements, or to any other object, what is to prevent the application of it to the purchase of the sovereignty itself, of a state, if a state were mean enough to sell its sovereignty?" Advocates of federally funded internal improvements need not have worried; Clay simply did not think a broad spending power was necessary to justify federal appropriations for roads and canals. As he saw it, the postal and commerce clauses as well as the war powers were more than adequate to the task. Roads and canals would, he promised, be as helpful to domestic commerce as "buoys, beacons, lighthouses [and] the surveys of coasts" were to foreign commerce. As for the idea that Congress had been vested with power over commerce to keep the states from imposing duties, Clay pointed out that another clause of the Constitution prohibited the

---

215. Richardson, *Messages and Papers of the Presidents*, 2:711–12, 726–31, 735–36, 748.

216. The speech of Mr. Barbour may be found in *Annals of Congress*, 18th Cong., 1st sess., January 13, 1824, 41:1005–13.

states from taxing imports—the commerce clause therefore served a different purpose.[217]

The president pursued his own course. In his 1822 annual message, Monroe suggested that additional funds be appropriated for the repair of the Cumberland Road. He repeated the point in his annual message of 1823.[218] Legislators, while not particularly supportive of the president's approach to the spending issue, proved unwilling to let the opportunity for internal improvements pass. At first there was but a trickle; in February 1823 Congress provided money for repairs to the Cumberland Road and authorized the appointment of a superintendent to oversee the work. The torrent began a year later with the General Survey Act, which passed easily through each house. Envisioned as a blueprint for a broad internal improvements program, the act authorized the president "to cause the necessary surveys, plans and estimates, to be made of the routes of such roads and canals as he may deem of national importance, in a commercial or military point of view, or necessary for the transportation of the public mail."[219] Within four years the federal government had commenced surveys of more than ninety projects under the authority granted by the act.[220] The projects included undertakings as varied as railroads in New England and a canal across northern Florida.[221] A May 1824 appropriation for improvements upon the Mississippi and Ohio rivers may well have qualified as the most critical measure.[222] Much of the money went to the army, which carried out each project itself. Aid also went to private corporations. On the last day of Monroe's presidency (March 3, 1825), Congress appropriated $300,000 for the purchase of stock in a company that had been chartered to build what became the Chesapeake and Ohio Canal.[223] A year later, Congress funded harbor dredging for the first time.[224]

Who could have guessed that the fever was about to break? Not John Quincy Adams, who succeeded James Monroe as president in 1825. Adams was probably the most thoroughly educated and experienced public servant in early nineteenth-century America. The epitome of virtue in his personal

217. Ibid., 1027–28, 1033–36.
218. Richardson, *Messages and Papers of the Presidents*, 2:759–860, 785.
219. 4 *Stats at Large* 22 (April 30, 1824), at 22–23.
220. Peterson, *Great Triumvirate*, 82; Sellers, *Market Revolution*, 152.
221. Hargreaves, *Presidency of John Quincy Adams*, 174.
222. 4 *Stats at Large* 32 (May 24, 1824).
223. Ibid., 124 (March 3, 1825).
224. Ibid., 150 (March 25, 1826).

life, Adams could also be cantankerous and severe. In time he earned a reputation for aloofness in his dealings with people that made even Andrew Jackson seem warm in comparison. He was certainly capable of wrath. His grandson Henry Adams recalled throwing a tantrum at age seven in order to avoid going to school, only to have his grandfather emerge from his study, grasp the boy by the hand, and escort him along the one-mile route to the schoolhouse—without uttering so much as a word during the trip.[225] Despite his chilly demeanor, Adams evinced a warm-blooded attitude toward the Constitution.[226] Like Hamilton, Marshall, Webster, and Clay, Adams was a conservative nationalist. In his view the Constitution did more than list a precise list of authorities; it also charged the government with the duty to protect property and foster commerce.

Because of the unusual circumstances surrounding the 1824 presidential contest, Mr. Adams's opponents held his administration under siege from the start. Their fervor stemmed in part from an alleged deal—the notorious "corrupt bargain"—that probably did not take place. Clay was said to have secured the presidential election for Adams in exchange for appointment as secretary of state, at that time the position of the heir apparent to the presidency. It was in this environment of suspicion that the new president, in his first annual message (December 6, 1825), made public his views on the powers of Congress. They were part Alexander Hamilton and part Old Testament. If the enumerated powers "may be effectually brought into action by laws promoting the improvement of agriculture, commerce & manufactures, the cultivation & encouragement of the mechanical and the elegant arts, the advancement of literature, & the progress of the sciences, ornamental and profound, to refrain from exercising them would be to hide in the earth the talent committed to our charge—would be treachery to the most sacred of trusts."[227] Critics pounced. Was the president suggesting that refusal to promote ends as far removed from the enumerated powers as literature and science constituted an offense against the Creator? Did strict adherence to the enumerated powers really constitute a "treachery to the most sacred of trusts?" As one his-

225. Henry Adams, *The Education of Henry Adams* (Boston: Massachusetts Historical Society, 1918; reprint, New York: Houghton Mifflin, 2000), 12–13.

226. Adams thought the plan of government presented by Alexander Hamilton at the Constitutional Convention of 1787—the chief feature of which was the effective abolition of the states—"theoretically better" than the plan adopted. *The Diary of John Quincy Adams, 1767–1848: American Political, Social and Intellectual Life from Washington to Polk*, ed. Allan Nevins (New York: F. Ungar, 1951), 477.

227. Richardson, *Messages and Papers of the Presidents*, 2:881–82.

torian wrote, "many Americans, including his predecessor in office, still wondered whether or not any other kind of reading [of the Constitution] might not be treachery."[228] Critics attacked the message for its implication that the Constitution authorized a federal role in areas not normally thought of as within Congress's sphere merely because such acts incidentally advanced one of the enumerated powers. In fact Adams had done no more than take the constitutional approach of Hamilton, Marshall, and Webster to its logical, albeit absurd, conclusion. In doing so, he inadvertently demonstrated a point that strict constructionists had long emphasized: if a government of limited powers is allowed unfettered discretion to choose the means by which it executes those powers, it will not remain limited for long.

The public did not care for the message, either. Recalling the abuses that occurred under the first Adams, many feared the policies of the son as potentially even more threatening.[229] Would not higher taxes follow in the wake of so ambitious a program? Some critics viewed appropriations for internal improvements as unnecessary—the states had taken up the slack. New York completed the Erie Canal in 1825, thus providing passage from the coast to the interior. Pennsylvania had by 1820 invested more than $1 million in turnpikes, and Ohio had built a canal from Lake Erie to the Ohio River.[230] The Erie Canal proved to be the most significant improvement. Its size (more than four hundred miles long) and cost ($7.5 million) made it the largest public works project ever undertaken in the Western Hemisphere. It funneled the produce and surplus income of the Great Lakes region into New York City, turning it into the leading port of North America. That the Erie Canal was completed without a dollar from Washington demonstrated that progress itself was not dependent upon federal appropriations.

Strict constructionists rushed to exploit the public's negative reaction to the president's message. Thomas Jefferson, now in his mideighties, drafted a declaration protesting federally funded internal improvements "usurpations" of state authority.[231] The Virginia legislature passed resolutions echoing Jefferson's sentiments; it even repeated the claim it had first made in 1798—that states were duty bound to "interpose" when necessary "for arresting the progress of evil."[232] James Madison was less extreme. He did suggest, in a

228. Dangerfield, *Awakening of American Nationalism,* 232.
229. Dangerfield, *Era of Good Feelings,* 349.
230. White, *Jeffersonians,* 489, 493.
231. Quoted in Mayer, *Constitutional Thought of Thomas Jefferson,* 220.
232. Ames, *State Documents on Federal Relations,* 141.

September 1826 letter to New York senator Martin Van Buren, that perhaps the time had come to simply remove the general welfare clause from the Constitution.[233]

For a time Washington remained unaffected by the hostile reaction. In a report of May 1826 the House Committee on Roads and Canals claimed that Congress had authority to construct a general system of internal improvements. The committee cited the commerce clause, the authority to establish postal roads, and the power to provide for the common defense in support of this assertion.[234] Lawmakers also considered a bill to distribute federal revenue to the states, with the proceeds to be used for internal improvements and education. Proponents defended the bill on the grounds that it would bring the decade-old debate over internal improvements to an end.[235] Meanwhile Congress went on spending. In May 1826 it appropriated $100,000 to buy stock in a Kentucky canal company. It also spent $160,000 on lighthouses and the removal of obstructions in waterways along the East Coast, with almost a third of the total going to the removal of impediments in Georgia's Savannah River. An act of May 20, 1826, provided $60,000 for piers.[236]

In the midterm elections of 1826–27, the forces in favor of federally funded internal improvements lost control of the House of Representatives. In their place emerged a strict constructionist majority that provided Americans with their first taste of divided government since the 1790s. The new majority did not share the president's enthusiasm for internal improvements. Andrew Jackson's supporters in particular wanted to deny Adams whatever credit it might have resulted from these projects. The twentieth Congress therefore took a giant step backward, at least from the administration's point of view. It did not, however, discard the habits of its predecessors, thus cementing the precedent it had pledged to destroy.[237] Ten years after it began, the greatest unilateral assumption of power yet undertaken by Congress still stood.

233. *Writings of Madison*, 9:252–55.

234. *Report of the Committee on Roads and Canals regarding the Chesapeake and Ohio Canal*, 19th Cong., 1st sess., May 1826, H. Rep. 228, 12–13.

235. *Register of Debates*, 19th Cong., 2d sess., February 1, 1827, 3:209–22.

236. 4 *Stats at Large* 162 (May 13, 1826); ibid., 170 (May 18, 1826); ibid., 175 (May 20, 1826).

237. An act of May 19, 1828 (ibid., 275), provided money for the Cumberland Road, removal of obstructions from Ashtabula Creek in Ohio and the Kennebec River in Maine, and piers at Oswego and Buffalo, New York. An act of May 23, 1828 (ibid., 282), provided money for lighthouses in Maryland and buoys for the Hudson River.

CHAPTER 4

# *The Market Republic,*
## *1829–1850*

Following the War of 1812, fundamental economic shifts began to occur. In time they greatly altered the role of government, particularly at the state level. Most of the changes arose out of the Industrial Revolution. Americans began to leave their farms and become wage earners. They became dependent upon state governments and political parties for protection from exploitation at the hands of employers, banks, and other powerful interests. As the need for legislative remedies increased the power of political parties, these institutions became increasingly susceptible to manipulation by the federal executive branch. An abundance of offices and contracts enabled presidents and their cohorts to buy the support of newspaper editors, convention delegates, and politicians in every town in America. The end result was the rise of an apparently decentralized party system that in fact enabled federal officials to manipulate political activity at even the local level.

The change that elevated American political parties—urbanization—presented a difficult challenge for a country in which economic security was viewed as the foundation upon which republics are built. By creating an urban populace that was largely impoverished, the Industrial Revolution seemed to threaten the country's future. This fear stemmed from the fact that Americans of the time were careful students of history and political science. They immersed themselves in what can be broadly described as the classical theory of republican government. Among the chief features of this theory was the idea that republics required "public virtue."[1] John Adams considered

---

1. Wood, *Creation of the American Republic,* 68.

virtue "the only foundation of republics."[2] Politicians often reminded their audiences that republics fell once their citizens became corrupted and public virtue destroyed.[3] On July 4, 1829, one speaker warned that "a profligate people cannot continue free."[4] After vote frauds marred the 1844 presidential election, an observer could not resist pointing out the obvious meaning of rampant electoral corruption: "the decay of virtue and honor, the only safeguard of a republic."[5]

What was public virtue? Edward Gibbon believed that it arose out of "a strong sense of our own interest in the preservation and prosperity of the free government of which we are members."[6] In a republican context, virtuous citizens were supposed to behave like disinterested jurors, voting in the best interests of their country instead of their own pecuniary interests. Americans derived their belief in the necessity of public virtue from history. They took special interest in the fortunes of the Roman Republic, and the last days of it in particular attracted their attention.[7] There was universal agreement about the root cause of Rome's fall. As a Philadelphia newspaper proclaimed in 1786, "Every page of history of the great revolution of Rome shows some instances of the degeneracy of Roman virtue and of the impossibility of a nation's continuing free after its virtue is gone."[8] Americans took note of how the Roman Republic supposedly lost its virtue: urbanization. During the second century B.C., aristocratic families enriched by Rome's overseas conquests purchased much of the land surrounding the capital city, forcing thousands of citizens to abandon their homesteads in the process. The dispossessed poured into the city of Rome. Poverty and hunger led them to sell the one asset they had left—their votes. While these farmers had once cast their ballots with only the interests of the Republic in mind, their votes were now determined by the wishes of those who paid for them. The situation was fatally exploited by Julius Caesar, who used grain and promises of land to bribe impoverished urban voters. Once in power, he tossed the republican government aside.

2. Quoted in Elkins and McKitrick, *Age of Federalism*, 535.

3. Wood, *Creation of the American Republic*, 423.

4. James T. Austin, *An Oration Delivered on the Fourth of July, 1829, at the Celebration of American Independence, in the City of Boston* (Boston: James Eastburn, 1829), 16.

5. Henry Clay, *The Works of Henry Clay*, ed. Calvin Colton, 7 vols. (New York: G. P. Putnam & Sons, 1904), 5:523.

6. Edward Gibbon, *History of the Decline and Fall of the Roman Empire*, 2 vols. (London, 1776; reprint, New York: Knopf, 1993), 1:13.

7. Bailyn, *Ideological Origins of the American Revolution*, 25–26.

8. *Philadelphia Packet*, August 8, 1786, quoted in Wood, *Creation of the American Republic*, 423.

This interpretation of Roman history is only partially correct—voters enjoyed the assistance of patrons long before the last years of the Republic.[9] Despite its flaws, the idea that the Roman Republic fell when its citizens left their farms had a great deal of appeal for the amateur political scientists of eighteenth- and nineteenth-century America. So did the notion that only landowners had the virtue and independence necessary to be responsible voters.[10] Because they could always find sustenance in the land, they were viewed as less susceptible to poverty and the temptation to sell their votes. James Madison believed that that "the class of citizens who provide at once their own food and their own raiment, may be viewed as the most truly independent and happy." Hence, they formed "the best basis of public liberty and its strongest bulwark of public safety."[11] In his *Notes on the State of Virginia* (1785), Thomas Jefferson declared that "corruption of morals in the mass of cultivators is a phenomenon of which no age nor nation has furnished an example."[12] He explained that corruption more easily arises in those "who not looking to heaven, to their own soil and industry, as does the husbandman, for their sustenance, [but] depend for it on the casualties and caprices of customers."[13]

John Adams also thought that landowners alone could form a stable electorate. Because the "balance of power in society, accompanies the balance of power in land," he thought that the preservation of "equal liberty and virtue" requires that society "make the acquisition of land easy to every member." Those who are "wholly destitute of property," he explained, were "too dependent on others to have a will of their own."[14] The *Hartford Courant* held that the widespread availability of freeholds ensured that when voters "exercise the important right of choosing men to act for them in a public capacity, they will act independently."[15] Land was readily available in

9. See Michael Crawford, *The Roman Republic* (Cambridge: Harvard University Press, 1993), 27–28.

10. As one historian summarized it, this view held that "the personal independence that resulted from the ownership of land permitted a citizen to participate responsibly in the political process, for it allowed him to pursue spontaneously the common or public good, rather than the narrow interest of the men—or the government—on whom he depended for his support." Drew McCoy, *The Elusive Republic: Political Economy in Jeffersonian America* (New York: W. W. Norton, 1980), 68.

11. Quoted in Carl J. Richard, *The Founders and the Classics: Greece, Rome and the American Enlightenment* (Cambridge: Harvard University Press, 1994), 165.

12. Thomas Jefferson, *Notes on the State of Virginia*, ed. William Peden (New York: W. W. Norton, and Chapel Hill: University of North Carolina University Press, 1954), 165.

13. Ibid., 165.

14. Adams to James Sullivan, May 26, 1776, in *Works of John Adams*, 9:376–77.

15. Quoted in Bailyn, *Debate on the Constitution* (January 7, 1788), 1:712.

the United States, and Albert Gallatin thought this was the most important element in the country's success.[16] In time the independent American farmer who benefited from this abundance became, like the yeoman of Elizabethan England, the stuff of patriotic myth. "The honest farmer," declared one play, "knows no dependence, except on Heaven."[17] Politicians referred to the electorate as the virtuous "yeomanry."[18] A sort of frontier asceticism could be found among Americans such as the New Jersey farmer who reported in 1797 that except for ten dollars spent on salt and iron, he "bought nothing to eat, drink, or wear, as my farm provided all."[19]

As political thinkers of early America glorified the self-reliant farmer, they vilified cities as decadent, crime ridden, and composed largely of itinerant laborers who were susceptible to political manipulation. Jefferson feared that the growth of cities would bring to America the same violent mobs he had seen in Paris.[20] Unfortunately for Jefferson and others of his ilk, cities had already become a fact of life in America, along with poverty. As early as the 1780s New England observers noted large numbers of urban poor.[21] American farmers themselves were hardly the picture of Roman virtue. The stay laws enacted to postpone the payment of debts during the 1780s demonstrated that farmers were capable of abusing public power for private gain. Yet the idea that enfranchisement of the urban poor would debase an otherwise virtuous electorate remained a persistent idea in America—at least behind closed doors—until well into the nineteenth century. It manifested itself most visibly in the form of laws that limited the suffrage to those who owned land.

Popular demand led the state legislatures to abolish property-based limitations on the suffrage during the period between 1820 and 1860. Great Britain, the only other large nation that allowed for some degree of republican government, did not move nearly as fast. In the Reform Act of 1832, Parliament extended the suffrage. Before the law's enactment, about one in ten men could vote; afterward, two of every ten could do so. Britain's laboring poor did not obtain the vote until the end of the century. The political evo-

16. Commager, Leuchtenberg, and Morison, *Growth of the American Republic*, 311.

17. Quoted in Sellers, *Market Revolution*, 9.

18. Quoted in Robert V. Remini, *Andrew Jackson and the Course of American Democracy, 1833–1845* (Baltimore: Johns Hopkins University Press, 1984), 339.

19. Quoted in Russel B. Nye, *Cultural Life in the New Nation, 1800–1830* (New York: Harper & Row, 1960), 129.

20. Jefferson, *Notes on the State of Virginia*, 164–65.

21. McCoy, *Elusive Republic*, 114.

lution of the United States during the antebellum period thus qualifies as something of an experiment, unique in its time. Could broad-based republican government survive in a nation increasingly made up of wage earners? The answer, of course, was yes. Yet the task of providing laborers with some semblance of legal protection—and in turn independence—proved to be among the most challenging tasks that faced government at any level during the nineteenth century. Success came neither quickly nor easily, and in fact did not really occur until long after antebellum America had passed into history. In the meantime, the urban population of the United States was almost completely defenseless even as it underwent explosive growth.

The percentage of Americans who lived in urban areas rose from less than 9 percent of the population in 1830 to more than 15 percent by 1850. The trend toward urbanization mirrored an equally revolutionary change in the labor force—by midcentury, more than a third of American workers toiled in nonagricultural pursuits.[22] The new cities quickly became centers of mass unemployment and poverty. This development stemmed largely from a severe labor glut that occurred during the 1830s and '40s, which itself grew out of several factors. Chief among them was immigration.[23] Even for those who could find work, wages were often too low to sustain a decent standard of living. The severe if short-lived depressions of the period inflicted widespread deprivation upon the residents of new cities; the downturn that followed the Panic of 1819 saw exports reduced by half.[24] Centers of trade were crippled, and some cities suffered a loss of population. Thirty percent of Pittsburgh's residents left the city.[25]

Widespread poverty left the inhabitants of the new cities extraordinarily susceptible to manipulation. Enterprising politicians bought the votes of impoverished males by the dozen in exchange for cash, liquor, or, in the case of immigrants, assistance in obtaining citizenship. The problem first manifested itself during the 1820s.[26] Electoral corruption reached an early peak in the election of 1844, when it probably cost Henry Clay the presidency. New York

22. U.S. Department of Commerce, *Historical Statistics of the United States, Colonial Times to 1857* (Washington, D.C.: U.S. Department of Commerce, Bureau of the Census, 1960), 14, 72.

23. Samuel Eliot Morison, *The Oxford History of the American People* (New York: Oxford University Press, 1965), 481.

24. Noble E. Cunningham Jr., *The Presidency of James Monroe* (Lawrence: University Press of Kansas, 1996), 85.

25. Dangerfield, *Awakening of American Nationalism*, 85.

26. Chilton Williamson, *American Suffrage from Property to Democracy, 1760–1860* (Princeton: Princeton University Press, 1960), 205.

proved crucial to the victor, Democrat James K. Polk, as its thirty-six electoral votes gave him a 170–105 victory in the Electoral College. Polk won the state by only 5,100 votes, and observers concluded that at least six thousand Democratic ballots in New York City were illegally cast.[27] The sale of votes alone did not reveal how precarious was the existence of the new laboring classes—or how far they were from possessing anything like public virtue. They enjoyed none of the protections necessary to maintain a stable urban population, such as unemployment and disability insurance. Nor did workers have the right of collective bargaining. Labor leaders sought help from the legislatures. Their goals included a ten-hour law (limiting the maximum workday to ten hours), mechanics' lien laws, public schools, secret ballots, and an end to the practice of imprisoning debtors. Labor also demanded the eradication of "paper money"—depreciated state banknotes through which workers were often defrauded of their meager wages.[28] In order to obtain these ends, the laboring classes—or at least skilled laborers—organized their own political parties in the late 1820s. Almost as soon as they took on any public identity at all, these entities were co-opted by local Jacksonians, or Democrats (the branch of the Republican Party that supported Andrew Jackson). Democrats overwhelmed these organizations by adopting labor's agenda as their own. In New York City, Tammany Hall persuaded the city council to pass a mechanics' lien law (albeit a weak one) in 1830.[29] Shortly thereafter, the state Democratic machine, the "Albany Regency," pushed a statewide mechanics' lien law through the legislature. It also secured the abolition of imprisonment for debt and reform of the militia system.[30] The Democratic Party and labor also came together in Massachusetts.[31] By the late 1830s labor leaders had dropped the pretense of neutrality, as Democrats throughout the urban North embraced their agenda.[32] In Congress Democrats such as Thomas Hart Benton won favor with the laboring classes by seeking to reduce tariffs on "necessaries" like coffee, tea, and salt, as well as those levied upon other slightly less critical items, such as woolens, flannels, and boots.

Within the growing ranks of urban laborers, there existed a group that

27. Remini, *Henry Clay,* 665.
28. Joseph G. Rayback, *A History of American Labor* (New York: Macmillan, 1959), 66.
29. Gustavus Myers, *History of Tammany Hall* (New York: Burt Franklin, 1968), 81.
30. Rayback, *History of American Labor,* 85.
31. Ronald P. Formisano, *The Transformation of Political Culture: Massachusetts Parties, 1790s–1840s* (New York: Oxford University Press, 1983), 241.
32. Bruce Laurie, *Working People of Philadelphia, 1800–1850* (Philadelphia: Temple University Press, 1980), 113.

became particularly dependent on the Democratic Party for protection: immigrants. Democrats had been viewed as defenders of the newly arrived ever since their predecessors, the Republicans, opposed passage of the Alien and Naturalization Acts in 1798. Upon Jefferson's election in 1800, Republicans further cemented their popularity with immigrants by abolishing the Naturalization Act. Other issues secured the alliance, the most important of which was the rise of nativism during the 1820s and '30s. Many of the newcomers were Irish Catholics; their arrival in such large numbers awakened the ancient hostilities of a native population that was of largely Anglo-Saxon descent. Economic difficulties also worsened frictions; many American-born workers blamed immigrants for the labor glut and the depressed wages that followed in its wake.[33]

Ties developed between nativist movements and those who stood in opposition to the Democrats. The Native American Party allied itself with the Whigs (the branch of the old Republican Party that opposed Andrew Jackson and the Democrats) in New York City's 1837 municipal elections.[34] During the 1844 presidential contest, Whigs played the nativist card by dropping hints that their candidate, Henry Clay, wanted to tighten immigration and naturalization laws. They also demonstrated their hostility to newcomers and the poor in general with their opposition to universal manhood suffrage. Jeffersonian Republicans and, later, Democrats embraced the idea, while Federalists and Whigs remained hostile to it.[35]

The relationship between the Democratic Party and the laboring classes was most firmly established not by labor laws or protection of the immigrant but by the rather arcane issue of money. During the early nineteenth century, state banknotes served as the primary currency. They proved wholly inadequate to the task. The notes passed at a discount, sometimes a substantial one, despite state laws requiring banks to redeem them at par and with specie (gold or silver). A note with a face value of a dollar might be worth as little as seven cents. The laboring classes despised state banknotes, because banks issued them in very small denominations (as little as six cents) so that businesses could pay workers with them.[36] Employers naturally sought the

33. Sean Wilentz, *Chants Democratic: New York City and the Rise of the American Working Class, 1788–1850* (New York: Oxford University Press, 1984), 268.

34. Glyndon G. Van Deusen, *The Jacksonian Era* (New York: Harper, 1959), 16–17.

35. Williamson, *American Suffrage*, 158–73, 260–63.

36. William M. Gouge, *A Short History of Paper Money and Banking in the United States* (Philadelphia: Ustick, 1833), 54, 57.

most depreciated bank paper they could find, and their workers were in no position to turn down these "shinplasters."[37]

Despite their abuses, state banks that issued these notes proved immune to legislative reform, largely because of the Supreme Court's *Dartmouth College* ruling, which set all corporate charters in stone. Even if a state bank's charter required it to redeem its notes in specie and it failed to do so, the legislature could not revoke its charter, as doing so would impair the contract between the state and the bank. Democratic state party organizations reacted by embracing "equal rights" platforms, the central tenet of which held that all citizens should operate under the equal protection of the law, and that none should be given exclusive privileges in the form of corporate charters that authorized the issuing of paper notes. Democrats also called for the repeal of those charters already issued, *Dartmouth College* notwithstanding.[38] When New York Democrats published what later came to be treated as the party's first national platform in 1836, the second plank spoke of the party's "unqualified hostility to bank notes," and the third held—in direct contradiction to *Dartmouth College*—that every law of incorporation passed by state legislatures could be repealed.[39]

Democrats focused most of their energy on passing laws that prohibited low-denomination notes. For a time the states held off on this course of action because employers threatened to go elsewhere. Popular outrage finally bubbled over during the mid-1830s. The largest public assembly in Philadelphia history took place outside Independence Hall on May 15, 1837, when a gathering opposed to paper money announced that it would support only those candidates who favored hard money (gold and silver coins), "the only just and legal currency."[40] Legislatures had already begun to respond—the number of states that prohibited paper notes in denominations of less than five dollars grew from three to thirteen during the mid-1830s.[41] In most of these states Democrats played a critical role in the process.[42] In Ohio a Democratic governor's proposal to ban small-denomination notes stalled

37. Sellers, *Market Revolution*, 162.

38. James Roger Sharp, *The Jacksonians Versus the Banks* (New York: Columbia University Press, 1970), 290, 301–2.

39. Thomas Hudson McKee, *The National Conventions and Platforms of All Political Parties, 1789–1905* (Baltimore: Friedenwald Co., 1906; reprint, New York: Da Capo Press, 1971), 35.

40. Sellers, *Market Revolution*, 358, 355.

41. Van Deusen, *Jacksonian Era*, 104.

42. Sellers, *Market Revolution*, 358–59.

until the Democrats took over the state assembly in 1835.[43] During his second term as president (1833–37), Andrew Jackson spent a great deal of time
campaigning for state bans of small-denomination notes. By the late 1830s
the hard money, or "locofoco," wing of the Democratic Party dominated the
politics of any region where labor was strong.[44]

While Democrats reached out to the urban working class, the Whigs
alienated it. When manufacturers demanded protective tariffs that would
enable them to increase the prices of their own goods, Whigs obliged, despite the hardships that resulted from higher taxes and higher prices. The
party opposed virtually every economic reform imaginable, such as laws limiting the workday to a maximum of ten hours. It also alienated immigrant
laborers by supporting state bans on the sale of alcohol. Even Whig support
for public schools stemmed in part from a nativist impulse to wean immigrants from the Roman Catholic Church. No wonder Democrats possessed
the support of labor and immigrants from the beginning. They won the allegiance of farmers as well, mainly by reducing land prices and protecting
squatters. Whigs, in contrast, preferred higher land prices and in turn increased revenues, which could be used to fund internal improvements.

The votes of urban laborers and farmers combined to make the Democrats the nation's majority party. They won four of six presidential elections
between 1828 and 1848; during the same period they usually controlled both
houses of Congress. Democrats also fared well at the state level, particularly
in the South and Northwest. More often than not, they also controlled the
state governments in Maine, New Hampshire, and New York. As industrialization and immigration endowed Democrats with majority party status, the
growth of the federal civil service left the party's state organizations dangerously susceptible to executive branch manipulation, at least when the party
controlled the presidency. The influence of federal officials within the states
grew dramatically during the 1830s and '40s. Federal offices were once and
for all completely politicized, so that an army of thirty thousand men loyal
to the president—and utterly dependent on him for employment—had legions encamped in every town. Many federal employees held positions in
one of the nation's eleven thousand post offices. Others toiled in one of the
111 customhouses that existed by 1840. An 1842 House report warned that

43. Michael F. Holt, *The Rise and Fall of the American Whig Party: Jacksonian Politics and the Onset of the Civil War* (New York: Oxford University Press, 1999), 53.
44. *New Yorker,* November 4, 1837, 2.

the growth of the civil list had combined with the practice of political removals to centralize the nation's political machinery.[45]

The practice of removing members of the opposition party from office
and barring them from appointment—the spoils system—became the rule
during the administration of Andrew Jackson (1829–37). While even the
highest estimates put removals during his two terms at no more than 20 percent, this number does not tell the whole story.[46] Jackson did not have to fire
many senior-level officeholders in order to turn them out; most held their
jobs for only four years under the Tenure of Office Act of 1820, so their places opened merely through the chief executive's refusal to renominate them.[47]
Succeeding administrations followed the Jacksonian approach, at least when
they took over the presidency from the opposition. In 1841 Whig postmaster general Francis Granger removed seventeen hundred postmasters before
the end of summer. When party leaders forced him to resign after the president vetoed a popular bank bill, Granger declared he would have terminated three thousand more had he been given another two weeks.[48] Following
the Democrats' takeover of the executive branch in 1845, they did much the
same. Their task was made easier by the Tenure of Office Act. Only 871 postmasters were removed in 1846, yet 4,958 were appointed. Some ten thousand
postmasters were thought to have resigned, many in the belief that the new
president would not renominate them.[49]

That incoming administrations cleaned house does not fully illustrate
the extent to which federal patronage centralized political power in antebellum America. In thousands of towns, the local federal facility—usually the
post office—became through its very size a hub of patronage and in turn a
center of political power. During the 1840 presidential contest, Democrats
had the nation's thirteen thousand postmasters, as well as temporary census workers, distribute campaign materials.[50] In rural areas, where post offices remained sparse, land offices provided the most sinecures. Originally

45. *Report of the Select Committee on Retrenchment*, 27th Cong., 2d sess., May 23, 1842, H. Rep.
741, 120–25, 4.

46. Richard E. Ellis, *The Union at Risk: Jacksonian Democracy, States' Rights and the Nullification Crisis* (New York: Oxford University Press, 1987), 18.

47. Matthew Crenson, *The Federal Machine: Beginnings of Bureaucracy in Jacksonian America*
(Baltimore: Johns Hopkins University Press, 1975), 65.

48. Norma Lois Peterson, *The Presidencies of William Henry Harrison and John Tyler* (Lawrence: University Press of Kansas, 1989), 39.

49. Leonard D. White, *The Jacksonians: A Study in Administrative History, 1829–1861* (New
York: Macmillan, 1954), 312.

50. Van Deusen, *Jacksonian Era*, 146.

set up under the Land Act of 1796, forty-two existed in 1830.[51] By 1835, Illinois alone had ten.[52] Each office required surveyors, registers, and assorted lower-level personnel. Those who headed these offices held immense political power, as the sheer number of places they controlled gave them a loyal faction with which they could impose their will in the informal nominating conventions of the era. For a time, the headquarters of the Indiana Democratic Party were located at the office of land register James P. Drake.[53] Land offices also played critical roles in Florida and Arkansas—when the latter became a state in 1836, the former surveyor was elected governor. Michigan Democrats also derived sustenance from land offices.[54] In Illinois, the political career of a young lawyer named Stephen Douglas received a boost when he served a stint as the land register in Springfield. The number of jobs he controlled enabled Douglas to arrange a Democratic convention. The assembled delegates promptly nominated Douglas for Congress—much to the chagrin of incumbent representative William May, who complained about the interloper to the Treasury Department.[55]

The importance of federal places in state politics received its most notorious demonstration in an episode involving a Mississippi land office, the U.S. Senate, and Andrew Jackson. In early 1831 the Senate passed a resolution critical of the appointment of persons to federal positions who were not residents of the state in which the job was located. Undeterred, President Jackson nominated Samuel Gwyn of Pennsylvania for the post of register at the land office in Clinton, Mississippi. The Senate rejected the nomination at the request of Mississippi senator George Poindexter, only to see the president give Gwyn a recess appointment. When Gwyn was nominated once more in 1833, the Senate again refused to go along. At that point the president declared that he would send no more nominations to the Senate until it approved Gwyn and repealed its resolution. The Senate backed down and confirmed Mr. Gwyn.[56] The episode has been cast as another chapter in the

51. *Report of the Select Committee on Retrenchment*, H. Rep. 741, 4.

52. Theodore Pease, *The Frontier State, 1818–1848 Illinois* (Springfield, Ill.: Centennial Commission, 1918), 176.

53. Donald B. Cole, *The Presidency of Andrew Jackson* (Lawrence: University Press of Kansas, 1993), 248.

54. William E. Nelson, *The Roots of American Bureaucracy, 1830–1900* (Cambridge: Harvard University Press, 1982), 28–29.

55. Robert W. Johannsen, *Stephen A. Douglas* (New York: Oxford University Press, 1973), 55–57, 61–64.

56. Edwin Arthur Miles, *Jacksonian Democracy in Mississippi* (Chapel Hill: University of North Carolina Press, 1960), 49–54.

struggle over appointments; it also indicated the growing importance of federal patronage—Mississippi Democrats feared that Gwyn would take over the state Democratic Party.[57] Their concerns proved well founded; in May 1834 Gwyn chaired the state's first Democratic convention. Largely because of administration influence, the state legislature shortly thereafter elected another new arrival and Jackson ally, Robert J. Walker, to the Senate.[58]

In the West, territorial government positions served as the chief source of patronage. The president appointed the governor, secretary, and judges in each territory, until five thousand "free inhabitants of full age" elected a legislature. Even then, the president selected the members of the upper house of the legislature. The territorial governors themselves also enjoyed extraordinary powers—they could remove all military and civil officers, including county and township officials. Nor did this influence dissipate after statehood was achieved. Politicians fortunate enough to receive appointments during the territorial stage had the advantage of familiarity among voters. The possibilities inherent in territorial patronage were demonstrated by an episode that occurred in the Deep South. A faction of Georgia politicians down on their luck departed for Alabama, where federal patronage in the form of territorial appointments enabled them to secure control of the first state government, after it was established in 1819.[59] One member of this group, a former Georgia congressman named W. W. Bibb, was appointed Alabama's territorial governor by James Monroe. Thereafter Bibb won the state's first gubernatorial election, though not without grumbling over what became known as the "Georgia faction."[60]

On the eastern seaboard, customhouses dominated. The Boston customhouse employed approximately sixty persons in 1842, Baltimore eighty, Philadelphia one hundred, and New York City almost five hundred—not including day laborers and watchmen.[61] In many eastern states, control of the local Democratic Party went hand in hand with the position of collector during the Jackson and Van Buren administrations. David Henshaw ruled Massachusetts Democrats by virtue of the fact that he was the collector of

57. Cole, *Presidency of Andrew Jackson*, 177.

58. Richard P. McCormick, *The Second American Party System: Party Formation in the Jacksonian Era* (Chapel Hill: University of North Carolina Press, 1966), 299–300.

59. Sellers, *Market Revolution*, 169.

60. Hugh C. Bailey, "John W. Walker and the Georgia Machine in Early Alabama Politics," *Alabama Review* 8 (1955): 191–92.

61. *Report of the Select Committee on Retrenchment*, H. Rep. 741, 204–38.

the Port of Boston.[62] A group of Democrats in the state legislature managed to cast Henshaw aside in 1835 by setting up a separate party organization, but they had to get the Jackson administration's approval before attempting the coup.[63] Similar realities characterized New York state politics. As early as 1845, the collector of the Port of New York, Cornelius Van Ness, concluded that possession of the customhouse meant control of New York City.[64] The numbers confirmed his assessment. At midcentury Gotham counted twenty-four hundred federal employees—all of whom owed their places to the president alone—while control of two thousand state and fourteen hundred municipal jobs was divided among multiple officials.[65]

Despite its awareness of the problem of patronage, Congress appeared to be in danger of losing its own independence to the executive branch. Members continued to accept appointment to federal offices. In addition, their newspapers—most prominent politicians had their own sheets—received printing contracts despite the 1808 statute that prohibited members of Congress from doing business with the federal government. Representative John Wentworth of Illinois obtained postal advertising for his newspaper, the *Chicago Democrat,* from the Polk administration.[66] Complaints over executive branch influence began to emanate from the Capitol. Perhaps the best-known response appeared in a series of resolutions offered by Henry Clay in the Senate in March 1834. Clay, like many other Whigs, had doubts about the power of the chief executive to remove federal officeholders, and a statement to that effect served as the first resolution. He also suggested that Congress prescribe tenure for appointees (it had already) and that Senate consent be required for the appointment of deputy postmasters.[67] By 1835 Clay sounded like an Antifederalist in his denunciation of the spoils system: "the official corps is distributed in every city, village and hamlet, having daily intercourse with society, and operates on public opinion ... aided by the executive, by the post-office department, and by a large portion of the public press, its power is invincible."[68]

62. Arthur M. Schlesinger Jr., *The Age of Jackson* (Boston: Little, Brown, 1953), 147.

63. Formisano, *Transformation of Political Culture,* 258.

64. White, *Jacksonians,* 12–13.

65. Amy Bridges, *A City in the Republic: Antebellum New York and the Origins of Machine Politics* (Ithaca: Cornell University Press, 1984), 132.

66. Don E. Fehrenbacher, *Chicago Giant: A Biography of Long John Wentworth* (Madison, Wisc.: American History Research Center, 1957), 61.

67. See, for example, the speech of John C. Calhoun of February 13, 1835, *Register of Debates,* 23d Cong., 2d sess., 11.1:418–21. Clay's resolutions may be found in ibid., 23d Cong., 1st sess., March 10, 1834, 10.1:836.

68. Colton, *Works of Henry Clay,* 8:23.

The Jackson administration's most notorious abuse in the area of patronage occurred in its manipulation of the press—the president appointed fifty-nine newspaper editors to federal office. They usually became postmasters, as these positions came with a franking privilege—free use of the mail. This tool provided an advantage of incalculable value in the eternal search for subscribers. Some newspapers had more than one employee on the federal payroll; David Henshaw's *Boston Statesman* had four, while Isaac Hill's *New Hampshire Patriot* had two. The lure of government jobs was supplemented with State Department printing contracts, fifty-five of which (out of a total of seventy-eight) were transferred to more favored newspapers following Jackson's inauguration in 1829.[69] Post office largesse also won friends for the administration. An 1834 investigation revealed that the editors of the *Boston Statesman, Albany Argus,* and *New England Patriot* all enjoyed mail delivery contracts.[70] Such formidable emoluments enabled the Jackson administration to construct an impressive fleet of publicly fed newspapers. Under the tutelage of editor Frank Blair, the *Washington Globe* served as the flagship of this armada. By 1837 the *Globe* provided guidance and material for a network of four hundred Democratic Party newspapers across the country (out of a total of twelve hundred).[71]

John Tyler embraced the system wholeheartedly upon taking over the presidency following William Henry Harrison's death in 1841. The Washington, D.C., *Daily Madisonian* was set up under New Hampshire Democratic boss Isaac Hill. In exchange, Hill received postal printing contracts and an effective monopoly on federal patronage in his home state.[72] Following a dispute with Henry Clay, Tyler stripped pro-Clay newspapers of their printing contracts.[73] The party press sustained a blow when the State Department's practice of handing out printing contracts to newspapers was discarded in 1842. After they regained the presidency and Congress in the 1844–45 elections, Democrats resumed the practice.[74] A Democratic newspaper, the *Washington Union,* was established under Thomas Ritchie, longtime

69. Smith, *Press, Politics, and Patronage,* 90, 87, 100.

70. *Report of the Committee on the Post Office and Post Roads regarding the condition of the Post Office,* 23rd Cong., 1st sess., June 9, 1834, S. Doc. 422, 28–31, 33, 81–82.

71. Cole, *Presidency of Andrew Jackson,* 250; Sellers, *Market Revolution,* 370.

72. Donald B. Cole, *Jacksonian Democracy in New Hampshire, 1800–1851* (Cambridge: Harvard University Press, 1970), 207.

73. Peterson, *Great Triumvirate,* 317.

74. Smith, *Press, Politics, and Patronage,* 110–113, 174.

editor of the *Richmond Enquirer*. President James Polk took an interest in Ritchie's work and occasionally rejected his editorials.[75]

If corruption of the press qualified as its most infamous practice in the area of patronage, the Jackson administration's use of federal jobs to dominate state Democratic organizations proved the most significant. It occurred at a time when the two-party system had revived to the point of forcing virtually every faction or pressure group into one of two channels—Whig or Democrat. One had to obtain the nomination of one of the two major parties in order to run for even the most modest public office. Office seekers at all levels thus had to prove their fidelity to the principles of the national party. It was not long before men such as Henry Wise of Virginia were complaining that even local elections turned on "federal" politics.[76] Under any circumstances, the focusing of all political activity through the prism of two national parties would have centralized the American political system to a degree that had not been contemplated by the Founders. The rise of nominating conventions doubled the effect, because just as the parties themselves became all important, they embraced a mechanism that left them extraordinarily susceptible to manipulation by federal officials. With the most places to offer, executive branch officers had a great deal of success in dominating these gatherings. As many areas of the country already tended to vote heavily for one party or the other, securing a party nomination was often equivalent to winning the general election.

Democrats pioneered the staging of conventions as well as the manipulation of these gatherings. Their skill stemmed in part from the experience many party leaders gained during their years as Jeffersonian Republicans. It was during this earlier period that men such as Martin Van Buren of New York learned how to control the nomination process while at the same time presenting a semblance of majority rule. This skill proved critical when the democratic trends of the early 1800s made the first method used for nominations—caucuses attended only by legislators—politically unacceptable. By the 1820s, nominating conventions had become the rule, at least wherever party organizations were intact. The chief means through which party leaders controlled conventions was to fill them with their supporters. Government workers who owed their jobs to elected officials came to be particularly

75. Paul Bergeron, *The Presidency of James K. Polk* (Lawrence: University Press of Kansas, 1987), 172–76.
76. Quoted in White, *Jacksonians*, 510.

numerous at these gatherings.[77] Contingents of officeholders used coordination, money, and occasionally brute force to ensure the nominations of candidates favored by the officials to whom they owed their jobs. They won access to nominating conventions by packing the primary meetings at which delegates were selected or by simply forcing their way into these gatherings.

During the 1820s imaginative politicians devised political machines in order to preserve their control over nominating conventions. Staffed by legions of party workers sustained by government jobs or contracts, these entities were devoted to carrying out the will of their patrons. The most successful machine was Martin Van Buren's Albany Regency in New York. Through its monopoly of seats on the Council of Appointment, the Albany Regency controlled some fifteen thousand offices in the state government, including sheriffs, district attorneys, and justices of the peace.[78] Even New York City's Tammany Hall came under its control.[79] For a time a reform popular in many states threatened these machines, when thousands of positions that had been filled by appointment were made elective.[80] The New York constitutional convention of 1821 reduced the number of appointive positions from fifteen thousand to just three thousand; the rest became elective.[81] New York officials thus saw their powers of patronage decline markedly in comparison to their local counterparts in the federal executive branch. In the rural West and South, where state government positions were fewer and were often elective, state officials also had difficulty competing with their federal counterparts. Of the situation in Kentucky, Democrat Amos Kendall bragged that the patronage of the post office alone exceeded the resources of the governor.[82] The disparity in power was worsened by the fact that control over state government jobs was often divided among different officials or commissions, while federal officeholders all answered to the same person, who could remove them at the drop of a hat.

The Democratic national convention of 1835 demonstrated the extent of presidential influence. Andrew Jackson sought to secure the Democratic presidential nomination for Vice President Martin Van Buren. Not all

77. McCormick, *Second American Party System*, 349.

78. Donald B. Cole, *Martin Van Buren and the American Political System* (Princeton: Princeton University Press, 1984), 73, 87.

79. Oliver Allen, *The Tiger: The Rise and Fall of Tammany Hall* (Reading, Mass.: Addison-Wesley, 1993), 32.

80. McCormick, *Second American Party System*, 29.

81. Cole, *Van Buren and the American Political System*, 74–76.

82. Cole, *Presidency of Andrew Jackson*, 48.

Democrats were so enthusiastic, particularly in the South, where Van Buren was viewed as having temporized over issues such as the tariff. By early 1834 disgruntled party members realized that Van Buren already had the nomination owing to the president's influence—Maine, New Hampshire, New York, Ohio, and Pennsylvania were said to be held "in chains."[83] When the Democratic convention met in Baltimore, it dutifully nominated the New Yorker. Critics charged that the nomination had been rigged for Van Buren through the use of federal patronage.[84] They may well have been right. Some states sent no delegates at all; two-thirds of those who did appear lived near Washington, D.C. Many of the delegates were either employed by or held contracts with the national government.[85] Congressman John Bell believed that the executive branch's manipulations originated with the state conventions that selected the delegates to the national convention. He found that the Ohio state Democratic convention of January 1834 included thirteen postmasters, three registers and receivers from the land office, two lighthouse keepers, two superintendents of the national road, one collector of customs, one inspector, one bearer of foreign dispatches, a commissioner under the treaty with the Kingdom of Naples, and four printers of the laws of the United States. By one estimate, 106 of the 117 delegates who attended the Ohio convention were either state or federal officeholders. The national convention also proved to be top-heavy with executive branch employees. New York alone sent seven postmasters, a collector of customs, and the superintendent of the New York customhouse.[86] No wonder the affair became known as the "officeholders' convention."[87]

By the middle of the nineteenth century, political power in America was rapidly accumulating in the hands of executive branch officials. This development conflicted with the original understanding of the federal government's role that made ratification possible. Instead of a modest institution concerned largely with foreign affairs and commerce, the national government had injected itself into domestic politics at even the local level. Political careers rose and fell with the approval of postmasters; newspapers on the federal payroll heeded the party line established in Washington; and exec-

83. Quoted in ibid., 254.

84. Van Deusen, *Jacksonian Era*, 110. See also speech of Congressman Bell in the House of Representatives of January 25, 1837. *Congressional Globe*, 24th Cong., 2d sess., 2.4:1455.

85. Cole, *Presidency of Andrew Jackson*, 256.

86. *Register of Debates*, 24th Cong., 2d sess., January–February 1837, 13.2:1467, 1518.

87. Cole, *Presidency of Andrew Jackson*, 256.

utive branch employees routinely flooded nominating conventions. Within fifty years of its founding, a theoretically confederated republic had erected one of the most centralized party systems on earth.

## TARIFFS AND THE AMERICAN SYSTEM

The disputes that dominated American political life during the 1820s seemed to render the idea of public virtue moot. Lawmakers spent a great deal of time fighting over "interest legislation"—the allotting of enormous material benefits to various factions. The forms these measures took were familiar by 1828—tariffs, internal improvement subsidies, cheap land, squatters' rights, pensions, and postal contracts, to name a few—yet the feeding frenzy took on a new intensity as the stakes became greater. Every level of American society had interests that were entwined with the policies of the national government, and no group could, like the mythical yeoman farmer, portray itself as above the fray.

As the election year of 1828 opened, pecuniary issues were the focus of attention. Aware of their weakness in the tariff-friendly North, the wing of the Republican Party that supported Andrew Jackson's presidential candidacy (soon to be known as Democrats) devised an awkward concoction of a tariff bill that contained rate hikes beneficial to a variety of interests. General Jackson was already popular in the South; his advocates in Congress believed a properly devised tariff could bring him northern support without hurting him at home. While they proved woefully mistaken in this calculation, the error did not impede the new party's rise. Only a handful of state political machines at the outset, the Jacksonian faction in time grew into the nation's dominant political party. The critical link was that which existed between the Albany Regency in New York and the Ritchie family of Virginia. Martin Van Buren was the major force behind the reestablishment of the New York–Virginia axis that had served as the backbone of the old Republican Party. The key figure, though, was Andrew Jackson. Americans knew him as the hero of the Battle of New Orleans, yet there was more to Old Hickory and his popularity than military success. Born in 1767 to Scotch-Irish immigrants in South Carolina, Jackson lost one brother in the Revolutionary War and for a time was jailed by the British at Camden, New Jersey. He later settled outside Nashville, where he speculated in land and practiced law. During the late 1790s he served a stint in the U.S. Senate before resigning to become a state judge. With their victory at New Orleans in 1815, Jackson and the men under his command enabled Americans to claim success in a war they had come perilously close to losing. Four years later, Jackson led the American force that drove the Spanish from Florida. By 1820 he was the country's most prominent military hero since Washington.

As was the case with Henry Clay, Jackson's humanity increased his appeal. Yet Jackson did not possess anything like the Kentuckian's warmth or vision. He was reputed to be ignorant, bellicose, and possibly mad. In fact, Jackson possessed a lucid mind, sound instincts, and a certain graciousness that tended to surprise people who met him. Reports of his temper were not completely without merit; he was certainly capable of tirades. Jackson was also competitive. He bred and raced horses at his Tennessee estate. A cockfighting enthusiast, he raised his own birds for competition and enjoyed some success in that pursuit.[88] Like other men of his time, Jackson did not accept insults lightly. His body carried metal from several gunfights. A bullet lodged in his chest in a duel led to an abscess in his lungs; another in his shoulder caused osteomyelitis. Jackson also suffered from chronic malaria, vertigo, and dysentery. Between his maladies, his chosen cures (sugar of lead and arterial bleeding), and his stoic refusal to be slowed by the scars of a hard life, Old Hickory was the spirit of the frontier incarnate.[89]

In Andrew Jackson Americans saw themselves and liked what they saw. State party leaders such as Martin Van Buren, Thomas Ritchie of Virginia, Isaac Hill of New Hampshire, and David Henshaw of Massachusetts liked the view as well. With almost a third of the population now living west of the Appalachians, they saw a western man with southern roots, a military hero and a longtime Jeffersonian Republican who could bring them the federal patronage they needed to secure their positions in their respective states. So confident were these men that they advised Jackson to be discreet on the main issue of 1828: tariffs. The general complied; his declaration of support for a "judicious" tariff had the hoped-for effect of meaning different things to different people. Following one of the most vicious presidential campaigns in American history, Jackson defeated John Quincy Adams in a contest that proved to be closer than expected.

Approximately six weeks after Jackson's election, the South Carolina leg-

88. Ben Perley Poore, *Reminiscences of Sixty Years in the National Metropolis,* 2 vols. (Philadelphia: Hubbard Brothers, 1886), 1:191.

89. Johnson, *History of the American People,* 268–69.

islature threw down the gauntlet over the Tariff of 1828. The issue had been working up to a boil for some time. Although the protectionist Tariff of 1816 derived much support from the South, matters changed shortly thereafter. The depression that followed the Panic of 1819 hit the region hard and turned it against protection. Even when hard times let up in the rest of the country, declining cotton prices prolonged the South's misery. From a high of eighteen cents a pound after the War of 1812, cotton dropped to twelve cents by the early 1820s. In 1827 it fell to nine cents a pound and did not surpass ten cents again until 1833.[90] The decline in cotton revenue and the South's dependence upon imports led southerners to object to the higher taxes and prices that resulted from protection. The southern contingent in Congress therefore began blocking what it had once supported. The Baldwin tariff bill of 1820 died largely because of a lack of support from southerners, who had no interest in increasing rates.[91] That same year John Taylor of Caroline defied thirty years of precedent when he claimed that the commerce clause did not authorize protective tariffs.[92]

In early 1824 Congress took up a bill to increase rates. Representative Philip Barbour of Virginia insisted that while protective tariffs might not violate "the letter of the Constitution," they surely violated its spirit. Congress could not, he reminded the House, use its enumerated powers to carry out ends over which it had no jurisdiction. It could not, for example, staff a needlessly large navy in order to keep members of the merchant marine employed. Nor could it impose needlessly steep taxes in order to aid manufacturers, as aid to manufacturers was not among the powers listed in Article I. Henry Clay avoided the constitutional issue altogether and instead appealed to the material interests of his fellow citizens. In a brilliant speech of March 31, 1824, Clay blamed the country's economic distress on the fact that its economy had grown and matured around a European war that no longer existed. Europe's commerce had resumed, and the continent was no longer dependent on American imports. We must, Clay asserted, encourage industry with protective tariffs in order to create a domestic market (of wage earners) for American agricultural commodities.[93]

The lure of higher profits produced the political support Clay needed to push through a tariff hike. Rates increased from an average of 25 per-

90. Sellers, *Market Revolution,* 277.          91. Peterson, *Great Triumvirate,* 73–74.
92. Taylor, *Construction Construed,* 212–22.
93. *Annals of Congress,* 18th Cong., 1st sess., March 1824, 42:1918–19, 1962–79.

cent under the 1816 act to 33 percent.[94] Clay viewed the Tariff of 1824 as a great success. Along with internal improvements, protection would serve as a critical element of what became known as the "American System"—Clay's platform for two decades to come and, by necessity, that of the Whig Party as well. This vaunted program promised aid to farmers in the form of tariffs on foreign commodities that would enable them to charge higher prices for their own crops, as well as internal improvements that would enable them to bring their produce to the marketplace. The American System offered labor higher rates on manufactured items in order to protect it from the competition of cheap European goods.

That a country once known for its hostility toward taxation of any kind could impose such burdensome taxes illustrated how much the national economy had already changed, at least in the North. In the South, where industrial development had yet to take hold, critics regarded the Tariff of 1824 as an abuse of the tax power—George McDuffie of South Carolina coupled it with the Stamp Act as "kindred acts of despotism."[95] Virginia and South Carolina passed resolutions holding that because a power to protect manufacturers appeared nowhere in the Constitution, the Tariff of 1824 was beyond the authority of Congress.[96] Northerners, on the other hand, embraced Clay's arguments. Their enthusiasm arose in large part from the rise of manufacturing. Many towns in the North already depended upon a single factory for jobs. Those who toiled in these facilities believed that protective tariffs were essential to their livelihoods. As they saw it, the American market was being flooded by cheap manufactured goods from Europe; only tariffs could stem the tide. This view spread during the depression that followed the Panic of 1819. Pennsylvania, which saw thousands of manufacturing workers lose their jobs, became the focus of pro-tariff agitation. In time, protection became the most important political issue in much of the North. John Sherman of Ohio recalled that he had "but two definite ideas in respect to the public policy of the U.S." when he entered the political arena in the 1840s. One was opposition to the Democratic Party, which he thought had too much of a southern tilt; the other was a "hearty belief in the doctrine of protection to American industries, as advocated by Mr. Clay."[97]

94. See 4 *Stats at Large* 25–26 (May 22, 1824).
95. Quoted in Orrin Leslie Elliott, *The Tariff Controversy in the United States, 1789–1833* (Stanford, 1892), 246.
96. Ames, *State Documents on Federal Relations*, 139 (South Carolina), 143 (Virginia).
97. John Sherman, *Recollections of Forty Years in the House, Senate and Cabinet*, 2 vols. (New York: Werner, 1895), 1:92.

The demise of yet another tariff hike in early 1827 led to a convention of pro-tariff forces that summer in Harrisburg, Pennsylvania; delegates from thirteen states attended.[98] It was the support of this interest group that congressional Jacksonians were seeking when they devised the Tariff of 1828 (the "Tariff of Abominations"). When the bill passed, southerners were furious. The average tax imposed by the act was 45 percent—among the highest rates in the world.[99] The Virginia legislature passed resolutions holding the Tariff of 1828 unconstitutional.[100] The rationale behind this view held that Congress could raise money only for ends included within the enumerated powers, and as the protection of manufacturers was not included, it could not impose taxes for that purpose. Closely connected to this notion was the idea that all federal taxation was necessarily subject to limits: no more could be taken from taxpayers than was necessary for the government to carry out its enumerated powers.[101]

Enter John C. Calhoun. Although once a proponent of protection (he helped secure passage of the Tariff of 1816), Calhoun had since changed course. At the request of a committee of the South Carolina legislature, he drafted what became known as the *Exposition and Protest*. Published in December 1828, the identity of its author remained secret. Similar to but more aggressive than the Virginia and Kentucky resolutions, it was never adopted by the South Carolina legislature. Instead, the assembly had copies of the document printed and distributed. The *Exposition and Protest* came to be known as the definitive statement of the "Carolina doctrine." Calhoun began the *Exposition* by pointing out that the national government was almost wholly supported by tariff revenues, most of which, he claimed, were paid by the South ($16 million out of a total of $23 million). He blamed this state of affairs on unchecked majority rule. Originally the tyranny of the majority in the United States had been limited by the enumeration of powers in the federal Constitution. This safeguard had since eroded. Nor could the federal judiciary be expected to check the other branches. State "interposition" appeared the only answer. "Power can only be restrained by power," Calhoun explained. Besides, he concluded, the Constitution was a contract among the states. "It appears to your committee to be a plain principle, founded

98. Peterson, *Great Triumvirate*, 154.

99. 4 *Stats at Large* 270–71 (May 19, 1828).

100. Ames, *State Documents on Federal Relations*, 157.

101. See the resolutions passed by the general assembly of Virginia in March 1826. Ibid., 143.

in common sense, illustrated by common practice, and essential to the nature of compacts, that where resort can be had to no superior tribunal . . . the
parties themselves must be the rightful judges, in the last resort, whether
the bargain made has been pursued or violated." Calhoun then took an odd
turn. While some might question the right of the state legislatures to interpose, no one could deny the right of state *conventions* to do so, since they
had ratified the Constitution. Conventions therefore had both the authority to declare federal laws unconstitutional and the right to decide in what
manner they ought to be rendered inoperative within the limits of their respective states.[102]

In the *Protest,* Calhoun claimed that protective tariffs were beyond the
authority of Congress. The power to impose duties is "only a means of effecting objects specified by the Constitution," and protection was not among
those objects. Nor could protective duties be justified by excessive expenditures that artificially created a need for more revenue. Thus the Tariff of
1828, whose real purpose was to aid manufacturers, violated the Constitution not only because Congress did not have the power to protect manufacturers, but also because the revenues thereby collected went to unauthorized
ends such as internal improvements. Perhaps realizing he was treading upon
new ground, Calhoun then backtracked. Even if Congress had the power
to impose duties for the protection of manufactures, "a tariff of which the
operation is grossly unequal and oppressive, is such an abuse of power as is
incompatible with the principles of free government and the great ends of
civil society, justice, and equal rights and protection." The commerce clause
did not authorize protective tariffs, Calhoun insisted, as the Constitutional
Convention viewed the tariff power as only "incidentally connected with the
encouragement of agriculture and manufactures." Besides, he concluded, the
commerce clause had never been understood to authorize tariffs so steep as
to prohibit the importation of foreign commodities.[103]

Although the ranks of those who embraced this view were growing, the
claim that protective tariffs were beyond the pale qualified as one of the
more specious interpretations of the Constitution offered during the antebellum period. The Tariff of 1789 expressly mentioned as among its objects

102. John C. Calhoun, *The Papers of John C. Calhoun*, ed. Clyde N. Wilson, 28 vols. (Columbia: University of South Carolina Press, 1959–2003) (hereafter *Papers of Calhoun*), 10:452, 454,
490, 496, 504, 508, 510, 512.
103. Ibid., 535–39.

"the encouragement and protection of manufactures."[104] As many members of the Congress that enacted that tariff had also been members of either the Constitutional Convention or the state ratifying conventions, it seemed an easy question. In a September 1828 letter, James Madison pointed out that the lack of a power to protect manufacturers had helped produce the Constitutional Convention. He also recalled that Antifederalist delegates to the state conventions made it abundantly clear in their arguments against ratification that they knew the impost power would be used to protect manufacturers.[105] Nor did the right of interposition have any basis in the Constitution—the document did not mention it and there is no evidence that anyone at the time of ratification believed the states retained such a right.

When the twenty-first Congress convened in December 1829, lawmakers understandably had no interest in reexamining the tariff question. Few expected the issue to enter the discussion when Senator Samuel A. Foot of Connecticut arose in the Senate to address the issue of federal land policy. There were several views as to how the public lands should be managed. Farmers demanded cheap lots, the western states wanted the land turned over to them, and easterners perceived a source of revenue from which the national government might fund internal improvements.[106] Senator Foot spoke for this eastern point of view when he addressed the Senate on December 30, 1829. Noting a report that 72 million acres remained unsold, he suggested that the surveys be suspended. Perhaps Congress should close some of the land offices. Three weeks later Senator Thomas Benton of Missouri offered a reply that was characterized by the sort of rabid sectionalism that would eventually prove disastrous. He accused the East of exploiting the West through a miserly land policy that discouraged would-be settlers with high land prices in order to maintain a "pauperized" labor force for its factories. Thus goaded, others joined the attack. On January 20, 1830, Senator Robert Hayne of South Carolina expressed sympathy for both his own section and the West: "it is our misfortune to stand in that relation to the

104. 1 *Stats at Large* 24 (July 4, 1789).

105. Madison to John C. Cabell, September 18, 1828, *Writings of Madison*, 9:316–40. Virginia saw one Antifederalist after another warn in 1787–88 that onerous taxes on imports would follow ratification. See, for example, "Objections of the Honorable George Mason", in Elliot, *Debates in the Several State Conventions* 1:495. For a more detailed analysis of the constitutional questions at issue in the dispute between South Carolina and the federal government, see David P. Currie, *The Constitution in Congress: Democrats and Whigs, 1829–1861* (Chicago: University of Chicago Press, 2005), 99–117.

106. Peterson, *Great Triumvirate*, 171.

federal government, which subjects us to taxation [tariffs] which it requires the utmost efforts of our industry to meet....The fruits of our labor are drawn from us to enrich other and more favored sections of the Union."[107]

As Hayne spoke, Massachusetts senator Daniel Webster was arguing a case before the Supreme Court, which was then located in the Capitol building. During a break he wandered into the Senate chamber and listened as Hayne attacked the East. Webster could not resist the urge to respond. After insisting that federal land policy was not unfair or miserly, he turned to fears of federal power. What if the national government's policies did lead to "consolidation"? In Webster's view, consolidation would strengthen the bonds of the Union. On January 25, Hayne declared that the South "repudiates the idea that a pecuniary dependence on the federal government is one of the legitimate means of holding the states together." The whole country was veering toward a state of dependence upon the national government through land and tariff policies. The South had it worst of all—as the country's major importer, it paid a disproportionate share of the tariff duties that provided most of the government's revenues. Hayne then turned to the protests over the tariffs that had been lodged by the legislature of his native state and insisted that South Carolina still had not gone as far in disputing federal authority as New England states had during the War of 1812. The greatest danger of all, he warned, stemmed from the idea that the federal government alone could judge the extent of its authority.[108]

Two days later, on January 27, 1830, Webster began his famous second reply to Hayne. It proved to be among the most famous addresses ever given by an American. For three hours on that day and the next, Webster's baritone voice carried his message to every corner of the Senate and its packed gallery. Following remarks aimed at demonstrating that the North asked only for moderate policies, Webster turned to the matter at hand. In his view, the federal lands should be treated as a "common fund; to be disposed of for the common benefit; to be sold at low prices for the accommodation of settlers, keeping the object of settling the lands as much in view as that of raising money from them." Webster then turned to the nullification doctrine. Although it was true that both American and English writers embraced a right of revolution, state governments had no power to nullify federal acts. "The great question is, whose prerogative is it to decide the

107. *Register of Debates*, 21st Cong., 1st sess., January 1830, 6.1:4, 24, 33.
108. Ibid., 36–38, 46–47, 58.

constitutionality of the laws?" The United States was but a confederation, he pointed out, if each state could decide for itself whether to obey the laws of the federal government. Even New England had not attempted nullification during the War of 1812 despite the fact that it viewed the embargo as unconstitutional. Nor did the Virginia and Kentucky resolutions support nullification—they only confirmed that states could complain about federal excesses. In Webster's view, the Supreme Court alone had authority to determine the legality of acts of the national government. If Americans did not like a particular clause of the Constitution, or if a "subsequent interpretation" proved offensive, they "know how to get rid of it."[109] Webster closed with an attack on the belief that the Union should be valued only to the extent that it served the cause of liberty.

> While the Union lasts, we have high, exciting, gratifying, prospects spread out before us, for us and our children. Beyond that, I seek not to penetrate the veil. God grant that, in my day, at least, that curtain may not rise. God grant that, on my vision, never may be opened what lies behind. When my eyes shall be turned to behold, for the last time, the sun in heaven, may I not see him shining on the broken and dishonored fragments of a once glorious Union; on states dissevered, discordant, belligerent; on a land rent with civil feuds, or drenched, it may be, in fraternal blood! Let their last feeble and lingering glance, rather, behold the gorgeous ensign of the republic, now known and honored throughout the earth, still full high advanced, its arms and trophies streaming in their original luster, not a stripe erased or polluted, nor a single star obscured, bearing for its motto no such miserable interrogatory as, what is all this worth! Nor those other words of delusion and folly, Liberty first, and Union afterwards; but everywhere, spread all over in characters of living light, blazing on all its ample folds, as they float over the whole heavens, that other sentiment, dear to every true American heart— Liberty *and* Union, now and forever, one and inseparable![110]

An admirer later claimed that the speech "fired the patriotic heart of the country."[111] It certainly contributed to the long process of casting a cloud over the states' rights doctrine that had driven national politics since 1798. What had once seemed the key to liberty suddenly appeared to be a divisive force. The federal government could be demonized if its critics could ensure its association with excesses such as the Sedition Act or burdensome tariffs. If the public mind came to associate it primarily with the Union—their own

109. Ibid., 64, 73–74, 77–79.
110. Ibid., 80.
111. Nathan Sargent, *Public Men and Events from the Commencement of Mr. Monroe's Administration in 1817 to the Close of Mr. Fillmore's Administration in 1853*, 2 vols. (Philadelphia: J. B. Lippincott & Co., 1875), 1:173.

country—then the foes of central power faced a much more difficult task.
In the spring of 1832 Congress took up the matter of tariffs once again.
With the national debt evaporating and South Carolina still hot, moderates
on both sides appeared ready to accept a decrease in rates. Henry Clay would
not have it. He supported a compromise bill in the Senate that, owing to
proposed changes in the way goods were valued, did not decrease rates at
all. In the House of Representatives, the majority appeared ready to accept
the argument that with the national debt on its way out, there was no need
for protective tariffs. Most Jacksonian Democrats operated under the impression that while tariffs fell within the pale, they had to have some connection
with the government's actual revenue needs. The only question remaining was
whether Congress would be able to resist the pressure of manufacturing lobbyists. Democratic representative Isaac Hill of New Hampshire summed up
the case against tariffs. He calculated that in 1832 the average family paid approximately $102.65 in duties on twenty-eight articles over the course of a
year—compared to $28.99 in 1790. Woolens carried a tax ranging from 45 to
150 percent. As a result, they cost twice as much in the United States as in
Britain. No wonder Tennessee senator Felix Grundy could declare that tariffs
inflict a "great injustice upon a large portion of the community." Senator Bedford Brown of North Carolina wholeheartedly agreed, saying that a government that "exerted its authority to take from one class of citizens the profits
of their labor to bestow them on another class, was . . . essentially despotic."[112]

Treasury Secretary Louis McLane devised a bill that cut tariffs on imported woolens, angering northern manufacturers. It reduced rates from an
average of 45 to 27 percent. After some tinkering moved the average tax back
up to 33 percent, Congress passed the bill, and the president signed it on
July 14, 1832. Rates on many items remained high—thirty-five cents per square
yard for manufactured wool.[113] South Carolina legislators were furious. Robert
Hayne wanted a bill with rates that averaged 15 percent—the so-called revenue standard—because it would provide adequate funds for the government's
revenue needs and no more.[114] The final bill, with its "exorbitant" duties, such
as a 57 percent tax on some woolens, would, he announced, "leave the responsibility [for] a measure fraught with . . . fatal consequences to others."[115]

112. *Register of Debates,* 22d Cong., 1st sess., February–March 1832, 8.1:233, 411, 675.
113. 4 *Stats at Large* 583, 584, 585 (July 14, 1832).
114. Peterson, *Great Triumvirate,* 202.
115. *Register of Debates,* 22d Cong., 1st sess., July 12, 1832, 8.1:1292.

In October the South Carolina legislature authorized the election of a state constitutional convention for the purpose of nullifying the Tariff of 1832. The vote produced a majority of nullifiers, and in November the convention met. It "nullified" the Tariff of 1832, effective February 1, 1833. The ordinance of nullification declared the tariff acts of 1828 and 1832 to be "unauthorized by the Constitution" and therefore "null, void, and no law, nor binding upon this state, its officers or citizens."[116] The ordinance barred state officials from enforcing payment of the tariff. It also declared that the Union would be dissolved if the federal government used force to collect the tariffs.[117] John C. Calhoun objected to this last provision. He had hoped to leave enforcement to the Supreme Court, as its directives could simply be ignored by South Carolina, much as Georgia had ignored the Court's assertion of authority over that state's dispute with the Cherokees.[118]

Outside South Carolina reaction to the nullification ordinance was almost universally negative. Thomas Ritchie of the *Richmond Enquirer* compared it with Federalist doctrines espoused during the War of 1812.[119] John Randolph disavowed it, and Virginia advised South Carolina to rescind the measure.[120] The legislatures of North Carolina, Georgia, Mississippi, and Alabama also passed critical resolutions.[121] The president had to walk a fine line; his majority coalition in Congress was built upon a South-West axis. Hence the moderate tone of his December 1832 annual message. Jackson called for additional rate reductions and an eventual end to the system of protective tariffs, as it brought "many evils." Manufacturers could not, he warned, expect people to pay high taxes for their benefit when the money raised was not required for any legitimate governmental purpose. When he finally addressed South Carolina's challenge in his Nullification Proclamation of December 10, 1832, the president took a hard line. He insisted that there were two alternatives available in the face of unconstitutional legislation: judicial review and amending the Constitution. Nullification was not an option. The power of a state to annul federal law was "inconsistent with the Union" and "contradicted expressly by the letter of the Constitution." Jackson then moved into the area of constitutional theory. Contrary to the

---

116. The text may be found in Benton, *Thirty Years' View,* 1:297.
117. Ibid.
118. McDonald, *States' Rights and the Union,* 108.
119. Ellis, *Union at Risk,* 9.
120. Cole, *Presidency of Andrew Jackson,* 168.
121. Ames, *State Documents on Federal Relations,* 180–87.

claims of some, the federal government was not merely a compact, he insisted, and therefore states had no constitutional right to secede. The states had irrevocably delegated a portion of their sovereignty to the national government. Jackson closed with two warnings: the laws of the United States would be executed, and "disunion by armed force is treason."[122]

The North applauded the message; Daniel Webster complimented the president for the sense of nationalism embodied in the proclamation. In a February 1833 speech the Massachusetts senator launched his own attack on the nullification doctrine and the compact theory on which it was built. If each state could decide for itself what federal laws to obey, the Constitution "would speak with as many tongues as the builders of Babel." While conceding that the Constitution was the "result of a compact," Webster insisted that the charter was by its own terms "fundamental law." A compact, he explained, depends on outside forces for its execution; a government does not. Nor did Webster accept the notion that the powers of the federal government had been bestowed upon it by the states. Instead, the people had established the Constitution in order to empower the federal government and limit the authority of the states.[123]

Southerners might have taken issue with Webster's claims regarding the nature of the Union had they not been preoccupied with what many viewed as the harsh line taken by the president. The old general—long viewed as a states' rights man—appeared to have betrayed them. Although most southerners did not accept the nullification theories of Calhoun, they wholeheartedly embraced the compact theory/states' rights approach to federal power.[124] Men such as Nathaniel Macon differed with Calhoun only with regard to the appropriate remedy; he held that states ought to secede if they found federal usurpations intolerable. Many southerners—perhaps a majority—embraced a right of secession. Three states claimed they had reserved the right to withdraw from the Union when they ratified the Constitution.[125]

122. Richardson, *Messages and Papers of the Presidents*, 3:1161–62, 1206, 1212–15, 1217.

123. Daniel Webster, "Constitution Not a Compact," in *The Papers of Daniel Webster: Speeches and Formal Writings*, ed. Charles M. Wiltse, 14 vols. (Hanover: University Press of New England, 1874–89), 1:580–85, 587–88, 595.

124. See, for example, *Blackstone's Commentaries*, ed. St. George Tucker 1:140–41 (Appendix, note D); see also Abel Upshur's essay in defense of the compact theory, in Upshur, *A Brief Enquiry into the True Nature and Character of Our Federal Government; being a review of Judge Story's Commentaries on the Constitution* (Philadelphia: J. Campbell, 1863; reprint, New York: Da Capo Press, 1971), 17–72.

125. The Virginia ratifying convention accompanied its ratification resolution with a pro-

These reservations were themselves of doubtful force, as the states lacked authority to unilaterally modify the charter's terms when they voted upon it. James Madison believed that a state could leave the Union only with the consent of the other states, as they formed the other parties to the constitutional compact.[126]

While the right of secession remained a matter of dispute, the view of the Constitution as a compact held sway throughout much of the nation. Jefferson and Madison had brandished it in their Kentucky and Virginia resolutions of 1798. Following Louisiana's admission to the Union, the Rhode Island legislature passed resolutions declaring the people of their state to be "one of the parties to the federal compact." In 1827 the South Carolina assembly called the Constitution a compact.[127] In 1852 the New Jersey legislature passed resolutions declaring the Constitution "a compact among the several states."[128] In 1859 Wisconsin described the Constitution as a compact; it also asserted a right to both identify infractions and determine the "mode and means of redress."[129]

While the president dismissed both the compact theory and a right of secession, he had no wish to use force in South Carolina. In late 1832 the Jackson administration moved federal troops in Charleston to island forts offshore in order to prevent conflicts with local residents. It also resolved a dispute between Georgia and the national government that arose out of the state's claim of jurisdiction over the Cherokee nation, thereby ensuring that South Carolina's neighbor did not follow her errant course.[130] Yet the president could not avoid preparing for the worst. In early 1833 he asked Congress for what became known as the "force bill." It authorized the use of armed force to collect tariffs, required that all federal taxes be paid in cash, and transferred customs cases from state to federal court. The proposal received a mixed response. Many recoiled at the news that a former general wanted authority to use military force to execute the laws.[131] Lawmakers

vision declaring the rights of the states to resume powers granted to the federal government if they are "perverted to their injury or oppression." Elliot, *Debates in the Several State Conventions*, 1:327.

126. James Madison, "Outline of the Form of Government of the United States" (September 1829), *Writings of Madison*, 9:356.

127. Ames, *State Documents on Federal Relations*, 43, 145.

128. Quoted in Arthur M. Schlesinger, "The State Rights Fetish," in *The Causes of the Civil War*, ed. Kenneth M. Stampp, 3d ed. (New York: Simon & Schuster, 1991), 66–70.

129. Ames, *State Documents on Federal Relations*, 304–5.

130. See McDonald, *States' Rights and the Union*, 98–102.

131. Ellis, *Union at Risk*, 90.

subjected the force bill to an extended debate. Fortunately, South Carolina had moved the date on which its nullification ordinance would go into effect, from February 1 to the end of the congressional session in early March. Prospects for compromise remained poor, as northeastern representatives fought to preserve high rates, while southerners refused to go along with a force bill until tariffs were reduced. The deadlock did not break until Treasury Secretary McLane and Representative Gulian C. Verplanck, chairman of the House Committee on Ways and Means, devised a bill that gradually lowered tariffs to their 1816 level. Henry Clay at that point sensed the change in the wind and proposed his own tariff reform bill. It provided for modest annual decreases between 1835 and 1841. No substantial reductions in tariff levels would occur until 1842, when rates would be reduced to a "revenue only" level of 20 percent.[132]

The trick was obvious. As Clay acknowledged privately, with real reductions put off so far in the future, pro-tariff forces would have plenty of time to amend the law and preserve high rates.[133] House members had their own cause for protest—revenue measures were not supposed to originate in the Senate. As so often happened, all opposition fell before the charms of the most gifted politician of the age. The compromise tariff won the approval of the House on February 26, 1833, and that of the Senate on March 1. A few days later, the House approved the force bill, and Jackson signed both measures on March 2, 1833.[134] The South Carolina convention repealed the nullification ordinance but passed another that declared the force act null and void.

The tariff battles and the nullification crisis damaged the relationship between the administration and the South. Jacksonian Democrats, desperate to make amends, linked high tariffs with that other hot issue, internal improvements, and claimed that both were the work of their opponents. Yet they did not terminate these subsidies. The benefits of access to transportation had become too obvious for that course of action to have been politically feasible. The value of Ohio's agricultural products more than doubled between 1825 and 1832, largely because newly constructed canals brought more of them to market.[135] Farmers throughout the country demanded roads and

132. *Register of Debates,* 22d Cong., 2d sess., February 21, 1833, 9.1:690; 4 *Stats at Large* 629, 630 (March 2, 1833).

133. Van Deusen, *Jacksonian Era,* 78.

134. For the text of the Force Act, see 4 *Stats at Large* 632 (March 2, 1833).

135. Francis S. Philbrick, *The Rise of the West, 1754–1830* (New York: Harper, 1965), 334.

canals. Whigs responded by calling for more spending on internal improvements. Democrats insisted that this was an issue for the states—though even in the legislatures they did not display the same enthusiasm for these projects as their opponents. Politically speaking, it was a losing proposition for Democrats. While the Whigs did well in those parts of the country that had been touched by the market revolution and hence understood the value of internal improvements, the Democrats derived strength from rural areas that loathed public expenditures and taxes alike.[136] As every year brought more of the country into contact with the outside world, the future, it seemed, belonged to the Whigs.

In the spring of 1830 Congress took up bills providing money for lighthouses, the Cumberland Road, a canal near the falls on the Ohio River, a second national road (from Buffalo to New Orleans), a thirty-mile stretch of the Washington Turnpike, and sixty miles of road in Kentucky between Lexington and Maysville. All passed except the Buffalo–New Orleans road bill. The House spent much time in late March and April haggling over the rather arcane question of what sort of road really qualified as "national" (and thus constitutional under the national benefit standard that had taken hold with some). Legislators could now cite, as one member did, more than fifty acts of Congress as precedents establishing the legality of appropriations for roads. Others referred to what they perceived as the public's acceptance of a broad spending power. When strict constructionists raised constitutional concerns, their opponents demanded—as Calhoun had in 1817—that they explain the legality of the Louisiana Purchase.[137]

Of all the measures passed by Congress in the spring of 1830, the appropriation for a road between Maysville, Kentucky, on the Ohio River, and Lexington quickly became the most famous. The road was widely seen as something of a sop to Henry Clay, a Lexington resident. President Jackson vetoed the bill. In a message of May 27, 1830, he explained his reasoning, and in so doing revisited the well-worn trails of the spending power debate. Jackson began by asserting that while the appropriation authority had once been limited to the enumerated powers, the continued use of that approach would weaken the federal government's ability to "fulfill the general objects of its institution." Hence the fact that recent administrations had "adopted

136. Cole, *Presidency of Andrew Jackson*, 251.
137. See, for example, *Register of Debates*, 21st Cong., 1st sess., March 1830, 6.1:656, 680, 712–13, 733.

a more enlarged construction of the power." The president nevertheless admitted that the general-local distinction was toothless. That it was "an unsafe one, arbitrary in its nature, and liable, consequently, to great abuses, is too obvious to require the confirmation of experience." The Maysville Road bill was clearly beyond the pale, he said—the measure was of a "purely local character." If allowed to become law, the bill would ensure that "no further distinction between the appropriate duties of the general and state governments need be attempted, for there can be no local interest that may not with equal propriety be denominated national."[138] The president also vetoed bills appropriating money for the Maryland turnpike, a canal, and lighthouses. He signed an appropriation for the Cumberland Road and several river and harbor bills.

Overall, the Jackson administration embraced an approach to internal improvements that was very similar to its tariff policies—strict constructionist/economy-in-government rhetoric contrasted sharply with utilitarian practice. Although most of the appropriations went for river and harbor projects or improvements in the territories, Jackson signed more internal improvements bills than any of his predecessors.[139] Congressional spending on these projects went up as well—from $312,000 in 1828 to $1,786,884 in 1836.[140] Overall, Congress spent $10 million on internal improvements and river and harbor subsidies during Jackson's presidency (1829–37)—more than all previous administrations combined, even when adjusted for inflation.[141] At the same time Jackson put a halt to the broad-based internal improvements program of the 1820s. Congress stopped subscribing to the stock of private corporations and ended federal involvement in the construction of canals. By 1840 the federal government had stopped building roads in the states. The Board of Engineers set up under the General Survey Act of 1824 was abolished in 1831.[142] Only appropriations for the improvement of rivers and harbors, as well as navigational aids, remained. Despite the federal government's retreat, the states ensured that the transportation revolution continued. State bond issues exploded; much of the revenue went to internal improvements. Several states took on so much debt building canals and

138. Richardson, *Messages and Papers of the Presidents,* 3:1050.

139. Peterson, *Great Triumvirate,* 196.

140. *Report of the Committee on Ways and Means regarding appropriations for improvements of rivers and harbors,* 24th Cong., 2d sess., January 31, 1837, H. Rep. 175, 2.

141. Cole, *Presidency of Andrew Jackson,* 67.

142. Peterson, *Great Triumvirate,* 196.

roads that they defaulted on their obligations during the depression of the early 1840s.[143]

Perhaps the most interesting aspect of the spending power debates of the Jacksonian period was the question of whether land sale revenues could be distributed to the states. At the time of its admission in 1816, Indiana received the right to use 5 percent of revenues from federal land sales in the state for roads.[144] Other states obtained similar arrangements upon their admission to the Union. Easterners complained of being slighted. In 1821 the Maryland legislature asked Congress to distribute western lands to the eastern states, with the revenue from the sale of those lands to be used for education and other specified ends. Nine states endorsed the plan, but it went nowhere after being submitted to Congress in 1822.[145] In February 1827 Senator Mahlon Dickerson of New Jersey proposed a bill to distribute $5 million in land sale revenues to the states annually for four years, with the funds to be used for internal improvements and education. From where did Dickerson believe the power to do such a thing arose? The general welfare clause.[146]

The distribution issue took on a bitter tone by the early 1830s, in part because of its relationship to the tariff question—increased spending required more revenue—and in part because of the resentment of western voters over federal land policies. Following the Webster-Hayne theatrics, Congress mulled over a bill to appropriate a township for the support of a school for the deaf in New York.[147] Precedent helped the bill's cause; in 1819 Congress had donated a township in the West to an asylum in Hartford, Connecticut (revenues from the sale of land in the township went to the asylum).[148] Some questioned whether aid for the New York school would be for the "common benefit." Edward Livingston of Louisiana thought the bill would render the national-local distinction toothless. "Why should we make an appropriation for the support of a deaf and dumb institution in New Jersey, and not of a marine hospital in any seaport town in the United States?" Robert Hayne made the same point. "Nothing can be more elevated in a na-

143. Johnson, *History of the American People*, 368–69.

144. Congress reserved 5 percent of the state's land sale revenues for the construction of roads in the 1816 statute authorizing the people of the Indiana territory to form a constitution and apply for statehood. 3 *Stats at Large* 289, 290 (April 19, 1816).

145. Peterson, *Great Triumvirate*, 84.

146. *Register of Debates*, 19th Cong., 2d sess., February 1827, 3:209, 222.

147. Ibid., 21st Cong., 1st sess., March 1830, 6.1:302.

148. 6 *Stats at Large* 229 (March 3, 1819).

tional point of view than to extend the blessings of education; but why not also make appropriations for lunatic asylums? Why not provide for the aged and poor?" Could anything "be more God-like than to relieve them? Why not include, also, alms-houses, and go on through all the circles of public and private calamities?"[149]

Into the fray stepped the new president. As with tariffs and internal improvements, Jackson had constituencies with sharply conflicting desires—the East wanted distribution; the South remained hostile to it. Many viewed it as unconstitutional. In his first annual message the president acknowledged demands for distribution. As a strict constructionist, Jackson made sure to hedge his bets. "Should this measure not be found warranted by the Constitution," he declared, "it would be expedient to propose to the states an amendment authorizing it."[150] Little movement occurred on the issue until early 1833, when Henry Clay lent his considerable skills to the cause. After much wrangling, he succeeded in affixing a distribution bill to the tariff compromise package. Congress would turn over excess land sale revenues to the states for five years, with the proceeds to be used for internal improvements, education, and the colonization of free blacks in Africa. Representative Clement Clay of Alabama pointed out that the land cessions made by the eastern states in the 1780s stipulated that the ceded lands were to be used for the benefit of the country as a whole. Despite this requirement, Clay continued, the distribution bill provided funds for objects that were "merely local." John C. Calhoun warned of the precedent that would be established—if Congress distributed land sale revenue by enacting the bill, it would eventually distribute revenue from other sources. The measure passed the Democratic House easily, 96-40, and later received the approval of the Senate.[151]

The president took a dim view of the bill and pocket-vetoed it in March 1833, despite the fact that it supposedly constituted a key element of the tariff compromise. In his veto message he suggested that the federal government should stop depending on land sales for revenue and instead reduce, or "graduate" downward, prices on unsold lots. At that point the land remaining in the hands of the federal government could be turned over to the states.[152] As Jackson's message indicated, Democrats were not pleased with

149. *Register of Debates,* 21st Cong., 1st sess., March 1830, 6.1:303–5.
150. Richardson, *Messages and Papers of the Presidents,* 3:1014–15.
151. *Register of Debates,* 22d Cong., 2d sess., March 1833, 9.2:1905–9, 234, 1920–21.
152. Richardson, *Messages and Papers of the Presidents,* 3:1288.

the prospect of the federal government serving as the nation's land dealer. John C. Calhoun's desperation to put an end to this pecuniary relationship led him to endorse the idea of turning all federal lands over to the states.[153] Yet the federal government plunged further into the land business with each passing year. One of the greatest real estate booms in American history took place during the 1830s, and it drove revenues from federal land sales through the roof—they tripled in 1835 alone.[154] The national debt evaporated and a surplus of some $30 million appeared almost overnight. Recognizing his opportunity, Henry Clay proposed another distribution bill in early 1836. Under its provisions, the state in which in a parcel of land was sold would receive 15 percent of the revenue from its sale; the rest would go to the other states. The bill did not stipulate the purposes for which the money could be spent.[155] The president immediately notified his allies in Congress that he would veto the bill if it reached his desk. Senate Whigs responded with an amendment providing that the funds would only be deposited with the states—Congress could demand their return at any time. Thus the measure did not constitute an exercise of the appropriation power but was merely a loan.[156]

Critics remained unmoved. Senator John M. Niles of Connecticut struck a common theme when he denounced distribution as an attempt "to do indirectly what it is now admitted we cannot do directly." Senator Isaac Hill of New Hampshire also looked upon the idea with contempt. The Framers, he insisted, "never contemplated the distribution of the funds of the nation, however raised, among the state governments."[157] Yet the president's objections melted away, in part out of concern for the presidential candidacy of his chosen successor, Vice President Van Buren.[158] The bill moved through Congress, and Jackson signed it on June 23, 1836. Within three years a depleted treasury could no longer afford to turn revenue over to the states. Several states refused to pay back the money they had been lent. By 1842 Congress found itself so short of funds that it had to postpone the steep reduction in tariffs that was scheduled to go into effect that year pursuant to the Compromise Tariff of 1833. Profligacy was replacing parsimony, and higher taxes were the result.

153. Peterson, *Great Triumvirate*, 281.
154. Cole, *Presidency of Andrew Jackson*, 232.
155. 5 *Stats at Large* 52, 56 (section 13) (June 23, 1836).
156. Remini, *Andrew Jackson and American Democracy*, 325.
157. *Register of Debates*, 24th Cong., 1st sess., March–April 1836, 12.1:1331; 12.2:849.
158. Benton, *Thirty Years' View*, 1:657–58.

## PECUNIARY LEGISLATION

Despite their intensity, the battles over tariffs and internal improvements did not demonstrate the full extent of the pecuniary relationship that developed between the national government and the American people during the early nineteenth century. Federal policies affected citizens in a variety of ways. Three areas of activity—the credit operations of the Bank of the United States, land policy, and the growth of military pensions—were the most visible examples of the increasing presence of the federal government in the lives of individual Americans. The second Bank of the United States drew much criticism because of the role its directors played in fuelling the speculative boom that helped trigger the Panic of 1819.[159] The events that followed the economy's downturn did not win the bank many supporters, either. Through its eighteen branches, the bank had extended loans in every part of the country. When the panic pulled down real estate prices, speculators and farmers defaulted on their debts. The bank reacted by suing its defaulters and obtained judgments against thousands of them. In time it came to own a great deal of property, particularly in the West. Large portions of Cincinnati ended up as bank assets, as did farmland in Kentucky and Ohio.[160] Enterprising politicians saw the opportunity presented to them and attacked the bank as an unscrupulous, predatory monster.

Federal land policies also affected many Americans. The Land Act of 1796 provided for the sale of minimum units of 640 acres at $2 an acre, with credit available but full payment due within a year. Over the next twenty-five years Congress passed additional acts reducing both prices and the size of the lots available. It also extended payment deadlines for those who had purchased land on credit. With passage of the Land Act of 1820, Congress stopped financing land purchases.[161] For those already snared in the trap of debt, the Relief Act of 1821 postponed installment payments and remitted interest charges.[162] Thousands of settlers did not bother to purchase public land before occupying and improving it. By one estimate, two-thirds of Illinois residents in 1828 were squatters.[163] Thus the obvious popularity of the Preemption Act of 1830, which granted squatters the right to buy the land

159. Dangerfield, *Era of Good Feelings*, 181–84.
160. Peterson, *Great Triumvirate*, 67.
161. 3 *Stats at Large* 566 (April 24, 1820).
162. Ibid., 612 (March 2, 1821).
163. Johnson, *History of the American People*, 292.

they occupied (up to 160 acres) at the minimum price before anyone else could bid on it.[164] The political benefits of settler-friendly land policies accrued almost exclusively to Democrats, as the party of Jefferson and Jackson embraced preemption acts sought by squatters as well as reduced land prices. Whigs, on the other hand, proved unwilling to discard the revenues provided by higher land prices. John Quincy Adams undermined western support for his administration when he insisted on maintaining higher land prices in order to obtain additional revenue.

Another area in which a pecuniary relationship developed between the federal government and the electorate was that of military pensions. Congress provided cash pensions for disabled veterans in 1790. An act of 1818 extended pensions to all Revolutionary War veterans—thirty thousand men applied, despite the fact that the Continental army never had anything close to that many soldiers in the field. Eighteen thousand applications were approved before legislators demanded reform. A retrenchment drive saw Congress order the Treasury Department to remove from the rolls a third of the persons whose applications had been approved.[165] A March 1823 statute restored payments for some who had been stripped of them, with the new and interesting proviso that they had to be poor.[166] In his first annual message, Andrew Jackson suggested that pensions should be extended once again to all veterans of the Revolutionary War.[167] Congress complied, and by 1837 the number of pensioners reached forty-two thousand.[168] An act of the following year added veterans' widows to the rolls.[169] Congress also gave thousands of acres to veterans in the form of land grants. While no one disputed the justice—indeed the necessity—of these measures, rumors of fraud were widespread. Federal law limited certain payments to disabled veterans; nonetheless a federal agent found in 1853 that of ninety Illinois men receiving disability benefits, seventy were able-bodied.[170]

With the exception of land policy, none of these relationships served as a source of exploitation during the antebellum period. Congress did not discover the full electoral potential of veterans' pensions until later in the cen-

---

164. 4 *Stats at Large* 420 (May 29, 1830).
165. Peterson, *Great Triumvirate*, 93.
166. 3 *Stats at Large* 782 (March 1, 1823).
167. Richardson, *Messages and Papers of the Presidents*, 3:1019.
168. *Report from the Commissioner of Pensions, War Department, November 11, 1837*, 25th Cong., 2d sess., November 1837, S. Doc. 1, 673–74.
169. 5 *Stats at Large* 303 (July 7, 1838).
170. White, *Jacksonians*, 413.

tury, and the Bank of the United States refused to allow political considerations to affect its loan practices. Still, pecuniary issues dominated national
politics between 1817 and 1845. Democrats tried to limit the federal government's intrusions into the economic sphere, while Whigs fought to establish
and preserve national programs and policies designed to foster development.
Americans everywhere found it difficult to ignore debates in a national capital that seemed increasingly capable of affecting their fortunes.

Among the most famous battles concerning the financial practices of the
national government was the question of whether to renew the twenty-year
charter of the Second Bank of the United States. The institution had served
as a positive influence since Nicholas Biddle's appointment as its president
in 1819. It imposed limits—albeit loose ones—on the ability of state banks to
issue paper money. A threat to renewal of the charter appeared in the person
of Andrew Jackson. Like many Americans, Jackson spent a lifetime developing a deep and visceral hatred for banks. He subscribed to the widespread
belief that these institutions served not as sources of capital but as parasites.
It appeared for a time that the president might acquiesce in a new charter
for the bank. In his second annual message, Jackson indicated that he could
accept a bank possessed of lesser powers, in part because it would serve as a
check on the issuing of paper money by state banks.[171] The president allowed
Treasury Secretary McLane to endorse a national bank in his annual report
of 1831. McLane knew his chief well enough to advise bank president Nicholas Biddle to refrain from applying for a new charter until after the 1832
presidential election. Unfortunately for the bank, Henry Clay decided to involve himself in the matter. He pressed Biddle to seek a new charter immediately. The president, as was his habit, took offense. Andrew Jackson had a
long list of enemies and Henry Clay was at the top of it, mainly because of
his alleged role in securing the 1824 election for John Quincy Adams. Biddle's decision to wage a preemptive public relations battle—complete with
purchased politicians and newspapers—did not endear the bank to the president, either.[172]

In July 1832 a bill extending the bank's charter passed Congress, but Jackson refused to go along. He issued a veto message that, although mainly a
populist diatribe, addressed the belief that decisions of the Supreme Court
were binding on the other branches. Some thought that *McCulloch v. Mary-*

171. Richardson, *Messages and Papers of the Presidents*, 3:1092.
172. Cole, *Presidency of Andrew Jackson*, 102–3.

*land* effectively barred members of Congress and the chief executive from questioning the constitutionality of a federally chartered bank. Jackson did not agree. "It is as much the duty of the House of Representatives, of the Senate, and of the President to decide upon the constitutionality of any bill or resolution which may be presented to them for passage or approval as it is of the Supreme judges when it may be brought before them for judicial decision." Thus "the authority of the Supreme Court must not . . . be permitted to control the Congress or the executive when acting in their legislative capacities, but to have only such influence as the force of their reasoning may deserve."[173]

After the veto, the bank issue was overshadowed by the nullification crisis. It flared up again when Jackson moved to finish off his enemy. Despite an almost complete lack of support for the move from his own cabinet and a House resolution declaring that federal deposits were safe, the president decided in 1833 to sever the federal government's connections with the bank. On Jackson's order, the Treasury Department stopped depositing money in it. Nicholas Biddle responded by tightening credit in the hope of forcing the administration to restore the deposits. A short-lived panic occurred; Jackson predictably stiffened and became obsessed with destroying the "monster." In September 1833 he ordered the secretary of the treasury to remove all federal deposits from the bank—$10 million, or half its total deposits. Of the members of Jackson's cabinet, only Roger Taney approved. When newly appointed treasury secretary William J. Duane refused to remove the deposits, Old Hickory replaced him with Taney, who issued the necessary orders on September 25. Five million dollars were withdrawn over the course of the following year. Biddle called in loans, hoping that agitated debtors would howl. He was right—they did—but the president refused to budge.[174]

Whigs claimed that Jackson had usurped the powers of Congress. Roger Taney responded on behalf of the president. He pointed out that the 1816 statute establishing a second national bank empowered the treasury secretary to withdraw federal money from those branches deemed unsafe (William Crawford had transferred money to state banks on those grounds in 1817).[175] Citing a statutory provision that required the treasury secretary to

173. Richardson, *Messages and Papers of the Presidents*, 3:1145.

174. Cole, *Presidency of Andrew Jackson*, 194–99.

175. Richardson, *Messages and Papers of the Presidents*, 3:1227. See also 3 *Stats at Large* 266, 274 (section 16) (April 10, 1816).

explain his reasons when he failed to deposit public money with the bank, the Senate—under the prodding of Henry Clay—asked the president to produce papers he had read to the cabinet concerning the deposit removals. Jackson refused. From late 1833 into 1834, the issue consumed the country, particularly after dislocations in the financial markets threatened to send the economy into a tailspin.

The irony of the bank war was that it worsened the paper money scourge. Before he left the administration, Treasury Secretary Duane warned the president that state banks would issue paper notes in even larger amounts once the federal government turned its funds over to them.[176] (It would have no choice once it withdrew its deposits from the Bank of the United States.) The president, although a hard-money man all the way, allowed his hostility to the Clays and Biddles of the world to obscure his judgment. No fewer than eighty-seven state banks obtained federal deposits by 1837.[177] With their balance sheets improved, these banks immediately issued more paper notes. The number of state banknotes in circulation exploded—from a value of $124 million in 1834 to more than $200 million in 1836.[178] The flood of paper caused the real estate boom that had been building since the late 1820s to enter its final, steepest phase. The administration responded by announcing in April 1835 that land offices would no longer accept paper bills in denominations of less than $5. In July 1836 the president issued his famous "specie circular," which provided that no paper bills of any denomination would be accepted as payment for federal land. The measure did not adequately slow the overheated economy, in part because actual settlers (as opposed to speculators) were exempt—they could continue to pay land offices with banknotes. Meanwhile, events in Europe pushed the staggering economy over the edge. When the Bank of England tightened credit in early 1837, New York banks followed suit, and those in debt were caught in the squeeze. Scores of companies went under as a result. A drain of specie from the West to the East Coast and then to Europe worsened matters. On May 8 a run on New York City banks began—more than $1 million in gold and silver was withdrawn, and soldiers were called in to guard the streets. Two days later the banks suspended specie payments. The Panic of 1837 had begun.

Into the ruins stepped Martin Van Buren. Elected to the presidency over three other contenders in 1836, the cautious and crafty New York Democrat

---

176. Van Deusen, *Jacksonian Era*, 81.
178. Van Deusen, *Jacksonian Era*, 105.

177. White, *Jacksonians*, 477.

had the misfortune of taking over at the end of a long period of economic expansion. In May 1837 the new president announced that despite intense pressure to withdraw it, the specie circular would remain in effect. Van Buren also called a special session of Congress, on the eve of which he issued a message in which he recommended the steps he felt would be necessary to restore confidence and prosperity. Chief among these was an independent treasury that would enable the national government to store its own revenues, thus depriving state banks of the assets they used to justify printing more paper notes.[179] Unfortunately for the new president, the combination of conservative Democrats and Whigs who controlled the Senate refused to enact his plan (it would not be passed until 1840). Congress did suspend distribution; it also gave pet banks (those that received federal deposits) additional time to resume specie payments. Despite these steps, the economy continued to worsen. In October 1839 more than eight hundred banks suspended specie payments.[180]

The ensuing depression led to Whig victories across the country in the elections of 1840–41. The party's presidential nominee, William Henry Harrison, embraced internal improvements and paper money, which was thought to be inflationary. Because the electorate was made up of cash-poor farmers who desired access to markets and higher commodity prices, Harrison's message had wide appeal. Nor did these same farmers—who had been the backbone of Jefferson's Republican Party—have much use for the narrow reading of the Constitution offered by Democrats (whose platform held that a "general system of internal improvements" was unconstitutional).[181] Worsening matters for Van Buren and his party was the failure of the Democratic-controlled Congress to pass a bankruptcy bill popular with voters in the Northeast. Given his handicaps, the president did fairly well in the election—another 8,100 votes in Pennsylvania, New York, New Jersey, and Maine and he would have won. As it was, he prevailed in only seven of thirty-three states.[182] Several of the states won by Van Buren, including Illinois, Alabama, and New Hampshire, were in parts of the nation that had not yet been fully integrated into the market economy. It was a bad sign for Democrats when they could carry only those portions of the country that did not know the value of in-

179. Richardson, *Messages and Papers of the Presidents*, 4:1541–63.
180. Peterson, *Presidencies of Harrison and Tyler*, 23.
181. McKee, *National Conventions and Platforms*, 41.
182. Major L. Wilson, *The Presidency of Martin Van Buren* (Lawrence: University Press of Kansas, 1984), 206.

ternal improvements, especially in light of the fact that, as Whigs won both houses of Congress, they would be able to carve up the country with roads and canals if they wished.

Most observers anticipated that the real power in Washington would now be Henry Clay. The president-elect—a sixty-eight-year-old former civil servant who had last held a position of leadership during the War of 1812—contributed to fears of an impotent administration when he let it be known that all matters would be decided by a majority vote of the cabinet, with the president getting one vote.[183] Even before Harrison took the oath of office, Clay started leaning on him. He demanded the nomination of his allies to the Treasury Department and the all-important post of collector of the Port of New York. While Harrison refused to go along with these requests, he acceded to Clay's call for a special session. The ostensible purpose would be tariff legislation—under the schedule set by the Tariff of 1833, the steep drop in rates that had been postponed for almost a decade was about to take effect. As distribution and the failure of many pet banks had already depleted the treasury, further rate reductions would create a risk of default unless something was done. The Kentucky senator also had other goals in mind. Clay made the terms of his program clear in early 1841: repeal of the independent treasury system, establishment of a national bank, and distribution of land sale proceeds to the states.[184]

At that point fate intervened, perhaps mercifully. In early April Harrison died of pneumonia and was replaced by John Tyler, a strict constructionist Whig from Virginia. (Had he lived, said one senator, Harrison would have been "devoured by the divided pack of his own dogs.") The conservative Tyler personified the conflict in the Whig Party that eventually destroyed it. Although he considered himself a Clay man, Tyler was as much of a strict constructionist as any Democrat. He sympathized with South Carolina during the nullification crisis (he held, as did many southerners, that a state could secede). Upon his succession to the presidency, Tyler surrounded himself with a coterie of strict constructionists, among them Henry Wise, Abel Upshur, R. M. T. Hunter, and Thomas Gilmer. That one party could contain both Tyler and Clay said a great deal about Whig ideology—or the lack thereof. Andrew Jackson explained the odd combination. Whig ranks contained remnants of the old Federalist Party, Clay's followers, and southerners

183. White, *Jacksonians*, 86.
184. Remini, *Henry Clay*, 582.

appalled by the Jackson administration's patronage policies. These groups did not see eye to eye on much of anything other than their hostility to Jackson. It remained to be seen if they could hold together once Old Hickory left the scene.

William Henry Harrison had promised that he would accept a bank if Congress decided one was necessary. John Tyler took a different view. During the 1840 campaign he told a group of Pittsburgh Whigs that he thought a bank was unconstitutional.[185] Harrison's death placed Tyler in the path of Clay's ambition. By 1841 Henry Clay had been seeking to implement elements of his American System for a quarter-century. He had been foiled repeatedly along the way; if parts of his program were enacted, other aspects succumbed to the limitations of less imaginative men. Strict constructionist majorities in Congress talked a broad internal improvements program to death; South Carolina's tantrums had stifled protection, and Jackson destroyed the bank. The election of 1840 appeared to bring Clay within reach of his goal, but fate intervened in the death of Harrison. The final battle in the war over the American System would not be a rout after all.

To bring the president along, Clay should have relied on his vast powers of persuasion. Instead he attempted to bully Tyler—himself a veteran of many partisan wars—just as he had bullied the aged Harrison. Clay began to ride herd as soon as Congress met in May 1841. He found little resistance—his party had majorities in both chambers, and all but three Whigs in the Senate and twenty in the House were said to follow his every command.[186] Clay proceeded to push the necessary legislation through Congress. Although the session had been called in order to revise the tariff, Whigs focused on other issues. Van Buren's hard-won independent treasury system was repealed in June after being in place less than a year. Next, the bank. At Clay's urging, Treasury Secretary Thomas Ewing submitted a plan to Congress. In order to allay Tyler's concerns, Ewing proposed to establish a bank in Washington, D.C., where, most everyone agreed, Congress enjoyed broad legislative powers. Its ability to establish branches would be dependent on state consent. (The president notified Senator William Rives of Virginia that he would veto any bank measure that did not include a consent clause.)[187] The bill floundered, in part because of the opposition of northern

185. Peterson, *Presidencies of Harrison and Tyler,* 28.
186. Peterson, *Great Triumvirate,* 305.
187. Van Deusen, *Jacksonian Era,* 157.

Whigs and in part because Clay himself did not care for it. The Kentucky senator then devised his own bill, which declared that Congress incorporated the bank under its powers as a national legislature. Allies of Tyler tried in vain to insert a consent clause. A Whig caucus that met in July came up with an amendment designed to address the president's concerns: it required state consent unless the bank deemed it necessary to establish a branch in that state.[188] The provision was toothless (Tyler called it "supremely ridiculous") but, driven by Clay, the Senate added it to the bill and it passed both houses of Congress.[189]

At a five-hour session on August 11, members of the cabinet tried to convince Tyler to sign the bill. He refused. The capital heard rumors of a plan to have the USS *Delaware,* then at anchor off Annapolis, head out to sea during a planned visit by the president, where it would remain until the expiration of the ten-day period during which the bill could be vetoed. Tyler canceled his trip to Maryland and shortly thereafter vetoed the bank bill.[190] In a message that accompanied the veto, the president failed to say how he had arrived at the notion that state consent was the criterion by which the constitutionality of legislation was to be judged. Instead, he declared that he had been a participant in the national debate over the issue during the past twenty-five years, and that, upon reviewing the "powers of this government to collect, safely keep, and disburse the public revenue and . . . to regulate commerce and exchanges," he could not bring himself to conclude that it had the authority to establish a bank.[191] As if to soften the blow, Tyler sent word to congressional leaders that he would go along with a national bank that had the power to establish branches—even without state consent—if those branches lacked the power to discount promissory notes. Congressional Whigs went along and devised a bill that met Tyler's specifications. They also replaced the word "bank" in the bill with the phrase "fiscal corporation of the United States." Congress passed the measure, with a sort of joker provision that had been added by Clay's allies. Designed to evade all but the closest reading, the clause empowered local branches to discount promissory notes despite Tyler's insistence that no such power be added to the bill.

188. Remini, *Henry Clay,* 588–90.
189. Quoted in Peterson, *Presidencies of Harrison and Tyler,* 69.
190. Benjamin Brown French, *Witness to the Young Republic: A Yankee's Journal, 1828–1870,* ed. Donald B. Cole and John J. McDonough (Hanover: University Press of New England, 1989), 121.
191. Richardson, *Messages and Papers of the Presidents,* 4:1917.

The president responded with a second veto. Four members of the cabinet resigned in protest.

As the constitutional questions at the center of the bank battle of 1841 had already been explored on numerous occasions, the congressional debates did not shed new light on the subject. The one exception was a discussion regarding the precedential value of Supreme Court decisions. Did *McCulloch v. Maryland* mean that Congress had to accept as binding the idea that a bank was constitutional, or could it decide the matter for itself? Whigs took the position that the Supreme Court had resolved the issue and that there was no use debating it further. As Isaac Bates of Massachusetts put it, if "doubt should arise" as to the constitutionality of a law, "the Constitution itself has provided its own appointed and legalized exposition of its meaning—the judicial power—commissioned by itself expressly for the purpose of resolving such doubt, and definitely settling such questions." Thus, "when invoked in due form, its decision becomes, in the highest sense, whatever any man may say to the contrary, res adjudicata—a part of the text engraven on the table of the Constitution by the power that made it—the people." Therefore all must abide by the Court's rulings, including *McCulloch v. Maryland,* because, "until reversed, the official oath to support the Constitution embraces it, as much as if there was no other provision in it." James Buchanan, Democratic senator of Pennsylvania, disagreed. "The idea of this question having been settled so as to bind the consciences of members of Congress when voting on the present bill, is ridiculous and absurd.... If all the judges and all of the lawyers in Christendom had decided in the affirmative [on the power of Congress to establish a bank] ... I must exercise my own judgment." In his view judicial opinions resolved only the matter before the Court, as well as "all future cases of the same character." Buchanan insisted that the Supreme Court in *McCulloch v. Maryland* had not held that it was constitutional for Congress to establish a bank, but only that the constitutional issue was to be decided by Congress itself. It was therefore odd that "keen-scented gentlemen rise in their places here and gravely contend that this very question has been so conclusively settled by the Court as to fetter our judgments and consciences, and compel us to abandon the use of our reason when legislating upon the subject."[192]

Clay and Tyler clashed in other areas as well during the summer of 1841.

192. *Congressional Globe,* 27th Cong., 1st sess., July 6, 1841, Appendix, 10:361 (Bates), and July 7, 1841, 10:162–163 (Buchanan).

Although the special session had been called in order to revise the tariff, Clay made sure that distribution got a hearing first. The states, starved for funds owing to a combination of excessive spending on internal improvements and hard times, wanted it badly.[193] Clay's allies devised a bill distributing federal revenue to the states. It provided that the funds should be spent on internal improvements such as railroads, turnpikes, bridges, and canals—on the condition that the federal government would not be charged for transporting either mail or troops on said improvements.[194] As there was no attempt to disguise the bill as a loan (as occurred in 1836), lawmakers offered a host of legal objections to it. John C. Calhoun claimed that the measure constituted the most substantial transgression of the Constitution in the country's history. Perhaps realizing that the bill might be viewed as an assertion of a general power of appropriation, proponents cited the territories clause in support of its legality. Discussion of the clause was complicated by the fact that, like the privileges and immunities clause, it had not received extensive discussion during ratification. Who could say what it had meant in 1787–88? Congressman Robert C. Winthrop of Massachusetts held that a broad power to dispose of land via the territories clause necessarily included an expansive authority to dispose of the proceeds from land sales. Congress had already exercised this power in granting land sale revenues to new states. Senator Oliver H. Smith of Indiana, chairman of the public lands committee, echoed Winthrop. He also pointed to the deeds of cession so popular with strict constructionists—these provided that the lands in question be used for the benefit of the states. Levi Woodbury of New Hampshire insisted that the territories clause merely empowered the government to dispose of lands in the same way a principal authorized an agent to dispose of property—by sale, not gift. As the government could not give the land away, it lacked authority to give away the proceeds of land sales. Other lawmakers warned that distribution would deplete the treasury and thereby increase pressure for higher tariffs. In fact, the House was already preparing a bill to increase rates—thus the conclusion of Charles Floyd of New York that it was an "absurdity" for Congress to distribute millions in land sale revenues even as it increased taxes and approved legislation authorizing the president to seek new loans.[195] In the end, Tyler signed the bill;

---

193. Peterson, *Great Triumvirate*, 311.
194. 5 *Stats at Large* 453, 455 (sections 8 and 9) (September 4, 1841).
195. *Congressional Globe*, 27th Cong., 1st sess., June–August 1841, Appendix, 10:332 (Cal-

he believed that it would encourage the legislatures to reduce state taxes. The president did secure one concession; at his insistence, Congress added a clause suspending distribution in the event that tariff rates surpassed an average of 20 percent.[196]

Other factions had their own projects, and all had to pass in order for the distribution bill to become law. Western states asked for and received a permanent preemption law (the Land Act of 1841), which gave squatters the right to buy federal lands they occupied before anyone else had the chance to do so.[197] Eastern states demanded a bankruptcy bill. This measure constituted perhaps the most interesting element of what became known as "the great logroll of 1841."[198] At the Constitutional Convention, the bankruptcy clause had hardly been discussed, even though it had been included among the enumerated powers. Congress passed a bankruptcy law in 1800 but quickly repealed it when it was abused.[199] The Whigs devised another bill during the tumultuous summer of 1841. Democrats—now in the minority—protested that it did not include provisions for banks and that it also allowed for voluntary bankruptcy. Joseph Trumbull of Connecticut insisted that there was no such thing as voluntary bankruptcy; the very phrase was "incomprehensible." Bankruptcy proceedings, he maintained, had always been triggered by a person's creditors when they feared the loss of money or goods that had been extended on credit. Samuel Gordon of New York insisted that because it covered all debtors, the measure constituted an insolvency bill. Charles Ferris of New York agreed. He pointed to the bankruptcy act of 1800 as an indication of the true meaning of "bankrupt"—it concerned merchants alone. Insolvency laws, by contrast, discharged the person of the debtor from prison by distributing his property among his creditors.[200]

Whigs were exasperated. The spectacle of Democrats declaring yet another bill beyond the pale led Jacob Howard of Michigan to complain that "the decisions of the courts go for nothing; the history of the government

houn); addition to the Appendix, xi–xii (Winthrop); Appendix, 456–57 (Smith); Appendix, 247–48 (Woodbury); 84 (Floyd).

196. Van Deusen, *Jacksonian Era*, 160; 5 *Stats at Large* 453, 454 (section 6) (September 4, 1841).

197. 5 *Stats at Large* 453 (section 10) (September 4, 1841).

198. Van Deusen, *Jacksonian Era*, 160–63.

199. 2 *Stats at Large* 19 (April 4, 1800). See also Charles Warren, *Bankruptcy in United States History* (Cambridge: Harvard University Press, 1935), 18–20.

200. *Congressional Globe*, 27th Cong., 1st sess., August 1841, 10:324 (Trumbull); Appendix, 209 (Gordon); addition to the Appendix, xxii–xxiii (Ferris).

and country goes for nothing; and each gentleman strives to be foremost in raising the clamor that the measure is unconstitutional." Justice Story, he pointed out, had affirmed the constitutionality of a general bankruptcy law. While there might have been a distinction between bankruptcy and insolvency in Britain (the former being involuntary and applicable only to merchants), no such classification had ever existed in the United States.[201] The measure passed the House and became law. It proved to be somewhat inconsequential; only thirty-four thousand Americans took advantage of it. Debtors disliked the bill because it lacked an exemption for real property. Creditors did not care for it either, and it was repealed within six months of its passage. Federal judges in Kentucky and Missouri held the act unconstitutional before Congress abolished it; the Kentucky decision was on appeal to the Supreme Court when the law was rescinded.[202] In the Missouri case, federal judge Robert Wells repeated what had been a common sentiment in Congress: the term bankruptcy applied only to merchants. He pointed out that this meaning was known to members of the Constitutional Convention, as were the meaning of insolvency acts, which he defined as laws that relieve persons from imprisonment for their debts following distribution of their assets to creditors. If, he concluded, the Convention intended to include all debtors, it would have said so. Wells found himself reversed by Supreme Court Justice John Catron, who was riding circuit in Missouri. The justice declared that because that it had been the intent of the Convention to remove from the states the power to abolish debts, the bankruptcy powers of Congress could not be limited to only one class of debtors (merchants).[203]

Overall, 1841 was far from a total loss for the Whigs. East and West had exchanged support for legislation each wanted badly in one of the earliest and most famous examples of the American tradition of logrolling. The Whigs had enacted laws that would endear them to every part of the country except possibly the Deep South, and they looked ahead with confidence. With the depression worsening, demand for protection echoed across the North. The national government's lack of adequate revenue further strength-

201. Ibid., Appendix, 494. See also Story, *Commentaries on the Constitution*, 2:47–49 (sections 1111–12).

202. Warren, *Bankruptcy in United States History*, 81, 86.

203. *In Re Klein*, 14 Federal Cases 719, 728 (1843). For a more detailed analysis of the constitutional aspects of the 1841 bankruptcy law and the congressional debate surrounding it, see Currie, *Constitution in Congress: Democrats and Whigs*, 126–36.

ened the resolve of pro-tariff forces—the national debt had gone from zero in 1836 to more than $13 million by 1842.[204] Under the Tariff of 1833, a reduction in rates was imminent. Yet Congress moved slowly, even as the treasury emptied and government workers went unpaid.[205]

When Congressional Whigs finally pushed through a tariff bill, they made the mistake of trying to keep distribution while raising rates above 20 percent. Tyler responded with a veto on June 29, and rates took a steep drop on July 1. Lawmakers did not take the hint; instead, they passed a second bill that raised rates and maintained distribution, only to see this one vetoed as well, on August 9. Despite his recent retirement from the Senate, Henry Clay continued to ride herd on wavering Whig legislators, demanding that they hold fast and push for a protective tariff while preserving distribution. The lines began to crumble despite his efforts, and a bill that increased tariffs and allowed distribution to lapse passed with just two votes to spare. The president signed the measure on August 30. Shortly thereafter he pocket-vetoed a separate bill that would have renewed distribution.

Congressional Whigs exploded. The presidency underwent the worst attack in its history. A committee headed by John Quincy Adams (now a congressman from Massachusetts) suggested an amendment reducing the margin necessary to override vetoes from two-thirds to a simple majority. Adams argued that the president had caused the legislative powers of the federal government to be left in a state of "suspended animation." It also concluded that there might be cause for impeachment of the president. The House approved the committee's report, and shortly thereafter a majority voted in favor of a constitutional amendment to allow simple majorities in each house of Congress to override presidential vetoes.[206]

While some tried to lay the conflicts of 1841 and 1842 at the feet of the president, even Daniel Webster admitted that the Clay and his supporters had brought about the tempest.[207] Nevertheless, Tyler paid the price, at least in the short run. Four of the five men he attempted to place upon the Supreme Court saw their nominations rejected or ignored by the Senate. A nominee for secretary of the treasury (Caleb Cushing) was voted down by the Senate three times in a single day. In March 1845 Tyler became the first president to have a veto overridden. Yet if he lost numerous battles, Tyler

204. Van Deusen, *Jacksonian Era*, 161, 164.
205. Peterson, *Presidencies of Harrison and Tyler*, 101.
206. *Congressional Globe*, 27th Cong., 2d sess., August 1842, 11:894–96, 907.
207. Peterson, *Presidencies of Harrison and Tyler*, 107.

arguably won the war. No federal bank emerged during his presidency, and the American System broke up on the rocks of strict construction in 1842, never to sail again. Four years later, in 1846, another independent treasury act would become law. That same year saw tariff rates drop to their lowest level in two decades. No other important domestic legislation (unrelated to slavery) would be passed before 1861. The period when the sections could be brought and bought together reached its peak in 1841 and then passed, never to be seen again. Pecuniary legislation and appeals to the pocketbooks of voters remained; in time they became permanent fixtures on the American political landscape.

### STRICT CONSTRUCTION IN THEORY AND PRACTICE

Despite the centralizing enticements offered by politicians, Americans relished and took pride in their federative system. No one disputed Andrew Jackson's declaration regarding the Constitution, that the "great mass of legislation relating to our internal affairs was intended to be left where the Federal Convention found it—in the state governments."[208] Some imbibed this view so deeply as to believe that if Congress "should suddenly cease to act, if it should fall asleep, or remain in a comatose state for a year or two, no great harm would result."[209] Alexis de Tocqueville, the French aristocrat who toured the United States in 1831 and subsequently wrote his classic *Democracy in America,* summed up the political pieties of his hosts with an almost wicked accuracy. Americans, he wrote, were "obviously preoccupied" with a fear that the "rights of sovereignty" would end up in the hands of the few. This obsession manifested itself in politics: "there is no subtler way of flattering the majority than to protest against the encroachments of central power." As Exhibit A, Tocqueville pointed to Andrew Jackson, "the spokesman of provincial jealousies." Power in the United States was flowing away from, not toward, the central government, Tocqueville maintained. Yet the Frenchman also acknowledged the existence of trends that seemed to undermine this conclusion. Extensive postal and transportation systems had combined with a "love of wealth" to make Americans much more mobile

208. Richardson, *Messages and Papers of the Presidents* 3:1015, quoted in White, *Jacksonians,* 508. In his annual message of 1850, Millard Fillmore declared that the federal government was "confined to the exercise of powers expressly granted, and such others as may be necessary for carrying those powers into effect." Richardson, *Messages and Papers of the Presidents,* 6:2615.

209. *North American Review* 71 (1850): 221–22, quoted in White, *Jacksonians,* 507.

than Europeans. Constant movement about the country made for a heightened sense of nationalism. In addition to these "commercial links," time had done much to dissipate the "fantastic alarms" over centralization that held so strong a grip on the American imagination in 1787–88: federal excesses had occurred, yet the sovereignty of the states had not been destroyed.[210]

To the extent that they came into contact with government, Americans of the early nineteenth century had far more interaction with state governments than with the federal government. In almost every area of the law, the legislatures had the stage to themselves. They alone regulated contracts, labor, and domestic relations; they alone devised and funded civil institutions such as schools and colleges. Americans embraced this arrangement, if they thought of it at all—the possibility of any other simply had not occurred to them. Yet, as Tocqueville noted, a perception that public authority was moving in the direction of Washington haunted some, especially in the South. Southerners were already more emphatic in defending in the primacy of the states. John Marshall noted this fact when he complained in 1833 that the phrase "states' rights" had "a charm against which all reasoning is in vain." The Virginia and Kentucky resolutions, he lamented, "constitute the creed of every politician, who hopes to rise in Virginia."[211] The nation's dominant political party during the antebellum period—the Democrats—embraced strict construction in order to preserve "states' rights." In the first platform devised at a national convention (1840), the party of Jefferson and Jackson made its position clear: "the federal government is one of limited powers, derived solely from the Constitution, and the grants of power shown therein ought to be strictly construed."[212] The party's success seemed to prove the wisdom of Tocqueville's wry observation: "It was by promising to weaken it [the federal government] that one gained control of it."[213] Although it would be going too far to credit their advocacy of strict construction with the Democrats' success—it had more to do with the party's antitax philosophy, its support for cheap land and the cause of labor—the two were not completely separate. Expansion of federal authority was widely portrayed as benefiting business interests at the expense of the rest of the country. The

210. Alexis de Tocqueville, *Democracy in America*, ed. J. P. Mayer and Max Lerner (New York: Harper & Row, 1966), 352–54, 360–61.

211. Quoted in Peterson, *Jefferson Image in the American Mind*, 39.

212. McKee, *National Conventions and Platforms*, 41.

213. Tocqueville, *Democracy in America*, 354.

Supreme Court's extension of the contract clause to corporate charters was the most notorious example of this trend. Democrats could therefore claim that centralization hurt the interests of labor.[214] Yet the strict construction of the Democratic Party—like that of the Republican Party before it—proved to be less than completely consistent. After all, who in 1800 had heard of distribution?

Whig politicians took a more relaxed approach. Most were well versed in the art of paying homage to strict construction and the Tenth Amendment, as most men in public life at midcentury had identified themselves as Jeffersonian Republicans during that party's dominant phase after the War of 1812. It cannot be said that Whigs concealed anything from the voters in repeating the expected platitudes; they too embraced the notion that the powers of the federal government consisted solely of those listed in the Constitution.[215] Despite their agreement on this point, the two parties still embraced very different, if not quite conflicting, attitudes toward the Constitution. While Democrats seemed obsessed with the restricted nature of federal authority, speakers in Whig-dominated New England treated the Constitution as one of several steps Americans had taken toward nationhood at the end of the eighteenth century. They also spoke with adulation of the Founders—not for crafting a precise list of enumerated powers but for creating a framework strong enough to last for ages. From this point of view, the Constitution served as a metaphor for a strong central government working to strengthen the bonds of the Union.[216]

The differences in the way they viewed the Constitution led the two parties to embrace different methods of interpretation. Republicans, and later Democrats, focused upon original intent in order to maintain the limits on federal authority established in 1787–88. Federalists and Whigs embraced the broad language of the text to justify the exercise of powers previously unimagined but necessary at present for the protection and encouragement of commerce. Yet they were not afraid to cite materials from the ratification

214. Schlesinger, *Age of Jackson*, 405.

215. The first plank of the 1852 Whig platform held that the federal government is "confined to the exercise of powers expressly granted by the Constitution, and such as may be necessary and proper for carrying [its] granted powers into full execution." McKee, *National Conventions and Platforms*, 44.

216. See, for example, the speech of Thomas Starr King, a New England preacher, of July 4, 1852, *An Oration Delivered before the Municipal Authorities of the City of Boston at the Celebration of the Seventy-Sixth Anniversary of the Declaration of Independence* (Boston: Rockwell & Churchill, 1892), 34–37.

period when it served their purposes. When Alexander Hamilton wrote several essays in 1796 arguing for a broad reading of the treaty clause, he pointed to the discussions of the clause in the state ratifying conventions in order to demonstrate that the delegates knew they were granting a formidable power.[217] Three decades later Joseph Story cited the ratification debates in support of a broad power of appropriation.[218] Jeffersonian Republicans and Democrats, by contrast, had always viewed original intent as their lodestar, though it was not always clear whose intent they had in mind—that of the Framers, the ratification conventions, or both? Thomas Jefferson thought the Constitution should be interpreted "according to the true sense in which it was adopted by the states."[219] In 1791 James Madison suggested that the intent of the Framers should be found in the text of the Constitution when possible, and that recourse in doubtful cases should be had to the "meaning of the parties to the instrument," which could be discerned from "contemporary and concurrent expositions."[220] Thirty-three years later, in 1824, Madison moved away from a textual approach when he claimed that the Constitution's meaning should be derived from the ratification debates, as the words of the text were too susceptible to manipulation.[221]

Original intent continued to dominate after the War of 1812. When it became known that James Madison and others had transcribed the proceedings of the Constitutional Convention, demand for publication of their notes became universal almost overnight. (The notes had not been published earlier because of a confidentiality agreement entered into by the delegates.) After the Convention journal was published in 1819 and the notes of delegate Robert Yates appeared in 1821, strict constructionists such as John Taylor of Caroline issued a number of angry tracts, including *New Views of the Constitution,* in which Taylor contrasted the Constitution of Hamilton, Marshall, and Webster with the one discussed in Philadelphia during the summer of 1787. Strict constructionists found additional ammunition in Jonathon Elliot's survey of the debates in the state ratifying conventions (1836) and in James Madison's notes of the Convention (1840). Antifederalist tracts written by Luther Martin and others also appeared again during the postwar

217. See *Papers of Hamilton,* 20:24–25.
218. See Story, *Commentaries on the Constitution,* 1:656–59 (sections 928–30).
219. Jefferson to Elbridge Gerry, January 26, 1799, *Writings of Jefferson,* 10:76–77.
220. *Annals of Congress,* 1st Cong., 3d sess., February 1791, 2:1945–46.
221. Madison to Henry Lee, June 25, 1824, *Writings of Madison,* 9:191. See also Madison to Thomas Ritchie, September 15, 1821, in Farrand, *Records of the Federal Convention,* 3:447–48.

period, taking their place alongside documents such as *The Federalist* as evidence of the popular understanding of the Constitution that existed at the time it was approved.[222]

Strict constructionists could now cite a multitude of sources in support of their constitutional interpretations. In 1842 Robert J. Walker of Mississippi cited Elliot's reports on the state ratification debates, including a speech by Alexander Hamilton at the New York ratifying convention, in arguing against the constitutionality of a bill to extend the right of habeas corpus to aliens accused of crimes in state courts.[223] In 1844 Thomas Bayly cited the Constitutional Convention's rejection of Ben Franklin's proposal to add the power to cut canals in arguing against the constitutionality of internal improvements.[224] In 1846 William L. Yancey cited James Madison's description of the commerce clause in *The Federalist*, No. 41 in arguing against the existence of power to fund internal improvements.[225] In 1854 J. W. Williams of New Hampshire cited the resolutions passed by the state nominating conventions regarding the limited nature of federal power.[226]

While willing to consult the ratification debates, broad constructionists rejected the notion that the Constitution's meaning was limited to the understanding of it expressed by delegates to the state ratifying conventions. Supreme Court Justice Joseph Story pointed out that the transcripts of the state conventions revealed conflicting interpretations of the charter. In addition, only about half of these transcripts survived, and even these were incomplete. Story argued that the words of the Constitution alone should guide its interpreters, at least when the text was clear.[227] In this belief he followed the approach of Alexander Hamilton, who held that under the "established rules of construction," the intent of the "Framers" should be deduced solely from the text of the Constitution.[228] If external sources had to be reviewed, Story believed, past acts of the federal government deserved more

222. Saul Cornell, *The Other Founders: Antifederalism and the Dissenting Tradition in America* (Chapel Hill: University of North Carolina Press, 1999), 288.

223. *Congressional Globe*, 27th Cong., 2d sess., Appendix, 11:611–15 (speech of June 21, 1842).

224. Ibid., 28th Cong., 1st sess., June 1844, Appendix, 13:650–51.

225. Ibid., 29th Cong., 1st sess., March 10, 1846, Appendix, 15:356–60.

226. Ibid., 33d Cong., 1st sess., Appendix, 23:1218–19.

227. Story, *Commentaries on the Constitution*, 1:306–12, 326 (sections 406, 407, 401, 405, 427).

228. *Papers of Hamilton*, 8:111. In *Gibbons v. Ogden*, Chief Justice Marshall called for a textual approach when he suggested that the powers of Congress should be "determined by the language of the instrument which confers them, taken in connection with the purposes for which they were conferred." 22 U.S. (1824) at 188–89.

serious consideration than the ratification debates. Nor did he accept the idea that the powers of the national government ought to be strictly construed. He dismissed the standard argument for this approach—the need to ensure that the bulk of governmental power remained with the states and not with the agent to which they had delegated certain tasks—on the grounds that the national government had been formed not by the states but through a grant of power from the American people. As the Constitution formed "a free and voluntary association of the people for their common benefit, security and happiness," no one "would deny the propriety of giving to the words of the grant a benign and liberal interpretation."[229]

Story and Hamilton seized upon an apparent weakness of the strict constructionist approach with their admonition that the Constitution's meaning, like that of any written document, should be extracted from the text itself and not from external sources. Yet Story acknowledged the limits of this criticism when he acknowledged that reliance upon the text alone could be expected only when the applicable provisions were clear. In fact, the Constitution is not clear—it is replete with broad phrases and vague clauses that are open to multiple interpretations. Story's dismissal of the theory behind strict construction—that it was necessary to protect the prerogatives of the states—was less compelling. In his claim that the Constitution had been formed by the American people rather than the states, Story engaged in a misreading of history as flagrant as that embodied in Calhoun's nullification theories. The Constitution had been ratified by the states in their individual capacities; it had never been approved by the American people as a whole. As John Taylor of Caroline pointed out, the American people had never assumed a collective legal existence beyond the state governments through which they might be said to have collectively brought forth the Constitution. The Treaty of Paris ending the Revolutionary War listed and recognized the independence of the states. The Articles of Confederation had been formed by the states, and the Constitution had been ratified by them. Additional amendments could become law only through the approval of the states.[230] Story's justification for dismissing the ratification debates was also subject to dispute. It is true that the debates of the Constitutional Convention and the state conventions were reported inadequately. If the evidence

229. Story, *Commentaries on the Constitution*, 1:299–302 (sections 402, 406–8, 410–24, 306, 313–20, 324).

230. Taylor, *New Views of the Constitution*, 172–77.

was less than complete, it was still voluminous. Was it really to be avoided, when the text itself constituted a monument to ambiguity?

If conservatives deviated from original intent in practice, they at least professed adherence to original intent. No matter how far they traveled from what their opponents viewed as the Constitution of 1787, Whigs insisted that their interpretations were in accord with the intent of the Framers, if not of those who ratified it.[231] While the intentions of the Convention itself were not always easily discerned, there is no question that the Whigs moved beyond the *popular* understanding of the Constitution evident when it was ratified in order to achieve what they saw as the intent of the men who wrote it. Strict constructionists, by contrast, treated the Constitution as a contract of adhesion that ought to be interpreted narrowly in favor of the party whose agreement was obtained by the warranties of the other. As certain representations had secured ratification, they believed, those same representations should govern its interpretation.

Democrats did their best to profit from what they saw as a sharp contrast in the way the two parties approached the Constitution. Some claimed that their different methods of interpretation formed the most important dividing line between the two parties. This belief dated to the battles of the 1790s; at the time of the bonus bill veto in 1817, Jefferson suggested that the fight over a broad power of appropriation formed the only question upon which the parties still differed.[232] In 1846 Congressman Jeff Davis of Mississippi claimed that the division between those who advocated a strict and a "latitudinous" approach to the Constitution formed the country's main political fault line.[233] Eight years later, Hiram Walbridge of New York explained that the "two great political parties sprung out of the adoption of the Constitution and the interpretation that should be given to the powers of that instrument."[234] In 1857 James Buchanan acknowledged that the question of whether the Constitution "should be liberally or strictly construed has more or less divided political parties from the beginning."[235]

While the language of original intent was spoken by both parties, the

231. See, for example, Daniel Webster's speech of May 18, 1840, in favor of making bankruptcy law applicable to all debtors. In speaking of the Founders, he declared that "their great object was to establish a uniform system throughout all the states." *Congressional Globe*, 26th Cong., 1st sess., Appendix, 8:794.

232. *Writings of Jefferson*, 10:91.

233. *Congressional Globe*, 29th Cong., 1st sess., March 16, 1846, Appendix, 15:434.

234. Ibid., 33d Cong., 1st sess., January 20, 1854, Appendix, 23:88.

235. Richardson, *Messages and Papers of the Presidents*, 6:2965.

waterline of federal power rose slowly but inexorably. Critics saw themselves forced to the conclusion that a method of interpretation alone could not be relied upon as an adequate limit to federal authority. Thus John Calhoun's 1834 lament: strict construction was "not worth a farthing without the right of interposition to enforce it; as the experience of more than forty years has shown."[236] Even northerners who did not share Calhoun's bleak outlook conceded that the federal government had moved beyond the boundaries established for it in 1787–88.[237] During the 1830s and '40s, Congress ventured into several new areas. In 1839 it spent $1,000 for the collection of agricultural statistics.[238] Fifteen years later it authorized the commissioner of patents to purchase seeds for distribution.[239] (The patent office had already begun collecting seeds from abroad.)[240] Legislators discovered that they could bolster their popularity by sending seeds to their constituents.[241]

During the 1840s Congress authorized establishment of the Smithsonian Institution and built a telegraph line. It bestowed enormous subsidies on shipping interests in exchange for the right to the use of ships in time of war. Congress also began donating enormous swaths of land to railroads. In 1850 it gave 2.6 million acres to Illinois, which subsequently transferred the land to the Illinois Central Railroad. In exchange, the federal government retained the right to transport U.S. mail and troops via those roads.[242] While these activities caused concern among those determined to prevent the accumulation of power in Washington, they did fall within the power of Congress. The Smithsonian was formed in Washington, D.C. (with a grant from a private donor), where Congress had broad powers of legislation. Purchasing the right to use ships in time of war qualified as necessary to the operation of a navy. Telegraph construction came within the scope of the war powers, and probably the postal power as well. They same could be said of railroads. Thus the conviction of Senator William Woodbridge: only land grants for the Michigan Central Railroad would enable the federal

236. Calhoun to Duff Green, September 20, 1834, *Papers of Calhoun*, 12:615.
237. "It is now apparent that the tendency of the system is to encroachments by the federal government upon the reserved rights of the states." Report of the Legislature of New York (February 23, 1833), *State Papers on Nullification* (Boston, 1834; reprint, New York: Da Capo Press, 1970), 136.
238. 5 *Stats at Large* 353–54 (March 3, 1839).
239. 10 *Stats at Large* 290, 292 (March 31, 1854).
240. White, *Jacksonians*, 441.
241. Poore, *Reminiscences of Sixty Years*, 1:373.
242. 9 *Stats at Large* 466 (September 20, 1850).

government to rush soldiers to the shores of Lake Michigan. While an attack from the north seemed unlikely, it was hard to deny that soldiers could
be more quickly transferred west by rail than by horse.[243] Strict constructionists, perceiving an onslaught, shot at everything that moved. Proposals for
novel federal action were invariably dismissed as beyond the pale. John C.
Calhoun insisted that Congress lacked authority even to publish the papers
of James Madison, despite their obvious utility to its ability to legislate (not
to mention to the cause of strict construction).[244] Some critics dared to raise
questions about federal activities that dated from the founding period. Martin Grover of New York claimed that marine hospitals—first established in
the 1790s—had deteriorated into poorhouses and were unconstitutional, as
they were not necessary to the exercise of war powers.[245]

That the assertions of strict constructionists were often specious did not
alter the fact that the federal government was slowly pushing outward the
limits of its jurisdiction. Some of the most notable and novel exercises of federal authority during the antebellum period occurred under the guise of the
commerce clause. From its earliest days, Congress had assumed authority to
legislate broadly in this area. A 1790 statute concerning the employment of
seamen in the merchant marine required written contracts and medicine on
all ships. It also established a mechanism for the recovery of wages. Licensing
and ship inspection laws were also passed during the 1790s. Additional regulations came during the Republican era; in 1813 Congress passed an act regulating the relationship between fishermen and their employers. In 1819 Congress limited the number of persons that be could taken on board passenger
ships and prescribed minimum provisions for each person. An 1847 statute
imposed safety requirements on oceangoing passenger ships.[246] In 1848 Con-

---

243. See, for example, the speech of John Bell of Tennessee of February 5, 1853 (the alternative would be to have men "drag cannon up the sides of mountains"), *Congressional Globe,*
32d Cong., 2d sess., Appendix, 22:221. In his first annual message, Franklin Pierce justified railroad land grants as an exercise of the territories power, under which the government acted as a
"proprietor" seeking to improve the value of federal lands. He also expressed his support, albeit
obliquely, for an intercontinental railroad on the grounds of its necessity to the nation's defense.
See Richardson, *Messages and Papers of the Presidents,* 6:2750–54.

244. See *Congressional Globe,* 24th Cong., 2d sess., February 20, 1837, Appendix, 4:252.

245. Ibid., 29th Cong., 1st sess., Appendix, 15:647 (speech of May 26, 1846). In March 1856
one lawmaker complained that marine hospitals could be found in towns as small as Napoleon,
Arkansas, and Ocracroke, North Carolina. Ibid., 34th Cong., 1st sess., March 3, 1856, Appendix,
25:217–22.

246. 1 *Stats at Large* 131 (July 20, 1790); 3 *Stats at Large* 2 (June 19, 1813); 3 Stat 488 (March
2, 1819); 9 *Stats at Large* 127 (February 22, 1847).

gress established the first lifesaving station.[247] Federal regulations expanded inland to cover steamboats, as almost weekly boiler explosions killed hundreds during the 1820s and '30s. An 1838 law provided for the inspection of boilers and required owners to employ engineers. An 1852 statute required annual inspections, authorized officials to order repairs, imposed design requirements, and provided for the licensing of pilots.[248]

Congress came close to exercising a general police power under its commerce clause authority when it imposed limits on what items could be imported into the country. In 1848 it banned adulterated drugs and provided for the inspection of imported medicines.[249] Some questioned whether the national government had reached the outer limits of its authority in this area. When Congress enacted a statute prohibiting the importation of obscene pictures, Justice Levi Woodbury wondered if the limits of federal authority had been transgressed.[250] Congress remained undeterred; it continued to act as if the commerce clause provided it with a broad police power. In 1860 it went so far as to prohibit the seduction of female passengers aboard vessels.[251] The terms of the law did not disclose what such a prohibition had to do with commerce.

Not surprisingly, strict constructionists began to view the commerce clause with dismay. As early as March 1841 the *Richmond Enquirer* announced that it had detected a new source of trouble to go along with other, more familiar suspects. "There have hitherto been said to be two 'sweeping clauses' in the Constitution, threatening to sweep off the rights of the states and the people; first the 'necessary and proper' clause; second the 'general welfare' clause." Now another appeared. "But a third sweeping clause has been sprung, which threatens to do as much mischief as its two predecessors. This is the power over commerce."[252] Like their Republican predecessors, Democrats insisted that the clause constituted nothing more than a power to establish the terms upon which foreign and interstate trade was to take place. Missouri senator Thomas Hart Benton claimed that the power

---

247. White, *Jacksonians*, 438.

248. 5 *Stats at Large* 304 (July 7, 1838); *Stats at Large* 10 (1855), 61 (August 30, 1852).

249. 9 *Stats at Large* 237 (June 26, 1848).

250. 5 *Stats at Large* 548, 566–67, section 28 (August 30, 1842). Justice Woodbury: "when [Congress] prohibited the import of obscene prints in 1842 it was a novelty, and was considered by some more properly to be left to the States." *The License Cases*, 46 U.S. 504, 630 (1847).

251. 12 *Stats at Large* 3 (March 24, 1860).

252. Quoted in Warren, *Supreme Court in United States History*, 2:169–70.

had never been exercised as it had originally been intended, since commercial treaties served the same purpose.[253] At the time of the Constitutional Convention, the commerce clause had been treated as merely empowering the national government to impose tariffs. In *The Federalist*, No. 42 James Madison described it as aimed at putting an end to trade wars between the states. Alexander Hamilton said as much in *The Federalist*, No. 22.[254] As early as 1811 William Crawford declared that Congress had already overrun the limits of the commerce clause. The power had been given to keep states from imposing tariffs on each other's goods, he claimed, not to authorize the construction of lighthouses.[255] John Taylor of Caroline wrote in 1823 that the commerce clause was intended to prevent nations from obtaining "unjust advantages over the U.S" and to keep "one state from making another tributary to itself" (through the enactment of discriminatory tariffs).[256]

River and harbor subsidies constituted the most visible exercise by Congress of its commerce clause powers. To justify them, proponents cited appropriations for aids to ocean-based navigation, which dated from 1789. In August of that year Congress provided funds for the construction of lighthouses, beacons, and piers on the Atlantic coast.[257] Yet it was never clear whether the first Congress viewed these acts as related to commerce or merely as an exercise of its power to establish a navy.[258] (The 1789 statute described its purpose as rendering navigation "safe and easy.") By 1810 Congress was spending $150,000 a year to maintain lighthouses, buoys, beacons, and piers.[259] Many legislators regarded these aids to navigation as having their constitutional basis in the commerce clause. Justice Story thought the clause authorized "appropriations for lighthouses and buoys, as well as the removal of obstructions from creeks."[260] Thus encouraged, Congress settled for the relatively painless route of basing river and harbor appropriations on the commerce clause—as opposed to treating them as subsidies carried out under the guise of the general welfare clause—for the balance of the ante-

253. Benton, *Thirty Years' View*, 1:149–54.

254. See Hamilton, *The Federalist*, No. 42, in Rossiter, *Federalist Papers*, 268, and Madison, *The Federalist*, No. 22, ibid., 144–45.

255. *Annals of Congress*, 11th Cong., 3d sess., February 1811, 22:139–40.

256. Taylor, *New Views of the Constitution*, 267.

257. 1 *Stats at Large* 53 (August 7, 1789).

258. Currie, *Constitution in Congress: Federalist Period*, 70.

259. 1 *Stats at Large* 53, 54 (August 7, 1789); 2 *Stats at Large* 557, 561 (February 26, 1810).

260. Story, *Commentaries on the Constitution*, 2:20–22 (sections 1074, 1075).

bellum period. With the arrival of the steamboat and the resulting ability of international commerce to reach far into the interior, towns on every stream lobbied for funds that had once been reserved for aids to ocean-based navigation. They naturally cited the improvements that had been made to East Coast harbors as precedent. Democrats attempted to impose some limits; Andrew Jackson declared shortly after the Maysville Road veto that he would accept surveys of only those rivers that qualified as "navigable streams from the ocean," passed through two states, and contained obstructions that prevented "commerce from passing through other states."[261] Despite Jackson's admonition, appropriations for improvements of rivers and even creeks became a fact of life during the 1830s.[262] The difficulty in keeping such measures from becoming law was greatly multiplied by the practice of adding or "logrolling" them together with more desirable appropriations.[263]

The embrace of the commerce clause as a source of authority for river and harbor appropriations made for some rather forced arguments. In June 1836 a Kentucky congressman moved to strike an appropriation of $200,000 for the Hudson River on the grounds that it was entirely in one state (the commerce clause empowered Congress to regulate commerce "*among* the states"). In response, a New Yorker indignantly rattled off statistics revealing the vast amount of freight that moved along the river. John M. Patton of Virginia decried the idea that Congress could do anything to "improve the facilities and increase the profits of trade between us and foreign nations, or between the several states." Such an approach would, he warned, "launch us into a boundless ocean of power never yet claimed or even dreamed of by the most latitudinous expounders of our Constitution." In Patton's view, the only clause that could justify improvements was the power to establish a navy, and the bill under consideration provided funds for rivers "where no ship of war, or sloop, or even barge from a man-of-war, is ever expected to be seen." River and harbor advocates nevertheless continued to cite the commerce power as justification for these appropriations. A New York congressman described a rivers and harbors bill as intended to "foster and protect

261. Jackson to Van Buren, October 18, 1830, in *Correspondence of Andrew Jackson*, ed. John Spencer Bassett, 7 vols. (Washington, D.C.: Carnegie Institute of Washington, 1926–35), 4:185–86.

262. Congress appropriated money for dredging Cattaraugus Creek in New York and Cunningham Creek in Ohio. *Report of the Secretary of War showing aggregate appropriations for improving rivers and harbors since July 1, 1836*, 29th Cong., 1st sess., July 23, 1846, S. Doc. 451, 6, 10.

263. An 1830 act that provided $50,000 for badly needed improvements on the Mississippi and Ohio rivers also appropriated funds for Ohio's Conneaut Creek. 4 *Stats at Large* 394, 395 (April 23, 1830).

commerce."[264] Seven years later, in 1843, Illinois congressman John Reynolds pointed to the commerce clause in defense of appropriations for the Mississippi River: the "high sea for commerce of the west." While "the river water is fresh, and has not the regular tides of the ocean in it . . . the Constitution must have the same application to it that it has to the Atlantic, as to commerce."[265] An 1846 commercial convention held at Memphis, Tennessee, issued a report holding that federal appropriations for dredging the Mississippi River and its major tributaries received authority from the commerce clause. It conceded that the general welfare clause bestowed no powers of any kind.[266] In 1848 the House Committee on Commerce issued a report holding that Congress possessed authority to fund river and harbor improvements when necessary for the protection of commerce with foreign nations or among the states.[267] Other legislators cited the naval and postal powers in support of the constitutionality of these expenditures.[268] In response, strict constructionists recalled Clay's attack on the power to establish a national bank and applied it to the power to fund internal improvements. It was a "vagrant power," said one lawmaker, that had been "chased from one end of the Constitution to the other."[269]

The hostility of John Tyler caused river and harbor appropriations to diminish during his presidency (1841–45). In 1838 Congress appropriated almost $2 million for improvements; six years later, in 1844, it spent less than $700,000—though the critical task of removing snags from the Mississippi and Ohio rivers took a huge step forward during this period.[270] In a De-

264. *Register of Debates*, 24th Cong., 1st sess., June 1836, 12.4:4380–82, 4441–42, 4456.

265. *Congressional Globe*, 27th Cong., 3d sess., Appendix, 12:127.

266. The "Report on the Memphis Memorial" may be found in *Papers of Calhoun*, 23:202–4.

267. The text of the report may be found in the *Congressional Globe*, 30th Cong., 1st sess., Appendix, 17:750. See also the speech of D. L. Seymour of New York of July 21, 1852: the clause in the Constitution to which "the power of improving rivers-and-harbors has been principally referred" is the power to regulate commerce among the states, foreign nations, and Indians (ibid., 32d Cong., 1st sess., Appendix, 21:845). See also speech of Charles E. Stuart of Michigan of July 3, 1852 (ibid., 32d Cong., 1st sess., Appendix, 21:868). See also the speech of James Thompson of Pennsylvania of March 1846, in which he claimed that the commerce clause authorized the construction of lighthouses on the Great Lakes (ibid., 29th Cong., 1st sess., Appendix, 15:488).

268. See speech of Andrew Stewart of Pennsylvania, March 14, 1846, ibid., 29th Cong., 1st sess., Appendix, 15:487.

269. See speech of Winfield Featherston of Mississippi, February 15, 1851, ibid., 31st Cong., 2d sess., Appendix, 20:180; and March 1846 speech of Thomas Bayly, ibid., 29th Cong., 1st sess., Appendix, 15:402.

270. Under a single act of July 1838, Congress appropriated more than $1.7 million for improvements. 5 *Stats at Large* 268 (July 7, 1838).

cember 1843 message following a veto of an internal improvements bill, Tyler claimed that the commerce power gave Congress nothing more than the authority to "adopt rules and regulations prescribing the terms" upon which citizens might "engage in trade" with residents of other states and nations. The president seemed to contradict himself when he defended aids for navigation on the East Coast, the Great Lakes (our "inland seas"), and the Mississippi River ("a great common highway") by claiming that they facilitated interstate and foreign commerce. The dredging of rivers "at far points in the interior" did not.[271] For not the last time, strict construction had veered dangerously close to absurd construction.

The Great Lakes failed to obtain adequate money for improvements during the 1840s, even as the amount of traffic moving through these "inland seas" exploded. The human and financial costs of this omission were staggering. John Wentworth of Illinois claimed that the bottom of the Great Lakes was rapidly filling with ships. It cost more to insure Chicago-to-Buffalo shipping than it did to cover New York-to-Liverpool traffic. Thirty-six ships in the previous year had been lost on the Great Lakes when captains had been unable to find shelter during storms (the Great Lakes were almost completely devoid of natural harbors).[272] Thus the retort of James Faran of Ohio: it was unfair of the East and South to fund improvements along the seaboard but to exclude dredging of rivers and harbors on the Great Lakes.[273] Robert C. Winthrop of Massachusetts countered with the stock reply of easterners: the first act for coastal improvements had been passed shortly after the Constitutional Convention, which many members of the first Congress had attended as delegates. River and harbor appropriations, however, did not appear until the 1820s, and thus were constitutionally suspect.[274]

The view that the commerce clause authorized improvements spread during the 1840s. One strict constructionist who did not accept the new thinking was Democrat James Polk of Tennessee, the former House Speaker and governor who succeeded John Tyler as president in 1845. In an August

271. Richardson, *Messages and Papers of the Presidents*, 5:2183, 2185. For the shortcomings of Tyler's analysis, see Currie, *Constitution in Congress: Democrats and Whigs*, 16–19.

272. *Congressional Globe*, 29th Cong., 1st sess., March 1846, Appendix, 15:452–53.

273. Ibid., 29th Cong., 1st sess., Appendix, 15:482. Congress did not completely exclude the Great Lakes during this period. Between 1836 and 1844 Chicago received $157,000 for its harbor, and Michigan City, Indiana, received $135,000. *Report of the Secretary of War showing aggregate appropriations for improving rivers and harbors since July 1, 1836*, S. Doc. 451, 9, 11.

274. *Congressional Globe*, 29th Cong., 1st sess., March 1846, Appendix, 15:484.

1846 veto message, Polk admitted that Congress had the power to construct lighthouses, beacons, buoys, and piers "for the purpose of rendering navigation safe and easy and of affording protection and shelter for our navy and other shipping." Polk did not cite any clause of the Constitution in justification of the practice. Instead he pointed to the "long acquiescence of [the] government through all preceding administrations." He dismissed the bill before him as containing appropriations for the improvement of rivers and harbors "upon which there exists no foreign commerce." Polk issued a second and more extensive veto message in December 1847. The legislation in question had as its self-proclaimed purpose the funding of internal improvements in the Wisconsin territory. It included only $5,000 for Wisconsin—the other half-million dollars went for various pork-barrel projects in the states. The president could find no power in the Constitution to fund internal improvements; the matter had therefore been left to the states. He expressly rejected James Monroe's attempt to graft a broad spending power onto the general welfare clause. There was no evidence, he maintained, that the Constitutional Convention intended to devise such a power or that the ratifying conventions intended to grant it.[275] Polk acknowledged that advocates of the constitutionality of river and harbor appropriations had more recently concentrated their efforts on the commerce clause, but he had no sympathy for that view, either. To those who believed the commerce clause authorized the bill before him, Polk propounded a sharp interrogatory. "If the definition of the word 'regulate' is to include the provision of means to carry on commerce, then have Congress not only power to deepen harbors, clear out rivers, dig canals, and make roads, but also to build ships, railroad cars, and other vehicles, all of which are necessary to commerce?" He did not buy it—in his view, the clause "confers no creative powers."[276] Polk's vetoes triggered a severe reaction on the part of northerners—Whigs and Democrats alike—as river and harbor appropriations dropped to just $24,000 by 1848. In Chicago—already a Democratic city—the vetoes placed party leaders such as Congressman John Wentworth in a tight spot. Ships in the harbor set their sails at half mast in protest, and cynics named a sandbar at the mouth of the Chicago River Mount Polk. (In downstate river coun-

275. Richardson, *Messages and Papers of the Presidents,* 5:2312–13, 2470.

276. "The power to regulate commerce seems now to be chiefly relied upon especially in reference to the improvement of harbors and rivers." Ibid., 5:2475. For a comprehensive discussion of Polk's approach to the constitutionality of internal improvement subsidies, see Currie, *Constitution in Congress: Democrats and Whigs,* 18–22.

ties, snags became Polk stalks.)[277] In neighboring Indiana there was widespread resentment over the termination of funding for work on the Cumberland Road and the harbor at Michigan City.[278] During the summer of 1847 an enormous rivers and harbors convention met in Chicago. A good deal of angry discussion took place, much of it over the "saltwater Constitution" that existed nowhere but in the minds of selfish easterners. The convention issued resolutions proclaiming that the commerce power and the right to "provide for the common defense" authorized federal funding of internal improvements.[279] The issue proved disastrous for Democrats in 1848, as many northerners held the failure of the party's presidential candidate, Lewis Cass, to attend the Chicago convention against him—despite the fact that he voted for river and harbor bills in the Senate. Cass was also hurt by the reduction of tariff rates in 1846 and the resentment that followed in the Northeast.[280] Democrats could ignore the demands for more vigorous governmental policies that came with the market revolution, but they did so at their own peril. By 1850 strict construction had, it seemed, become more untenable than ever.

### STRICT CONSTRUCTION AND THE TANEY COURT

Confusion over the meaning of the commerce clause was not limited to Congress. The Supreme Court struggled with it as well. The Court's difficulties arose in part from the increasingly popular idea—at least among lawyers—that the clause prohibited all state legislation affecting interstate commerce. The debate within the high court over the meaning of the clause that took place between 1835 and 1860, as played out in opinions that ran into the hundreds of pages, proved so convoluted that no one was able to draw much guidance from it. The confusion stemmed in part from the vague language of the clause itself and in part from the fact that the "exclusivity" question had ramifications for American Federalism that arguably surpassed the spending power issue in importance. If, as men such as Daniel Webster

277. Pease, *Frontier State,* 334.
278. Logan Esarey, *History of Indiana from Its Exploration to 1922* (Dayton, Ohio: Dayton Historical Publishing Co., 1922), 1:541.
279. Bessie Louise Pierce, *History of Chicago: The Beginning of a City,* 2 vols. (New York: Knopf, 1937), 1:425–28.
280. Van Deusen, *Jacksonian Era,* 258, 260. See also Joseph G. Rayback, *Free Soil: The Election of 1848* (Lexington: University Press of Kentucky, 1970), 263.

and Joseph Story believed, the commerce clause alone rendered void all state measures that affected interstate or foreign commerce, hundreds of state statutes were unconstitutional. Understandably, the justices did not embrace that tack. Yet it was not until the 1850s that they found an approach to the commerce clause that was acceptable to even a bare majority of the Court. When agreement finally arrived, the justices settled upon a method that was almost completely devoid of any connection with the intent of the Founders—or any real limitation upon federal authority.

This encroachment occurred despite the fact that Democratic presidents stocked the Supreme Court with a majority of strict constructionists during the period between 1829 and 1849. To the horror of Whigs, Jackson nominated his crony and hatchet man, Roger Brooke Taney, to succeed John Marshall as chief justice in 1836. Although he had been a Federalist at one time, Taney entered the national stage as a Democrat. The Maryland lawyer provided the Jackson administration with the legal acumen necessary to stand up to an opposition party that included Daniel Webster and Henry Clay. In 1836 Jackson nominated Philip Barbour of Virginia to the Supreme Court. Barbour had been one of the House of Representatives' most doctrinaire and skillful interpreters of the Constitution. He served a term as Speaker and helped crush the Adams administration's internal improvements program. Many southern Democrats favored him over Van Buren for the Democratic vice presidential nomination in 1832. In 1841 Peter Daniel was appointed to the Court. The Virginian subscribed to the restrained conception of federal authority that increasingly held sway in his native state and throughout the South. In 1845 Levi Woodbury became an associate justice. As a member of the Supreme Court of New Hampshire, he voted with the majority when it held that the state's reorganization of Dartmouth College did not violate the contract clause.

The Taney Court issued the first of several difficult decisions involving the commerce clause in 1837: *Mayor of the City of New York v. Miln*. Masters of vessels arriving at New York City were required by state law to turn in passenger lists. Counsel for Miln claimed the statute constituted a regulation of foreign commerce and that this power was vested exclusively in Congress. The state countered that the law was merely a police regulation, and the Supreme Court agreed (Justice Barbour writing for the court). The case was the first in which a justice explained the limits of the commerce clause by pointing out what sort of state acts it did *not* render inoperative. In his concurring opinion, Chief Justice Taney carved the broadest possible swath for the states. Permissible laws, he wrote, included all those "whose operation was within the territorial limits of the state, and upon the persons and things within its jurisdiction." Justice Story dissented. While he conceded that the states could enact "health laws," even these could not conflict with Congress's "power to regulate commerce."[281]

A more difficult test occurred ten years later in the License Cases (1847). The Court refused to invalidate three state laws that prohibited or taxed the sale of liquor in small containers. While the laws were designed to discourage the consumption of alcohol, some viewed them as impermissible regulations of foreign commerce and/or taxes upon imports. The justices could not agree on a single opinion and issued six different ones, even though all agreed the laws were permissible. John McLean, Levi Woodbury, and Robert Grier held that the laws did not regulate commerce but concerned only health and morals and thus qualified as permissible regulations under the states' police powers. Chief Justice Taney pointed out that the statutes had as their primary purpose the discouragement of alcohol consumption and not the raising of revenue. State legislatures were free, in Taney's view, to reduce alcohol consumption, as they possessed the power to "guard the health or morals of citizens, although such laws may discourage importation." States could enact such laws even if the acts constituted regulations of foreign commerce, so long as they did not conflict with federal statutes.[282] (During the 1840s and '50s eleven states banned the sale of alcohol.) Taney attacked the notion that the Founders viewed the commerce clause as prohibiting all state legislation affecting interstate or foreign commerce. The Constitution, he pointed out, contained explicit bans of state legislation in certain areas, such as the rule against issuing paper money.[283] Thus, if the Founders had intended to ban all state legislation that affected interstate commerce, they would have used words expressly prohibiting it. Justice Woodbury pointed out that banning the sale of an item was not the same thing as prohibiting the importation of it. Besides, he continued, there were already numerous state laws on the books aimed at intemperance, and who ever regarded bans on Sunday liquor sales as prohibiting imports? Legislatures had long acted to keep out all manner of persons and things, such as opium and lot-

281. 36 U.S. 102, 130, 139, 156 (1837).
282. 46 U.S. 504, 592–93, 627–31, 631–32, 577–78 (1847).
283. Article I, Section 10, contains approximately eighteen such prohibitions.

tery tickets, Woodbury concluded, despite the fact that such laws obviously reduced commerce.[284]

Antebellum confusion over the commerce clause reached its height in 1849 with the Supreme Court's opinion in the Passenger Cases. The litigation arose out of New York and Massachusetts statutes that provided for the collection of money from arriving passengers and shipmasters. The proceeds were used to fund marine hospitals. A 5-4 majority found the statutes unconstitutional. Although no one wrote for the majority (the justices could not agree on a single line of reasoning), John McLean held that the commerce power encompassed navigation, that it was exclusive, and that the laws in question constituted impermissible regulations of foreign commerce. There was clearly a national policy of encouraging immigration, he claimed, and the states could no more prohibit the introduction of immigrants or retard the process with taxes than they could impose a tax upon persons arriving from other states. Justice John Catron believed that the laws impermissibly regulated the same subject matter as federal statutes enacted to protect immigrants from exploitation. Nor were the laws enacted under the states' police powers, in his view; rather, they were revenue measures that attempted to tap into foreign commerce.[285]

Chief Justice Taney dissented. The power of states to keep out particular classes of persons had, he thought, been recognized in *Groves v. Slaughter* (1841).[286] (In that case, the Supreme Court held that a provision of the Mississippi constitution barring the importation of slaves did not violate the commerce clause.) If they could ban persons, surely they could tax those wishing to enter. In addition, the Supreme Court had already rejected the idea that passengers qualified as commerce in *New York City v. Miln* (1837).[287] Taney repeated the point he had made in the License Cases: if the Constitutional Convention had intended to prohibit all state regulations of interstate and foreign commerce, it would have said so with an explicit ban. Justice Woodbury issued perhaps the most thoughtful dissent. He acknowledged widespread confusion over state laws in the areas of commerce, taxation, and the "police power," and he observed that what one person might consider "matters of taxation" another might consider "matters of commerce." Woodbury insisted that state laws on the books "for local purposes," such as those that imposed quarantines or prohibited paupers, criminals, or poisons, qualified

284. 46 U.S. at 504, 579, 620, 621, 628.
286. 40 U.S. 449 (1841).

285. 48 U.S. 283, 403–9, 441–44 (1849).
287. 36 U.S. 102 (1837).

as local measures and hence were constitutional even though they affected foreign commerce.[288]

The justices were finally able to agree on a compromise approach in *Cooley v. Board of Wardens of the Port of Philadelphia* (1852). The Court refused to invalidate a Pennsylvania law requiring that all ships entering its waters use local pilots. Speaking for the Court, Justice Benjamin Curtis observed that Congress had authorized the continuation of state pilotage laws in 1789. The most important aspect of the decision came with Curtis's description of the appropriate line between state and federal authority over commerce. "Whatever subjects of this power are in their nature national, or admit only of one uniform system, or plan of regulation, may justly be said to be of such a nature as to require exclusive legislation by Congress."[289] Unfortunately, Curtis failed to explain how future courts should determine what subjects were "national" and thus required uniform legislation. Nor did his method appear to contemplate the more restrictive notions of the commerce power that characterized the ratification debates.

The commerce clause and the confusion surrounding it created a situation ripe for the expansion of federal authority, simply because, without the original understanding attached, the justices were able to affix to the clause whatever meaning they liked. Yet the Court's interpretation of the commerce clause did not have any immediate adverse effects. The same could not be said for the Court's activities in other areas. *Dartmouth College v. Woodward* continued to bear fruit during the 1830s and '40s. Under the holding of that case, state legislatures could not revoke corporate charters because doing so would violate the contract clause. Interested parties thereafter began extracting ridiculously favorable charters from state legislators, confident in the knowledge that regardless of the circumstances involved in their passage (such as bribery), the federal courts would protect their investment. New Jersey granted the Camden & Amboy Railroad a charter under which no one else could build competing lines across the state.[290] In effect, a private corporation obtained the exclusive right to provide land-based transportation between the nation's two largest cities (New York City and Philadelphia). Similar monopolies were handed out in other states. In July 1841 Con-

288. 48 U.S. at 471, 545–46.
289. 53 U.S. 299, 317–20 (1852). As Curtis pointed out, Congress had specifically authorized state legislatures to enact pilotage laws when it first enacted legislation on the subject in 1789. See 1 *Stats at Large* 53, 54 (August 7, 1789).
290. See *Camden & Amboy Railroad v. Briggs*, 22 (N.J. App.) 623 (1850).

gressman Lewis Tappan attacked the *Dartmouth College* ruling on the floor of the House of Representatives. It created a situation in which "our legislation has run so much towards promoting private interests, and the encouragement of monopolies that we have insensibly raised up a host of interested men to clamor for the preservation of their privileges, under the named of vested rights, and the perpetuity of their monopolies, under the specious character of contracts."[291] *Dartmouth College* also impeded attempts to limit the excessive issuing of banknotes because it made bank charters irrevocable. Without the right to revoke charters, the states found it difficult to ensure that banks did not violate them by printing notes in excessive amounts or by refusing to redeem them.

*Dartmouth College* proved to be the among the most unpopular Supreme Court decisions of the first half of the nineteenth century. Democrats responded to the decision by arguing that it was flawed and should be reversed—corporate charters were not contracts, and the charters of state banks could be repealed if necessary.[292] Many states attempted to remedy the situation with general incorporation laws under which anyone could form a corporation if they filed the necessary paperwork with state officials.[293] These statutes did not provide the exclusive privileges, such as issuing paper notes, that lobbyists often included in special charters. Consequently, private acts that recognized a particular corporation's existence and rights remained the favorite among business interests even after the onset of general corporation laws. It was not until the 1870s, when state constitutions were amended to prohibit the use of private acts to establish corporations, that legislatures stopped granting charters packed with special privileges.[294]

Approximately a third of the constitutional law cases tried by the Supreme Court during Chief Justice Taney's tenure concerned the contract clause.[295] Much of the litigation revolved around laws that improperly al-

---

291. *Congressional Globe*, 27th Cong., 1st sess., Appendix, 10:196.

292. For contemporary essays arguing that the *Dartmouth College* decision was in error and that corporate charters did not fall within the scope of the contract clause, see "The Supreme Court of the United States: Its Judges and Jurisdiction," *United States Democratic Review* 1, no. 2 (January 1838): 162–63; "Speech of Charles J. Ingersoll to Pennsylvania Convention on Legislative and Judicial Control of Charters," *United States Democratic Review* 5, no. 13 (January 1839): 99–144; and "The Repeal Question," *United States Democratic Review* 9, no. 38 (August 1841): 107–10.

293. Bray Hammond, *Banks and Politics in America from the Revolution to the Civil War* (Princeton: Princeton University Press, 1957), 578–79.

294. Mark W. Summers, *The Plundering Generation: Corruption and the Crisis of the Union, 1849–1861* (New York: Oxford University Press, 1987), 100.

295. Currie, *Constitution in the Supreme Court*, 211.

tered contracts between private citizens. Other contract clause suits concerned state regulations of business enterprises that had been the recipients of corporate charters. The large number of suits in this area stemmed from the conviction—rapidly spreading among lawyers and judges—that the contract clause prohibited acts that even incidentally affected the value of these charters. An early example occurred in *Charles River Bridge v. Warren Bridge* (1837), the first major contract clause case decided by the Supreme Court after Taney's appointment as chief justice. It revolved around the rather extraordinary question of whether the state of Massachusetts could authorize the construction of a second bridge across the Charles River. According to the attorneys for the Charles River Bridge, which had been constructed under a 1795 law, the state could not, for a second bridge would impair the value of its charter by reducing the amount of tolls the bridge owners would collect. (Traffic would be lost to the new bridge, which was nearby and over which travel was free.) As occurred in *Dartmouth College*, attorneys for the Charles River Bridge treated the law primarily as a taking of private property; they offered only a few comments about the contract clause. Attorneys for the Warren Bridge owners did not ask the Court to overturn *Dartmouth College*. Instead, they pointed out that the Charles River Bridge charter did not explicitly prohibit construction of other bridges across the river. Writing for the Court, Taney held that the question was whether the owners of the Charles River Bridge had been granted the exclusive right to operate bridges across the Charles River. Finding no such promise in their charter, Taney refused to accept the argument that it implied one. The state legislature was therefore free to issue a charter for the construction of a second bridge. Thus the principle was born that corporate charters bestowed only those rights explicitly granted.[296] Justice Story, Daniel Webster, and others of their school were infuriated; they saw the decision as an attack on property rights. That the Supreme Court had allowed the *Dartmouth College* doctrine to stand, despite its tenuous reasoning and disastrous consequences, was of little consolation to these critics.

In an 1854 case *(Piqua v. Knoop)*, the Supreme Court held void a state law raising taxes on the grounds that it violated the contract clause. An 1845 Ohio general incorporation statute detailed the steps by which banks could be formed. The same law also listed the taxes that the banks thereby in-

296. 36 U.S. 420, 453–61, 465, 544–52 (1837).

corporated would pay. The Ohio legislature subsequently attempted to raise taxes beyond the level mentioned in the general incorporation act; banks formed under the 1845 law sued. In his opinion for the Court, Justice John McLean ruled that the 1845 law constituted a contract and that the state could not increase taxes on banks organized under it. Associate Justice John Archibald Campbell pointed out in dissent that more than fifty banks had been incorporated under the act and that no consideration had been paid for what the majority called a contract. In addition, the law explicitly reserved the power to raise taxes beyond the level set in the general incorporation law. It provided that the legislature of Ohio "imposes no limit on its power, nor term to the exercise of its will, nor binds itself to adhere to this or any other rule of taxation."[297] In a companion case, Justice Peter Daniel warned that the *Dartmouth College* doctrine placed the states at the mercy of corrupt legislatures. "I never can believe in that, to my mind suicidal doctrine, which confers upon one legislature, the creatures and limited agents of the sovereign people, the power, by breach of duty and by transcending the commission with which they are clothed, to bind forever and irrevocably their creator, for whose benefit and by whose authority alone they are delegated to act, to consequences however mischievous and destructive."[298]

The Taney Court issued its last major contract clause decision in 1856. Ohio drafted a constitution in 1851 that purported to repeal the 1845 general incorporation statute. The Supreme Court held that the state had once again exceeded its lawful authority because the 1845 law was a contract— Ohio could not repeal it with a new constitution any more than it could with a statute. The offending portion of the 1851 state constitution was therefore void. In dissent, Justice Campbell complained again of the legacy of the *Dartmouth College* decision. The "courts cannot look to the corruption, the blindness, nor the mischievous effects of state legislation, to determine its binding operation." Thus, the Court "becomes the patron of such legislation, by furnishing motives of incalculable power to the corporations to stimulate it, and affording stability and security to the successful effort."[299] In early 1859 the *Dartmouth College* doctrine came under attack in the House of Representatives. Philemon Bliss recalled the strange history of the contract clause's interpretation. "Does the state, tired of monopoly, seek to grant to

297. *Piqua Branch of the State Bank of Ohio v. Knoop*, 57 U.S. 369, 415 (1854).
298. *Ohio Life and Trust Company v. DeBolt*, 57 U.S. 416, 443 (1854).
299. *Dodge v. Woolsey*, 59 U.S. 331, 371 (1856).

others the same privilege hitherto given alone to a corporation, or to otherwise change the law creating it, we find the Court making the strange discovery that all charters are contracts, and beyond the control of the state." The disastrous consequences produced by *Dartmouth College* and its progeny led Bliss to observe that an independent federal judiciary in the American sense of the term was something of a novelty, and a destructive one. When the British coined the phrase "independent judiciary," they were speaking of the need to protect judges from the Crown. The judges of that nation had always been subject to removal by Parliament.[300]

While the structural defects of the federal judiciary remained, the difficulties surrounding corporate charters and the unsavory means used to obtain them eased in time. By 1865 fourteen states had added clauses to their constitutions providing that all powers not expressly bestowed upon corporations via their charters were retained by the state.[301] In 1880 the Supreme Court ruled that the states could not under any circumstances surrender their police powers.[302] Corruption did not disappear; on the contrary, the Gilded Age saw it reach unprecedented heights. Yet the venality that overtook the country's legislative bodies by the end of the century received encouragement during the antebellum period from the *Dartmouth College* decision of 1819.

### SLAVERY AND THE CONSTITUTION, 1789–1820

Disputed exercises of federal power worsened sectional friction and distrust of the federal government during the early nineteenth century, even as a heightened sense of nationalism manifested itself throughout the country. The Louisiana Purchase and the embargo alienated New England; steep tariffs offended the South, and federal ownership of vast tracts of land within supposedly sovereign states frustrated the West. Democrats recoiled from the growth of the congressional spending power as well as the Supreme Court's excesses, while Whigs looked with disgust upon the Jackson administration's use of federal offices to accumulate power over state parties and newspapers. It was in this tense if optimistic atmosphere that the issue of

---

300. *Congressional Globe*, 35th Cong., 2d sess., February 7, 1859, Appendix, 28:73.

301. Wright, *Contract Clause of the Constitution*, 84.

302. *Stone v. Mississippi*, 101 U.S. 814 (1880). (The state of Mississippi made the mistake of prohibiting lottery sales after allowing a corporation to be formed for the purpose of selling lottery tickets.)

slavery appeared on the scene. For four decades it imposed increasing pressure on the nation's political system, in no small part because of the growing ability of federal officials to impose their views upon all parts of the nation. Centralization and discord over slavery led southerners to fear that their northern brethren—already perceived as inadequately mindful of the limits of federal authority—would use the growing power of the national government to undermine the "peculiar institution." Northerners suspected that the South's disproportionate influence in Washington would result in a proslavery agenda being forced upon them. Western expansion worsened tensions, as each section feared being surrounded by territories and states devoted to a hostile social system.

During the second half of the eighteenth century, northern states began abolishing slavery. Many northerners feared that ratification would burden them with responsibility for slavery in the South.[303] In response, Federalists assured northerners that they need not worry about a problem over which they had no control.[304] Suspicions lingered in part because the Constitution provided protections for the slave-owning southern states that seemed disproportionate. It apportioned seats in the House of Representatives according to the number of free persons and three-fifths of the total number of "all other persons" in each state. This provision gave southern states additional representatives for their slaves, though the slaves could not vote. (Federalists argued that because direct taxes were tied to property—including slaves— representation should be as well.)[305] Article IV, Section 2 obligated northern states to return escaped slaves to their southern masters. Article I, Section 8 withheld the power to ban the importation of slaves until 1808. The Constitutional Convention was paralyzed for a time by this clause; northerners accepted it only when southerners dropped their demand for a provision requiring the approval of two-thirds of each house for tariffs.

Further indignities for the North followed ratification. Congress passed a Fugitive Slave Act in 1793 despite the fact that none of the enumerated powers mentioned the subject. The fugitive slave clause appeared in an area of the Constitution—Article IV, Section 2—that imposed obligations

303. See, for example, the article by "Phileleutheros" in the *Hampshire Gazette*, May 21, 1788, in Storing, *Complete Anti-Federalist*, 4:268–69.

304. See "General William Heath on Slavery," January 30, 1788, in Bailyn, *Debate on the Constitution*, 1:915.

305. James Madison, *The Federalist*, No. 54, in Rossiter, *Federalist Papers*, 336–41.

upon the states. It did not appear to bestow authority upon Congress. With the Louisiana Purchase of 1803, the United States government greatly increased the extent of territory in North America that was open to slavery. The purchase of Florida (1819) provided the institution with additional space. And then there was the political influence of slaveholders—a southern-dominated party (Republicans and later Democrats) dominated national politics between 1801 and 1861. Finally, the nation's capital had by 1820 become the world's greatest slave-trading market, to which slave families were brought to be broken up, with their members sold and taken away to all parts of the South.

If slavery benefited from the ratification of the Constitution and the success of the government thereby established, it remained a subject of regret throughout the nation during the late eighteenth and early nineteenth centuries. In 1774 Thomas Jefferson—himself a slaveholder—declared that abolition of the institution was the "great object of desire in the colonies."[306] In 1784 the Confederation Congress came within a single vote of prohibiting slavery in all the territories, and three years later it banned it in the Northwest, with every state voting in the affirmative (the Northwest Ordinance). During the 1790s Americans formed antislavery societies, most of them in the South.[307] In 1807 Congress prohibited the importation of slaves, effective January 1, 1808. Southerners toyed with the idea of abolition in their own states until well into the nineteenth century. In a June 1819 letter, James Madison—also a slaveholder—described a plan for gradual emancipation with compensation for owners. He called for the program to be carried out at national expense on the theory that it was a national evil, albeit with the obligatory proviso that a constitutional amendment had to be enacted before it could be put into to effect.[308] During his famous clash with Daniel Webster, Senator Robert Y. Hayne of South Carolina acknowledged the evil of slavery, though he insisted that the present generation had no responsibility for it ("we of the present day found it already made to our hands").[309] As late as 1832 Virginia gave serious consideration to a plan for gradual emancipation.[310]

306. Instructions to first delegation of Virginia to the Continental Congress (1774), *Writings of Jefferson*, 1:201.
307. Louis Filler, *The Crusade against Slavery* (New York: Harper & Brothers, 1960), 15.
308. *Writings of Madison*, 8:437–47.
309. *Register of Debates*, 21st Cong., 1st sess., January 1830, 6:46.
310. Peterson, *Great Triumvirate*, 257.

Yet the heyday of the southern antislavery movement had already passed by 1830. Most southern politicians had come to view protection of the institution as equivalent to the defense of their section. The change of heart stemmed from the fact that slavery had made a stunning comeback from its eighteenth-century decline. The invention of the cotton gin in 1793 eased the removal of seeds and caused the price of cotton to drop substantially. Reduced cost led to an increase in demand and therefore in production. The number of bales that passed through New Orleans on their way to foreign lands exploded, from thirty-seven thousand in 1816 to almost a million in 1840. In 1850 more than a billion bales left the country.[311] While planters had resigned themselves to the inevitable demise of an unprofitable system in 1780, by 1850 they gazed upon the raw material for the world's textile industry. Slavery had evolved from a colonial relic into a critical element of the Industrial Revolution.[312]

As slavery became more popular in the South, it gave increasing offense in the North. This change in outlook first manifested itself in the controversy surrounding the admission of Illinois in 1818. As had been the case with Indiana and Ohio, the state's earliest settlers were largely southerners. Many brought slaves with them in violation of the Northwest Ordinance, which banned the institution in the Northwest. Illinois tried to enter the Union with a state constitution that, while it appeared to abolish slavery, allowed it to exist in other forms.[313] Thirty-four members of the House of Representatives therefore voted against admission.[314] Although the state was admitted after repealing its "black codes," the Illinois legislature subsequently reenacted them.[315] Illinois was only the calm before the storm. In February 1819 the House took up a bill authorizing a constitutional convention in the Missouri territory—the first step toward admission. Congressman James Tallmadge Jr. of New York suggested an amendment declaring "all free who should be born into the [Missouri] territory after its admission into the Union." Lawmakers immediately perceived the significance of the proposal. As Speaker John Taylor of New York put it, the question was simple: "Has Congress the power to require of Missouri a constitutional prohibition against the fur-

311. Commager and Morison, *Growth of the American Republic*, 521.

312. Johnson, *History of the American People*, 312.

313. Don E. Fehrenbacher, *The Dred Scott Case: Its Significance in American Law and Politics* (New York: Oxford University Press, 1978), 85.

314. For the debate and vote, see *Annals of Congress*, 15th Cong., 2d sess., November 1818, 33:305–11.

315. Dangerfield, *Awakening of American Nationalism*, 110.

ther introduction of slavery, as a condition of her admission to the Union?" Mr. Taylor thought the answer was yes. If Congress has the power to admit new states, surely it has the power to refuse to admit them, "and much more has it the power of prescribing such conditions of admission as may be judged reasonable." Ohio, he pointed out, had been admitted with the proviso that nothing in its state constitution violate the Northwest Ordinance. Conditions had been imposed on the admission of Indiana, Illinois, and Mississippi as well.[316]

It was hard to argue with Taylor's position—though the question remained as to how Congress would enforce such an agreement once the state was admitted and became a sovereign member of the Union. Henry Clay (a slaveholder) insisted that Congress could not require that Missouri ban slavery in exchange for admission. If Tallmadge's amendment became law, he warned, it would violate the privileges and immunities clause. John Taylor disagreed—slaveholding was not among the privileges contemplated by the clause. Phillip Barbour of Virginia thought Congress lacked the power to demand that Missouri ban slavery in exchange for admission. As he saw it, even the Northwest Ordinance was void—the states that had been carved out of the Northwest Territory could allow slavery if they wished to do so. Barbour explained that Virginia had ceded its claims to lands in the Northwest on the condition that the states carved out of it would be equal in their independence to the rest of the states—retaining, like them, the power to establish slavery.[317]

In February 1819 the House added the Tallmadge amendment to the Missouri bill by a vote of 87-76.[318] The Senate refused to go along, and the matter stood deadlocked when Congress adjourned in March 1819. Newspaper editors, politicians, and citizens debated the admission bill with an ardor not seen since the ratification debates. While the question of whether Congress could ban slavery as a condition of admission proved exceedingly difficult, the territories question was a simple matter. Although the territories clause did not receive extensive discussion during the ratification struggle, its terms appeared broad enough to encompass a power to ban slavery.[319] In

316. *Annals of Congress,* 15th Cong., 2d sess., February 1819, 33:1166, 1172, 1182. For a more detailed survey of the constitutional aspects of the Missouri Compromise debates, see Currie, *Constitution in Congress: Jeffersonians,* 235–49.

317. *Annals of Congress,* 15th Cong., 2d sess., February 1819, 33:1182, 1187.

318. Ibid., 1214.

319. U.S. Constitution, Article IV, Section 3.

August 1789, two years after the Confederation enacted the Northwest Ordinance banning slavery in the Northwest, the first Congress—which included nineteen members of the Constitutional Convention—adopted it.[320] In 1819 President Monroe's cabinet agreed unanimously that Congress could prohibit slavery in the territories.[321] James Madison disagreed; in a November 1819 letter he insisted that the powers granted by the territories clause did not include authority to ban slavery in the territories.[322]

When the sixteenth Congress met for its first session in December 1819, the Missouri question once again took center stage. A complication developed when Maine applied for statehood. Henry Clay claimed that Kentucky was forced to wait eighteen months to be admitted alongside Vermont during the 1790s. Maine could wait as well. On January 26 Henry Storrs of New York proposed a compromise: in exchange for the admission of Missouri without a ban on slavery, a dividing line would be extended in the western territories along the thirty-eighth parallel, north of which slavery would be prohibited. Most southern representatives did not take issue with the assertion of a power to ban slavery in the territories; only one argued that such a prohibition was beyond the powers of Congress. Alexander Smythe of Virginia believed the territories clause bestowed only a custodial power over property; it did not provide "political jurisdiction." Southerners were far more concerned with the attempt to impose conditions upon Missouri's admission as a state. Complete discretion for Congress in this area would be dangerous, in their view. Surely Congress could not, one legislator asked, admit a state on the condition that it authorize Congress to "stipulate for the regulation of [its] press?" Charles Pinckney of South Carolina agreed. Even if a power to admit states implied a power to refuse to admit them, it did not follow that Congress had authority "to insist upon any terms that impair the sovereignty of the admitted state as it would otherwise stand in the Union."[323]

In early January the House passed a bill authorizing a constitutional convention in Maine. Upon receiving it, the Senate attached an amendment admitting Missouri. Shortly thereafter, Senator Jesse Thomas of Illinois pro

320. See 1 *Stats at Large* 50, 51 (August 7, 1789).

321. Nevins, *Diary of John Quincy Adams*, 231–32.

322. *Writings of Madison*, 9:6.

323. *Annals of Congress*, 16th Cong., 1st sess., December 1819, 35:831, 940, 1003, 992–93, 399. Another lawmaker held that the prohibition of slavery in a prospective state would constitute a taking of property without due process of law (ibid., 998).

posed to amend the bill with a clause prohibiting slavery in the Louisiana Territory north of 36´30˝. The institution would therefore be allowed in only a small portion of the territory (the area that would become the states of Oklahoma and Arkansas). The amendment was adopted and the Senate approved the bill. The House initially rejected the compromise; two weeks of lobbying resulted in passage of the Missouri bill, with the Thomas amendment attached, on March 2, 90-87.[324] Fifteen northern representatives who changed their votes made the difference.[325] To the chagrin of politicians on both sides of the aisle, the controversy arose again later in 1820 and divided the nation once more. Missouri devised a constitution that required the enactment of legislation prohibiting free blacks from entering the state. Some believed that this provision violated the Constitution's privileges and immunities clause. A House committee reported that it could not answer the question with any certainty, as it was the one clause in the Constitution whose meaning was the most "difficult to construe."[326] The clause had largely been ignored during the ratification debates. Thus the limits of strict construction—how could the meaning of a part of the Constitution be limited to the intent of the Founders and the ratifying conventions if that intent was unknown?

Henry Clay thought the bar upon entry by blacks violated the U.S. Constitution. Yet he still favored admission, on the theory that the federal courts would do away with the offending provision.[327] Others were not so sure.[328] To placate them, Senator John Eaton of Tennessee proposed an amendment declaring that Congress did not assent to any portion of the Missouri state constitution that violated the privileges and immunities clause. The matter ended up in the hands of a joint committee, which in February 1821 suggested a proviso similar to that proposed by Eaton. It added a clause requir-

324. Ibid., 363, 1586–87.

325. Dangerfield, *Era of Good Feelings*, 228.

326. *Annals of Congress*, 16th Cong., 2d sess., November 1820, 37:453. The clause received virtually no discussion either at the Constitutional Convention or during ratification. Thus the committee's warning that while no other clause was more conducive to a "beneficial connection of the states," the privileges and immunities clause held out the potential for constructions that would "completely break down" the "defensive power" of the states and thereby "lead more directly to their consolidation" (ibid., 454).

327. Remini, *Henry Clay*, 185–86. Three years later, Justice Bushrod Washington confirmed the House committee's concerns with a description of the rights granted by the clause that could not have been more vague: "Protection by the government; the enjoyment of life and liberty, with the right to acquire and possess property of every kind, and to pursue and obtain happiness and safety." *Corfield v. Coryell*, 6 Federal Cases 546, 551 (1823).

328. See, for example, the speech of Gideon Tomlinson (Connecticut) of February 12, 1821, in *Annals of Congress*, 16th Cong., 2d sess., 37:1096–97.

ing that the Missouri legislature pass an act declaring its assent to the condition, whereupon the state's admission "shall be considered as complete."[329] Both houses of Congress approved the measure, and the president signed it in March 1821. In response, the Missouri legislature passed a resolution declaring the action requested by Congress to be unnecessary—nothing in its constitution violated the privileges and immunities clause. President Monroe, eager to bring the episode to a close, declared Missouri admitted to the Union on August 10, 1821. Four years later, in 1825, the Missouri legislature passed a law prohibiting free blacks from entering the state.[330]

The hostility unleashed by the Missouri Compromise dispute led many to fear that the Union might fail. Southerners would not tolerate conditions on the admission of new states; the North, for its part, made clear it would not sit quietly while the continent was converted into a vast slave pen. No wonder Henry Clay wrote to John Quincy Adams that the entire episode had led him to consider a rather stunning possibility—that within five years the Union could be "divided into three distinct confederacies."[331]

### SLAVERY IN THE AGE OF JACKSON

Many Americans shared Clay's fears for the future of the Union. This concern was partially responsible for the negative light in which even northerners viewed abolitionists and their demand for the eradication of slavery throughout the United States, even in the South. Nevertheless, the movement accumulated momentum during the 1830s. Based in New England and upstate New York, abolitionism followed the tailwinds of that great religious revival known as the Second Great Awakening.[332] The cause derived additional strength from Europe's disavowal of the institution. Parliament prohibited slavery throughout the British Empire in 1833, and the continent's other colonial powers followed its lead. By midcentury most of the nations of Latin America had outlawed the practice. In the United States, new organizations formed to carry the abolitionist message to the country. William Lloyd Garrison launched his *Liberator* in Boston in 1831, and the American Antislavery Society was formed in 1833. By 1838 it had 1,350 chapters and almost 250,000 members.[333]

329. Ibid., 41, 1830.
331. Quoted in Remini, *Henry Clay*, 182.
333. Filler, *Crusade against Slavery*, 67.

330. Dangerfield, *Era of Good Feelings*, 242.
332. Sellers, *Market Revolution*, 202.

The cause of abolition won far more enemies than friends during its nascent phase. Between northern contempt for the movement and southern determination to protect slavery, members of Congress got no argument when they proclaimed their belief that the federal government did not have the power to abolish the institution in the states. In March 1790 the House adopted a resolution holding that Congress had "no authority to interfere in the emancipation of slaves, or in the treatment of them within any of the states."[334] Daniel Webster began his second reply to Hayne by insisting that he had no designs on slavery; so far as he knew, no northern member of Congress had ever introduced legislation aimed at emancipating slaves in the South.[335] Charles Sumner, the fiery antislavery senator from Massachusetts during the 1850s, declared it a mistake to say that antislavery elements in the North "seek to interfere, through Congress, with slavery in the states."[336] Tempestuous southerners such as John Randolph and John C. Calhoun on occasion imputed such motives to their northern brethren; their protests fell on deaf ears simply because no northern politician—not one—claimed any such power for Congress, at least in peacetime.[337] Even abolitionists themselves acknowledged that the Constitution did not give the national government power over slavery in the states. William Lloyd's description of the Constitution as a "covenant with death and an agreement with hell" stemmed from the embittered belief that it bound the North to slavery and at the same time withheld from the federal government the ability to do anything about it. The 1848 Free Soil Party platform also took the view that slavery in the states was not the "responsibility" of the national government.[338] John Quincy Adams was alone in daring to depart even slightly from this consensus. In an 1836 speech he pointed out that in the event of armed conflict in the South, Congress could, under its war powers, abolish slavery in the region.[339]

Even as they despised abolitionists, northerners objected to the extension of slavery into areas under the supervision of the national government,

<hr />

334. *Annals of Congress*, 1st Cong., 2d sess., March 23, 1790, 2:1524.

335. *Register of Debates* 21st Cong., 1st sess., January 27, 1830, 6.1:61.

336. *Congressional Globe*, 33d Cong., 1st sess., February 20, 1854, Appendix, 23:269.

337. See the January 31, 1824, speech of John Randolph, in which he claimed that the commerce clause did not authorize the general survey bill: "If Congress possesses the power to do what is proposed by this bill, [it] may . . . emancipate every slave in the United States." *Annals of Congress*, 18th Cong., 1st sess., 41:1308.

338. See McKee, *National Conventions and Platforms*, 67.

339. *Register of Debates*, 24th Cong., 1st sess., May 25, 1836, 12.4:4047.

i.e., the capital and the territories. As Charles Sumner later explained, "since we at the north are responsible for slavery wherever it exists under the jurisdiction of Congress, it is unpardonable in us not to exert every power we possess to enlist Congress against it."[340] The northern desire avoid any contact with slavery collided sharply with southern designs on Texas. Although some Americans thought it formed a part of the Louisiana Purchase, Texas had been part of Mexico from the time of that country's birth in 1821.[341] It did not take long before Texans developed a long list of grievances. By 1830 the gap proved insurmountable, as American immigrants made up three-quarters of the population of Texas.[342] A people accustomed to governing themselves chafed at the Mexican government's heavy-handed and corrupt rule. They also took offense when it announced the abolition of slavery in 1829. After years of smoldering and false starts, Texans finally won their independence at the Battle of San Jacinto in April 1836. The Jackson administration and southerners wanted to recognize Texas's independence before it was lost. Many saw this as the first step toward admission to the Union. Southern planters viewed the rich black soil of east Texas as ideal for growing cotton; they also wanted to ensure that Texans did not succumb to British pressure to abolish slavery. A Democratic Congress recognized the independence of Texas in March 1837. Southern elements pressed for admission, and the minister of Texas to the United States suggested it in August 1837. Northerners remained opposed. John Quincy Adams spoke to the fears of many when he warned of a conspiracy among proslavery interests to annex Texas.[343] (Presumably it had not been that when Adams tried to obtain it as secretary as state.) Henry Clay declared his opposition out of fear that annexation would trigger war with Mexico.[344] Senator Thomas Hart Benton of Missouri equated the acquisition of Texas with the dissolution of the Union.[345] The Massachusetts legislature confirmed his fears when it passed resolutions holding that annexation would force the states of New England to secede.[346]

With such powerful elements lined up against annexation, it is a wonder

---

340. *Congressional Globe*, 33d Cong., 1st sess., February 20, 1854, Appendix, 23:269.

341. See May 21, 1844, speech of Robert Dale Owen of Indiana, ibid., 28th Cong., 1st sess., Appendix, 13:696–97.

342. Johnson, *History of the American People*, 373.

343. Fehrenbacher, *Dred Scott Case*, 124.    344. Remini, *Henry Clay*, 486–87.

345. Van Deusen, *Jacksonian Era*, 186.

346. Schlesinger, "State Rights Fetish," 69.

that Texas ever became a state. That it did so had much to do with John C. Calhoun, the Democratic Party, and presidential politics. The austere Calhoun had much more in common with John Quincy Adams than with the other two giants of the age, Daniel Webster and Henry Clay. Adams and Calhoun both combined personal virtue with a capacity to behave like recalcitrant schoolboys when others appeared to threaten their ambitions or ideas. Although both men worked closely with Whigs, by the mid-1830s the two shared little more than contempt for the spoils policies of the Jackson administration.[347] With Jackson's return to private life in 1837, the absence of a common enemy weakened bonds within the Whig Party, and the strange amalgamation that could include both John Quincy Adams and John C. Calhoun began to lose its cohesiveness. While other conservative southerners remained with the Whig Party, Calhoun found it far too centralizing for his taste. Fortunately, the Democratic Party awaited. Although its strict constructionism had been watered down, the party's approach to the Constitution still qualified as more restrained than that of the Whigs. In addition, the Democrats, like the Republicans before them, had always possessed a strong southern contingent. It was only natural that with Jackson out of the way, Calhoun—with presidential ambitions at least as consuming as those of Clay—would lead his followers back into the Democratic fold. He announced the move in a November 16, 1837, letter to the Edgefield (South Carolina) *Advertiser.* National politics would now return, he predicted, to the "old and natural division of state rights and national."[348]

Calhoun's move proved to be one of the most critical events of the antebellum period. By herding the most determined proslavery elements back into the Democratic Party (Calhoun himself owned about eighty slaves), he provided them with a vehicle that would eventually bring them national power. As for Texas, Calhoun personally did little to advance the cause of annexation and a great deal to hurt it. Nevertheless, by bringing southern radicals back into Democratic ranks, he gave the party a proslavery tinge, and in the process kept annexation near the center of its priorities. The Whigs, by contrast, split over Texas. While John Tyler embraced annexation, the party's northern wing remained violently opposed to the idea. In early 1844 the administration completed work on a treaty of annexation and sub-

347. Calhoun attacked the tactics of the Jackson administration as centralizing in his 1835 Senate report on federal patronage. See *Report of the Select Committee on Executive Patronage,* 23rd Cong., 2d sess., February 9, 1835, S. Doc. 108.

348. *Papers of Calhoun,* 13:639.

mitted it to Congress. It provided that as many as five states could be carved out of the annexed territory.[349] Approval by two-thirds of the Senate appeared most unlikely.

The leading candidates for president in early 1844, Martin Van Buren and Henry Clay, both went on record against annexation that spring. In what became known as the Raleigh letter, Clay equated annexation with war. He reminded his countrymen that "it was never in the contemplation of the Framers of the Constitution to add foreign territory to the confederacy." He could not go along with the purchase of land when it was sought for the competitive advantage it would give to one section. Such a thing would, he feared, "sow the seeds of the dissolution of the Union."[350] In two letters sent to newspapers a short time thereafter, Clay modified his position. He announced that he would go along with annexation if it could be completed without war. The North took offense; the South perceived a lack of nerve.[351] Van Buren's demise was even more avoidable. By the spring of 1844 he had won the endorsement of twelve state Democratic conventions.[352] Yet the New York native—at one time perhaps the sharpest politician in the country—repeated Clay's error and issued a letter advising Americans to postpone annexation until Mexico recognized the independence of Texas.[353] Enter James K. Polk. A classic dark horse, Polk took the Democratic presidential nomination from Van Buren when the New Yorker failed to obtain the required two-thirds vote of the delegates at the party's national convention. Unlike Clay and Van Buren, Polk embraced the annexation of Texas as well as Oregon. Clay nonetheless appeared to be the early favorite. Hoping to assist Polk, Andrew Jackson, with less than a year to live, talked the incumbent John Tyler into withdrawing from the contest. In a move worthy of Old Hickory, Polk shored up his northern support with equivocations on the tariff, even while he privately assured southerners of his intention to lower rates. In the end, Polk won, though not by much and perhaps through fraud.

As it turned out, Texas did not have to wait for Democrats to take over the executive branch to gain admission to the Union. Instead, the Tyler administration, in one of the most boldly unconstitutional acts of the antebel-

349. 5 *Stats at Large* 797–98 (March 1, 1845).
350. Commager, *Documents of American History*, 305.
351. Holt, *Rise and Fall of the American Whig Party*, 180–81.
352. Cole, *Van Buren and the American Political System*, 390.
353. See Van Deusen, *Jacksonian Era*, 182.

lum period, accomplished that task itself. In a June 1844 vote, the treaty an-
nexing Texas did not come close to winning the approval of two-thirds of
the Senate, as was required for the ratification of treaties. The administration
thereafter sent what it called an annexation resolution to the House. Northern politicians were apoplectic. As Congressman J. R. Ingersoll of Pennsylvania put it in January 1845, "agreements between independent nations
are treaties, and nothing else."[354] Southern lawmakers suddenly discovered
the merits of a more latitudinarian approach to the Constitution. Democrat
James Bowlin of Missouri declared that while he was a "strict constructionist" and belonged to the party that "believes the rights of the states and the
liberties of the people are only secure whilst we adhere strictly to the Constitution," he thought the resolution legal. In Marshallesque tones he argued
that the power of acquiring territory was an "attribute of sovereignty" that
necessarily belonged to every "independent nation." He pointed to the increasingly common habit among national leaders of entering into compacts
and insisted that legislatures could do so as well.[355] Despite objections, the
resolution passed, and Tyler signed it in early March. Texas was admitted as
a state later that year. The legislatures of Massachusetts, Connecticut, Vermont, and Ohio issued statements declaring that Congress lacked the authority to annex Texas.[356]

While Texas dominated the headlines, other episodes involving slavery
and federal power also worsened sectional conflict during the late 1830s and
early 1840s. When abolitionist tracts began arriving in southern post offices,
postmasters destroyed these materials pursuant to the request of local officials. Both northerners and southerners were troubled by this unprecedented assumption of authority by federal officers, but the practice continued for
more than two decades after a law prohibiting it was passed in 1836. Abolitionist petitions received equally poor treatment in Congress, where Democratic majorities tabled them for several years rather than force southern
lawmakers to listen as they were read. While the practice did not violate
the right of petition (as some suggested), it certainly created the impression
that antislavery sentiment was not welcome in the nation's capital. Perhaps
the most appalling episode involving slavery and federalism occurred in the

354. *Congressional Globe,* 28th Cong., 2d sess., Appendix, 14:56.
355. Ibid., 93–94.
356. Ames, *State Documents on Federal Relations,* 230; see also Schlesinger, "State Rights Fetish," 69.

South itself. Fear of slave revolts led a handful of states to enact laws requiring that black sailors visiting southern ports be incarcerated in the local jail until their ships set sail (lest they incite nearby slaves to violence). Justice William Johnson held a South Carolina statute of this type to be an impermissible regulation of foreign commerce, but the decision was not enforced. These episodes produced mistrust of the federal system on both sides of the sectional divide. Northerners saw federal authority stifling antislavery sentiment, while southerners feared losing control of the flow of persons and ideas into their own states and cities.

Following the elections of 1844–45, Democrats returned to power in both Congress and the executive branch. Led by a strong-willed president who was also an experienced legislator, they pushed through the last pieces of important legislation not related to slavery to be enacted before 1861. Despite Tyler's acquiescence, the Tariff of 1842 established rates that were egregiously steep. Imported wool and flannels each came with a 40 percent sales tax. Boots carried a tax of $1 a pair—more than a day's wages for most Americans.[357] With large Democratic majorities in both houses of Congress, the Polk administration pushed through a substantial reduction in rates during the summer of 1846. Taxes under the Walker Tariff averaged just 20 percent by one estimate—the lowest in decades.[358] Many Democrats expressed satisfaction with the measure, and the president called it the most important of his administration.[359]

By the fall of 1845 neither low tariffs nor hard money qualified as the chief cause of Democrats. In an indication of the fact that proslavery elements increasingly dominated the party, annexation held that honor.[360] Slaveholders looked upon land west of the United States, and especially California—reports indicated Mexican control was a mere fiction—as the natural frontier for southern civilization and slavery. First there was Oregon. For years the United States and Great Britain had been unable to set a border. In 1827 they agreed to a joint occupation of the area. By 1845 further organization became imperative, as American settlements were sustaining Indian attacks on an almost weekly basis. James Polk asserted American claims to

357. 5 *Stats at Large* 548, 559, 554 (August 30, 1842).

358. James M. McPherson, *Battle Cry of Freedom: The Civil War Era* (New York: Oxford University Press, 1988), 192.

359. Milo Milton Quaife, ed., *The Diary of James K. Polk during His Presidency*, 4 vols. (Chicago: A. C. McClurg, 1910), 2:28.

360. Van Deusen, *Jacksonian Era*, 199.

that portion of the Oregon territory south of the fifty-fourth latitude. When the British proposed to partition the territory at the forty-ninth latitude, the president—with one eye on the burgeoning conflict with Mexico—accepted the offer. The Senate ratified the treaty in June 1846.

Following the admission of Texas, Mexico broke off relations with the United States, and the Mexican president recommended war. The Americans obliged. In the fall of 1845 General Zachary Taylor stationed four thousand troops south of the Neuces River. As Mexico viewed that river as its border with Texas, it understandably saw Taylor's presence as an act of war. Polk sent John Slidell to offer the Mexican president up to $40 million for New Mexico, California, and recognition of the Rio Grande River as the international boundary. Unfortunately, Slidell's mission became known, and the intensely negative reaction of the Mexican public made a deal impossible.[361] The following spring Americans took matters a step further. Taylor marched to the Rio Grande and blockaded it. When that failed to provoke a response, the president decided to ask Congress for a declaration of war. Before he could do so, word arrived that sixteen hundred Mexican regulars had crossed the Rio Grande and captured or killed sixty-five American soldiers. In response, the Democratic Congress declared war and authorized the president to call up fifty thousand volunteers.

The military conduct of the war may be sketched quickly. American armies marched south and west into Mexican territory and only occasionally came across their hosts. General Stephen Watts Kearney arrived in Santa Fe in August 1846; meeting little resistance, he headed for California. The state fell to American forces before the end of the year. General Zachary Taylor took Monterey, Mexico, in September 1846 and prevailed at Buena Vista six months later. In early 1847 General Winfield Scott executed a brilliant amphibious landing on the Mexican coast near Veracruz; shortly thereafter he took Mexico City. The Americans finished off the Mexican army at Huamantla in October 1847. Early the following year, the two sides brought the war to a close with a treaty under which Mexico ceded New Mexico, upper California, and private claims to lands north of the Rio Grande in exchange for $15 million.

Despite the relative ease with which American troops secured victory, criticism of the war quickly became very sharp. Politicians of all sections suddenly found themselves apprehensive of the future at a time when they might

361. Ibid., 219–21.

have been jubilant. John C. Calhoun warned that "Mexico is to us the forbidden fruit; the penalty of eating it [is] to subject our institutions to political death."[362] Many in the North saw the conflict as a step toward the admission of more slave states into the Union.[363] Joshua Giddings, an antislavery Democrat from Ohio, decried the carrying of "bloodshed and suffering to the heart of a sister republic." Where, he asked, was General Taylor when the Mexicans attacked him in 1846? The whole country knew the answer—in Mexican territory. The conflict with Mexico was, Giddings concluded, "a war of conquest, commenced and carried on for the purpose of dismembering Mexico." Daniel King of Massachusetts warned that "the fixed determination of the administration is that the [conquered] territory shall be slave territory."[364]

Already northern legislators had taken steps to head off what they feared as the Polk administration's long-term goal. On August 8, 1846, Congressman David Wilmot suggested that Congress condition an appropriation for the war on the requirement that "neither slavery nor involuntary servitude shall ever exist in any part of said territory [lands obtained from Mexico], except for crime, whereof the party shall first be duly convicted." The House approved the amendment the same day, 85–79, and sent the bill to the Senate.[365] As everyone knew it must, the measure died there when the session ended on August 10. Wilmot's proviso reawakened a volcano that had been dormant for two decades. It would pour forth steam almost continuously during the next fifteen years. Northern determination to keep slavery out of the territories hardened, while southerners insisted that it must follow the flag. While it is true that support for the proviso stemmed in part from a racist determination to keep blacks out of the territories,[366] inconsistency did nothing to slow the spread of antislavery sentiment in the North. First the state legislatures acted—every single assembly in the North but one passed resolutions endorsing Wilmot.[367] Southerners countered with the issue of fairness: men from their section were serving in the army, and it would be a great injustice to deny them access to the lands for which they had fought.[368]

362. Quoted in Peterson, *Great Triumvirate*, 423.

363. Van Deusen, *Jacksonian Era*, 240.

364. *Congressional Globe*, 29th Cong., 2d sess., Appendix, 16:48, 51, 295.

365. Ibid., 29th Cong., 1st sess., August 12, 1846, 15:1217–18.

366. See James M. McPherson, *Ordeal by Fire*, vol. 1, *The Coming of the Civil War* (New York: McGraw-Hill, 1981), 42.

367. Commager and Morison, *Growth of the American Republic*, 619.

368. See the January 1847 speech of J. A. Seddon of Virginia, *Congressional Globe*, 29th Cong., 2d sess., Appendix, 16:77.

At least some southerners feared that Wilmot would result in the creation of enough free states to enable northerners to amend the Constitution for the purpose of abolishing slavery throughout the nation.[369]

It was perhaps inevitable that southerners would label unconstitutional a course of action whose connection to the enumerated powers was not entirely self-evident. In early 1847 the Virginia legislature passed a resolution holding that Congress lacked the power to prohibit slavery in the territories.[370] A year later the Alabama state Democratic convention announced its agreement with this view and repudiated the Missouri Compromise in the process. It called for secession if Wilmot passed.[371] In the House, Thomas H. Bayly of Virginia claimed that many southerners had always viewed the Missouri Compromise as unconstitutional. In the spring of 1847 John C. Calhoun offered several resolutions in the Senate. One provided that the "territories of the United States belong to the several states composing this Union," and that Congress cannot "discriminate" between the states. Another held that the "enactment of any law which . . . deprive[s] the citizens of any of the States of this Union from emigrating, with their property, into any of the territories of the United States, will make such discrimination." Such a law would "be a violation of the Constitution, and the rights of the States from which such citizens emigrated, and in derogation of that perfect equality which belongs to them as members of this Union, and would tend directly to subvert the Union itself."[372] No vote was taken on the resolutions, as only days remained in the session and Congress was more concerned with a war-related appropriation bill. Calhoun's statement nonetheless played a critical role in the coming years, as proslavery southerners embraced his state-based approach to the territories question. Yet it was no more rooted in the Constitution than Calhoun's other brainchild, nullification. Nothing in the proceedings of the federal Convention or the ratification debates hinted at state ownership of the territories or at the notion that territorial laws must affect immigrants from all sections equally. It is true that the cessions of the 1780s included stipulations regarding those regions. Virginia's deed of cession for the Northwest Territory (1783) provided that the lands ceded were to be used "as a common fund for the use and benefit

369. See Gustavus Schmidt to Peter Conrey, July 1847, *Papers of Calhoun*, 24:488–92.

370. Ames, *State Documents on Federal Relations*, 244–47.

371. Allan Nevins, *Ordeal of the Union*, vol. 1, *Fruits of Manifest Destiny, 1847–1852* (New York: Charles Scribner's Sons, 1947), 12.

372. *Congressional Globe*, 29th Cong., 2d sess., February 19, 1847, Appendix, 16:347, 455.

of such of the United States as have become, or shall become members of the confederation or federal alliance of said states."[373] Prohibitions of slavery were not viewed as violations of these provisions during the 1780s. The Northwest Ordinance, with its ban on slavery in the Northwest, was enacted without protest in 1787. As Congressman George Rathbun of New York pointed out, there was a time when slavery had been regarded as an evil throughout the Union.[374]

The idea that all federal legislation must affect the states or sections equally did not withstand examination, either. The constitutionality of laws turned on the question of whether they bore a necessary relationship to the exercise of one or more of the enumerated powers. Sectional fairness had nothing to do with it. From the beginning, it had been universally accepted that tariffs would favor the North. Conversely, Americans knew the Fugitive Slave Act of 1793 would favor the South. Calhoun's previous statements on the issue also undermined his argument. In 1837 he offered several resolutions in the Senate, one of which appeared to concede the legality of prohibitions of slavery in the territories, as it attacked such bans only on substantive grounds.[375] As Calhoun had already demonstrated a willingness to label policies with which he disagreed (i.e., protective tariffs) unconstitutional, the question arises as to why he failed to attack a territorial ban on slavery on those grounds in 1837.[376]

Some of Calhoun's fellow southerners found it difficult to embrace his approach. Accustomed to citing historical evidence for the original understanding of the clauses of the Constitution, they were not disposed to making broad generalizations about the rights of the states. Many therefore stuck to the old approach. The going proved difficult. As had occurred three decades earlier in the debate over the spending power, northerners offered an endless barrage of congressional acts in support of their view that Congress had the power to ban slavery in the territories.[377] The 1845 resolution admitting Texas proved to be especially popular—it prohibited slavery north of thirty-six degrees latitude in the annexed territory—as most of the legis-

373. Commager, *Documents of American History*, 121.

374. *Congressional Globe*, 29th Cong., 2d sess., Appendix, 16:179.

375. Ibid., 25th Cong., 2d sess., 55.

376. See Benton, *Thirty Years' View*, 2:697, for the argument that Calhoun's 1847 resolutions conflicted with the stances he took in 1820 and 1837.

377. See speech of Aylett Buckner of Kentucky, *Congressional Globe*, 30th Cong., 2d sess., February 17, 1849, Appendix, 18:225–26.

lators who now denied the existence of such a power had voted for it.[378] Unlike the fight over the spending power, southerners had nothing so compelling as the ratification debates to cite in response to the claim that Congress could ban slavery in the territories. They tended to avoid the most glaring difficulties altogether. Almost no one bothered to explain the 1789 statute adopting the Northwest Ordinance. As for the ordinance itself, Congressman Franklin Welsh Bowdon of Alabama held that it constituted a compact and not a statute. Therefore it could not serve as a precedent for future legislation.[379] When northerners pointed out that the alleged compact lacked the requisite two parties, Senator John Berrien of Georgia claimed that the state of Virginia served as the second party (the other states being the first party). Thomas Bayly of Virginia dismissed the Northwest Ordinance on the grounds that the Confederation lacked the authority to enact it. Another legislator made much of the fact that the ordinance had been passed prior to ratification of the Constitution. Some argued that ratification rendered it void.[380] Even if the Confederation lacked authority to enact the Northwest Ordinance, that fact did not have any bearing on the authority of Congress to adopt it in 1789. Thus the question at the center of the debate: why did the first Congress approve an act that everyone understood to prohibit slavery in the Northwest Territories if it lacked the power to do so?

In March 1847 thirteen northern representatives broke down under administration pressure and provided the votes necessary to pass a war appropriation bill that did not have the Wilmot Proviso attached to it.[381] The administration's legislative victory was overshadowed by electoral disaster. In the midterm elections of 1846-47, the Democrats lost both houses of Congress for only the second time in twenty years. Although the defeat had more to do with the war and the Walker Tariff (which was unpopular in the North) than with Wilmot, this was little consolation to the president, who now faced the prospect of convincing an antiwar Congress to bring Mexi-

378. See, for example, the comments of Congressman Richard Brodhead of Pennsylvania, ibid., 30th Cong., 1st sess., June 3, 1848, Appendix, 17:651. See also 4 *Stats at Large* 797–98 (February 17, 1849).

379. *Congressional Globe,* 29th Cong., 2d sess., January 26, 1847, Appendix, 16:137–39.

380. Ibid., 31st Cong., 1st sess., February 12, 1850, Appendix, 19:205; ibid., 30th Cong., 1st sess., May 16, 1848, Appendix, 17:575. Franklin Pierce held this view; see Richardson, *Messages and Papers of the Presidents,* 6:2879.

381. *Congressional Globe,* 29th Cong., 2d sess., February 21, 1849, 16:573. See also Chaplain W. Morrison, *Democratic Politics and Sectionalism: The Wilmot Proviso Controversy* (Chapel Hill: University of North Carolina Press, 1967), 37, 189.

can territory into the Union. The new Whig majority made clear that it was not going to be helpful. First the House devised a resolution declaring that the war had been "unnecessarily and unconstitutionally begun by the President of the United States."[382] It then fastened the Wilmot Proviso on a war-related appropriation in early 1848. Deadlock resulted, with grave consequences. During the summer of 1848, Indians began attacking American settlements in Oregon.[383] An ad hoc provisional government proved unequal to the task of imposing order, and formation of a territorial government became imperative. The need to organize the Mexican cession complicated matters. The president suggested banning slavery altogether in Oregon and extending the Missouri Compromise line through the Mexican cession to the Pacific Ocean. The House of Representatives would not go along. It passed a bill that prohibited slavery in Oregon without extending the Missouri Compromise line. As southerners insisted upon organizing the territories in the Southwest first, the Oregon bill languished in the Senate.

In July 1848 a committee chaired by Senator John M. Clayton of Delaware proposed a compromise plan: territorial governments would be formed in three western territories: Oregon, California, and New Mexico. While a ban on slavery that had been devised by Oregon's provisional government would remain in force, the territorial governments of California and New Mexico would be barred from legislating on the issue. Any disputes that occurred concerning "title to slaves" would be turned over to federal courts, with a right of appeal to the Supreme Court. The proposal instilled fear in senators on both sides. George Badger of North Carolina called it a "complete surrender of the rights of the south." John Hale of New Hampshire had no confidence in the "Supreme Court, as now constituted," because the Constitution had been "interpreted as variously as the Bible." Despite misgivings, the Senate passed the Clayton compromise bill, 33 to 22. The measure received a rough welcome upon its arrival in the House. H. P. Putnam of New York reminded his colleagues that the Constitution vested authority to legislate for the territories in Congress and not the Supreme Court. J. H. Crozier of Tennessee predicted that the section disappointed by the ruling would disregard it. Caleb Smith of Indiana warned his fellow northerners that southern lawmakers favored the Clayton amendment because it would result in the recognition of a constitutional right to bring slaves into

382. *Congressional Globe*, 30th Cong., 1st sess., January 3, 1848, 17:95.
383. Bergeron, *Presidency of James K. Polk*, 204.

the territories. The Whig-dominated House tabled the measure on July 28, 1848. The Senate thereafter backed down and accepted a House bill that organized the Oregon territory alone and banned slavery within it.[384]

The task of organizing California and New Mexico in a manner acceptable to both sides proved to be an enormously difficult one. Many saw extension of the Missouri Compromise line to the Pacific Ocean as the answer. In an August 1847 letter, Secretary of State James Buchanan—a leading candidate for the 1848 Democratic presidential nomination—embraced extension. The Polk administration's mouthpiece, the *Washington Union,* endorsed the idea as well. Northerners wanted nothing to do with it. Vice President George M. Dallas proposed leaving the matter of slavery to the settlers themselves, who could act through their territorial governments. The idea received its most famous endorsement in the "Nicholson letter," written by Michigan senator Lewis Cass. A hero of the War of 1812 and Andrew Jackson's secretary of war, critics had long suspected Cass of being, as one historian put it, "more concerned with how he was affected by his votes than how his votes affected the country."[385] In the Nicholson letter Cass went a long way toward accepting the now standard position among southern Democrats—that Congress lacked the power to ban slavery in the territories—when he declared it "hardly expedient" to exercise a "doubtful and invidious authority . . . which would give to Congress despotic power, uncontrolled by the Constitution, over most important sections of the common country."[386] Such a power would enable Congress to regulate anything it chose, even domestic relations. "If the relation of master and servant may be regulated or annihilated . . . so may the relation of husband and wife, of parent and child, and of any other condition which our institutions and the habits of our society recognize."[387] Territorial legislatures, however, could ban slavery, Cass held. He was careful to hedge his bets, as many southerners insisted that a ban on slavery remained beyond the powers of settlers until statehood. "They [the territorial legislatures] are just as capable of doing so as the people of the states; and they can do so at any rate as soon as their

384. *Congressional Globe,* 30th Cong., 1st sess., 17:1002–5, 1001, 988, 1007, 1077–78; and July–August 1848, Appendix, 18:1126, 1081. See 9 *Stats at Large* 323, 329 (section 14) (August 14, 1848).

385. See Rayback, *Free Soil,* 114–15, 17.

386. Quoted in Frank B. Woodford, *Lewis Cass: The Last Jeffersonian* (New Brunswick: Rutgers University Press, 1950), 252.

387. Quoted in Andrew C. McLaughlin, *Lewis Cass* (Boston: Houghton Mifflin, 1899; reprint, New York: Chelsea House, 1980), 237.

political independence is recognized by their admission into the Union."[388]

The Nicholson letter and the doctrine of popular sovereignty it made famous was no more rooted in the Constitution than nullification or state ownership of the territories. If Congress could not legislate concerning slavery in the territories, then how could institutions that it created, such as territorial legislatures? Eager for a resolution, elements in both sections embraced Cass's approach despite its defects. Moderate northern Democrats saw it as a way to preserve party unity on the eve of a presidential election.[389] To them, popular sovereignty promised to remove a rather needless issue from the agenda—most territories, it was thought, were not appropriate for the type of intensive agriculture that used slave-based labor. Southerners embraced popular sovereignty because of its implication (in their view) that Congress lacked authority to prohibit slavery. Thus the somewhat hollow endorsement of popular sovereignty offered by Jacob Thompson of Mississippi: "Where then resides the power to legislate for the territories? I unhesitatingly answer in the language of General Cass in the Nicholson letter, 'in the people of the territories, under the general principles of the Constitution.'"[390] The last phrase—"under the general principles of the Constitution"—was critical. In using it, Thompson expressed a widely held belief that the residents of a territory could not address the subject of slavery until they drafted state constitutions in preparation for admission to the Union.

In the midst of this debate, the country held a presidential election. Despite widespread opposition to the war, its chief hero, General Zachary Taylor, came home in December 1847 to a huge reception at New Orleans. Although a slaveholder, Taylor obtained the Whig nomination with almost no objection because his military fame and lack of a political record made him irresistible to party leaders. Taylor confirmed their confidence by refusing to take a stand on any key issues, explaining that he had not had time to investigate them.[391] In perhaps his closest brush with ideas, the general straddled party and sectional lines through an embrace of Whig ideology: Congress, he declared, should set policy on such matters as the tariff, the currency, and internal improvements. For Democrats, the election of 1848 was an unmitigated disaster. Lewis Cass succeeded in taking the nomination from James

---

388. McLaughlin, *Lewis Cass,* 237.
389. Rayback, *Free Soil,* 119.
390. *Congressional Globe,* 30th Cong., 1st sess., June 27, 1848, Appendix, 17:721.
391. Van Deusen, *Jacksonian Era,* 252.

Buchanan. For many southerners, the senator paled in comparison with Taylor. As the general was a slaveholder, surely he could be relied upon to protect the interests of their section. Many northern votes turned on the economy. A recession hit in the summer of 1848 and worsened steadily during the fall. Prices dropped precipitously—surely the Walker Tariff was responsible.[392] Internal divisions also hurt the Democrats. A convention of antislavery or "Free Soil" Democrats nominated Martin Van Buren for the presidency on a separate ticket. The Free Soil platform called for the federal government to prohibit slavery wherever it could under the Constitution (in the territories and national capital). When Zachary Taylor won the presidential election, the split within the Democratic Party probably made the difference.

Hostilities with Mexico came to an end in the fall of 1847, but the war did not draw to an official close until July 1848, when the Treaty of Guadalupe Hidalgo was ratified. The United States spent thirteen thousand lives and more than $100 million.[393] In exchange, the American people received nearly half of Mexico (albeit the empty half), and more grief than they could have imagined. The trouble began in California, where the discovery of gold in 1848 caused the new territory to fill up to the point of statehood almost overnight. Its citizens devised a constitution that prohibited slavery, and southern members of Congress reacted with hostility. Since 1820 states had been admitted in pairs (one each from the North and South), and with no proslavery territory ready for statehood, California would give the North a numerical advantage in the Senate. With the admission of Oregon and Minnesota imminent, the imbalance promised to grow worse.

After Californians overwhelmingly approved a state constitution banning slavery in the fall of 1849, the president suggested that a territorial government was unnecessary and that California should seek admission to the Union immediately. Ten years earlier the southern states might have welcomed California as a coequal member of the Union, but sectional considerations now altered their course. A whole group of slavery-related issues called out for adjustment, and southerners determined that these should be addressed before they would go along with admission. New Mexico and Utah needed territorial governments, the border between New Mexico and

392. See Holt, *Rise and Fall of the American Whig Party*, 310, 367.
393. Van Deusen, *Jacksonian Era*, 245.

Texas had to be adjusted, and the Fugitive Slave Act of 1793 (in their view) needed to be strengthened.

In retrospect, the package of legislation that followed has an air of inevitability. It did not at the time. For months in early 1850, the prospect of deadlock and even disunion hovered over the country. Northerners worked themselves into a fury over the idea that one section should have to make concessions to another in order for a state to enter the Union. Many would have been perfectly happy if Mexican law—with its prohibition of slavery—remained intact in the West. Assorted southerners talked of disunion as the only acceptable alternative if Congress banned slavery in the Southwest.[394] Georgia's legislature passed a law obligating its governor to call a state convention if California was admitted.[395] Intense feelings were evident on both sides when the thirty-first Congress met for its first session in December 1849. Thirteen Free Soil Democrats in the House refused to caucus with their party, leaving it with only a plurality of seats. The House split into factions over the election of Speaker; it did not settle on Democrat Howell Cobb of Georgia until December 22. The president exacerbated frictions when he called for the admission of New Mexico as well as California, despite the fact that it was occupied by only a smattering of Pueblos and Mormons—neither of whom had demonstrated any interest in joining the Union. The president's suggestion was ignored; in the House, opponents organized a filibuster of the California statehood bill.

With prospects for success diminishing by the day, the most prominent legislator of antebellum America stepped forward to offer a compromise plan. Henry Clay, seventy-two years old and still disappointed over the Whigs' decision to pass him up in 1848, believed that he might be able to bring lawmakers of both sections together and resolve the crisis. In a speech of January 29, 1850, Clay offered eight resolutions in the Senate. They provided for the admission of California as a state and the organization of New Mexico as a territory without any mention of slavery (Mexican law would presumably remain intact); assumption of the debts of Texas in exchange for settlement of its border dispute with New Mexico; prohibition of the slave trade in Washington, D.C.; and a strengthened fugitive slave act. Clay added declarations holding the abolition of slavery in Washington, D.C., to

394. David M. Potter, *The Impending Crisis, 1848–1861* (New York: Harper & Row, 1976), 94.
395. Philip Shriver Klein, *President James Buchanan* (University Park: Pennsylvania State University Press, 1962), 213.

be inexpedient and regulation of the interstate slave trade to be beyond the powers of Congress.[396] The speech broke a long-building tension. Americans held enormous meetings to show their support for Clay against what was perceived as a growing threat of secession.

Senator Henry S. Foote of Mississippi declared that he would go along with the admission of California if two conditions were met. First, all of the other slavery-related questions before the country would have to be "satisfactorily adjusted"; second, another slave state would have to be admitted in order to preserve sectional balance in the Senate.[397] While Foote and other southern members of Congress gambled aggressively, an aged and dying John C. Calhoun still surpassed them in the extremism of his rhetoric. Escorted into the Senate on the afternoon of March 4, 1850, the South Carolina senator was so weak from the effects of tuberculosis that John Mason of Virginia had to read his speech for him. Calhoun began with the obvious: the South was discontented. The sections had been virtually even in population in 1790, but the gap was now more than 2 million and growing. There was already a northern advantage in states, as Delaware (where slavery was dying) was already neutral. This gap would continue to widen with the admission of California, Minnesota, and Oregon. The danger inherent in this loss of sectional balance had manifested itself, Calhoun argued, in the exclusion of southerners from the territories, as well as in "a system of revenue and disbursements, by which an undue proportion of taxation has been imposed upon the south, and an undue proportion of its proceeds appropriated to the north." Nor was there any real hope of correcting the situation, as the national government had grown beyond the ability of others to check it, in part owing to its insistence upon determining the extent of its own powers. Thus the federal Republic of 1789 no longer existed; it had been replaced by "a great national consolidated democracy." While separation would not come through a "single blow," the cords of the Union were already snapping. The Baptists and Methodists had split along sectional lines, and the Presbyterians were about to do so. The South should therefore be ready to secede if the Union failed to serve its original purposes. As for the legislation before Congress, Calhoun largely ignored it, though he declared that California should not be admitted, because her citizens had formed a state constitution without authorization from Congress. He closed with a word of advice for

396. *Congressional Globe*, 31st Cong., 1st sess., January 29, 1850, 19.1:244–46.
397. Ibid., 247.

his fellow southerners—agree to no compromise but that which conceded to the South an "equal right" in the territories and ensured the return of fugitive slaves.[398]

As one historian put it, Calhoun "overshot the mark."[399] Clay had so completely defused the forces of radicalism that there was not much of an audience for the South Carolina senator's brand of pessimism. With the light of compromise still bright, the third member of the great triumvirate, Daniel Webster, arose to give the most anticipated speech of the session. Like Calhoun and Clay, he had been born during the American Revolution; like them he was near the end of his illustrious career in 1850. To everyone's surprise, Webster embraced Clay's plan to admit California and bring southerners back into the fold with the adjustment of other slavery-related issues. He did so in words that rang familiar to American schoolchildren until well into the twentieth century. "Mr. President, I wish to speak today, not as a Massachusetts man, not as a northern man, but as an American and a member of the Senate of the United States. I speak today for the preservation of the Union. Hear my cause." After reciting the events of the past five years that had produced so much bad feeling, the great lawyer turned to the issues at hand in the hope of finding middle ground. Webster reminded the Senate that the proposed California constitution and its prohibition of slavery had been devised by a state convention that included a large contingent of southerners. It was hardly the product of abolitionists. Nor was this the only instance of southern antislavery sentiment; both sections had been antislavery in outlook when the government was founded. This view manifested itself in the Northwest Ordinance and the Constitutional Convention's grant of a power to ban the importing of slaves after twenty years had passed. Since that time, the South had changed. It had taken a proslavery turn and dragged the federal government along with it—thus the purchase of so much slave territory. Yet the most recent additions would provide no slave territory at all, for the lands obtained were not suited to that kind of agriculture. Why did the North insist on a law prohibiting slavery where it could not exist? "I would not," Webster announced, "take pains to reaffirm an ordinance of nature, nor to reenact the will of God." He endorsed the compromise measures before Congress, including the provision to strengthen the fugitive slave act. He turned again, though, and warned southern rad-

398. *Papers of Calhoun*, 27:188–92, 194–95, 199–200, 202–9.
399. Nevins, *Ordeal of the Union*, 1:283.

icals that secession could never work—northerners would not accept losing access to the mouth of the Mississippi River.[400] Webster had tried to appease both sides by suggesting that each had legitimate grievances. Nonetheless, antislavery elements attacked him ferociously. For many, the moral issues at stake were far too grave to allow for compromise. Nor did the disappointment ease quickly. For decades to come, Webster's endorsement of the fugitive slave bill tarnished his reputation in his native New England.

William Seward gave what was in essence the response of Webster's own region to his call for compromise. The New York senator began by dismissing demands for measures that would restore sectional balance on the grounds that a price should not be paid for California's admission. He then turned to the view that the Constitution required equal access to the territories for slaveholders. In perhaps the most famous remark of his career, Seward pointed out that "there is a higher law than the Constitution, which regulates our authority over the domain, and devotes it to the same noble purposes." The territories, he continued, formed a part of the "common heritage of mankind, bestowed upon them by the Creator of the universe. We are his stewards and must so discharge our trust as to secure in the highest attainable degree their happiness." To introduce slavery into the territories would violate that trust. Seward claimed that no free state would establish slavery within its borders at the present day—nor would any of the slave states, if they could choose. The institution was clearly on its way out, and he favored laws that "check its extension and abate its strength." Seward went on to make it clear that he intended to work for the demise of slavery within the confines of the Constitution. "I would," he insisted "adopt none but lawful, constitutional, and peaceful means, to secure even that end." Make no mistake, though; Seward announced as his goal the termination and not merely the limitation of slavery. In doing so, he hinted that federal expenditure might prove the solution. "There is no reasonable limit to which I am not willing to go in applying the national treasures, to effect the peaceful, voluntary removal of slavery itself."[401]

The people of the far northern tier of states applauded; the American Antislavery Society published ten thousand copies of Seward's speech.[402] Others were less enthusiastic. The New York senator's fellow Whigs attacked

400. *Congressional Globe*, 31st Cong., 1st sess., March 7, 1850, Appendix, 19:269–76.
401. Ibid., 262, 265, 268.
402. Peterson, *Great Triumvirate*, 467.

him for his failure to endorse the administration's plan. What proved memorable for most was the "higher law" phrase. Henry Clay demanded to know where Seward had obtained his "credentials of prophecy."[403] Almost a decade later, southerners blamed it for much of the posturing that occurred in the interim. "The law of conscience," James Jackson of Georgia announced in 1859, had usurped the Constitution. It was in fact "a crown of absolute sovereignty placed upon the brow of every man, submitting to his option obedience or disregard of every law, under the plea that the thing he calls conscience will not permit him to obey the law."[404] Perhaps Jackson's interpretation was too harsh. Seward did not renounce the Constitution, and he acknowledged implicitly that the national government had no authority to abolish slavery in the states. Yet even if he had called for means of emancipation of doubtful legality, such as the compensation of slaveholders, was there not precedent for such an act? Jefferson had transgressed the Constitution in order to buy Louisiana—surely it would be at least as acceptable to do so in order to end slavery. The idea was not seriously considered, and practically speaking it was irrelevant. As events would prove, nothing short of armed force would secure emancipation.

On May 8, the committee of thirteen reported its compromise plan. The central piece of legislation—the omnibus bill—provided statehood for California and territorial governments for New Mexico and Utah. It did not restrict the powers of either territorial legislature over slavery. Both territories would be admitted "with or without slavery," as their constitutions provided. The bill encompassed other matters as well, such as the Texas–New Mexico boundary and fugitive slaves. Shortly thereafter, the committee agreed to amend the bill so that any disputes that might arise in New Mexico or Utah over title to slaves could be appealed on an expedited basis to the Supreme Court.[405] It also agreed to a provision formally extending the Constitution to the territories, thus easing fears that Mexican law, which prohibited slavery, would remain intact in the West. As spring turned into summer, most observers expected the bill to pass, even as Free Soil elements insisted on a Wilmot-like provision expressly banning slavery in the new territories. The

403. Quoted in Allan Nevins, *The Emergence of Lincoln*, vol. 1 *Douglas, Buchanan, and Party Chaos, 1857–1859* (New York: Charles Scribner's Sons, 1950), 301.

404. *Congressional Globe*, 35th Cong., 2d sess., February 10, 1859, Appendix, 28.2:104.

405. For the text of the committee's report, see ibid., 31st Cong., 1st sess., May 8, 1850, 19:944.

Taylor administration constituted the most formidable obstacle to compromise. The old general simply could not accommodate himself to the idea that a price ought to be paid for the admission of California.

On July 9, 1850, the president died. He was probably a victim of the healing arts as they existed at that time—a simple case of gastroenteritis was treated with opium, quinine, and the drawing of enormous quantities of blood.[406] Taylor's successor, Millard Fillmore, a moderate Whig from Buffalo, New York, immediately placed the weight of executive branch patronage on the side of the compromise measures.[407] Several northern Whig newspapers that opposed compromise lost federal printing contracts.[408] Despite the support of the president, Clay, Webster, and the middle of the country, the omnibus bill failed. In stepped Stephen Douglas, the fast-rising Democratic senator from Illinois. He broke up the omnibus package into several smaller bills on the theory that each alone might elicit a level of support the entire measure could not. Douglas also strengthened the fugitive slave bill and provided additional money for Texas in exchange for its agreement to cede disputed land to New Mexico. The tinkering worked. The breakup of the omnibus package allowed southern moderates to join their northern brethren in voting to admit California, while a handful of northerners in turn voted for the fugitive slave bill. Twenty-eight congressmen who had previously voted against assumption of the debts of Texas changed their votes and went along with it.[409] The defections produced something of a scandal; many in the North were convinced that legislators from their section had been bribed. Most Americans did not care. For the moment, at least, the Union remained.

406. Commager and Morison, *Growth of the American Republic*, 628.
407. Remini, *Henry Clay*, 753.
408. Holt, *Rise and Fall of the American Whig Party*, 547.
409. Elbert B. Smith, *The Presidencies of Zachary Taylor and Millard Fillmore* (Lawrence: University Press of Kansas, 1988), 188.

# CHAPTER 5

# The Fall of the Republic, 1850–1861

## SLAVERY, CITIES, AND PARTIES

While the country drew a sigh of relief with the passage of the compromise acts, underlying tensions worsened. The Whig Party began to disintegrate despite the fact that it was the more moderate party in a time when virtue was supposedly prized. There were several reasons for this, among them the passing of both Daniel Webster and Henry Clay in 1852. The continued un-popularity of tariffs in the South also played a role. The most important fac-tor was the Fugitive Slave Act of 1850. Heavy-handed enforcement of the law kept the antislavery movement alive at a time when the other compro-mise measures might have put it to sleep. It also caused northern Whigs to move toward a more militant antislavery position. Northerners such as Wil-liam Seward abandoned the president, and by the time Millard Fillmore left office in 1853, his support was limited to the southern wing of the party.

In demanding vigilant enforcement of the Fugitive Slave Act of 1850, southerners embraced a law that Congress probably did not have author-ity to enact. The fugitive slave clause, Article IV, Section 2 of the Constitu-tion, imposed duties upon the states. Article I, Section 8 listed the powers of Congress; it said nothing regarding fugitive slaves. Nonetheless, Congress enacted the Fugitive Slave Act of 1793 with no protests concerning its au-thority to do so.[1] The act gave slaveholders the right to recapture slaves in the northern states and provided for an extradition process that included

---

1. 1 *Stats at Large* 302 (February 12, 1793). Justice Story attempted to explain this anomaly by pointing out that Congress had enacted other laws with no obvious relation to the enumerated powers, such as acts apportioning representatives and executing treaties. See *Prigg v. Pennsylva-nia*, 41 U.S. 539, 618–19.

none of the safeguards required by the Bill of Rights. The 1850 Fugitive Slave Act also denied suspected fugitives the right to a jury trial and arguably violated the Constitution.[2] In discharging one Sherman Booth, accused of aiding a runaway, the Wisconsin Supreme Court held the law void.[3] The decision led to southern complaints that northern states were now engaging in their own brand of nullification.[4] The U.S. Supreme Court reversed the decision of the Wisconsin court, pointing out that the states had no authority to interfere with the enforcement of federal law.[5] The Court did not bother to justify its conclusion that the law fell within the pale. (While on circuit, Justice McLean justified the lack of provision for a jury on the grounds that fugitive slave proceedings were statutory and not common law in nature.)[6] The Wisconsin legislature responded to the Court's corrective with resolutions declaring that the states "had the unquestionable right to judge of [constitutional] infractions," as well as a right to engage in "positive defiance" of acts of the federal government that were beyond its powers.[7] Wisconsin's stand, although futile, demonstrated that the term "states' rights" was not yet a term of derision in the North.

The Fugitive Slave Act of 1850 spawned one of the most far-reaching exercises of federal power in the antebellum Republic. All citizens were "commanded to aid and assist in the prompt and efficient execution" of the law. In effect the act required every able-bodied man in the North to make himself available for service in a federal law enforcement agency for the purpose of sending others into bondage. The law also barred suspected fugitives from testifying in the cases brought against them. Commissioners received payment of $10 when they returned a suspected fugitive to the South and only $5 when they allowed the accused to remain in the North. Predictable results followed: of 343 suspected slaves brought before federal commissioners in the 1850s, 332 were removed to the South, while only eleven regained their

---

2. 9 *Stats at Large* 462 (September 18, 1850). In 1855 the Massachusetts legislature passed resolutions declaring the law unconstitutional, as no such power appeared in the Constitution. Ames, *State Documents on Federal Relations*, 288.

3. *In re Sherman M. Booth*, 3 Wisc. 13, 67–71 (1854). The plaintiff's attorney pointed to the fact that the enumerated powers did not say anything about fugitive slaves, as well as the lack of a jury trial, in arguing that the act was unconstitutional (49–54).

4. See, for example, the February 27, 1860, speech of Robert Toombs of Georgia, *Congressional Globe*, 36th Cong., 1st sess., 29.1:888–90.

5. *Ableman v. Booth*, 62 U.S. 506 (1859).

6. *Miller v. McQuerry*, 17 Federal Cases 335 (1853).

7. Quoted in Schlesinger, "State Rights Fetish," 70.

freedom.[8] Inevitably, some of those taken south were not runaway slaves. Northern states responded with attempts to frustrate the purpose of the law. Between 1854 and 1858, six legislatures enacted statutes giving the right to a jury trial and the writ of habeas corpus to suspected fugitives.[9] Antislavery leaders advised citizens against cooperating with federal officials attempting to execute the Fugitive Slave Act.[10] Northerners impeded its enforcement in spite of the six-month jail term and $1,000 fine imposed upon those found guilty of obstructing it. People were willing to resist the law in part because northern juries proved unwilling to convict those who had been indicted for violating it.[11] State officials helped defeat the purpose of the measure by arresting slave catchers and charging them with kidnapping or assault.[12]

Heavy-handed enforcement of the Fugitive Slave Act was not the only development that worsened sectional friction during the 1850s. Two distinct economies were emerging side by side, one in the North and one in the South. At midcentury the South produced as much as two-thirds of the annual worldwide cotton harvest. While this abundance gave the region a disproportionate share of the nation's richest men, its almost complete dependence on "king cotton" prevented the rise of a consumer class and in turn blocked the development of manufacturing.[13] It also left virtually all whites in the region economically dependent upon slavery. By one count, a third of all white families in the South owned slaves by 1860.[14] Most slaves lived not on vast plantations but on middling farms, toiling alongside three or four others as well as their master. In 1850 only five Kentucky residents owned more than a hundred slaves; about thirteen thousand owned four or fewer.[15] Even southern laborers perceived value in the institution; like their northern brethren, they feared that 4 million liberated blacks would flood the labor market and drive down wages.

8. 9 *Stats at Large* 462, 463, 465 (sections 3, 5, 9); McPherson, *Battle Cry of Freedom*, 80.

9. Don E. Fehrenbacher, *The Slaveholding Republic*, completed and edited by Ward M. McAfee (New York: Oxford University Press, 2001), 238.

10. Allan Nevins, *Ordeal of the Union*, 1:351.

11. White, *Jacksonians*, 527.

12. In September 1854 Chicago authorities arrested a band of slave catchers and charged them with aggravated assault after they were caught escorting an alleged fugitive through the city. "The Fugitive Slave Case," *Chicago Tribune*, September 12, 1854, 2.

13. Emory M. Thomas, *The Confederate Nation: 1861–1865* (New York: Harper Collins, 1993), 13–14.

14. McPherson, *Ordeal by Fire*, 1:31. Another estimate has only a quarter of all southern families owning slaves. Thomas, *Confederate Nation*, 6.

15. Nevins, *Ordeal of the Union*, 1:424.

As the South fixed itself to slavery's mast, the Northwest embraced free labor and the market revolution. Increased demand for wheat, labor-saving implements such as the reaper, improved transportation routes, and some of the most fertile soil in the world led hundreds of thousands to take up farming in the prairie states during the 1840s and '50s. In an area that had been virtually unknown to whites as recently as the 1790s, some 8 million people—one of every four Americans—dwelled in 1860. Like their eastern brethren, residents of the Northwest favored a vigorous exercise of governmental power. Railroads required land grants. Those near the Great Lakes demanded harbor improvements. Manufacturers—who came to western cities almost before the workers did—sought protective tariffs. Democrats seemed congenitally incapable of meeting these demands; opposition parties were only too happy to fill the void.

Although two of the nation's three regions appeared to have less to gain from strict construction, the party most identified with that doctrine—the Democrats—managed to hold on to the reins of power. In 1852 it won its fifth presidential election in seven attempts. It also secured overwhelming majorities in both houses of Congress in the elections of 1852–53. The party's continuing strength stemmed from the very changes that were supposedly rendering it obsolete. It patronized the burgeoning urban population, drawing strength from those cauldrons of the Industrial Revolution that dotted the North. The populations of New York City, Philadelphia, Cleveland, Cincinnati, Chicago, and other cities held deep within themselves populations that preferred and in fact depended upon the Democrats for protection from powerful interests such as banks and employers. Thus the party of strict construction, rather then being swallowed whole by the tidal wave of the Industrial Revolution, rode high upon it, with sails full.

The cities themselves fairly exploded during the 1840s and '50s, largely because of immigration. Between 1845 and 1855 almost 3 million persons arrived in America—some 15 percent of the nation's population in 1845.[16] The deluge was the largest since the inundation of the Roman Empire by the Goths in the fifth century A.D. Most of the newcomers settled in the cities. As early as 1850 immigrants made up a third of the populations of Philadelphia and Boston.[17] St. Louis, Milwaukee, and Chicago all had more for-

16. U.S. Department of Commerce, *Historical Statistics of the United States, Colonial Times to 1957* (Washington, D.C.: U.S. Department of Commerce, Bureau of the Census, 1960), 57.

17. John F. Coleman, *The Disruption of the Pennsylvania Democracy, 1848–1860* (Harrisburg: Pennsylvania Historical and Museum Commission, 1975), 64.

eign-born than native residents by the end of the 1850s.[18] The American city thus became a metropolis almost overnight. New York City and Brooklyn teemed with nearly a million inhabitants by 1860. Philadelphia passed half a million and Baltimore, Boston, Cincinnati, and St. Louis all exceeded 150,000.[19] This growth served as testimony to the changing face of northern labor; so did the fact that by 1860 a majority of workers in the North toiled in nonagricultural pursuits.[20] Many held one of the 1.3 million manufacturing jobs available in 1860.[21] Pennsylvania alone had 150,000.[22] Despite this growth, many persons had trouble obtaining work of any kind. As throughout the antebellum period, the 1850s saw working men and women suffer from a glut in the labor supply.[23] Even for those who could find work, exploitation awaited. Despite the attacks upon it by Jacksonians, paper money survived, and employers continued to pay workers with depreciated notes that were almost never worth their face value. The problem worsened during the boom of the 1850s, as state banks proliferated at a rate unseen since the mid-1830s.[24] Banknotes increased accordingly. Democrats responded by continuing the fight against paper money and sought bans on the notes in the legislatures and in Congress.[25] They had only limited success, and Americans continued to complain bitterly over the use of "shinplasters."[26]

Nativism also linked urban laborers to Democrats during the 1850s. For a time, nativist elements appeared to be on the verge of succeeding the Whigs as the nation's second political party. Their agenda understandably terrified the newly arrived. One group suggested extending the residency requirement for citizenship to twenty-one years. In many states the American Party defeated attempts to end Protestant instruction in the public schools. (The textbooks were often anti-Catholic.) After building steadily in popularity for twenty years, the nativists were enabled by a unique set of cir-

18. Kenneth Stampp, *America in 1857: A Nation on the Brink* (New York: Oxford University Press, 1990), 37.

19. Nevins, *Emergence of Lincoln*, 1:309.

20. McPherson, *Battle Cry of Freedom*, 40.

21. U.S. Department of Commerce, *Statistical Abstract of the United States, 1923* (Washington, D.C.: U.S. Department of Commerce, 1924), 289.

22. Coleman, *Disruption of the Pennsylvania Democracy*, 6.

23. Nevins, *Ordeal of the Union*, vol. 2, *A House Dividing, 1852–1857* (New York: Charles Scribner's Sons, 1947), 279.

24. Nevins, *Emergence of Lincoln*, 1:184–85.

25. In 1854 Congress prohibited notes under $5 from the capital. 10 *Stats at Large* 599 (December 27, 1854).

26. See "Nebraska Shinplasters," *Chicago Tribune*, December 21, 1857, 2.

cumstances to stage a shocking triumph in the state and congressional elections of 1854–55. They won control of the Massachusetts legislature and just missed doing so in New York. Nativists also elected more than one hundred members of the thirty-fourth Congress, including a plurality of the House of Representatives.[27]

Owing in large part to the hostility of nativist parties, Catholic immigrants—who made up a sizeable portion of the laboring classes—formed the strongest Democratic voting block by midcentury. Michigan Irish Catholics voted Democratic at the astounding rate of 95 percent between 1854 and 1860.[28] Abraham Lincoln barely won his hometown of Springfield, Illinois—a longtime Whig bastion—when he ran for president in 1860, mainly because of a recent influx of Irish Catholic immigrants. Ten percent of the city's population in 1850, they made up 20 percent of it in 1860.[29] The Democrats profited hugely from the deluge of immigrants. New York City, which had elected Whig mayors as late as 1850, was overwhelmingly Democratic by 1860.[30] The significance of this development for the national political scene was enormous. During the 1850s the Democrats' embrace of proslavery legislation lost the party support in much of the North, but not in urban areas, where large, persecuted, and helpless populations could not afford to turn away from their Democratic patrons. In states such as New Jersey, the growth of cities made up for votes the Democrats lost because of their extreme proslavery positions.[31] By the end of the 1850s city dwellers were virtually the only voters in the North who still supported the party of Jefferson and Jackson—the rest had been lost to the opposition. As New York congressman Horace Clark put it in 1860, the section's Democrats had been "driven to take refuge within the walls of our northern cities."[32] Its leaders were infuriated by the party's declining influence. Familiar with the myriad ways that business interests used their influence with Whigs and Republicans to obtain policies injurious to the average American, i.e., protective tariffs, they saw the growing antislavery movement as a ploy. Recalling Jeffer-

27. Martis, *Historical Atlas of Parties*, 107.

28. Ronald P. Formisano, *The Birth of Mass Political Parties: Michigan, 1827–1861* (Princeton: Princeton University Press, 1971), 305.

29. Kenneth J. Winkle, "The Second Party System in Lincoln's Springfield," *Civil War History* (December 1998): 10.

30. Bridges, *City in the Republic*, 141.

31. William Gillette, *Jersey Blue: Civil War Politics in New Jersey, 1854–65* (New Brunswick: Rutgers University Press, 1995), 72–73.

32. Quoted in Potter, *Impending Crisis*, 443n60.

son's dismissal of the dispute that preceded the Missouri Compromise as a Federalist plot, Democratic leaders saw the movement against slavery as a political trick devised by the stewards of wealth to undermine the party that alone served the interests of the American people.

For a time, the support of the urban North enabled the Democratic Party to retain majority status despite its unpopular approach to slavery-related issues. At the same time, the party's northern wing became increasingly susceptible to domination by officials in the federal executive branch. A quality of subservience had been evident for years; even in Jefferson's day northern Republicans had been less ideological and more willing to compromise than their southern brethren. This trait was viewed as a weakness. When John Randolph used the term "doughface" at the time of the Missouri Compromise to describe northern congressmen, he did not intend it as a compliment.[33] In later years, critics applied the label to northern congressmen suspected of placing offices and contracts ahead of the interests of the nation. During the Mexican War, northerners complained that the South enjoyed an effective majority in the House of Representatives, as it "had bought up dough-faces enough to control us."[34] By 1848 charges that northern Democratic congressmen had been bribed en masse by the Polk administration in exchange for votes approving war-related appropriations had become commonplace. And, as if the term "doughface" did not make it clear, critics began referring to northern officeholders who were suspect on the slavery question as "hunkers." (They were said to "hunker" for places.) Such men were, as Salmon Chase put it, always "submitting to slaveholding dictation for the spoils of office."[35]

Southern-dominated administrations had been using the powers of office to defend slavery for some time. As early as 1835 the Jackson administration took printing contracts away from William Cullen Bryant's *Evening Post* after it defended abolitionism.[36] James Polk reportedly offered executive branch places to legislators whose support for proslavery legislation had cost them their seats.[37] The State Department kept the Democratic press in line during the Mexican War with the help of an 1846 law that reintroduced the

33. Quoted in Remini, *Henry Clay*, 183; see also Summers, *Plundering Generation*, 225.
34. Quoted in Summers, *Plundering Generation*, 225–26.
35. *The Salmon P. Chase Papers*, ed. John Niven, vol. 2, *Correspondence, 1823–1857* (Kent: Kent State University Press, 1993), 181–82.
36. Cole, *Van Buren and the American Political System*, 274.
37. Summers, *Plundering Generation*, 224.

practice of retaining two newspapers in each state to print the laws. Secretary of State James Buchanan thereafter built up a fleet of obedient Democratic editors who defended what were regarded as the proslavery policies of the Polk administration.[38]

In no area did executive branch patronage and the slavery question collide with more explosive results than in the Democratic organizations of the northern states. Upon taking office in the spring of 1845, the Polk administration antagonized New York Democrats by giving most of the critical plums to the state party's small but influential Hunker wing. What had been a private feud became public after Governor Silas Wright—leader of the Free Soil Democrats in New York—lost his bid for re-election in the fall of 1846. Many Democrats, including Wright himself, blamed the Hunker wing of the party—and the inflated power it enjoyed thanks to its control of the state's federal offices.[39] Even the president held the Hunkers responsible for Wright's loss.[40] The intraparty war continued in 1847, when Congressman Preston King of New York proposed a bill banning slavery in the territories. New York Hunkers, furious with King, held rump elections for the 1847 state Democratic convention. This was no mean feat. To hold elections throughout the state required money and men. Administration Democrats were able to succeed only because they controlled local federal offices, such as the postmasterships. In doing so, they usurped the powers of the state Democratic organization in Albany, which normally arranged those elections itself. In one district, New York Democrats elected a man of their own choosing (A. Harrigan) delegate to the state convention, only to have a squad of customhouse officers appear, seize the ballot boxes, and announce that one Jeremiah Towler was the winner.[41] Thus the *Jefferson (New York) Democrat*'s dismissal of "mock delegates with mock credentials."[42] Empire State residents complained bitterly of "dependents on federal patronage who had attempted to override the sentiments of the New York state Democratic Party" and "pervert its opinions" as well as "dictate its candidates."[43] By the time the New York Democratic convention assembled at Syracuse in September 1847,

38. Smith, *Press, Politics, and Patronage*, 175.
39. John A. Garraty, *Silas Wright* (New York: Columbia University Press, 1949), 375.
40. Quaife, *Diary of Polk*, 2:218 (November 6, 1846).
41. "A Bird's Eye View of the Late Democratic State Convention," *Syracuse Convention: Albany Atlas Extra*, October 1847, 11.
42. *Jefferson Democrat*, October 7, 1847, quoted in ibid., 16.
43. "Resolutions of the Fourth Assembly District of the state of New York," ibid., 15.

Free Soilers had worked themselves into a fury—Silas Wright had dropped dead at his farm earlier that summer, and many blamed the Hunkers for his demise. Before his failure to obtain re-election as governor, many northern-ers expected Wright to be the Democratic candidate for president in 1848. When the state convention met, it included a large number of delegates who had not been elected but who still insisted on participating.[44] Free Soil-ers appeared to have the votes for a resolution against the extension of slav-ery in the territories. Convention chairman Robert Morris—who was also the New York City postmaster—declared the resolution out of order, refused to announce the result of a vote on it, and adjourned the convention.[45]

The influence of federal officials in local politics grew along with the civil list. The federal apparatus more than doubled in size between 1840 and 1860, growing from 23,700 places to 49,200.[46] While the total number of state jobs slightly exceeded those in the federal executive branch through-out the antebellum period, control over state officers was divided between governors and other senior-level officers, as well as various commissions and committees.[47] Almost all federal employees remained subject to removal by the president. Nor did the federal payroll include the thousands of postal contractors and laborers in the customs warehouses. Ostensibly employed by private interests, they owed their jobs to officials in the upper levels of the executive branch.[48] Census workers rounded out the civil list. In 1850 federal marshals hired deputies and assistants for every county in the country. Whig Party leaders put the new civil servants to work in state elections, lobbying voters.[49] One observer estimated that, overall, 150,000 persons at midcentu-ry held positions under the direct control of the president.[50] Of course, even this number paled in comparison to the civil establishments of Europe; on the other hand, government workers on the continent were not subject to the caprices of an individual who could remove them at the drop of a hat.

44. "Remarks of John Van Buren," ibid., 2.

45. Rayback, *Free Soil*, 75–76.

46. U.S. Commerce Department, *Statistical Abstract of the United States, 1923*, 766.

47. Summers, *Plundering Generation*, 24. State and local government spending exceeded federal spending by about 50 percent in 1850 (2.92 percent of the gross national product to 1.93 percent). Susan B. Carter, ed., *Historical Statistics of the United States, Millennial Edition*, 5 vols. (Cambridge: Cambridge University Press, 2006), 5:6 (table Ea-A).

48. Roy Franklin Nichols, *The Disruption of American Democracy* (New York: Macmillan, 1948), 94.

49. Holt, *Rise and Fall of the American Whig Party*, 417.

50. Summers, *Plundering Generation*, 175.

In its usefulness as a tool through which federal officials could impose their will upon state party organizations, no Tammany Hall chieftain could have designed a better system than the federal civil service. Most communities, down to the smallest hamlet, enjoyed a post office—more than eighteen thousand existed in 1850, and another ten thousand would be added by 1860. Some had enormous staffs; New York City's post office employed three hundred by 1860. In large and small towns alike, the term postmaster became synonymous with party leader.[51] In the cities, where bosses needed additional reinforcements in order to control conventions, customhouses provided extra muscle—up to a thousand persons worked in New York City's. Five naval yards along the East Coast added further heft—more than ten thousand workers toiled in them by the fall of 1858.[52] Party leaders maximized the influence to be derived from such a large and dependent bureaucracy through removals. By midcentury the practice had gained acceptance among all but the most pious of reformers; no one protested when Postmaster General Thomas Ewing removed or forced out more than half of the postmasters before Zachary Taylor's death in July 1850.[53]

The spoils system gave federal officials control over thousands of party workers. These legions proved enormously useful at the polls, where success often depended upon which candidate mustered the most party workers to distribute ballots to voters. Federal employees also played a decisive role at nominating conventions. A lack of rules meant that these gatherings continued to be the informal affairs they had been during the 1830s. Consequently they remained susceptible to domination by those willing to use brute force. New York City conventions were particularly bad; during the late 1840s and 1850s they often disintegrated into intimidation and violence, as party bosses used "rowdies" to control them.[54] More often political bosses simply packed these "wide-open, walk-in primaries"—which were often held in taverns—

51. U.S. Commerce Department, *Statistical Abstract of the United States, 1923*, 359; *Report of the Special Committee appointed to investigate whether the President of the United States or any other officers of the government have, by money, patronage or other improper means, sought to influence the action of Congress*, 36th Cong., 1st sess., June 16, 1860, H. Rep. 648 (hereafter Covode Committee Report), 520; Mark L. Berger, *The Revolution in the New York State Party Systems* (Port Washington, N.Y.: Kennikat Press, 1973), 44.

52. *Report of the Select Committee on Naval Contracts and Expenditures*, 35th Cong., 2d sess., February 24, 1859, H. Rep. 184 (hereafter Navy Yards Report), 73.

53. Summers, *Plundering Generation*, 27.

54. Edward K. Spann, *The New Metropolis: New York City, 1840–57* (New York: Columbia University Press, 1981), 327–28.

with their own followers.[55] Because they could deploy so many underlings, federal officials loomed large at these affairs. The susceptibility of nominating conventions to executive branch influence increased considerably as a reform popular among the states took on new force around 1850. Beginning in the first quarter of the century, the states abolished thousands of appointive government offices. The positions themselves remained but became elective.[56] This change stripped state government leaders of the offices necessary to buy support; it also sharply increased the relative influence of local federal officers. This disparity increased sharply between 1848 and 1854, when nine states enacted new constitutions. Many reduced the number of appointive offices available. Ohio made all of the senior posts in the state bureaucracy elective, including those in the judiciary. Maryland made similar changes, and by 1855 the state governor had but 160 jobs at his disposal.[57]

Federal officials thereby obtained enormous power relative to other politicians, simply because they controlled the most jobs. For northern Democrats the situation proved to be a huge problem during the 1850s, as successive administrations of their own party sent legions of federal officeholders to take over state nominating conventions for the purpose of extracting proslavery planks or candidates. By the end of the decade, northern Democrats could not, as one observer put it, so much as hold a meeting without the administration trying to influence or control it.[58] Federal meddling advanced furthest in states where the party of the president was weakest, as few cared to oppose federal officeholders seeking to appease their bosses. In Massachusetts the Democratic Party was so anemic that it constituted little more than a union of postal and customs employees. Party leaders Robert Rantoul and Benjamin Hallett of the *Boston Times* and Postmaster Charles Greene winnowed Free Soil elements so effectively that an antislavery plank obtained but a single vote at the state Democratic convention of 1847.[59] Critics joked that New England Democrats in the federal civil service embraced unpopular policies in order to ensure there would be just enough Democrats

55. Edwin G. Burrows and Mike Wallace, *Gotham: A History of New York City to 1898* (New York: Oxford University Press, 1999), 823.

56. McCormick, *Second American Party System*, 29.

57. Summers, *Plundering Generation*, 32; Holt, *Rise and Fall of the American Whig Party*, 660 (Ohio); Jean H. Baker, *The Politics of Continuity: Maryland Politics from 1858 to 1870* (Baltimore: Johns Hopkins University Press, 1973), 21 (Maryland).

58. Summers, *Plundering Generation*, 31, 224.

59. Rayback, *Free Soil*, 78.

to fill the available offices. The reaction of Democratic Party regulars to a report in the *Springfield Republican* demonstrated that such jokes were not far off the truth. When the paper asserted that the Democratic ticket in one Massachusetts county was selected by a convention consisting of five delegates, all of whom had been postmasters, one of the delegates angrily informed the editor that there had been twelve delegates to the convention— only three of whom were postmasters.[60]

Federal executive branch officials also enjoyed enormous political leverage in the new states. Even after a territory's admission to the Union, federal officials continued to operate from a position of strength, as new states tended to have smaller, elective bureaucracies. Federal land offices, however, offered dozens of appointive positions. Men such as Asahel Bush of Oregon used executive branch patronage to obtain influence; in exchange they provided badly needed support to Democratic administrations unpopular for their proslavery policies. Whigs naturally complained; in his "higher law" speech, William Seward claimed that the "concentration of the slave power enables you [the South], for long periods, to control the federal government, with the aid of the new states." He went on to advise southern senators to vote for California's admission, as her senators and representatives would vote with the South.[61] He was right, they did. California, Oregon, Iowa, and Minnesota all provided Democratic votes at a time when they became hard to find elsewhere in the North (all four states elected doughface Democrats to the Senate during the 1850s).[62]

Some states in the West saw the rise of formidable political machines that thrived on their alliances with proslavery Democratic administrations. In Oregon, boss Asahel Bush and his "Salem clique" lived on federal printing contracts and enjoyed veto power over federal jobs in the territory. The star of the group was Joe Lane, a former Indiana resident who came to the territory after serving in the Mexican War. President Polk appointed him territorial governor. Lane later served in the House as a territorial delegate and won friends at home by obtaining large appropriations for roads.[63] With statehood in 1859, Oregon sent Lane to the Senate. He ingratiated himself so thoroughly with the proslavery extremists at the head of the party

60. Summers, *Plundering Generation,* 31, 310n24.

61. *Congressional Globe,* 33d Cong., 1st sess., Appendix, 23:268.

62. Summers, *Plundering Generation,* 229.

63. James E. Hendrickson, *Joe Lane of Oregon: Machine Politics and the Sectional Crisis, 1849–61* (New Haven: Yale University Press, 1967), 60, 90–91, 113, 44, 102–3.

that they put him on the national ticket in 1860. California's Democratic machine—"the Chivalry"—proved even more successful. Led by doughface senator William Gwyn, it "assessed" 10 percent of the salaries of all resident civil servants. The Chivalry also had federal employees appear at the polls to hand out Democratic ballots to voters.[64] It borrowed a tactic from Democrats back East and had the state government run up enormous printing bills so that contractors could make generous contributions to the party.[65] For a time it flirted with the idea of having southern California secede so that another slave state might be formed.[66]

Americans reacted with pointed hostility to this state of affairs. Federal civil servants in the North found themselves increasingly viewed as agents of a powerful proslavery faction in Washington—the "slavocracy"—that would stop at nothing to preserve and extend its influence. These fears seemed to receive confirmation from reports linking federal executive branch officials with that other scourge of the age—electoral corruption. With the rise of large, impoverished urban populations, the buying and selling of votes grew from the mere source of irritation it had been during the Jacksonian period into a genuine plague. To many, the extent of the problem appeared to confirm Jefferson's suspicion that cities and self-government were incompatible. The growth of electoral bribery in combination with worsening corruption in the legislatures and in Congress led some to conclude that public virtue— the most critical ingredient in any republic—was in serious jeopardy.[67] After the 1858–59 midterm elections, which had been badly marred by fraud, President James Buchanan felt obligated to address these concerns with a letter warning of the consequences of electoral corruption.[68] As congressional investigations would reveal, his administration was involved in the frauds up to its ears.[69]

Electoral corruption and the use of federal employees to control nominating conventions were two critical elements of the national political machine that emerged during the 1850s; another was the party press, which

---

64. David C. Williams, *David C. Broderick: A Political Portrait* (San Marino, Calif.: Huntington Library, 1969), 99.

65. "From the Pacific Side," *New York Times*, September 26, 1853, 2.

66. Fehrenbacher, *Slaveholding Republic*, 293–94.

67. Summers, *Plundering Generation*, 62–63, 54–56, 169–70.

68. James Buchanan, letter of November 22, 1858, *The Works of James Buchanan*, ed. John Bassett Moore, 12 vols. (Philadelphia: J. B. Lippincott, 1910) (hereafter *Works of Buchanan*), 10:233–34.

69. See Covode Committee Report, 388–93.

continued to feed at the public trough. While partisan editors faced competition in the form of a new generation of large, independent newspapers, politicians discovered that the so-called independent press could be particularly useful, precisely because voters thought it was above influence and thus relied more heavily on it.[70] Candidates made a habit of securing the support of these newspapers through the purchase of advertisements. Nor did the old-fashioned party paper disappear—the vast majority of newspapers remained partisan sheets dependent on government printing contracts.[71] It was in part because of their explicit party identification that newspapers retained fervently loyal readers. Voters of upstate New York continued to rely on the *Albany Argus,* the newspaper of the old Regency machine.[72] The wife of an Alabama senator later recalled three lessons learned in childhood: read the Bible, have pride in her family and section, and know the (Democratic) *Richmond Enquirer.*[73] Politicians themselves certainly did not think the day of the party sheet had passed; if they had the wealth or influence to establish their own, they almost always did so. Robert Barnwell Rhett had his *Charleston Mercury,* James Buchanan his *Press.* When Stephen Douglas of Illinois lost control of his newspaper in the early 1850s, he immediately set up a new one—the *Chicago Times.*[74] Americans hungrily accepted their offerings. They devoured newspapers at a pace unmatched by any other people on the planet. Almost every household, even on the frontier, received a newspaper, usually through the mail.[75] Newspapers possessed enormous influence in part because Americans remained an acutely political people. They debated the issues of the day to the point of exhaustion and stood in the open for hours, listening to the speeches of prominent orators such as Edward Everett of Massachusetts. Editors devoted entire pages to the transcripts of congressional debates that had been initially published in the *Congressional Globe.* At midcentury, politics was very much the national sport, and newspapers were almost alone in their ability to satiate the public's appetite for it.[76] Editors naturally used this power to spread their views and those of the politicians upon whom they depended for support.

The continued success of the party press, in combination with electoral

70. Summers, *Plundering Generation,* 47.     71. Stampp, *America in 1857,* 31.
72. Summers, *Plundering Generation,* 39.
73. Peterson, *Jefferson Image in the American Mind,* 38.
74. Nevins, *Ordeal of the Union,* 2:336n92.
75. McDonald, *States' Rights and the Union,* 89.
76. Nevins, *Ordeal of the Union,* 1:57.

corruption and the use of offices to control the nation's dominant political party, vested in federal officials a staggering amount of power. Two Democratic administrations exploited this situation during the 1850s to promote the agenda of proslavery southerners. Thus one of the great ironies of the antebellum Republic: the group that most fervently embraced the belief that federal power ought to remain limited profited enormously from the unwillingness of the country to heed its warnings.

KANSAS

While the compromise acts quelled talk of secession, underlying differences continued to produce rancor and distrust. To each section the federal government appeared as both an ally and a threat—capable of limiting slavery's expansion and also possessed of the means to stifle antislavery sentiment. As it became clear that sectional discord would continue to haunt the country despite the compromise acts, control of the federal apparatus was increasingly viewed by elements in both the North and the South as a matter of the gravest importance.

Stephen Douglas took the early lead in the race for the 1852 Democratic presidential nomination. Owing in part to what was viewed as youthful impetuousness, the Illinois senator ran out of steam by the time of the national convention. Party leaders reasoned that Douglas would have plenty of opportunities in the future to cash in on his role in pushing through the Compromise of 1850. Democrats did not have many alternatives. Some favored U.S. Supreme Court Justice Levi Woodbury of New Hampshire—a rare northerner with spotless strict constructionist credentials—until he expired in September 1851. Woodbury's backers then turned to another orthodox Democrat from New Hampshire, Franklin Pierce. With the help of southern delegations, Pierce prevailed over James Buchanan of Pennsylvania at the June 1852 Democratic convention in Baltimore. The Whigs selected General Winfield Scott of Virginia when President Fillmore let the nomination slip through his hands. It may not have been worth having. A southern faction abandoned the party after the nomination despite the fact that Scott was a slave owner; a northern group left a few weeks later.

General Scott was well known to the country as one of the heroes of the Mexican War. Franklin Pierce, while a successful public servant, did not enjoy anything approaching Scott's name recognition. Son of Revolutionary War hero Benjamin Pierce, he had been active in New Hampshire politics since the 1820s. He rose steadily from state representative to speaker of the statehouse to U.S. representative and senator. During his long career, Pierce earned a reputation as a doughface (he was accused of it as early as 1836). Many northern Democrats who participated in national politics during the antebellum period could have been accused of the same thing; the fact remains that Pierce seems to have earned the title more than almost any other northerner. When fellow New Hampshire Democrat John Hale voted against the annexation of Texas in 1844 despite the state legislature's request that he vote for it, Pierce led the drive for Hale's scalp and succeeded in having the senator removed from the party ticket.[77] Years of service to his party won Pierce an officer's commission at the beginning of the Mexican War; serving alongside southerners cemented his sympathy for the South.

It is not clear that any issues divided the candidates in the 1852 presidential election. Both men called for adherence to the Compromise of 1850 and resisted attempts to revive slavery-related questions. Democrats made much of an 1845 letter of Scott's in which he appeared to embrace nativism; Whigs for their part dismissed Pierce as a drunkard. Pierce won the election by a comfortable margin in the Electoral College, carrying twenty-seven of thirty-one states (though his margin in almost all of them was close). The immigrant vote—which had increased substantially since 1848—proved critical to his victory.[78]

Although the new president had to overcome a reputation as a doughface to win the election, he gave important cabinet appointments to two men who thrived on sectional politics: Jeff Davis of Mississippi (secretary of war) and Caleb Cushing of Massachusetts (attorney general). Davis served with distinction in the Mexican War; thereafter he sought to position himself as the heir to Calhoun's mantle in the Senate. Caleb Cushing, by contrast, had been ostracized in his native state. The Massachusetts lawyer compiled one of the longest and strangest careers of any figure in American public life during the nineteenth century. Cushing entered Harvard at thirteen and became fluent in four languages, went to law school, and taught mathematics before leaving in his early twenties. During the 1830s he served in the U.S. House of Representatives alongside John Quincy Adams, where he presented antislavery petitions until the nervous Democratic majority put

77. Cole, *Jacksonian Democracy in New Hampshire*, 182, 218–24.
78. Holt, *Rise and Fall of the American Whig Party*, 761.

an end to the practice.[79] Cushing voted against the admission of Arkansas because its constitution withheld the power to abolish slavery from the legislature.[80] In the early 1840s he began to turn, and he was among the last northerners willing to serve in John Tyler's cabinet. Cushing played a critical role in opening China to American trade; James Polk rewarded him with a brigadier general's commission. As with Pierce, the experience of serving alongside southern men in the Mexican War deepened Cushing's sympathy for the South. Upon returning home he gained a reputation as one of the North's most notorious doughfaces. In the process Cushing became a despised figure in his own state of Massachusetts; voters twice rejected him as a candidate for governor. When he received an appointment to the state supreme court, antislavery elements howled.[81]

Between the president's history as an enemy of Free Soil Democrats, Cushing's unholy conversion, and the presence of Jeff Davis in the War Department, antislavery Democrats held out little hope for federal appointments when the Pierce administration came to life in March 1853. To the surprise of all Washington, the new regime doled out favors to Free Soilers and Hunkers alike.[82] Eager to unite the party, Pierce sacked newly appointed collector of the Port of New York, Greene C. Bronson, when Bronson refused to employ Free Soilers. While the president filled the vacancy with another Hunker (or Hardshell, as they were called in New York), he also named John A. Dix, a Free Soiler, assistant collector. This approach extended to members of Congress: the administration promised each Democratic representative and senator—including Free Soilers—three or four positions in the executive branch for their supporters.[83] For a time, the strategy worked—once again, federal largesse appeared to be serving the cause of conciliation. Antislavery zealots such as Salmon Chase of Ohio naturally complained. He would have preferred a policy that excluded Free Soilers altogether instead of one that offered "bribes to antislavery Democrats to desert their principles."[84]

In exchange for appointments, the administration expected Free Soil

79. See Edward Lee Miller, *Arguing about Slavery: The Great Battle in the United States Congress* (New York: Knopf, 1996), 242–44.

80. Sister M. Michael Catherine Hodgson, O.P., *Caleb Cushing: Attorney General of the United States, 1853–57* (Washington, D.C.: The Catholic University of America Press, 1955), 25n72.

81. Nevins, *Ordeal of the Union*, 2:49.         82. Ibid., 2:70.

83. White, *Jacksonians*, 397–98.

84. Niven, *Salmon P. Chase Papers*, 2:378 (December 14, 1853).

Democrats to bring their antislavery agitation to an end. When Massachusetts Democrats entered into electoral coalitions with Free Soil elements, Attorney General Cushing sent them an extraordinary letter, warning that "to support or vote for free soilers in Massachusetts" would be to aid those interested in the "persistent agitation of the slavery question" and was "therefore hostile in the highest degree to the determined policy of the administration." Such a thing would not be allowed. "If there be any purpose more fixed than another in the mind of the President . . . it is that the dangerous element of abolitionism, under whatever guise or form it may present itself, shall be crushed out, so far as his administration is concerned."[85] Bay State residents reacted to the warning much as their forebears had reacted to the Stamp Act. Bostonians held a huge rally at Faneuil Hall at which Charles Francis Adams—son of John Quincy Adams—angrily denounced "Cushing's Ukase."[86] The idea of executive branch officials dictating to state parties struck many as wholly at odds with the federal system. One Massachusetts Democrat complained that "if we are to acknowledge the right of this administration to intermeddle in the [state] elections . . . we may as well give up having a state administration & become an empire at once."[87] Similar disturbances occurred elsewhere in the fall of 1853, as executive branch officials attempted to stamp out Free Soil sentiment. When Free Soilers bolted the New York state Democratic convention in September, Attorney General Cushing attacked the move as an "organized insurrection of a portion of the Democratic Party against its necessary chief, the President."[88] The following month, California Democrats issued a rebuke. Furious over the administration's meddling in their intraparty squabbles, they published "The Address of the Majority," in which they complained of the "interference of the federal power and patronage with our domestic policies."[89] By the time the thirty-third Congress met in December 1853, it was evident that the administration's attempts to stifle Free Soil sentiment had backfired, as Democrats throughout the North complained of its attempts to impose its will upon state parties.[90]

85. Quoted in Hodgson, *Caleb Cushing*, 222.
86. Nevins, *Ordeal of the Union*, 2:74.
87. Quoted in Hodgson, *Caleb Cushing*, 86–87n17.
88. Ibid., 82.
89. Quoted in Williams, *David C. Broderick*, 87.
90. Nevins, *Ordeal of the Union*, 2:76; see speech of Hiram Walbridge in the House of Representatives of January 20, 1854, *Congressional Globe*, 33d Cong., 1st sess., 23.1:88–89.

It was in the midst of these frictions that the issue of slavery in the territories reappeared. A disastrous series of events for the administration, the Democratic Party, and the country had its origin in a dispute over the appropriate route for an intercontinental railroad. In early 1853, Senator Stephen Douglas proposed a bill providing for the organization of the Nebraska territory—a necessary prerequisite to the construction of a railroad through the area. The House passed the measure, and Senate approval—long thought unlikely—appeared to be within reach. The key change came from Missouri senator David R. Atchison, who announced that he would go along with the organization of the Nebraska territory despite the fact that it would probably mean another free state.[91] The bill stalled when Senator Atchison's fellow southerners decided to oppose it. Douglas took up the matter again when the thirty-fourth Congress convened in December 1853. Armed with another Nebraska bill, he set out to neutralize all possible sources of opposition. As the Democratic majority in each house of Congress approached 70 percent, the bill's prospects once again turned solely on the question of whether southerners would accept it. Unfortunately for Douglas, Atchison resumed his initial opposition to the measure. The Illinois senator would obviously have to do something more to win southern support. That he had not done so already must have come as a surprise to Douglas, given a clause within the bill. It provided that the states carved from the Nebraska territory would be admitted "with or without slavery," as their constitutions provided at the time of admission. The phrase had been borrowed from the 1850 acts organizing the territories of New Mexico and Utah.[92] Those newly conquered territories had never been subject to the prohibition of slavery in areas north of 36´30˝ contained in the Missouri Compromise. Nebraska, however, was north of 36´30˝ and within the region formerly known as the Louisiana territory—the area from which slavery had been banned by the Missouri Compromise.

In a bid to obtain political cover, Douglas included a clause declaring that in explicitly empowering the people of Kansas and Nebraska to legislate on the subject of slavery, the act merely carried out the principles of the Compromise of 1850—all slavery questions ought to be decided by territo-

91. See speech of David Atchison, *Congressional Globe,* 32d Cong., 2d sess., March 3, 1853, 22:1111.

92. Nevins, *Ordeal of the Union,* 2:94. For the acts organizing New Mexico and Utah, see *Stats at Large* 9 (1862), 446 and 453 (both September 9, 1850).

rial residents themselves.[93] One week later, Achibald Dixon, a Whig senator from Kentucky, proposed an additional amendment. It provided that the Missouri Compromise's ban on slavery north of 36´30˝ would not apply to territory "contemplated by this act, or to any other territory of the United States; but that the citizens of the several states or territories shall be at liberty to take and hold their slaves within any of the territories of the United States, or of the states to be formed therefrom, as if said act . . . had never been passed."[94]

President Pierce informed Douglas that he opposed Dixon's amendment, and the administration newspaper, the *Washington Union*, attacked it as likely to inflame sectional frictions. Such was his determination to win passage of the bill that Douglas added the clause to it anyway. He also altered the measure so that it provided for two territories—Nebraska and Kansas—in order to exploit southern hopes for an additional slave state. With the help of Jefferson Davis, Douglas overcame Pierce's resistance. The two men persuaded the president to write the section repealing the Missouri Compromise himself. This was a critical move. It ensured Pierce's support and made clear that the bill was a party measure.[95] The pertinent clause now provided that the Constitution and all federal laws would apply in the new territories, "except the eighth section of the act preparatory to the admission of Missouri into the Union, approved March 6, 1820, which was superseded by the principles of the legislation of 1850, commonly called the compromise measures, and is declared inoperative."[96]

The Compromise of 1850 "superseded" the Compromise of 1820. How? The president did not say. Douglas proposed a substitute bill with the new amendment the next day (Monday, January 23), and the *Washington Union* promptly endorsed it.[97] Leading Democrats took the hint and began pushing the line that the Missouri Compromise had already been repealed and that, since 1850, the ruling principle in the territories had been popular sovereignty. This was patently false—no one had ever heard of the idea that the Congress had, through the acts of 1850, repealed the Missouri Compromise. Slaveholders did not start trickling into the northern half of the territories with their chattel in tow. It was true that the laws organizing New Mexico

93. Nevins, *Ordeal of the Union*, 2:95.
94. *Congressional Globe*, 33d Cong., 1st sess., 23.1:175.
95. See Nevins, *Ordeal of the Union*, 2:99, 110.
96. *Congressional Globe*, 33d Cong., 1st sess., January 23, 1854, 23.1:222.
97. Ibid., 221–22.

and Utah provided for popular sovereignty even though both territories extended north of 36´30˝. Yet those regions were part of the Mexican cession. The adoption of popular sovereignty in those territories could not be fairly described as having repealed the Missouri Compromise and its prohibition of slavery in the Louisiana territory. Thus the Kansas bill, and not the acts of 1850, constituted a revolutionary change in policy. As of January 1, 1854, the whole of the territorial United States had been organized, and sectional compromises resulted in the prohibition of slavery in all of the territories north of 36´30˝ except Utah and New Mexico. Barring the purchase of more land, the thorniest of all slavery-related issues had been resolved. Douglas's bill, if passed, would repeal the most important of these sectional adjustments (the Missouri Compromise), and in the process drag the issue of slavery in the territories back into the spotlight.

Northerners were incensed. The Missouri Compromise was widely viewed as a critical sectional adjustment that had contributed immeasurably to national harmony. Hostility to the Kansas bill overtook the whole of the region almost overnight. Many towns held public meetings at which citizens bitterly attacked it. Five northern legislatures passed resolutions condemning the measure.[98] Northern objections were not completely principled. Many northerners simply did not want blacks in Kansas—just as they did not want them in Illinois or Iowa (both of which had enacted laws prohibiting blacks from entering). Whatever their motives, northerners were furious. This frustration manifested itself in the congressional debates of early 1854. Most infuriating to antislavery legislators was the claim that the Missouri Compromise had been discarded in 1850. Senator Ben Wade of Ohio, after pointing out that many in his section held the Missouri Compromise in almost as high regard as they did the Constitution itself, asked who, six months earlier, thought it had been repealed? Stephen Douglas insisted that the Missouri Compromise had been "superseded by a principle" (popular sovereignty) in 1850. Wade was not having it. While he had not been in Senate at that time, he had read the transcripts of the debates—no one had expressed the view that the bills organizing the New Mexico and Utah territories repealed the Missouri Compromise.[99]

Debate in Congress ranged back and forth from the merits of the legislation to the legality of prohibiting slavery in the territories. Richard Brod-

98. Nevins, *Ordeal of the Union*, 2:146.
99. *Congressional Globe*, 33d Cong., 1st sess., February 6, 1854, 23.1:337–38.

head of Pennsylvania recalled that many southern legislators who now denied the legality of such a ban had spent four years (1846–50) campaigning to extend the Missouri Compromise line to the Pacific. Lewis Cass insisted that Congress lacked the power to ban slaves in the territories, as "political jurisdiction is entirely withheld" from it. John M. Clayton of Delaware questioned why Congress should allow the people of Nebraska to vote on the issue. The residents of a territory did not always deserve the right of self-government, in his view. Utah, with its own "peculiar institution"—a Mormon "theocracy"—constituted one such case. Representative L. D. Campbell of Ohio suggested that, if nothing else, time had settled the question of the legality of the Missouri Compromise, just as it had with the Louisiana Purchase. Presley Ewing of Kentucky disagreed. He held that the Missouri Compromise was unconstitutional, at least with respect to the states that had been carved out of the Louisiana Purchase. He also attacked the notion that precedent should be viewed as having settled the matter—if it had, why did so many continue to insist that a national bank would be unconstitutional? There was also the matter of sectional equity. The Louisiana Territory had been purchased with money from the "common treasury." Thus "common justice require[s] that it be held for the benefit of all the people of all states." J. C. Allen of Illinois agreed that the Missouri Compromise violated the Constitution to the extent that it applied to states. He also pointed out that at least a portion of Utah had been part of the Louisiana Purchase—to that extent, at least, the 1850 measures allowing popular sovereignty repealed the Missouri Compromise. Thomas H. Bayly of Virginia hauled out Calhoun's trustee doctrine. The public lands, he insisted, were "held by this government in trust" for the benefit of the states, and Congress could not dispose of them in a way that disregarded that trust. Israel Washburn of Maine believed that the power of legislation with respect to Nebraska (including the power to ban slavery) must reside "somewhere within the American political system because that power had been transferred to the U.S. from France at the time of Louisiana Purchase." He thought it came within the scope of the territory and treaty powers of Congress. George Bliss of Ohio held that although there might not be any express constitutional authority to legislate for the territories, all sides had acquiesced in the exercise of such a power ever since Congress first purchased foreign territory "with just as little constitutional authority." Bliss insisted that if the territorial legislatures could not enact laws banning slavery, they could not pass laws to protect it, either. As slavery existed only where it was recognized by positive (statutory) law, the institution could never exist in the territories—no one had the power to introduce it.[100]

The most memorable aspect of the battle over what became known as the Kansas-Nebraska Act was not the debate over federal power in the territories. That ground had been turned over before and would be again. The most significant element of the episode, at least in the context of federal power, was the executive branch's use of the powers of office to win approval of the Kansas bill. State Democratic organizations were subjected to a withering assault by the executive branch. In resorting to scorched-earth tactics, administration officials acknowledged the difficulty of the task that lay before them. While most observers expected the Senate to pass the bill—there were too many doughface Democrats in that body for defeat to have been a possibility—the House was another matter. Democratic representatives from the North recalled 1846–47, when voters, irritated over the war, the Walker Tariff, and river and harbor vetoes, decimated their ranks and turned the House over to the Whigs. Given the uproar already in progress over the Kansas bill, political oblivion awaited any northern Democrat who dared to vote in favor of it.

Legislators received no sympathy from the president. In an article said to have been written by Attorney General Caleb Cushing, the *Washington Union* stated that the bill merely implemented the principles of the Compromise of 1850, and therefore "cannot fail to command the support of all Democrats who are standing faithfully" on that measure as the "final and permanent settlement of the slavery question."[101] Democratic editors in the North were expected to spout this doctrine or face losing their place at the public trough. When many nevertheless criticized the bill, the administration pulled the reins in a manner so efficient and ruthless that it left even long-time observers in awe. President Pierce himself told a group of Connecticut citizens visiting the executive mansion that he would discipline the editor of the *Hartford Times* (a Democratic newspaper that enjoyed federal contracts) for printing anti-Nebraska letters.[102] Secretary of State William Marcy withheld contracts from anti-Nebraska newspapers.[103] Some Democratic printers

---

100. Ibid., February–April 1854, Appendix, 23:249, 277, 390–91, 245, 251–54, 405–6, 493, 504.
101. Quoted in Hodgson, *Caleb Cushing*, 148–50.
102. Nevins, *Ordeal of the Union*, 2:147.
103. Ivor Debenham Spencer, *The Victor and the Spoils: A Life of William L. Marcy* (Providence: Brown University Press, 1959), 280.

attempted to toe the line. Of the party's editors in New England, one reporter wrote that they had been "pensioned on government money . . . their
servile echo is thus secured." As public anger mounted, however, editors began to defect. Throughout the North an odd correlation developed—most of
the dwindling number of sheets that continued to support the Kansas bill
also happened to be on the federal wagon. The editor of the *Milwaukee News*
received printing contracts and at the same time found the bill reasonable;
the postmasters who operated the *Kenosha Democrat* and the *Racine Democrat*
also embraced it. Their thinking was undoubtedly summed up by Congressman John Wentworth, proprietor of the *Chicago Democrat.* When asked why
he refused to publish letters critical of the Kansas bill, the former champion
of the Wilmot Proviso acknowledged his fear of party leaders in Washington:
"I have too many favors to ask . . . to quarrel with them."[104]

The administration's campaign did not begin in earnest until March 21,
when a procedural vote in the House sent the Kansas measure to the Committee of the Whole, which was scheduled to consider some fifty other pieces of legislation first.[105] As this was seen as something of a test vote and
a defeat, the administration launched a furious lobbying campaign. All the
members of the cabinet save one appeared at the Capitol to lobby House
members.[106] Attorney General Cushing promised Massachusetts Democrats
that support for the administration would bring them federal jobs worth
more than $1 million in aggregate salaries, while the state government jobs
Free Soilers could offer were worth no more than $75,000.[107] Stephen Doug-
las sought to keep northwestern Democrats on board. He had to contend
with the belief, already widespread among lawmakers, that a vote for the bill
would bring an end to one's career in Washington. It was at this point that
the administration's patronage policies—places for all Democrats, including
Free Soilers—began to pay dividends. With so many independent-minded
Democrats given places for their friends, the president's influence extended
to all elements of the party. The administration had only to threaten to remove what had already been given in order to win support for the bill.[108]
President Pierce was remarkably direct about it; he warned New York repre-

104. Quoted in Summers, *Plundering Generation,* 49, 211.
105. *Congressional Globe,* 33d Cong., 1st sess., March 21, 1854, 23.1:703. See also Potter, *Impending Crisis,* 165.
106. Nevins, *Ordeal of the Union,* 2:154.
107. Leonard L. Richards, *The Slave Power: The Free North and Southern Domination* (Baton Rouge: Louisiana State University Press, 2000), 187.
108. Summers, *Plundering Generation,* 210–11.

sentatives visiting the executive mansion that their access to federal patronage would be taken away if they did not vote for the Kansas bill.[109] Perhaps the most notorious incident involved Democratic senator Hannibal Hamlin of Maine. Cushing approached him early in the fight and offered additional offices for his supporters if Hamlin would support the measure. When that failed, Pierce called the senator to the executive mansion and asked him what he would do if the administration made it a party test. Hamlin insisted he could not support the bill without losing his self-respect.[110] At that point Pierce warned Hamlin of the fate of Hugh White and John C. Calhoun, both of whom had crossed Andrew Jackson. Hamlin was unmoved.[111]

For at least a few lawmakers, honey took the place of vinegar. The State Department successfully dangled vacant consulates in Chile, London, and Turin before the eyes of legislators. Congressman William Tweed of New York secured the removal of a postmaster so that an ally could have the post. The administration's campaign picked up momentum during the spring. Of the five Democratic-controlled legislatures in the North that were in session, four—those of New Jersey, Ohio, Pennsylvania, and California—ignored popular sentiment and refused to pass anti-Nebraska resolutions, largely out of fear that members would lose their access to federal patronage.[112] John Cochrane, surveyor for the Port of New York, extracted resolutions endorsing the Kansas bill from the state Democratic general committee.[113]

Difficulties remained. With northern Whigs opposed to the measure and increasing numbers of Democrats realizing it would be their end if they voted for it, success remained in doubt all through April. By May matters had begun to turn; Alexander Stephens of Georgia proved effective as the administration's floor leader in the House. On May 8 the Committee of the Whole decided to lay aside eighteen other bills in order to take up the Kansas measure immediately. Two weeks later, on May 22, the House passed the bill, 113 to 100. Twenty-one members did not vote. The Senate approved it on May 25 (35–13), and the president signed the Kansas-Nebraska Act on May 30, 1854.[114]

Proslavery southerners rejoiced. The North fumed at yet another victory

109. Roy Franklin Nichols, *Franklin Pierce* (Philadelphia: University of Pennsylvania Press, 1958), 324.

110. H. Draper Hunt, *Hannibal Hamlin: Lincoln's First Vice-President* (Syracuse: Syracuse University Press, 1969), 82.

111. Nichols, *Franklin Pierce*, 334.

112. Summers, *Plundering Generation*, 210–11, 208.

113. Berger, *Revolution in the New York State Party Systems*, 21.

114. *Congressional Globe*, 33d Cong., 1st sess., May 1854, 23.2:1131–32, 1254, 1321.

for the "slavocracy." From the moment of its passage Democrats could not agree on a single interpretation of the law. Northerners, including Douglas, viewed it as a further extension of popular sovereignty, while southerners continued to insist that no federal entity, including territorial legislatures, could prohibit slavery in the territories. They saw the bill as empowering the people of Kansas and Nebraska to address the issue of slavery only at the time when they devised state constitutions in preparation for statehood.[115] Perhaps the only area of agreement was the widespread view that purchased votes had decided the matter. Southerners saw the bill's passage as confirming their expectations that northern representatives would "bluster" and then end up "knocking themselves under to the highest bidder."[116] Northerners also suspected that venality had played a role.

By the time of the 1854–55 elections, the North had worked itself into a collective fury. Most of the heat focused on Stephen Douglas. The senator joked that he could have traveled from Boston to his home in Chicago "by the light of my own effigy."[117] The administration made the mistake of attempting to stifle northern anger. When state Democratic organizations held nominating conventions in the summer and fall of 1854, contingents of federal officeholders attempted to impose their will. In New York the Democratic state convention took place in Syracuse. By the end of the first day, federal officeholders had so dominated the proceedings that the *New York Times* could report that "the custom-house, thus far, is ahead."[118] The platform committee, which included both the collector and the surveyor of the Port of New York, drafted resolutions that only mildly criticized Kansas-Nebraska. The resolutions disavowed attempts to reenact the Missouri Compromise. Angry over the committee's refusal to condemn the administration in stronger terms, former congressman Preston King and more than one hundred other delegates left the convention. Federal officeholders ensured that Democratic state conventions in New Hampshire, Vermont,

---

115. Nevins, *Ordeal of the Union*, 2:157. Section 14 of the Kansas-Nebraska Act provided that it was "true intent and meaning of this act not to legislate slavery into any Territory of State, nor to exclude it therefrom, but to leave the people thereof perfectly free to form and regulate their domestic institutions in their own way, subject only to the Constitution of the United States." 10 *Stats at Large* 277, 283 (section 14).

116. Quoted in Summers, *Plundering Generation*, 212.

117. Quoted in Johannsen, *Stephen A. Douglas*, 451.

118. Quoted in "New York Democratic State Convention," *New York Times*, September 7, 1854, 1.

Maine, and Pennsylvania also sided with the administration.[119] In Illinois, Stephen Douglas secured resolutions endorsing Kansas-Nebraska.[120]

The administration reaped its harvest in the elections for the thirty-fourth Congress, which extended from September 1854 to November 1855. The party of Jefferson and Jackson not only lost the House of Representatives, its ranks were absolutely decimated—the number of seats held by northern Democrats dropped from ninety-three to twenty-three.[121] In Pennsylvania, administration Democrats retained only six of twenty-five seats.[122] In New York they won only two of thirty-one seats.[123] Democrats lost even New Hampshire and Maine, both of which had been longtime party strongholds. Iowa also fell; it elected its first Whig governor, and the legislature replaced Augustus Dodge, one of the Senate's most notorious doughfaces, with Free Soiler James Harlan.[124] Past services earned Dodge an appointment as minister to Spain. Democrats did better in the South; the party fared well in parts of the region where it formerly had little luck, such as North Carolina.[125] If the Democrats were badly crippled by the election, the Whig Party did not even survive it. In its place emerged a coalition of Free Soil Democrats, antislavery Whigs, and nativists, or "Know-Nothings." These elements eventually coalesced into the Republican Party. Essentially the Whig Party reformed, the new party defined itself by its absolute opposition to the further extension of slavery in the territories. Republicans also intended to remove slavery, or the possibility of it, from the Kansas and Nebraska territories and therefore called for repeal of the act of the same name.

Even as a revolution overtook the North, the administration held to its disastrous course. Executive branch officers plagued northern Democrats whenever they dared to meet. New York "Softshells" returned to Syracuse for their annual convention in September 1855. (The New York state Democratic Party split into two wings during the decade, largely over the determination of one faction, the Hardshells, that party members opposed to the extension of slavery—Softshells—should not have access to federal patronage.) To their chagrin, the state's Softshells found upon arriving in Syracuse that executive branch employees intended to serve as hosts. All told,

119. Berger, *Revolution in the New York State Party Systems,* 46–47.
120. Johannsen, *Stephen A. Douglas,* 450.
121. McPherson, *Battle Cry of Freedom,* 129.
122. Coleman, *Disruption of the Pennsylvania Democracy,* 75.
123. Nevins, *Ordeal of the Union,* 2:341.        124. Johannsen, *Stephen A. Douglas,* 451.
125. Nevins, *Ordeal of the Union,* 2:345.

some eighty members of the convention held federal office, and another fifty sought what one historian called "preferment."[126] When administration Democrats attempted to prevent the passage of resolutions critical of the president, Softshell Democrats erupted. One upstate delegate warned that when "people from the City of New York" ask us to "go against the will of our constituents," they forget that "there is a state of New York, which is in favor of principle and not wedded to the office holders of New York and their masters at Washington."[127] Ward Hunt of Oneida, another delegate obviously not employed by the executive branch, painted the scene before him. "And here we see the customhouse agents, inside and out—secret agents, as well as open agents—post office agents and the delegates from the City of New York, standing here in one firm phalanx of customhouse supporters, and reliers upon presidential influence, urging us to sacrifice all to that influence."[128] In the end, administration strength prevailed. The convention rejected resolutions critical of Pierce.[129] When the Pennsylvania Democratic state convention refused to pass pro-administration resolutions, one reporter suggested that such a thing would "require a larger body of customhouse officials."[130]

Similar machinations took place in the Kansas territory during 1855 and '56, with far more disastrous results. With free states now outnumbering slave states and two more likely to come in soon (Minnesota and Oregon), proslavery forces knew they would not have another opportunity to increase their ranks for some time. They determined that Kansas should become a slave state. The slaveholders of Missouri demonstrated particular interest in the affairs of their western neighbor. Like Delaware and Maryland, Missouri in the early 1850s appeared to be slowly shedding slavery. A dwindling if vocal group of slaveholders remained along the western edge of the state. This faction did not take well to the news that northerners were pouring into Kansas at breakneck speed. Missourians took matters into their own hands and crossed into Kansas to vote in the election for a territorial delegate to Congress. Their actions were clearly illegal, as the Kansas-Nebraska

126. Summers, *Plundering Generation*, 213.
127. "The Soft Convention: Trouble between the Customhouse and the Rural Districts," *New York Times*, August 31, 1855, 8.
128. "The Softs at Syracuse: The Administration in Danger," ibid., September 1, 1855, 8.
129. Summers, *Plundering Generation*, 213.
130. "Troubles and Dissensions at the Democratic State Convention," *New York Times*, July 9, 1855, 3.

Act provided that only "actual residents" could vote.[131] With ballots cast by Missourians making up more than half of the votes cast, proslavery forces won the election for a territorial delegate to Congress. They probably would have won even without the assistance of their neighbors, as proslavery men constituted a majority of the territory's voters at that point.[132]

The frauds were repeated in the elections for a territorial legislature held the following March; proslavery elements won easily. Out of a total vote of 6,300 ballots, 4,900 were cast illegally by Missourians.[133] Under the Kansas-Nebraska Act, the territorial governor, Andrew Reeder, had to certify the results. The proslavery faction in Kansas pressured him to do so quickly, before the extent of the fraud became known. The governor refused to accept some returns, but on the excuse that he could not question a particular district's vote unless a resident of it complained, he certified approximately two-thirds of the victorious candidates as having won their elections. A proslavery legislature convened in the spring of 1855. Having saddled the Kansas territory with a fraudulently elected government, Reeder quit his post and traveled east to warn the president of what he had wrought. Pierce refused to act on the grounds that he lacked authority to do so. The territorial legislature meanwhile adopted the entire code of the state of Missouri, including its laws protecting slavery. In order to ensure that no future Free Soil legislature would repeal the acts, it also banned nonslaveholders from office. Another measure criminalized antislavery speech—up to two years in prison for those who denied the right to bring slaves into the territories. Finally, voters had to take an oath to support these laws before exercising the franchise.[134]

Free Soil Kansans, indignant over the conduct of the territorial legislature, held a constitutional convention in the fall of 1855. It drew up a proposed state constitution banning slavery, and the territory's voters adopted it by an overwhelming margin in December 1855 (1,731-46), despite the fact that the convention did not have authority to meet. Free Soil Kansans formed their own "free state" legislature—also completely illegal—and it met in early 1856 in Topeka. Meanwhile, factions associated with the two

131. 10 *Stats at Large* 277 at 285 (section 23).
132. Nevins, *Ordeal of the Union*, 2:313; Potter, *Impending Crisis*, 201.
133. Nevins, *Ordeal of the Union*, 2:385.
134. See ibid., 2:387. For a discussion of the numerous violations of the Constitution perpetrated by the territorial government, see the August 7, 1856, speech of William Seward, *Congressional Globe*, 34th Cong., 1st sess., Appendix, 25:1108–9.

sides began to skirmish, and the first of perhaps a hundred persons to die as a result of armed conflict in the territory was shot in November 1855. On one occasion fifteen hundred Missourians and proslavery Kansans encountered a thousand Free Soilers near the town of Lawrence; only the frantic pleas of Senator David Atchison of Missouri prevented a bloodbath.

In a special message of January 1856, the president recognized the pro-slavery legislature on the grounds that Governor Reeder had certified the returns. He blamed Reeder as well as northern emigrant aid societies for the troubles in the territory. As for the reported electoral frauds in Kansas, it was not, he declared, the duty of the president to ensure the purity of elections in either the states or the territories.[135] The House of Representatives voted in mid-March to investigate the electoral frauds. Later that spring a House committee arrived in Kansas and took depositions. One Free Soiler after another testified, and the report—some twelve hundred pages in length—obliterated the president's claims about the source of all the trouble.[136] Pierce continued to focus on Free Soilers; he sent the army into Kansas, where it broke up one of their meetings. In May 1856 the territory's chief justice, Samuel LeCompte, persuaded a grand jury to indict several members of the free state legislature as well as the editors of two Free Soil newspapers for the "inflammatory and seditious language" of their publications.[137] The House committee that had gone to Kansas (the Howard Committee) issued its report on July 2, 1856. It contained accounts of intimidation of voters and even election judges by proslavery elements. The committee did not miss the significance of what it heard, noting that the "invasion" was the first of its kind in the nation's history in which "an organized force from one state has elected a legislature for another state or territory."[138] Republicans made much of the testimony. Senator William Seward of New York concluded that the territorial legislature stood on a foundation of "force and fraud."[139] Even John Clayton of Delaware acknowledged that matters had gone awry. And all this for a territory that had a population of only twenty

135. Richardson, *Messages and Papers of the Presidents*, 6:2885–91.
136. *Report of the Special Committee appointed to investigate the troubles in the territory of Kansas*, 34th Cong., 1st sess., July 2, 1856, H. Rep. 200.
137. Quoted in Larry Gara, *The Presidency of Franklin Pierce* (Lawrence: University Press of Kansas, 1991), 123, 119.
138. *Report of the Special Committee appointed to investigate the troubles in the territory of Kansas*, 35.
139. *Congressional Globe*, 34th Cong., 1st sess., August 7, 1856, Appendix, 25:1110.

thousand, while Minnesota had 120,000 persons—yet the latter still had not gained admission.[140]

As the consequences of its Kansas policy unfolded, the Pierce administration took up the daunting task of securing re-election. From the beginning, its prospects appeared exceedingly poor. Democratic Party leaders looked at the returns from the 1854–55 elections and knew that Franklin Pierce could not win. While he might well carry the South, no northern state except possibly Illinois or Indiana would support him in 1856. Pierce nevertheless fought on, but he failed to use the civil service effectively in his own behalf. As happened to Tyler in 1844, executive branch employees labored on behalf of other candidates even as they paid lip service to the president. In always critical New York, Pierce could only hold the Softshell wing of the party; even that success probably stemmed from the fact that its convention was attended almost exclusively by federal officeholders.[141] Hardshells supported James Buchanan, who was serving as minister to Great Britain. At the Democratic convention in Cincinnati, Buchanan narrowly prevailed over Stephen Douglas. Party leaders realized that the election might well turn on Pennsylvania, as New York had been lost to Free Soil sentiment. The "old public functionary," as Buchanan called himself, was a native of the Keystone state. He had another advantage as well—he had been out of the country for the past four years and had thereby managed to avoid taking a stand on Kansas-Nebraska.

The Republicans nominated forty-three-year-old John C. Fremont, a former army officer famed for both his exploration of the far West and his military exploits in the Mexican War. Fremont also hailed from Pennsylvania—thus giving the Republicans hope in the state on which the election hinged. His military background kept Fremont out of politics and thus, like Buchanan, he offered the signal advantage of having not uttered so much as a word about Kansas-Nebraska. The new party saddled its nominee with a platform that proved troublesome. It declared in bold terms the power and duty of Congress to prohibit in the territories those "twin relics of barbarism, polygamy and slavery."[142] (The Mormons of Utah embraced polygamy. Republicans introduced legislation banning the practice only to have Democrats, fearful that such a law might set a precedent for the prohibition of

140. Ibid., July 2, 1856, 25:766–67.
141. Berger, *Revolution in the New York State Party Systems*, 102.
142. McKee, *National Conventions and Platforms*, 98.

slavery, resist.) In calling for a ban on slavery in the West, Republicans implicitly renounced the Compromise of 1850, which allowed for the possibility of slavery in New Mexico and Utah. The new party thereby provided fodder for the network of Democratic newspapers that cast it as a collection of
scheming abolitionists.

For a time, nativists posed a greater threat to Republicans than their own
platform did. The American Party promised to deprive Fremont of support in
such critical states as Pennsylvania and New Jersey. This possibility remained
even after the party split along sectional lines. New York Whig Party boss
Thurlow Weed came to the rescue. When the northern wing of the American Party held a nominating convention, he bribed enough delegates to secure the nomination for House Speaker Nathaniel Banks. In accordance with
a plan devised in advance, Banks withdrew in favor of Fremont. The southern
wing of the party nominated Millard Fillmore. What appeared to be a major
threat to the Republicans had turned back on the Democrats—southerners
would split between Fillmore and Buchanan, while the northern antislavery
vote would go exclusively to Fremont. To the horror of the South, the Republicans appeared to have the presidency within their reach.

Tensions mounted in early 1856. In May Senator Charles Sumner of
Massachusetts delivered a savage attack upon South Carolina senator Andrew Butler and Stephen Douglas. Butler's nephew, Congressman Preston Brooks, nearly killed Sumner by striking him over the head repeatedly
with a cane while the senator sat at his desk. Additional fuel for the fire arrived within hours of the Sumner incident in the person of John Brown. A
miscreant whose only proven skill was fathering children (at least twenty),
Brown appears to have merged his misfortunes in life with the sin of slavery.
He determined that the cleansing should come through violence. Already
in Kansas looking for a fight, Brown reacted with outrage to a raid upon
Lawrence, a tiny hamlet occupied by Free Soilers. Brown and several other
men dragged five Kansas residents of southern origin from their homes on
the night of May 24, 1856. As family members watched, Brown and his cohorts hacked their victims to death. Among those killed were a father and
his two sons; Brown murdered them in front of the boys' mother. An hour
later, Brown and his followers crushed the skull of a member of the territorial legislature as his wife watched.[143] Brown's acts (the "Pottawatomie Mas

143. Potter, *Impending Crisis*, 212.

sacre") triggered new violence in Kansas, as free state and proslavery bands alike spent the summer of 1856 roaming the territory, murdering anyone they found who appeared to be with the enemy. Senator David Atchison of Missouri joined a band hunting for Brown. In August the administration's luck finally changed. A new territorial governor—John Geary—intercepted a large group of Missourians, and peace returned to Kansas for the first time in months. Newspapers across the country printed the good news; Democrats sighed in relief.

The presidential campaign proved an oddity, and not merely because it coincided with anarchy in the territories. Buchanan battled Fremont in the North and Fillmore in the South. Fillmore's candidacy terrified Democrats, because if he won so much as two southern states, Buchanan would be unable to secure a majority in the Electoral College. Republicans naturally made much of the conflict in Kansas, but they did not pass up other opportunities presented by the Pierce administration. They promised river and harbor legislation in the Northwest and took special care to make their latitudinarian views known in Michigan, where the president's veto of a bill to deepen a channel through the St. Clair Flats remained unpopular. Republicans promised protective tariff reform throughout the North. Both parties claimed to support a transcontinental railroad.

Democrats took up the challenge with some hope of success. Governor Geary had deflated the Kansas issue, at least for the moment. The party took a discreet approach to slavery-related matters; its platform emphasized the Compromise of 1850 instead of Kansas-Nebraska (though it did endorse the Kansas principle of "non-interference by Congress with slavery in state and territory"). The platform dodged the all-important question of *when* territorial legislatures gained the right to ban slaves, saying only that the Democratic Party recognized the right of the people of a territory "to form a Constitution, with or without domestic slavery, and be admitted into the Union upon terms of perfect equality with the other states."[144] The Buchanan campaign avoided the issue altogether. Instead, a collection of wily party veterans, including John Slidell of Louisiana, Jesse Bright of Indiana, Howell Cobb of Georgia, Congressman J. Glancy Jones of Pennsylvania, and lobbyist W. W. Corcoran, ran a campaign that portrayed Republicans as extremists. They took over the party press from the feckless Pierce administration, turned the *Washington Union* into a campaign sheet, and sent pamphlets out to "Keystone Clubs" under the congressional frank.[145] They also levied large assessments (campaign contributions) from customhouse workers, naval yard employees, and postmasters.[146] Isaac Fowler, the New York City postmaster, donated $250,000 in post office funds on the promise that the department would be paid back after the election (it was not).[147] Contractors such as W. C. N. Swift made substantial contributions in exchange for naval contracts.[148] Between their control of the federal civil service and the support of business interests—who feared secession would follow if Fremont was elected—the Buchanan campaign obtained an almost bottomless reservoir of cash. Much of the largesse went to Pennsylvania, where party leaders purchased advertising in order to obtain the support of newspapers.[149] The Buchanan campaign accumulated enough funds to send materials to every home in Philadelphia.[150]

Matters looked bad for the Democrats when the first returns from the state elections became known in September. (A poor showing in the state contests invariably led to defeat in the presidential election.)[151] Maine—a reliably Democratic state until 1854—went Republican again, with all six congressional seats going to the new party. In the following weeks Republicans won in other northern states as well, including Ohio, Vermont, and Iowa. In response, Virginia governor Henry Wise organized a drive for a sectional convention in order to demonstrate the consequences of a Fremont victory.[152] The *Washington Union* and other Democratic sheets predicted that secession would follow if Republicans prevailed in November.[153] As the campaign neared its end, odd rumors began to seep out of Pennsylvania. The *New York Times* reported on October 9 that while the election of Fremont was an "almost certainty," some $70,000 had been raised by Buchanan supporters on Wall Street in order to secure a Democratic victory. This would

145. Nichols, *Disruption of American Democracy,* 55–56.
146. Summers, *Plundering Generation,* 240.
147. Nevins, *Ordeal of the Union,* 2:495–96.
148. Nichols, *Disruption of American Democracy,* 59.
149. Nevins, *Ordeal of the Union,* 2:507.
150. Nichols, *Disruption of American Democracy,* 59.
151. Although an 1845 statute provided for all states to vote for president on the second Tuesday in November, politicians viewed the state elections that began in early fall as a reliable indicator of how people would vote in November. If a party did poorly in state elections, turnout among its supporters inevitably dropped in the presidential election.
152. Potter, *Impending Crisis,* 263.
153. Nevins, *Ordeal of the Union,* 2:498.

be done, the article continued, through "gigantic frauds" that were about to be perpetrated in Philadelphia through the "addition of several thousands of bogus names" to the voter rolls. Federal employees were said to have mailed campaign materials to what seemed like every adult male in Pennsylvania. As the *Times* put it, "whole platoons of federal office-holders in Washington are busied night and day dispatching their pestilent stuff."[154]

As late as October 16—two days after the state election was held—the *New York Times* predicted that the Republicans would win by four thousand votes. It was not to be. By the next day, October 17, the results became known—Democrats had won the state by almost three thousand votes over the combined returns of the Republicans and the American Party.[155] Subsequent investigations revealed that Democrats obtained several thousand fraudulent votes by illegally naturalizing immigrants and then having them cast Democratic ballots. Election judges in Philadelphia later declared illegal five hundred votes in one ward alone.[156] A single marine court clerk testified that he had printed 2,700 counterfeit naturalization forms.[157] The city's overall returns made it obvious that something had gone badly awry—with a population at least two hundred thousand less than that of New York City, Philadelphia residents somehow produced six thousand more votes than New Yorkers had ever cast in a single election.[158] It became apparent that the Democratic frauds in Pennsylvania exceeded their margin of victory. Democrats won the Indiana state elections by 5,800 votes, and observers looked with skepticism upon that result as well. Repeat voters were common, and Illinois residents were said to have wandered across the Wabash River to cast ballots.[159] Kentuckians crossed the Ohio.[160] Jesse Bright's Democratic machine voted thousands of nonresident railroad construction workers. As in Pennsylvania, the frauds appeared to exceed the Democrats' margin of victory.[161] Once the results of the Pennsylvania and Indiana state elections became known, the Democrats were all but assured of winning in November.[162] And so it was. Buchanan, despite obtaining only 45 percent of the popular vote, carried nineteen states, to eleven for Fremont. While he won

154. "Where There's So Much Smoke, There Must Be Some Fire" and "The Franking Privilege," *New York Times*, October 9, 1856, 4.

155. Nevins, *Ordeal of the Union*, 2:507.    156. Summers, *Plundering Generation*, 241.
157. Nevins, *Ordeal of the Union*, 2:508.    158. Summers, *Plundering Generation*, 241.
159. Nevins, *Ordeal of the Union*, 2:508–9.    160. Summers, *Plundering Generation*, 241.
161. Nevins, *Ordeal of the Union*, 2:508–9.    162. Potter, *Impending Crisis*, 264.

only four northern states—Indiana, Illinois, Pennsylvania, and New Jersey—Buchanan had his closest call in the South. If Fillmore had won another eight thousand votes in Kentucky, Louisiana, and Tennessee, no one would have won a majority of electoral votes and the matter would have been decided in the House of Representatives.[163] Edmund Ruffin, as radical a southern rights man as any, noted rumors that "enormous sums of money were sent from the city of New York and . . . New England to buy votes in Pennsylvania, which turned the vote in that state." If this was true, he continued, the victory was "worth less than I had before estimated."[164] In the end, the *New York Herald* may have said it best: Buchanan won the presidency "with infinite labor, at vast expense, and by the skin of his teeth."[165]

### DRED SCOTT

During the winter of 1856–57, Franklin Pierce waited grimly for the end of his term. As the first elected president who failed to be renominated by his own party, he surely felt the pangs of humiliation during his final months in office. A spirit of defiance infused his last annual message, when he claimed that the troubles in Kansas had been exaggerated for political purposes and falsely accused the Republicans of advocating abolitionism. Perhaps the most important point in Pierce's message was his declaration of what had become gospel in the Democratic Party: prohibitions of slavery in the territories, including the now dead Missouri Compromise, were unconstitutional.[166] Pierce's attorney general, Caleb Cushing, issued an opinion embracing that view some fourteen months earlier, in October 1855.[167] None of this might have mattered—Pierce and Cushing would be gone soon enough—except for the fact that, as anyone who read the papers knew, the Supreme Court was preparing to involve itself in the issue.[168]

Northerners placed no more trust in the Supreme Court in 1857 than they had in 1848, when John Clayton of Delaware proposed a bill allowing expedited appeals to it in cases involving slaves in the New Mexico

163. Ibid., 264n83.

164. Quoted in Nichols, *Disruption of American Democracy,* 80.

165. Quoted in Fish, *Civil Service and the Patronage,* 166.

166. Richardson, *Messages and Papers of the Presidents,* 6:2931–40.

167. See *Digest of the Official Opinions of the Attorney General of the United States, 1789–1881,* 16 vols. (Washington, D.C.: U.S. Government Printing Office, 1885–89), 8:571–76.

168. Fehrenbacher, *Dred Scott Case,* 305.

and Utah territories. Throughout the early 1850s Free Soil politicians made it abundantly clear that they did not believe the Supreme Court could be trusted with the territories question. They arrived at this state of pessimism largely because the Supreme Court had a majority of southerners. That one of the Union's three sections could have a majority of seats on the high court stemmed from the old circuit-riding system—the justices still traveled through circuits where they served as appellate judges. (They would continue to do so until the end of the century.) The country was divided into circuits to which each justice was assigned to hear appeals and occasionally preside over trials. By custom, only residents of the states within a circuit could be appointed to its seat on the Supreme Court. Justice Story's demise in 1845 thus resulted in the appointment of another New England native—Levi Woodbury of New Hampshire. Because settlement of the Southwest slightly preceded that of the Northwest, it obtained two federal circuits—and thus two Supreme Court seats—in 1837, while the Northwest was left with only one. In time the population of the northwestern states exceeded that of the southwestern states, but by that point sectionalism had made the addition of circuits—and in turn Supreme Court justices—impossible. (Genuine concern over the size of the court also played a role.) By the 1850s the Supreme Court had, in a sense, been gerrymandered. The two smallest circuits—both in the South—had populations of well under a million, while the next-smallest had 1.4 million.[169] In contrast, the seventh circuit, which included Illinois, Indiana, Michigan, and Ohio, had 4.1 million people.[170] Other factors added to northern mistrust of the Supreme Court. The Senate, which Democrats controlled for all but six years between 1829 and 1861, rejected or refused to act upon several Whig Supreme Court nominations, including those of John Crittenden (1829), John Read (1845), and George Badger (1853). By the time of the Whig Party's demise, only one of their rank, Benjamin Curtis, had obtained a seat on the high court (though Justice John McLean sought the Whig presidential nomination on at least one occasion).

Despite its southern bent, the Supreme Court embraced a rather generous approach to the powers of Congress over the territories. In *American Insurance Company v. Canter* (1828), the Court ruled that the Florida terri-

---

169. Warren, *Supreme Court in United States History*, 2:220–23, 289.
170. Nevins, *Emergence of Lincoln*, 1:101.

torial legislature possessed authority to set up its own courts and that these in turn could exercise admiralty jurisdiction. Some wondered if Congress could authorize the establishment of a judicial system that was not subject to the requirements of Article III of the Constitution. (Among the variations of the Florida tribunals was the fact that the judges did not enjoy lifetime tenure.) Chief Justice Marshall thought the subject called for broad discretion. In legislating for the territories, he wrote, "Congress exercises the combined powers of the general and of state government."[171] Twelve years later the Court affirmed the federal government's right to lease mines on the public lands in *United States v. Gratiot* (1840). In so doing, it expressly dismissed the notion that the power of Congress over the territories was subject to special limitations. "Congress has the same power over it [the territories] as over any other property belonging to the United States; and this power is vested in Congress without limitation; and has been considered the foundation upon which the territorial governments rest."[172] In *Cross v. Harrison* (1854), the Court affirmed the right of the federal collector at San Francisco to collect duties prior to the formation of a territorial government. On behalf of the Court, Justice James Wayne held that congressional power over the territories arose from the new states clause as well as the territories clause. In his view, it was subject to no limits except those found in the Constitution itself.[173]

Despite such broad precedents, northerners expected the worst as the Court prepared to issue its decision regarding a slave named Dred Scott in early 1857.[174] Dr. John Emerson, an army surgeon, had taken Dred Scott from Missouri to Fort Armstrong, Illinois, in 1834. Two years later Emerson and Scott traveled to Fort Snelling, in what was at that time the Minnesota territory—formerly part of the Missouri territory and thus subject to the Missouri Compromise. The following year, the two returned to Missouri. In 1843 Emerson died and left Scott to his in-laws in St. Louis. Scott brought suit in Missouri state court, claiming that Dr. Emerson inadvertently freed him when the two traveled to Illinois. Scott prevailed at trial but the Missouri Supreme Court reversed the decision in 1852.[175] At that point abolitionists took an interest in the matter. They helped Scott bring suit in federal court in St. Louis by selling him (fictitiously) to a New York resident. Scott in-

171. 26 U.S. 511, 546 (1828).                  172. 39 U.S. 526, 537 (1840).
173. 57 U.S. 164, 193 (1854).                  174. Nevins, *Emergence of Lincoln*, 1:88.
175. *Scott et al. v. Emerson*, 15 Missouri 577 (1852).

voked diversity jurisdiction in order to sue his new owner in U.S. District
Court. The court agreed that Scott was a Missouri citizen for jurisdictional
purposes; it also ruled that under the laws of Missouri, he remained a slave.
Scott appealed the decision to the Supreme Court in 1854 and the justices
heard arguments in the spring of 1856. They put a decision off until 1857 for
the purpose of having the case reargued—though some believed the Court
wished to avoid trouble on the eve of a presidential election.[176]

Dred Scott derives much of its drama from the Supreme Court's han-
dling of a difficult issue; it also carries an air of tragedy, or at least waste, in
that the justices were given so many opportunities to avoid addressing it at
all. Scott's attorneys did not even cite the Missouri Compromise before the
Court; instead they pinned their hopes on the fact that their client spent a
year in Illinois. The Court could have focused on that issue and relied on a
recent decision that seemed to be controlling. In Strader v. Graham (1851), the
Court held that whether a slave brought into the North and then returned
to the South became free depended upon the laws of the state where the
slave had been held in bondage.[177] For a time it appeared that the Court was
going to rely on Strader and hold that under the laws of Missouri, Scott remained a slave. A majority agreed on the substance of an opinion to that effect, and Justice Samuel Nelson of New York was assigned to write it.[178] Perhaps in the mistaken belief that it could resolve it, a majority of the Court
decided to take up the broader issue of the powers of Congress in the territories. With the decision to go all the way, the lobbying began. Justice John
Catron wrote the president-elect on February 19 to inform him that the majority had decided to rule the Missouri Compromise unconstitutional and
that he intended go along. Catron went on to make an extraordinary request
of Buchanan, asking him to "drop [Justice Robert] Grier a line, saying how
necessary it is—& how good the opportunity is, to settle the question by an
affirmative decision of the Supreme Court, the one way or the other."[179] Buchanan complied with the request and Grier shortly thereafter wrote back of
his intent to vote with the majority.

The new president was not finished. In his inaugural address he did his
best to prepare the country for what he surely knew would come as un-
pleasant news to much of it. Buchanan began by acknowledging a difference of opinion on the question of when territorial legislatures could ban

176. McPherson, Battle Cry of Freedom, 171.      177. 51 U.S. 82 (1851).
178. McPherson, Battle Cry of Freedom, 171.      179. Works of Buchanan, 10:106n1.

slavery. Fortunately, he said, the issue would soon be resolved. It was a "judicial question," he announced, which "legitimately belongs to the Supreme Court of the United States. To their decision, in common with all good citizens, I shall cheerfully submit."[180] A week after the inauguration, the Supreme Court handed down its opinion in *Scott v. Sandford*. Although the broad outlines of the ruling were already known, it nonetheless stunned and angered people throughout the North. In his opinion for the majority, Chief Justice Taney held the Missouri Compromise void as a violation of the Constitution. Even worse, he ruled that blacks—including those who lived in the North—were not citizens. They could not therefore invoke the diversity jurisdiction of the federal courts.[181] In Taney's view, blacks were considered "a subordinate and inferior class of beings" when the Constitution was written. They "had no rights or privileges but such as those who held the power and the government might choose to grant them." He arrived at this conclusion despite conceding that every person who was a citizen of a state at the time of the Constitution's formation necessarily became a citizen of the new "political body" that came to life with the Constitution. Did blacks enjoy citizenship in any state in 1787–88? Taney thought not. He pointed to a long list of discriminatory laws enacted in the 1780s and concluded that blacks occupied a degraded status throughout the country when the Constitution was written. Certain constitutional provisions, such as the fugitive slave clause, as well as early acts of Congress that referred only to whites, confirmed in Taney's view the belief that blacks were not members of the political community formed in 1787–88.[182]

Despite ruling that the Court did not have diversity jurisdiction over the case, Taney moved on to the question of whether Congress had authority to prohibit slavery in the territories. The territories clause, he began, had only been added to the Constitution to authorize the federal government to manage the lands possessed by the United States in 1787. The Constitutional Convention's use of the terms "rules and regulations" in the clause indicated that it did not intend to confer a general power of legislation. The 1789 act of Congress that carried into effect the Northwest Ordinance and its ban on slavery did not constitute an exercise of the powers of Congress under the

180. Richardson, *Messages and Papers of the Presidents*, 7:2962.

181. 60 U.S. 393, 405 (1857). The plea in abatement argued against Scott's citizenship because "he is a negro of African descent; his ancestors were of pure African blood, and were brought into this country and sold as negro slaves" (396–97).

182. Ibid., at 404–16, 419–22.

territories clause. Instead, it executed the provisions of what was in effect a treaty. The 1789 statute therefore possessed no weight as a precedent for subsequent laws that prohibited slavery in the territories.[183]

The chief justice turned to the question of where Congress obtained its authority to purchase foreign territory, presumably because only by answering that question could he determine the extent of the congressional power over territory. The new states clause of the Constitution "plainly" contains such a power, he wrote—though the territories could not be kept in that condition permanently; Congress must eventually admit them into the Union. Even before admission, persons residing in the territories could not be governed as "mere colonists"; such a thing would be inconsistent with the limited nature of federal power. Where did the territorial powers of Congress end? The chief justice did not say. As for the powers of the territorial legislatures, Taney held that the degree to which self-government might be allowed in a territory depended upon its particular condition. In all cases, Congress must avoid "infringing upon the rights of person or rights of property of the citizen who might go there to reside, or for any other lawful purpose." Exactly what rights did he have in mind? Taney pointed to the obvious: Congress could not make laws concerning religious establishments in the territories. "Nor can Congress deny the people the right to keep and bear arms, nor the right to trial by jury." He was not done. "The rights of property have been guarded with equal care. . . . [They] are united with the rights of the person, and placed on the same ground by the Fifth Amendment of the Constitution, which provides that no person shall be deprived of life, liberty, and property, without due process of law." Thus, "an act of Congress which deprives a citizen of the United States of his liberty or property, merely because he came himself or brought his property into a particular territory of the United States, and who has committed no offense against the laws, could hardly be dignified with the name of due process of law." No other federal entity could do such a thing either. "If Congress itself cannot do this—if it is beyond the powers conferred on the federal government—it will be admitted, we presume, that it could not authorize a territorial government to exercise them." Thus the conclusion that would have been unimaginable only a few years earlier: the Missouri Compromise was "not warranted by the Constitution, and is therefore void."[184]

183. Ibid., at 438–40.
184. Ibid., at 446–52.

Seven of the Court's nine justices agreed with at least part of Taney's opinion; six held the Missouri Compromise unconstitutional. Justice John Catron thought the 1820 law violated the Treaty of Louisiana's requirement that citizens of Louisiana have free enjoyment of their property. Justice Peter Daniel embraced John C. Calhoun's trustee approach. In his view, Congress served only as the "agent or trustee for the United States." It could not "without a breach of trust and fraud appropriate the subject of the trust to any other beneficiary . . . than the United States, or to the people of the United States, upon equal grounds, legal or equitable." Nor could it appropriate lands to "one class or portion of the people to the exclusion of others, as all citizens have 'rights of purchase, settlement, [and] occupation' in the national territories." The Northwest Ordinance was void, in his view, because it conflicted with Virginia's 1780 deed of cession, which required that the lands be used to benefit the country as a whole.[185]

In his dissenting opinion, Justice Benjamin Curtis pointed out what appeared to be a glaring error in the opinion of the chief justice: if Dred Scott could not sue in federal court because he lacked citizenship, what right did the Court have to address the merits of the case, and in particular to determine the constitutionality of the Missouri Compromise?[186] Curtis refused to accept the idea that blacks were not citizens in any state in 1787. At that time New Hampshire, Massachusetts, New York, New Jersey, and North Carolina all provided that every free, native-born inhabitant enjoyed citizenship automatically. With its invention of the notion of national citizenship, the majority had, in Curtis's view, asserted an authority "to create privileged classes within the states, who alone can be entitled to the franchises and powers of citizenship of the United States." He did not buy it. The constitutional power to establish rules for naturalization did not imply authority to establish criteria for American citizenship—it was "confined to removal of the disabilities of a foreign birth." Nor did the fact that blacks were subject to legal limitations mean they were not citizens—women and children were also subject to limits, and no one suggested they did not enjoy citizenship.[187]

As for the issue of congressional power in the territories, Curtis point-

---

185. Ibid., at 526–27, 489–91.

186. Ibid., at 565. For the view that the Court had to rule on the validity of the Missouri Compromise in order to decide the jurisdictional question, see Fehrenbacher, *Dred Scott Case*, 332, and Currie, *Constitution in the Supreme Court*, 266–67.

187. 60 U.S. at 572–73, 577–78, 583.

ed out that while its own words described the Northwest Ordinance as a compact between the original states and the people of the Northwest Territory, there were few people and no states in the region at that time. They could hardly serve as a party to a treaty. Clearly the August 1789 statute adopting the ordinance constituted more than the implementation of a treaty. It served as "an assertion by the first Congress of the power of the United States to prohibit slavery within this part of the territory of the United States." The existence of this authority was confirmed by the numerous statutes passed between 1790 and 1848 that either applied the ordinance's prohibition to newly formed territorial governments or in some other way evinced a federal power to ban slavery in the territories.[188] Nor did Curtis buy the notion that the due process clause of the Fifth Amendment bestowed upon slaveholders the right to enter the territories with their chattel. Congress had repeatedly banned slavery in the territories, and yet no one, at the time at which those measures were passed, suggested that they constituted a violation of the due process clause. When Virginia provided by law in 1778 that all slaves brought in from outside the state were free upon entry, no one claimed that the statute violated the due process clause of the state constitution. (The right to own slaves normally arose out of statute and had not been viewed as a right protected by constitutions.)[189] As for the idea that the Treaty of Louisiana forever protected slavery in the Missouri territory, Curtis pointed out that Congress could modify or repeal treaties with subsequent legislation. All of this led the lone Whig justice to a rather unhappy conclusion: the Court had substituted its own beliefs for the intent of the Founders. This boded ill for the country and the Constitution. "When a strict interpretation of the Constitution, according to the fixed rules which govern the interpretation of laws, is abandoned, and the theoretical opinions of individuals are allowed to control its meaning, we have no longer a Constitution; we are under the government of individual men, who for

188. Ibid., at 617–18. Section 5 of the law authorizing the formation of a constitution and state government in the Ohio territory required that neither could be "repugnant" to the Northwest Ordinance. 2 *Stats at Large* 173 (April 30, 1802). In 1790 Congress accepted deed to western lands claimed by North Carolina. 1 *Stats at Large* 106 (April 2, 1790). In 1848 Congress extended the Northwest Ordinance's provisions to Oregon. 9 *Stats at Large* 322 (August 14, 1848).

189. 60 U.S. at 624–27. American jurists followed the rule handed down by a British court in *Somerset v. Stewart*, when it granted a writ of habeas corpus to a man who had been held in bondage in a British colony, on the grounds that Parliament had not established the institution and it could exist only through statute. The court held that there was no common law presumption in favor of servitude. 20 Howell St. Tr. (G.B.) 1 (1772).

the time being have power to declare what the Constitution is, according to their own views of what it ought to mean."[190] The chief justice had clearly erred. His fabrication of the notion of federal citizenship in order to exclude blacks was particularly egregious. Despite a handful of attempts by Federalists and Whigs to usurp their authority in this area, the states enjoyed exclusive power to confer citizenship and the privileges that came with it.

Taney fared somewhat better in his evaluation of the Northwest Ordinance and the 1789 act that provided for its continuance under the new government. The ordinance by its own terms constituted a compact. In providing for its continuation, Congress arguably executed a treaty—it did not exercise its powers of legislation. Thus all subsequent laws applying the terms of the ordinance to the Northwest also arguably occurred under the treaty power. Congressional promises to refrain from prohibiting slavery in certain territories did not evince a power to ban slavery, because a promise to refrain from doing something does not always imply the authority to do it. Congress arguably had not attempted to ban slavery through its legislative powers until the Missouri Compromise—and that is where the argument of Taney fell apart. While southern critics at that time argued with great fervor that conditions upon the admission of a state were unenforceable, almost no one denied the constitutionality of a ban on slavery in the Louisiana Territory. Congress thereafter enacted additional prohibitions in territories such as Oregon that were not subject to the Northwest Ordinance; in doing so it was not executing a treaty.[191]

Of all the bad wood in the ruling, none proved more rotten—or more significant in the long run—than Taney's citing of the due process clause of the Fifth Amendment in defense of the right to take slaves into the territories. Historians have, it is true, normally downplayed the clause's significance to the decision, largely because Taney's reference to it comes at the end of his opinion and takes up less than a paragraph.[192] In fact, the due process clause is the basis for the entire ruling. The most critical part of the opinion revolves around Taney's analysis of the powers of Congress in the territories. Unable to come up with a standard by which to evaluate the constitutionality of territorial laws, the chief justice resorted to the Bill of Rights, including the Fifth Amendment.

190. Ibid., at 629, 621.
191. See 9 *Stats at Large* 322, 329 (section 14) (August 14, 1848).
192. See Fehrenbacher, *Dred Scott Case*, 403.

Taney's error occurred in his application of the due process clause to an act of Congress.[193] The phrase had a long history in Great Britain, where it served to limit the power of the monarchy by requiring that courts and Crown officials observe certain procedural safeguards before taking the lives, property, or freedom of British subjects. The phrase had been given a similar interpretation in the United States, where it had been placed in the federal and in several state constitutions in order to check abuses of authority by courts and law enforcement officials. It was not thought of as limiting the power of legislative bodies to pass laws concerning property or any other subject. Contrary to Taney's assertion, the Missouri Compromise law did not result in the confiscation of property—it merely prohibited settlers from bringing a particular type of it into the territories. As Justice Curtis pointed out, the federal government had (via the territorial legislatures) banned many kinds of property in the territories, such as whiskey and firearms.[194] In applying the due process clause to an act of Congress, the Supreme Court greatly altered the meaning of the clause and in turn vastly expanded its own power. A limitation on federal executive officers had evolved into a doctrine whose vagueness threatened to give the Court an effective veto power over all federal legislation affecting property. When viewed from this perspective, the nature of the abuse perpetrated in the *Dred Scott* ruling changes drastically. Instead of whittling an enumerated power (the territories clause) down to nothing, the Supreme Court gave the Fifth Amendment—and in turn its own authority—a scope that was unduly broad.

Unfortunately, Taney's attempt to smuggle the rights of slave owners into the Constitution under the guise of the due process clause was not the anomaly that it appeared to be. Everyone conceded that slaves met the legal definition of property and that, since 1800, judges had steadily expanded legal protections for property. This burst of judicial activism arose out of the fact that most of the state constitutions included only piecemeal safeguards. For a time judges invalidated offensive laws on the grounds that they conflicted with "natural rights." In the egalitarian atmosphere of the early nineteenth century, the spectacle of judges holding laws void merely because they disliked them proved unpopular. Judges changed their approach; they cited at least one constitutional clause when they invalidated statutes

193. For Justice Curtis's critique of Taney's interpretation of the due process clause, see 60 U.S. at 627.
194. Ibid., at 631.

that impaired what were viewed as property rights.[195] In doing so, they often had to resort to creative interpretations. The most infamous manifestation of this practice at the federal level was *Dartmouth College v. Woodward* (1819), in which the Supreme Court held that charters qualified as contracts and therefore could not be withdrawn or even modified by legislatures.

In the 1830s lawyers began to cite due process clauses found in some state constitutions as a source of protection for what were deemed property rights. The long and well-known history of the phrase made for some questionable decisions. In 1833 a rather creative attorney convinced the North Carolina Supreme Court that a law providing for the election of court clerks (the positions had been appointive) violated the due process rights of the incumbents, as it divested them of their offices.[196] Five years later, a law requiring lawyers to swear they had not participated in duels was held void by an Alabama court on the grounds that it violated their due process rights.[197] The most visible example of this trend occurred in response to the movement to give married women a degree of control over their own wages and property, which had been managed by their husbands. Sixteen state legislatures expanded the property rights of women during the 1840s and '50s.[198] When the New York legislature enacted a law establishing property rights for married women, a state judge pronounced it a violation of their husbands' rights under the due process clause of the state constitution.[199] In *Wynehamer v. The People* (1856), the New York Court of Appeals held unconstitutional a state law requiring the immediate destruction of all liquor in the hands of dealers. The court explained that the statute constituted an act so offensive as to be beyond the powers of government "even by the forms which belong to due process of law."[200] As one commentator pointed out, the decision effectively amended the state constitution's due process clause so that it prohibited the taking of life, liberty, or property regardless of whether due process was followed.[201] No wonder the rule of law handed down in *Wynehamer* was not adopted by other states—on the contrary, it was roundly criticized

195. Edward S. Corwin, "The Extension of Judicial Review in New York, 1783–1905," 15 *Michigan Law Review* 281, 292, 293 (1917).

196. *Hoke v. Henderson*, 15 (4 Dev.) N.C. 1 (1833).

197. *Ex Parte Dorsey*, 7 (Porter) (Ab.) 293 at 328–29 (1838).

198. Nevins, *Ordeal of the Union*, 1:131–32.

199. *White v. White*, 5 (Barb.) N.Y. 474 at 482 (1849).

200. 13 N.Y. 378 (1856) at 420.

201. Edward S. Corwin, "The Doctrine of Due Process of Law before the Civil War," 24 *Harvard Law Review* 366, 468 (1910–11).

by judges across the country. As a Rhode Island jurist explained, "Pushed to its necessary conclusion, the argument goes to the extent, that once make out anything real or personal is property, as everything in a general sense is, and legislation as to its use and vendability . . . must stop at the precise point at which it stood when the thing first came within the protection of this clause."[202]

The temptation to expand the scope of the Constitution's due process clause first afflicted the U.S. Supreme Court in 1854. The suit before the Court arose out of the activities of Samuel Swartwout, collector of the Port of New York during the Jackson administration. At the close of Jackson's term, Mr. Swartwout absconded to Europe with more than $1 million in customs revenues. He subsequently purchased lands in the United States; the Treasury Department issued distress warrants to void the land sales and recover the lost revenue. Swartwout challenged the procedure in federal court as a violation of his rights—the property of a citizen, he claimed, could only be taken following a trial. The Supreme Court found otherwise in *James B. Murray v. The Hoboken Land and Improvement Company* (1856). Speaking for the majority, Justice Curtis pointed out that an 1820 statute authorized the Treasury Department to sell the property of revenue officers in order to recover the amounts due on their accounts with the government. The question therefore seemed simple—Congress had authorized by statute the debt collection process used, so there was no way the actions of the Treasury Department could be described as something other than due process of law. The Court upheld the law, but Justice Curtis went on to make clear that he too saw something new in the clause. "The article is a restraint on the legislative as well as on the executive and judicial powers of the government, and cannot be so construed as to leave Congress free to make any process 'due process of law.'"[203]

In the years following *Dred Scott*, speakers on both sides interpreted the decision as barring Congress from prohibiting slavery in the territories because such bans would violate the property rights of individual slaveholders under the due process clause. In contrast, the doctrine that such bans violated the rights of *states* in the territories lost favor. Speaking in Jonesboro, Illinois, Republican senatorial candidate Abraham Lincoln explained the ruling: if Congress passed an act "by which a man who owned a slave on one

202. *State v. Keeran*, 5 R.I. 497 (1858) at 506, quoted in ibid., 474.
203. 59 U.S. 272, 276 (1856).

side of a line would be deprived of him if he took him on the other side," it would be "depriving him of that property without due process of law."[204] A year later, Jefferson Davis declared that the Supreme Court had ruled that the Constitution extended to the territories, "and as it recognized property in slaves, so authorized their introduction into the territories."[205] Robert Toombs echoed this approach in 1861, when he spoke of the South's demand that "the common government . . . use its granted powers to protect our property."[206] Perhaps the most graphic indication that Taney's view had taken over occurred in 1860, when demands for a territorial slave code were heard. Jeff Davis and others based this campaign squarely upon the notion that slaves qualified as property under the Constitution. As they saw it, since Congress was obligated to protect property, it had to enact a slave code for the territories if the federal courts proved unwilling to protect the rights of slaveholders.[207] One of the Democratic platforms of 1860 provided in its first plank that all citizens have an equal right "to settle with their property in the territory."[208] The significance of this change in approach stems from the fact that Taney cited the due process clause alone in support of the proposition that the Constitution recognized slaves as property.[209] Thus the clause alone supports Taney's property-based argument that was adopted by so many during the late 1850s. The chief justice's emphasis on due process therefore constituted more than a mere flourish—it played a pivotal role in the decision and in turn altered the way Americans perceived the issue, which became a matter of property rights rather than sectional equity.

The federal judiciary assisted slave owners in other areas as well during the 1850s, with decisions that were often just as devoid of historical support. The most prominent example of judicial activism in defense of slavery (other than *Dred Scott*) arose out of the view that slaveholders possessed a right of "transit": they could take their slaves with them as they traveled, even through free states. When New York abolished slavery in 1817 (effective in 1827), it made an exception for visiting slave owners; they could keep their chattel in

204. Abraham Lincoln, *Abraham Lincoln: His Complete Works*, ed. John G. Nicolay and John Hay, 12 vols. (New York: Century Co., 1907) (hereafter *Works of Lincoln*), 1:357.

205. Jefferson Davis, speech of July 6, 1859, at Mississippi Democratic convention, in *Jefferson Davis, Constitutionalist: His Letters, Papers and Speeches*, ed. Dunbar Rowland, 10 vols. (New York: Little & Ives, 1923), 4:77.

206. *Congressional Globe*, 36th Cong., 2d sess., January 7, 1861, 30.1:168–69.

207. Ibid., 36th Cong., 1st sess., February 2, 1860, 29.1:658.

208. McKee, *National Conventions and Platforms*, 110.

209. 60 U.S. at 450.

the state for up to nine months.[210] During the 1830s and '40s, almost all of the northern states did away with even that right. (California was one of the few exceptions. It had more slaves during the 1850s via a right of sojourn than either New Mexico or Utah, both of which had slave codes.)[211]

Slaveholders viewed this situation as intolerable. Southern transportation routes still went through the Northeast during the 1850s. Surely a man traveling from the southern states to Philadelphia in order to sail for New Orleans ought to be able to bring his servants along. Federal judge John Kane thought so. In *Wheeler v. Williamson* (1855) he took up the matter of a North Carolina man who had been deprived of slaves he brought into Pennsylvania. In ruling for the plaintiff, Judge Kane gutted an 1847 Pennsylvania statute that abolished what had been a six-month right of sojourn for slaveholders. In his view, the law applied only to persons who intended to remain in the state permanently. The legislature undoubtedly intended to leave "the right of transit for property and person, over which it had no jurisdiction, just as it was before, and as it stood under the Constitution of the United States and the law of nations." Kane based this conclusion squarely upon, of all things, the commerce clause. The power of Congress over commerce necessarily extended to the transportation of human beings as well as goods—any other result would invite the same sort of chaos that reigned during the 1780s. If a state "can control the rights of property of strangers passing through its territory; then the sugar of New Orleans, the cotton of Carolina, the wines of Ohio, and the rum of New England may have their markets bounded by the states in which they are produced; and without any change of reasoning, New Jersey may refuse to citizens of Pennsylvania the right of passing along her railroads to New York."[212] Thus a constitutional right to transport slaves into all parts of the Union, even northern states, was born.[213] Kane was clearly in error; in 1841 the Supreme Court upheld a Mississippi law that banned the importation of slaves *(Groves v. Slaughter).*[214] Surely Pennsylvania was also free to ban slaves, including those who were passing through with their masters.

The next battle over the right of transit took place in New York. When

210. Paul Finkleman, *An Imperfect Union: Slavery, Federalism, and Comity* (Chapel Hill: University of North Carolina Press, 1981), 72.

211. McPherson, *Battle Cry of Freedom*, 181, 76–77.

212. *U.S. ex rel. Wheeler v. Williamson*, 28 Federal Cases 686, 692 (1855).

213. Finkleman, *Imperfect Union*, 260.

214. *Groves v. Slaughter*, 40 U.S. 449 (1841).

Jonathon Lemmon moved his family and slaves from Virginia to Texas in November 1852, he took them through New York City. Despite a warning from his ship's captain not to take his slaves ashore, Mr. Lemmon did so. Local abolitionists sought relief pursuant to an 1841 law revoking what had been a nine-month right of sojourn, and a New York judge promptly freed Lemmon's slaves.[215] Proslavery southerners erupted. The *Richmond Daily Dispatch* declared that if a slaveholder could not pass through northern states with his slaves in tow, "then the union no longer exists."[216] Mr. Lemmon appealed, only to have the New York Supreme Court affirm the trial court's decision. In so doing, it dismissed the idea that comity—a doctrine under which courts apply the laws of other jurisdictions in appropriate cases—bestowed a right of sojourn. The judges held that if Mississippi could bar the importation of slaves and not violate the commerce clause, then so could New York.[217] Undeterred, Mr. Lemmon appealed to the highest tribunal in the state—the New York Court of Appeals. Lemmon's attorney, Charles O'Conor, based his argument upon the U.S. Constitution as well as comity. In his view, the New York law constituted a regulation of interstate commerce—a function that belonged exclusively to Congress. The law also violated the privileges and immunities clause, in O'Conor's view. It required more of a state than allowing the nonresident the same rights its citizens enjoyed. "Its object was to exempt him from state power, not to subject him to it."[218] The Buchanan administration sheet, the *Washington Union*, made the same argument. In an editorial of November 17, 1857, it suggested that the privileges and immunities clause bestowed a right of sojourn to "every citizen of one state coming into another state," for they had a right to the protection of that "property which is recognized as such by the Constitution of the United States, any law of a state to the contrary notwithstanding."[219]

The New York Court of Appeals ruled against Lemmon. In a 5-3 decision, it held constitutional the law that freed slaves immediately upon entry into the state. In the view of the majority, the privileges and immunities clause ensured that visitors enjoyed the same rights as New Yorkers while in the state. They did not bring all the rights they enjoyed in their home

---

215. *The People v. Lemmon*, 5 N.Y. 681 (1852); see also Finkleman, *Imperfect Union*, 296–97.
216. Quoted in Finkleman, *Imperfect Union*, 298–99.
217. *Lemmon v. The People*, 26 Barbour 270, 287–89 (1857).
218. *Lemmon v. The People*, 20 N.Y. 562, 578–79, 580 (1860).
219. Quoted by Charles Stuart of Michigan on the floor of the Senate, *Congressional Globe*, 35th Cong., 1st sess., March 22, 1858, Appendix, 27:199.

state along with them. The court acknowledged that if Congress had enacted conflicting regulations concerning the subject of slave transit, the law would have been unconstitutional. In dissent, Justice Thomas Clerke made clear that he had no doubt that the New York law violated the Constitution. The privileges and immunities clause provided a right of "ingress to and from any other state," and under no circumstances could the host legislature go so far as to remove the visitor's property.[220]

Popular reaction to *Dred Scott*—the Supreme Court's first invalidation of a major federal law—flowed through two channels. Southern editors who had grown old complaining of judicial tyranny now spoke of that "great tribunal . . . before whose decisions all parties and all factions must give way."[221] Republicans pointed to Taney's determination that Scott lacked standing to bring the suit and insisted that his subsequent comments constituted nothing more than *obiter dictum*. Congressman Orris Ferry declared in early 1860 that the Supreme Court had issued a "political decision, not called for by the case, which is entitled to the same respect as a similar opinion uttered by an equal number of able, upright, and learned men in any other station would be, and no more."[222] The Connecticut legislature passed resolutions declaring that the justices had "volunteered opinions which are not law."[223] Republicans announced that they would ignore *Dred Scott* and continue to seek a ban on slavery in the territories. The decision thus proved toothless as well as wrong. While Congress passed no laws prohibiting slavery in the territories before 1861, its failure to do so stemmed from a lack of votes and not from acquiescence in the Court's ruling.

The opinion did not receive the discussion in Washington it arguably warranted—it purported after all to resolve the issue that had dominated congressional debate for the previous ten years. When the thirty-fifth Congress convened in December 1857, it spent almost all of its time focusing on a proslavery constitution that had been devised by a fraudulently elected convention in Kansas. In effect, the even more explosive question of Congress's authority to deny a prospective state admission to the Union pushed

220. *Lemmon*, 20 N.Y. at 608, 614–15, 635–37.

221. Quoted in Stampp, *America in 1857*, 101.

222. *Congressional Globe*, 36th Cong., 1st sess., February 10, 1860, 29.1:734. See also the comments of William Pitt Fessenden of February 8, 1858, in the Senate, ibid., 35th Cong., 1st sess., February 8, 1858, Appendix, 27:616–17. See also speech of Representative D. W. Gooch of Massachusetts of May 3, 1860. ibid., 36th Cong., 1st sess., Appendix, 29.4:291.

223. Ames, *State Documents on Federal Relations*, 298.

aside the question of whether it could ban slavery in the territories. While Washington largely ignored *Dred Scott,* northerners proved more than willing to fill the vacuum. Editors discovered the wisdom of Jefferson's warnings regarding the dangers of a usurping federal judiciary, while others hauled out the old Republican remedies, i.e., appointing judges for terms instead of for life.[224] A New York state legislative committee issued a report critical of *Dred Scott* that quoted the Virginia resolutions of 1798.[225] The legislatures of Massachusetts, Maine, Connecticut, and Vermont also passed resolutions attacking the decision.[226] Three years later, Senator John Hale of New Hampshire could be heard on the floor of the Senate quoting at length Jefferson's diatribes against the Supreme Court.[227] Republicans—who saw a ban on the further expansion of slavery in the territories as their chief goal—took note of the obvious political ramifications of *Dred Scott.* As one historian put it, the ruling constituted "nothing less than an order for their party to disband."[228]

While *Dred Scott*'s notoriety stems largely the fact that it was the first case in which the Supreme Court invalidated a significant federal law, the ruling is also deeply entwined with the evolution of American federalism and the growth of federal power. In attempting to strip hundreds of thousands of blacks in the North of their rights as citizens of the United States, the Supreme Court usurped the powers of the legislatures. In extending the domain of slavery over an area that comprised two-thirds of the national domain, the justices exacerbated fears in the North of the "slavocracy" or "slave power" and the government it was said to control. The decision and its aftermath also revealed the nation's inability to manage the consequences of the most significant expansion of federal power that had occurred thus far: the assumption of the right to purchase territory. The sections could not agree on how to manage the new lands, and the losing side in the contest resorted to spurious interpretations of the Constitution in an attempt to impose its will. In the process, it badly inflamed sectional animosities and mistrust of the national government. Finally, *Dred Scott* was the first manifestation of the federal judiciary's willingness to use novel interpretations of the Bill of Rights to invalidate laws it viewed as unwise. This practice would even-

224. Stampp, *America in 1857,* 107.                      225. Fehrenbacher, *Dred Scott Case,* 433.
226. Nevins, *Emergence of Lincoln,* 1:114.
227. *Congressional Globe,* 36th Cong., 1st sess., February 14, 1860, 29.1:762–63.
228. Stampp, *America in 1857,* 104.

tually inflict far more injury upon the states than on Congress. In the years after the enactment of the Fourteenth Amendment (1868), federal judges steadily eroded the powers of the states by expanding the scope of the Bill of Rights—often in ways that were far removed from the original understanding of those rights—to bring them into conflict with state legislation. This practice converted federal judges into quasi-colonial governors armed with a veto power over both the state and national legislatures. The judges usually exercised these powers with reticence when evaluating federal legislation; state laws, by contrast, fell in droves. This process began with *Dred Scott* and Justice Taney's conversion of the due process clause into a broad limitation upon the legislative powers of Congress.

### THE TWILIGHT OF STRICT CONSTRUCTION

With the demise of the Whigs, the conservative approach to the Constitution embraced by Democrats might have been expected to prosper during the 1850s. It did not. As more farmers saw the benefits of quick and cheap transport of goods, they demanded transportation improvements such as turnpikes and railroads. Their elected leaders—federal as well as state— sought to comply, and the Constitution was read accordingly. Democratic Party leaders perceived a declining appreciation of the limits of federal power. In an 1852 letter to Franklin Pierce, Connecticut Democrat Gideon Welles warned that an increase in states and population had led many Americans to view Washington as "*the* government" and the states as mere "subordinate corporations." He constantly heard "erroneous opinions" on the subject of federal authority from citizens who called themselves Democrats.[229] Worsening sectional tensions also eroded popular support for strict construction. Northerners came to associate this approach to the Constitution with overbearing slave owners. The never-ending debate over the powers of Congress with respect to the territories made many tire of hearing southern politicians cry wolf.[230]

Broad-minded legislators still did not attack the limits upon federal power directly; as in previous years, indirect routes were taken. The territo-

---

229. Quoted in Nevins, *Ordeal of the Union*, 1:157–58 (letter of December 16, 1852).
230. In 1854 Robert Toombs of Georgia complained that the terms "strict construction" and "states' rights" had come to serve as "by-words of reproach." *Congressional Globe*, 33d Cong., 1st sess., July 20, 1854, Appendix, 23:1210.

ries clause in particular continued to attract the minds of imaginative lawmakers. In early 1854 Congress took up a bill to fund the construction of insane asylums. The states had only just begun to copy Britain's example and
provide shelter for impoverished persons suffering from mental illness. (The
matter had formerly been left to town or county governments.) Dorothea
Lynde Dix, a New England–born progressive, successfully lobbied eleven
states to set up asylums between 1845 and 1852.[231] Realizing—as have a thousand reformers since—that she could kill a flock of birds with one stone if
she simply concentrated her efforts in Washington, Ms. Dix traveled to the
capital to lobby members of Congress. After convincing lawmakers to establish St. Elizabeth Hospital in the District of Columbia, she turned her attention to a more ambitious project: a bill providing grants of land to each
state, with the sales proceeds to be used to establish insane asylums.

Despite the novelty of her proposal, Ms. Dix could be forgiven if she approached her task with optimism. The federal government had given away
millions of acres to states, veterans, and railroads—thus the necessary precedent seemed to be available. An asylum bill found only limited resistance,
and it passed both houses of Congress in April 1854.[232] In the tradition of
his strict constructionist predecessors, the president vetoed on constitutional
grounds a spending bill that appeared to have bipartisan support. In a veto
message of May 3, 1854, Pierce began by making the obvious points: if Congress could provide for the indigent insane, it could provide for the indigent
who are sane. Such an approach would "transfer to the federal government
the charge of all the poor in all the states." As Congress should provide for all
the poor, if any, this was the real question presented by the bill. The president
made quick work of that idea. "No one of the enumerated powers touches
the subject or has even a remote analogy to it." Pierce attacked the claim that
Congress might devote federal lands to ends for which it could not appropriate general revenues. "In a constitutional point of view it is wholly immate-
rial whether the appropriation be in money or in land." As for the fact that
Congress had long put aside land in new states for public schools, Pierce held
that the federal government possessed the same powers retained by any land-
owner. It could "augment the value of [its] residue and in this mode encourage the early occupation of it by the industrious and intelligent pioneer." As

231. *Concise Dictionary of American Biography*, ed. Joseph Hopkins (New York: Scribner's,
1964), 237.
232. Nichols, *Franklin Pierce*, 349.

for previous acts that might have crossed the line, the president expressed the usual Democratic indifference to precedent. "Congress," he declared, "may sometimes have failed to distinguish accurately between objects which are and which are not within its constitutional powers."[233]

Lawmakers did not take kindly to the president's exposition. George Badger of North Carolina pointed to the broad language of the territories clause— it allowed Congress "to dispose of" federal property. Badger recalled that past arguments against measures such as distribution assumed they would benefit some parts of the Union more than others. In his view, all sides implicitly agreed that if those bills had been more equitable in their benefits, they would have been constitutional. Badger pointed out that over the previous two decades, Congress had given away land for everything from railroads and canals to colleges and government buildings. It had granted Iowa a permanent share of proceeds from the sale of federal land in the state. Vermont senator Solomon Foot asked how it could be legal for the government to sell land at rock-bottom prices but not legal for it to give away land for nothing. "It is a burlesque upon the Constitution to say that it authorizes you to sell your lands for the consideration of a pepper-corn, if you please to do it, but that it gives you no authority to dispose of them or give them away upon consideration of great public benefit."[234]

Three weeks later, on June 19, 1854, Senator William Seward of New York addressed Pierce's assertion that the federal government lacked authority to care for the poor. He noted that Congress had established hospitals for members of the merchant marine. The New York senator then changed course and denounced the idea that he or anyone else thought the general welfare clause bestowed a power of appropriation. "No member of Congress has advocated the principle since this bill was inaugurated, half a dozen years ago. The principle is obsolete, if it ever had advocates. No statesman has advocated it, in or out of Congress, for a period of forty years." Seward believed that the territories clause authorized the asylum bill and that nothing in the measure conflicted with the state cessions of the 1780s. He did not accept the claim that grants must enhance land values in order to be constitutional; it was undermined by the fact that the federal government did not raise land prices in order to reflect increases in the value of its holdings.[235]

233. Richardson, *Messages and Papers of the Presidents,* 6:2781, 2783, 2786–88.
234. *Congressional Globe,* 33d Cong. 1st sess., May 1854, Appendix, 23:626–27, 630–31, 807.
235. Ibid., June 15, 1854, 23:959–60.

The president had his defenders. Andrew Butler of South Carolina be-lieved that because the territory in the West had been purchased with tax revenues, it only made sense that the distribution of it should be subject to the same limitations as appropriations of tax revenue. The alternative, he warned, would lead to the use of the public lands to "promote the fine arts, painting, and poetry." R. M. T. Hunter of Virginia also spoke of the prece-dent that would be set by the bill. "If you can endow an asylum for the in-sane, you can also endow schools and colleges. If you can endow schools and colleges upon conditions, which is a power assumed in this bill, you may prescribe the terms on which the endowment may be made, and the mode in which this trust is to be executed." Hence, "you may take charge here, in this general government, of the whole system of public instruction within the states." Hunter warned that the devotion of land sale revenue to ends not listed in Constitution would render the enumerated powers a nullity. It might even lead to the purchase and emancipation of slaves. Clement Clay of Alabama attacked the idea that the word "dispose" in the territories clause was to be taken literally. If a planter sent cotton to a broker in New Orleans or Mobile, the broker would not understand a request that he dispose of the merchandise as a license to "give it away." Congress, Clay insisted, stood in the position of a trustee or agent who could not discard his principal's wares. "He holds the property not for his own or himself, but in trust for the ben-efit of another." The territories clause empowered Congress to dispose of the property of the United States as well as land—yet did anyone believe Con-gress could give away the munitions or dockyards that belonged to the fed-eral government?[236]

Lewis Cass supported the veto. He pointed out that the powers granted by the territories clause, like those derived from the treaty and commerce clauses (which also contain broad language) were necessarily subject to limi-tations. Cass insisted that past land grants had either served as part of the compacts entered into between Congress and new states in exchange for ad-mission, or had added to the value of real estate remaining in the hands of the federal government, i.e., grants for railroads, canals, and schools. Sena-tor Isaac Toucey of Connecticut—like Cass, one of the few remaining strict constructionist northern Democrats in the Senate—also weighed in against the bill. "The federal government has no jurisdiction whatever over the sub-

236. Ibid., May 1854, 23:649, 651, 798, 969–70.

ject of providing for the indigent insane of the states. You cannot pass a law regulating their condition." Toucey recognized that at bottom the question remained whether "the public moneys, which have passed into other forms of public property, now, in their new forms [are] exempt from the restraints of the Constitution." He thought not. Toucey closed by warning that the territories clause, "in the hands of liberal constructionists, threatens to become the Pandora's box of the Constitution."[237]

No lobby or faction rose up in outrage over Pierce's veto of the indigent insane bill. The same could not be said for his river and harbor vetoes. Since the 1830s, northwestern Democrats had moved toward unanimity on the question of whether river and harbor improvements were constitutional. As they saw it, appropriations for piers, harbors, lighthouses, and navigational aids on the East Coast rendered the question moot. Nor could it be doubted that the lack of improvements was retarding commerce—by 1850 hidden obstructions on the lower Mississippi River were destroying $3 million worth of property each year.[238] With the conversion of many Democrats to the cause and a Whig in the executive mansion, river and harbor subsidies flowed with ease during the early 1850s. From a low of $25,000 in Polk's last year in office, the annual appropriation reached almost $2 million in 1852.[239] In the spring of 1854, House members cobbled together the largest rivers and harbors bill yet—a $2.5 million monstrosity that appeared to have as its aim the dredging of every creek in the country.[240]

Senator Robert Toombs of Georgia objected to the national benefit standard (still in vogue with some as the sole limit on the spending power) as unworkable. "It is a fraudulent term used to deceive, having no definite meaning, and to which no signification is intentionally attached." Nor did he believe that precedent helped the bill's cause. Congress did not fund harbor improvements in the thirty years after the Constitution was ratified. Toombs tossed in the other standard objections as well: the Constitutional Convention considered and rejected a power to carry out internal improvements (canals); the government enjoyed only those powers granted to it; the term "to regulate" as used in the commerce clause could not reasonably be interpreted to authorize internal improvements. On the contrary, the power to

237. Ibid., June 1854, 23:981, 990–91.
238. Nevins, *Ordeal of the Union*, 2:216.
239. See 10 *Stats at Large* 56 (August 30, 1852).
240. For a description of the bill, see *Congressional Globe*, 33d Cong., 1st sess., July 28, 1854, Appendix, 23:1145–46.

regulate commerce involved nothing more than authority to "prescribe the rules under which commerce should be carried on." Hence the conclusion: "Until it can be shown by some astute logician, that, to regulate commerce, means to carry or transport commodities, they must utterly fail in showing there is any express grant of power over this subject." As for the lighthouses on the East Coast, the Georgian declared that these had been necessary for the navy. He offered a unique argument for why Congress need not address itself to the problem of snags in rivers. They were mere nuisances, Toombs explained, and therefore the common law itself obligated legislatures to remove them. He also reminded the Senate that Congress had repeatedly authorized states to levy tonnage duties for the purpose of raising money for navigational aids and harbor improvements. Baltimore had levied them since 1791. Since that time, ten states had received permission from Congress to impose their own duties. Why could not other states ask for this authority? The senator then took a rather sharp turn that undermined his own argument, or at least exposed him to charges of hypocrisy. Because the bill was going to pass, and although he did not think it "a right principle to act upon," Toombs felt it his duty to express his support for a $70,000 appropriation for dredging the Savannah River. The senator justified the expenditure on the grounds that two hundred thousand bales of cotton passed through Augusta, Georgia, each year.[241]

Lewis Cass of Michigan offered perhaps the most moving argument in support of the constitutionality of river and harbor appropriations. He told of an occasion during the War of 1812 when the Royal Navy bottled up Oliver Hazard Perry's fleet in the harbor of Erie, Pennsylvania. The Americans looked to be cornered, as a sand bar at the mouth of the harbor kept them from making a run for it. They only escaped when a storm blew the British ships further out into the lake. The American sloops still had to be stripped of their heavy cannon and tipped on their sides before they could be eased across the bar at the mouth of the harbor. Perry and his men were able to replace their cannons before the Royal Navy returned, but only barely. The Americans subsequently defeated the British at the western end of the lake, preserving American sovereignty in the Northwest. A great deal of territory had almost been lost, Cass pointed out, when the expenditure of a few hundred dollars to dredge the harbor entrance would have made it possible

241. Ibid., July 28–31, 1854, 23:1154, 1175–76, 1178, 1197.

to move the fleet out into the lake without having to strip each ship bare.[242]

The president vetoed the river and harbor bill and, as if looking for a fight, waited until the second session of the thirty-third Congress convened, in December 1854, before issuing his veto message. Pierce began by listing those powers that had been cited in support of the constitutionality of internal improvements: the right to establish post roads, authority to raise an army and navy, and the commerce and territories clauses. The president conceded that if a particular project appeared truly necessary to the exercise of one of these powers, it was constitutional. At the same time he insisted that because a general power to effect improvements was so substantial, the Constitutional Convention would have explicitly granted such a power if it intended to grant it at all. As for river and harbor appropriations, Pierce believed their late vintage rendered them suspect.[243] The naval power, on the other hand, authorized appropriations for East Coast improvements such as lighthouses, beacons, and piers. The president acknowledged that more projects had been funded than were warranted by military considerations. Pierce then turned to the task of devising a method for determining what river and harbor improvements ostensibly related to commerce were constitutional. He dismissed one standard popular with some—improvements only for areas that could be reached by foreign commerce—as not workable because foreign trade penetrated so deeply into the heart of the country. The president settled upon another standard, though one equally arbitrary: an 1845 statute that extended the admiralty jurisdiction of the federal courts to all waters capable of carrying twenty-ton ships.[244]

Members of Congress noted that the president appeared to concede the constitutionality of at least some improvements. That the way might be open for future assistance was of little consolation to shipping interests. Residents in the Great Lakes region reacted with particular anger. Ships in Chicago once again lowered their sails to half mast in protest.[245] Although 350,000 tons of freight moved through the Great Lakes in 1855, there were few

242. Ibid., July 29, 1854, 23:1170.
243. Richardson, *Messages and Papers of the Presidents*, 6:2792–94, 2797. Pierce referred to two 1824 appropriations—one for the dredging of the Mississippi and Ohio rivers, and another for improving the harbors on Presque Isle in Lake Erie and Plymouth Beach in Massachusetts. 4 *Stats at Large* 32 (May 24, 1824), and 38 (May 26, 1824).
244. Richardson, *Messages and Papers of the Presidents*, 6:2797, 2799, 2802. See 5 *Stats at Large* 726 (February 26, 1845).
245. Johannsen, *Stephen A. Douglas*, 438.

harbors with entrances deep enough to allow ships entry in rough weather. When unusually severe gales during the winter of 1854–55 inflicted huge losses, the president's stock in the Northwest dropped even further.[246] Pierce and his allies in Congress held firm; Great Lakes states received money for navigational aids, but no money for harbor dredging was forthcoming.[247] By the spring of 1856 Pierce appeared to be almost consciously trying to antagonize his critics. On May 19 he vetoed a bill that would have provided funds for dredging the mouth of the Mississippi River.[248] A week later he vetoed a measure of equal necessity—it would have provided funds for the deepening of a channel in the St. Clair Flats near Detroit, the shallow depths of which often cut the Great Lakes in half. In Pierce's view the measure would not contribute to the "common defense," as the channel would be dredged to a level of only twelve feet and thus of no use to naval vessels.[249] The president also rejected an appropriation for the Baltimore harbor. Robert Toombs endorsed Pierce's approach, if not his vetoes. He dismissed the claim that Congress had always funded improvements conducive to commerce. Toombs insisted that all of the appropriations for coastal improvements signed by Jefferson and Madison—still the guiding lights of strict constructionists—had been necessary for the protection of the navy. Lewis Cass disagreed. He thought the August 7, 1789, law funding navigational aids clearly "recognizes the principle that a regulation of commerce is not a mere declaratory power as to the mode in which it shall be carried on, but that it also includes the means of 'facilitating and securing it.'" Thus the surveys for the merchant marine.[250] For once, Congress had the last word with a strict constructionist president; it overrode vetoes of the bills appropriating money for dredging the Mississippi River, St. Clair Flats, and the Baltimore harbor.[251]

Enter James Buchanan. The Pennsylvania Democrat took an approach to congressional spending that was even more restrictive than that of his predecessor. Consequently, appropriations for river and harbor improvements

---

246. Nevins, *Ordeal of the Union*, 2:227–30.

247. See, for example, 10 *Stats at Large* 335 (August 3, 1854).

248. See Richardson, *Messages and Papers of the Presidents*, 6:2919.

249. Ibid., 6:2919–20.

250. *Congressional Globe*, 34th Cong., 1st sess., July 1856, Appendix, 25:1043, 743.

251. 11 *Stats at Large* 24 (July 8, 1856) (two appropriations in the amount of $145,000 for the St. Clair Flats); ibid., (July 8, 1856) (an appropriation for dredging at the mouth of the Mississippi River); ibid., 44 (August 16, 1856) (an appropriation for deepening the Patapsco River and dredging the Baltimore harbor).

all but disappeared during the late 1850s. Congress appropriated funds only for aids to navigation along the coasts and on the Great Lakes. Even the Mississippi River did not qualify for federal funds during this last hurrah of strict construction; the president vetoed an appropriation for additional dredging in early 1860. (There was no evidence, he explained, that prior appropriations had improved navigation on the river.)[252] Buchanan's most controversial river and harbor veto occurred in connection with the Great Lakes. By the time he took office, northwestern congressmen had been demanding assistance for almost two decades. In 1859 Representative Israel T. Hatch of New York claimed that more than twelve hundred people had lost their lives on the Great Lakes between 1854 and 1858 because too few harbors had been built.[253] Hatch and his allies found more cause for grief when Buchanan repeated Pierce's error and vetoed an appropriation to deepen the channel through the St. Clair Flats in early 1860. In a veto message, Buchanan pointed out that the Army Corps of Engineers had already cut a channel twelve to fifteen feet deep through the flats. The army assured him that this was adequate. (Thus a channel too shallow to qualify for aid during Pierce's administration had become too deep to justify assistance under that of his successor.) In Buchanan's view, the state of Michigan ought to fund any additional dredging that it deemed necessary. As for the commerce clause, Buchanan insisted that it did not include a power to "create or construct." Nor did it grant authority to "improve the navigation of water courses." It had been born of interstate tariff wars and had not been conceived of as authorizing general improvements—the Constitutional Convention had rejected inclusion of that very power when it rejected an authority to cut canals. Hence the failure of Congress to make any appropriations for that purpose until the 1820s. The only improvements that were legally permissible, the president concluded, were those related to national defense.[254]

Buchanan next knocked heads with Congress over a bill to distribute land revenues to the states for the establishment of agricultural colleges. Not even the most tortured interpretation of the enumerated powers could extract authority for the federal government to involve itself in agriculture or education, yet the move to do so had been in the works for some time. Both houses of Congress established committees on agriculture during the 1820s.

252. Richardson, *Messages and Papers of the Presidents*, 7:3138.
253. *Congressional Globe*, 35th Cong., 2d sess., February 21, 1859, Appendix, 28.2:203–5.
254. Richardson, *Messages and Papers of the Presidents*, 7:3132–35, 3137.

In his 1849 annual message (probably written by William Seward), Zachary Taylor declared that the aid provided to agriculture by the federal government thus far had been "wholly inadequate."[255] Some would have been surprised to learn that Washington had offered any assistance at all. The patent office had already published statistics on crop yields and distributed seeds. By midcentury its reports were hugely popular.[256] In 1856 the patent office sent out agents to determine the grasses found in each state.[257] This was a modest start, to be sure, but the foot was in the door. Perhaps sensing the possibilities, the U.S. Agricultural Society established a permanent office in Washington in 1858.

Congress had long put aside land in each territory for the benefit of primary and secondary schools. During the early 1850s lawmakers embraced the idea of giving the states land sale revenues for colleges. The states heard the call as well, and while some, such as Michigan, established their own institutions, others held off in the hopes that Congress would grant a portion of its land sale revenues to the states.[258] In early 1859 a bill to turn 6 million acres over to the states for the "benefit of agricultural and the mechanical arts" appeared on the verge of passage in the Senate. The critics did not take long to come out of the woodwork. The federal treasury was turning into a "source of alms," they warned.[259] Supporters pointed out that the bill donated less than a sixth of the amount of land that had been given to veterans and railroads.[260]

Senator James Mason of Virginia complained that the bill proposed to use "the public lands as a means of controlling the policy of the state legislatures." It would mean "misusing the property of the country in such a mode as to bring the appropriate functions of the state entirely . . . under the discretion of Congress by a controlling power, and it is doing it in the worst and most insidious form—by bribery, by direct bribery." What senator, he asked, would dare vote for a bill to appropriate $10 million for the establishment of agricultural colleges? Yet this bill not only aimed at that end, it also required the states to report to the federal government on the progress

255. Ibid., 7:2556.
256. George T. Kurian, ed., *A Historical Guide to the United States Government* (New York: Oxford University Press, 1978), 24.
257. Nevins, *Ordeal of the Union,* 2:190.
258. Ibid., 191.
259. Nichols, *Disruption of American Democracy,* 236.
260. Nevins, *Emergence of Lincoln,* 1:451.

of each school. An agriculture department would be next, Mason warned. James Harlan of Iowa pointed out that the states need not accept the revenue. Besides, he argued, there had been no constitutional authority for the Smithsonian, the naval academy, or the coastal survey. James Green of Missouri wondered whether the federal government would now establish medical and law schools as well. As for the Smithsonian, he noted that its assets had been donated. Congress served as the trustee of that institution—it did not own it.[261]

James Simmons of Rhode Island pointed out that Congress had always put aside land for schools in each township in the territories.[262] Yes, answered Green, but these had merely been inducements to settlement. From where, Simmons asked, did Congress derive authority to induce settlement? Green did not answer the question directly; instead he claimed that land grants to new states formed part of the compact that served as the act of admission. The new states would not tax federal land, and Congress in turn granted them one township for their state capitals and two for higher education.[263] Jeff Davis of Mississippi admitted that on at least one occasion not related to admission, Congress had donated land to a state. Like an irritated father warning a child not to repeat a sibling's behavior, Davis insisted that the act constituted a "very bad precedent" and "should not be followed." Jacob Collamer of Vermont did not accept the "inducement to settle" explanation for the practice of putting aside the sixteenth and thirtieth section of each township for schools—the Founders viewed that provision as one whose purpose was education.[264]

The Senate passed the agricultural colleges bill, 25-22.[265] At that point the president weighed in on the side of parsimony and purified constitutionalism. In a veto message of February 24, 1859, he began with what he thought was a common assumption—that Congress could not use general tax revenues "for the purpose of educating the people of the respective

---

261. *Congressional Globe*, 35th Cong., 2d sess., February 1, 1859, 28.2:718–20.

262. Ibid., 721. In the Ordinance of 1785, Congress provided for the division of public land into townships, with one section in each township set aside for public schools.

263. Ibid. At the time of admission, each state received land for various purposes, including schools (for which one section was reserved in every township). An entire township was also reserved for a college. Congress often provided that each state would receive 5 percent of the revenues from land sales within the state, with the proceeds also going toward education. See, for example, the act authorizing the people of the Illinois territory to form a state constitution. 3 *Stats at Large* 428 (section 6) (April 18, 1818).

264. *Congressional Globe*, 35th Cong., 2d sess., February 1, 1859, 28.2:721–22.

265. Ibid., 857.

states." The consequences would be disastrous. "Should Congress exercise such a power, this would be to break down the barriers which have been so carefully constructed in the Constitution to separate federal from state authority." For the idea that land sales proceeds were not subject to the limitations of the Constitution, he had no sympathy. To assume that the Founders intended to enumerate the powers of Congress and at the same time gave it absolute authority over the public domain would conflict with the "well-known jealousy of federal power which prevailed at the formation of the Constitution." The more likely interpretation "would be that as the Constitution confined Congress to well-defined specific powers, the funds placed at their command whether in land or money should be appropriated only to the performance of duties corresponding to these powers." As for the ambitions of some with respect to the phrase "to dispose of" in the territories clause, Buchanan pointed out that a trustee in the position of Congress would not be viewed as having authority to "give away the fund entrusted to his care." "Dispose" only meant "making sale of the lands or raising money from" them. The president closed by repeating the now common explanation for the constitutionality of land grants. The federal government was "a great landed proprietor." It was therefore "both the right and duty of Congress as trustee to manage these lands as any other prudent proprietor would manage them for his own best advantage."[266]

In one sense, strict constructionists won the seventy-year battle over appropriations that extended from Washington's first administration to Buchanan's. The idea that Congress could appropriate funds for any purpose conducive to the general welfare fell out of favor almost as soon as Hamilton introduced the idea. Imaginative legislators did not retreat; they simply focused on other clauses that seemed to suit their purposes. Their generous readings of the commerce and territories clauses, while annoying to many, did not wreak the havoc that would have followed if lawmakers had embraced a broad spending power via the general welfare clause. Yet if Congress refrained from a frontal assault on the limits of its authority, it repeatedly demonstrated a determination to address subjects beyond its realm—albeit under the guise of privileges formally granted to it. The Constitution omitted the subject of education, yet who would deny that the desire to promote the

266. Richardson, *Messages and Papers of the Presidents*, 7:3078–81. See also Currie, *Constitution in Congress: Democrats and Whigs*, 28–31, regarding Democrats' use of the trustee doctrine to justify land grants.

diffusion of knowledge produced the college land grant bill? Nor did it mention poor laws, yet who would claim the indigent insane bill stemmed from
any motive other than charity? Passage of these measures by both houses of
Congress evinced a belief among a large contingent of the political class—
Democrat as well Whig—that the federal government might cast its eyes
upon those great subjects beyond its designated realm, and promote them
when possible through disingenuous constructions of its enumerated powers.
Advocates of strict construction may have prevailed in the antebellum battle
over congressional appropriations in the sense that lawmakers felt it necessary
to link projects to one or more of the enumerated powers. Yet strict constructionists failed to prevent broad constructions of these powers from taking
hold in the minds of a majority of lawmakers. These incidents demonstrated
that, left to its own devices, Congress would not exercise continual vigilance
in limiting itself to its enumerated areas of authority. They also provided important precedents for future incursions. The deluge that occurred during the
following century, while hardly contemplated in land grants or river and harbor appropriations, followed a path that had been smoothed by the erosion of
the Constitution's limits that took place between 1789 and 1861.

## LECOMPTON

Following the Supreme Court's decision allowing slavery throughout
the territories, proslavery Kansans set about the task of adding another slave
state to the Union. They received a great deal of assistance from the federal
executive branch, dominated as it was by men eager to aid what they saw as
the cause of the South. Administration officials used the ample influence of
federal offices in Kansas to strengthen one group of settlers at the expense
of another. They later used executive branch patronage in the northern states
in an effort to obtain congressional approval of their work. Like *Dred Scott*,
the Kansas episode led many to believe that a "slave power" in Washington,
D.C., was using the federal government to expand slavery.

Despite the fact that the Democratic Party was increasingly seen as a
pawn of the "slave power," it fared well in the state elections of 1857, winning control of virtually every northern legislature outside New England.[267]
It also expanded its base in the South at the expense of the now defunct

267. Stampp, *America in 1857*, 257.

Whig Party. When the thirty-fifth Congress met for its first session in December, Democrats held large majorities in each house. Newly arrived lawmakers took heart from the fact that all was quiet in Kansas. In early 1858 a harsh winter drove out half of the slave owners in the territory, further easing tensions. The exodus demonstrated that it was pointless to try to make Kansas a slave state. Unfortunately, the proslavery territorial legislature could not see what was obvious to everyone else. In early 1857 it scheduled elections for a constitutional convention that would meet in the fall—the first step in applying to Congress for statehood. The legislature gerrymandered the districts from which convention delegates would be elected in order to ensure that proslavery forces enjoyed a majority on the floor of the convention. It also vested complete authority over the elections in proslavery sheriffs and county commissioners. In the hope of disenfranchising Free Soilers, the legislature barred all persons who entered the territory after March 15, 1857, from voting in the convention elections. Territorial governor John Geary vetoed the convention bill, but it was passed over his veto. Geary resigned his post and headed east, warning newspapers along the way of what was about to unfold.[268]

As it was apparent that the Free Soil majority in the territory would never approve a proslavery constitution, the president hoped to bring Kansas into the Union as a free but Democratic state. In order to accomplish this goal, he sent Robert J. Walker (secretary of the treasury under James Polk) to the territory as the new governor. Walker's political skills were considerable, but he stumbled almost immediately upon arrival. In his first message as governor he declared that its climate made Kansas unfit for slavery. Aware that the impending convention would be tainted by the circumstances of its election, he warned that failure to submit a draft constitution to a popular vote would cause Congress to reject it. Proslavery elements in Kansas and southerners reacted angrily—what right did a federal official have issuing directions to a prospective state's constitutional convention?[269] Even as Walker preached moderation, officials at the federal land office used jobs at their disposal to aid the territory's proslavery faction. This group won the June 1857 elections for the convention, in part through fraud and in part because the state's Free Soil residents refused to vote—they correctly believed that the contest would be rigged. The president at that point made the tac-

---

268. Nevins, *Emergence of Lincoln*, 1:137–40, 162.
269. Ibid., 1:151–52, 162–63.

tical error of hardening the resolve of his newly appointed governor, writing to Walker that he was willing to "stand or fall" on the question of submitting the yet-to-be-drafted constitution to the territory's "bona fide" residents for their approval.[270]

The constitutional convention met at Lecompton, Kansas, in September 1857. The delegates embraced the approach of Chief Justice Taney in drafting a constitution that protected slavery. It declared the right of property to be "higher than any constitutional sanction." Thus the "right of an owner of a slave to such a slave and its increase is the same and as inviolable as the right of the owner of any property whatever."[271] Despite the efforts of Buchanan administration officials, the delegates discarded the idea of popular ratification. The convention provided for a referendum not on the whole of the constitution but only on the slavery question. Kansans could take a constitution with slavery or one without it. However, the one without slavery provided that the right of property in slaves already in Kansas could not be violated. Nor could the offending clause be corrected immediately, as the constitution barred amendments for seven years.

The president reaffirmed his support for a fair referendum as late as October 22, 1857. The *Washington Union* nevertheless endorsed the Lecompton constitution only weeks later, on November 18. Buchanan probably changed his mind because of pressure from southerners. Many took offense over what they viewed as meddling by federal officials in the political disputes of what would soon be a sovereign state. Southerners also wished to know why northerners were so fixated on the fact that Lecompton would not be submitted to a popular vote. Most of the constitutions of the southern states had not been submitted to the voters and, until the 1840s, neither had those of the North. By one count, only thirty of the sixty-three state constitutions enacted between 1776 and 1858 had been popularly ratified. Of the nine state constitutions in effect in 1858 that had not been ratified by the voters, eight were in the South.[272]

So indignant were the legislatures of Alabama and Georgia that they ordered their respective governors to call state conventions for the purpose of considering secession if Congress rejected the Lecompton constitution.[273]

270. "From Washington," *New York Times*, April 19, 1860, 1.
271. Quoted in McPherson, *Battle Cry of Freedom*, 164.
272. Klein, *President James Buchanan*, 305.
273. Ibid., 309.

Northern assemblies, for their part, passed resolutions condemning the work of the Lecompton convention; the region's newspapers dismissed it as a fraud.[274] Northern Democrats began warning Buchanan to change course. In a cabinet meeting of November 26, Governor Walker called the Lecompton constitution a fraud. Treasury Secretary Howell Cobb and Attorney General Jeremiah Black insisted that it allowed for a vote on the only thing that mattered—slavery.[275] On December 2, Senator Stephen Douglas of Illinois—by now the leader of northern Democrats—went to the executive mansion and told the president that he would oppose Lecompton. Buchanan replied that "no Democrat had ever yet differed from an administration of his own choice without being crushed." He warned Douglas of the fate of party members who had differed with Andrew Jackson over the bank. The senator's reply made clear that he was unmoved: "Mr. President, I wish to remind you that General Jackson is dead, sir."[276] Congressman John Haskin of New York also met privately with the president. He later recalled Buchanan's words: "from forty years political experience, he was satisfied that any man who went against the administration of his party would be without the pale of his party, and that would be the end of him politically."[277]

In a speech of December 9, 1857, Stephen Douglas announced his opposition to Lecompton on the floor of the Senate. To those who saw a conspiracy to bar the admission of another slave state, the senator pointed out that Congress had recently ordered the Minnesota territory to submit its proposed constitution to a popular vote.[278] The administration took another hit on December 15, when Robert Walker resigned as governor of the Kansas territory. Walker made public the contents of a letter he sent to Secretary of State Lewis Cass, in which he complained that the federal surveyor general in Kansas had used "immense patronage," extending to "many hundred of employees," to control the territorial convention.[279] The vote on the Lecompton constitution took place on December 21, 1857. Free Soil settlers stayed home in protest, and the proslavery version of the constitution passed easily. The modest size of the overall vote undermined the territory's prospects for admission; so did revelations of extensive electoral fraud. The constitution's

---

274. Nevins, *Emergence of Lincoln*, 1:236–38.
275. Potter, *Impending Crisis*, 315.
276. Quoted in Johannsen, *Stephen A. Douglas*, 586.
277. Covode Committee Report, 283.
278. *Congressional Globe*, 35th Cong., 1st sess., December 9, 1857, 27.1:14–15.
279. Nevins, *Emergence of Lincoln*, 1:267.

prospects took perhaps their worst hit in early January, when a second (non-binding) referendum on Lecompton saw it defeated overwhelmingly. Significantly, the total vote cast in this second contest far exceeded that of the first. The second referendum had been arranged by the newly elected anti-slavery majority in the territorial legislature at the request of the new governor, F. P. Stanton. When it received word of the move, the Buchanan administration sacked its new appointee.

By the end of January, a block of anti-Lecompton Democrats from northern states (twenty-six out of a total of fifty-three) had formed in the House of Representatives. Still the administration remained confident. It expected to push Lecompton through, just as Pierce had won passage of the Kansas-Nebraska Act four years earlier. Pierce had overcome a deficit of twenty-one votes in 1854; surely Buchanan and his allies could find sixteen votes in 1858.[280] Almost as if anticipating a fight, the Buchanan administration issued a surprising declaration shortly after it came into office: all employees in the federal executive branch would leave office once their terms ended. The order applied only to federal officeholders in the North.[281] The practice of removals had been around for thirty years, but never before had it been applied by an administration to members of its own party. The decision vested immense power in the president—he could now use the entirety of a vast civil list to buy, blackmail, or otherwise secure northern congressional votes. The administration went to great lengths to ensure that newly empty offices in the North went only to sympathetic Democrats. In New York, members of the Hardshell wing of the party received places owing to their support for Buchanan at Cincinnati, despite the fact that they were greatly outnumbered by Softshells.[282] Uncooperative Democrats received nothing. Supporters of Stephen Douglas found themselves shut out even before their leader's clash with the president. In California, the administration bestowed patronage upon doughface senator William Gwyn and the Chivalry while almost completely excluding Free Soil senator David Broderick.[283] The administration aided Jesse Bright's Indiana machine by nominating former governor Joseph Wright (a Free Soiler) for the mission in Berlin. Had he not been

280. Nichols, *Disruption of American Democracy*, 162, 167.

281. Fish, *Civil Service and the Patronage*, 166.

282. Stewart Mitchell, *Horatio Seymour of New York* (Cambridge: Harvard University Press, 1938), 203.

283. Williams, *David C. Broderick*, 156–63.

appointed, Wright would probably have won election to the Senate. With Wright out of the way, Bright engineered the election of an ally, Dr. G. N. Fitch, to the seat.

Its harsh approach to patronage was an enormous gamble for the Buchanan administration. In withholding favors from Free Soilers, the president departed sharply from the approach of his supposedly inept predecessor—Pierce had given jobs and contracts to both Free Soilers and administration Democrats. With their scorched-earth tactics, Buchanan and his cohorts left themselves with only limited influence over the Free Soil wing of the party. The president also gambled aggressively in Kansas. Like Pierce, Buchanan made a habit of appointing proslavery partisans to the federal posts in the territory, such as the land offices and Indian agencies.[284] He probably regretted it. According to Robert J. Walker, critical portions of the Lecompton constitution had been devised by federal officeholders who, despite genuine admonitions to the contrary from the administration, drafted a proslavery document.[285] Congressional investigations later revealed that federal officeholders in the territory had also been deeply involved in the territory's electoral frauds. The trail had not been hard to follow. Investigators found a box of ballots from the December 21, 1857, vote on the Lecompton constitution under a woodpile near the land office.[286]

The administration also sought to impose its will on the party press. Twenty-nine editors who enjoyed federal jobs or contracts were stripped of them when Buchanan took over in 1857.[287] The available largesse went to those editors from whom cooperation could be expected. The proprietor of the *Milwaukee News* became a postmaster. In Connecticut, the editor of the *Bridgeport Republican Farmer* obtained a post with the Treasury Department, and the publisher of the *New London Star* became a surveyor, as did the editor of the *New Haven Register* (who also held a State Department contract).[288] The administration focused most of its attention on Pennsylvania. Almost as populous as New York and not nearly as extreme on slavery questions, the state would serve as the focus of the administration's political operations for the duration of the Buchanan presidency. The flagship newspaper was the *Phila-*

284. Stampp, *America in 1857*, 151.       285. Nevins, *Emergence of Lincoln*, 1:267–68.
286. Potter, *Impending Crisis*, 318.
287. Smith, *Press, Politics, and Patronage*, 201.
288. Mark W. Summers, "Dough in the Hands of the Doughfaces? James Buchanan and the Untameable Press," in *James Buchanan and the Political Crisis of the 1850s*, ed. Michael J. Birkner (Annbury, N.J.: Associated University Press, 1996), 80, 74.

*delphia Argus,* which was owned by Congressman Thomas Florence. Along with the *Pennsylvanian,* the *Argus* enjoyed post office printing contracts.[289]

The battle over the Lecompton constitution began in early 1858, when the president submitted it to Congress along with a message defending it as both legal and fair. He explained his prior insistence on a referendum by claiming that he merely wanted the slavery question submitted to a popular vote. Buchanan claimed that the people of Kansas would be able to alter the state constitution immediately upon admission, since a provision banning amendments for seven years was not enforceable. Thus, if Kansans wanted to abolish slavery, the quickest way to achieve that end would be statehood under Lecompton. If Congress rejected Lecompton, Kansans would not be able to ban slavery in the immediate future because "it has been solemnly adjudged by the highest judicial tribunal known to our laws that slavery exists in Kansas by virtue of the Constitution of the United States."[290] Northern Democrats held fast. Their careers may have depended upon it. As early as November 1857, newspapers predicted that any northern Democrat who voted to approve Lecompton would not survive.[291] Anger over the Kansas-Nebraska Act had decimated their ranks four years earlier, and members realized that the Lecompton constitution was every bit as unpopular. Thus a vote for admission would mean a short stay in Washington, and all the patronage in the world could not change that—even an executive branch job might last only until the next administration.

The congressional debates that followed were among the most the most acrimonious in the nation's history. Administration men such as Henry M. Phillips of Pennsylvania followed the party line: the people of the territory did not need permission from Congress to hold a constitutional convention; popular approval of the entire constitution was not required by law or custom; the only divisive issue (slavery) had been submitted to a popular vote; the proceedings at Lecompton had been authorized by the territorial legislature; and Kansas voters could amend the constitution immediately via a state convention, as the clause barring amendments for seven years applied only to the legislature.[292] Senator James Mason of Virginia focused on al-

289. Nichols, *Disruption of American Democracy,* 211.
290. Richardson, *Messages and Papers of the Presidents,* 6:3008–10.
291. Nevins, *Emergence of Lincoln,* 1:237.
292. *Congressional Globe,* 35th Cong., 1st sess., March 4, 1858, Appendix, 27:71–74. Section 14 of the Lecompton constitution provided only one means for the formation of a convention— upon an affirmative vote of two-thirds of both houses of the legislature and the approval of a subsequent referendum by voters.

legations of electoral fraud. "I should like to know what popular election has been in many parts of the states of this Union—and I will not designate them further—under great popular excitement, where frauds have not been charged upon both parties, precisely the same as they are charged in Kansas." In his view, the real question before Congress was whether it was willing to admit more slave states to the Union. Other southerners agreed. Robert Toombs of Georgia insisted that Congress could not deny a state admission either because it allowed slavery or in response to alleged defects in its constitution. Free Soilers and Republicans focused on Kansas itself. Perhaps realizing that some might be moved by the argument that the state constitution could be amended immediately by the state's voters, they insisted that under Lecompton, only the legislature would be able to call a constitutional convention (only a convention could amend the constitution). As the state legislature was likely to be proslavery given gerrymandering, it is doubtful that it would have cooperated. In addition, as D. W. Gooch of Massachusetts pointed out, the Lecompton constitution itself purported to ban constitutional conventions until after 1864.[293]

As both houses of Congress moved closer to a vote near the end of March 1858, throngs packed the galleries. Eventually they were allowed on the Senate floor. Although eight anti-Lecompton men now occupied seats formerly held by senators who had voted for Kansas-Nebraska, everyone knew the measure would pass the upper house. Still, opponents kept up a steady beat of criticism. Charles Stuart of Michigan noted that the newly elected territorial legislature of Kansas had renounced the Lecompton constitution. Hence the observation of John Crittenden of Kentucky: when states had applied for admission in the past, they had done so with "unequivocal evidence of universal consent." Given the January 4 vote (the nonbinding referendum in which Lecompton was overwhelmingly rejected), that was not the case with Kansas. Despite Crittenden's wisdom, the Senate passed the Lecompton bill on March 23 by a vote of 33-25.[294]

Prospects for passage in the House worsened with the news that federal officials in Kansas had conspired to hide evidence of electoral fraud in the first referendum on Lecompton. Realizing that the bill would fail, members on both sides began to move toward a compromise. On March 29 a group of northern Democrats informed the president that they would vote for the

293. Ibid., March 1858, Appendix, 27:78, 81–82, 126, 229.
294. Ibid., Appendix, 176, 212–13; 1264–65.

measure if he agreed to the addition of a clause that recognized the right of Kansans to amend the state constitution immediately. The president refused to budge. Free Soilers spent the final hours of the debate pointing to the congressional investigations that revealed massive electoral fraud in Kansas.[295] The final verdict came on April 1: 120 to 112 in favor of a substitute bill that provided for a popular vote on the whole of the Lecompton constitution. Administration forces regrouped to salvage what they could. One of Jesse Bright's lieutenants, Representative William H. English of Indiana, proposed a rather extraordinary measure. Lecompton would be submitted to another vote in Kansas with the following proviso: acceptance of the constitution would bring immediate statehood and a land grant of 23.6 million acres, far in excess of the allotment normally given to new states. Rejection would mean no statehood until the territory's population reached 93,000 (the size of the average U.S. House district) and a land grant of only 4 million acres.[296] Despite blistering attacks from newspapers and complaints that the administration was offering Kansans a "land bribe," northern Democrats accepted the bill, and it passed.[297] Kansas voters nonetheless rejected Lecompton that August.[298] The campaign to add another slave state had been lost. As one historian put it, each of the steps taken by the Buchanan administration in the Lecompton debacle "had a certain plausibility" and might even have qualified as legal. Yet the electoral fraud clearly made the overall result unacceptable.[299] The episode demonstrated that Congress could review the affairs of a territory that applied for statehood. The power to admit new states, it appeared, necessarily carried at least a modicum of discretion with it.

It had been an intense battle outside Washington as well as within it. Those newspaper editors on the federal dole who came out against Lecompton lost their places at the trough. J. W. Gray of the *Cleveland Plain Dealer* was stripped of his postmastership.[300] So was the editor of the *Quincy (Illinois) Herald*.[301] Douglas papers, including the *Chicago Times* and *Illinois State*

295. See speech of F. H. Morse of New York of March 31, 1858, ibid., Appendix, 312–15.
296. Ibid., 1437, 1765–66.
297. The English bill passed the House on April 30, 1858, by a vote of 112 to 103. Ibid., 1905–6.
298. Two years later the territorial legislature in Kansas passed a bill (over the governor's veto) prohibiting slavery in the territory. The law was never tested in court.
299. Potter, *Impending Crisis*, 314.
300. Nevins, *Emergence of Lincoln*, 1:290.
301. Summers, "Dough in the Hands of the Doughfaces," 84–85.

*Register,* saw their printing contracts taken from them.[302] The editors of the *Albany Argus* and the *Rochester Union* endorsed Lecompton; they were suspected of seeking postmasterships.[303] A Jonesboro, Illinois, editor who had opposed Lecompton changed his mind after his son was appointed a federal marshal.[304] The *Chicago Tribune* complained that editors throughout southern Illinois remained quiet in the hope of joining the post office.[305] Members of Congress were told that it was a party measure and that all Democrats were expected to support it. As the weekly counts indicated that the necessary votes were still lacking, the administration resorted to the use of federal jobs, contracts, and even officer commissions to buy votes. (Hostilities with the Mormon nation in Utah required expansion of the army.) In the Senate, few resources had to be expended, though it was said that George Jones of Iowa and Philip Allen of Rhode Island—both near the end of their terms—sought diplomatic posts (Jones obtained one). Senator Fitch of Indiana reportedly allowed patronage concerns to guide his vote.[306] More largesse was distributed in the House. Critics charged that an Ohio congressman came on board after his son's appointment as postmaster and assurances that he would be appointed a U.S. marshal after he left office. The administration gave naval and army contracts to firms associated with cooperative representatives. The bribery continued with the English bill. The brother of Representative J. H. Ahl of Pennsylvania received a contract to supply the army with three hundred mules at $55 per animal. Joseph McKibben of California was offered a township of land as well as the imminent and unexpected departure of his father from the federal civil service.[307] Washington printer Cornelius Wendell—who held a virtual monopoly on federal printing contracts in the capital during the Buchanan administration—gave $5,000 to the roommate of Congressman Lawrence W. Hall of Ohio just before the vote.[308] By his own estimation, Wendell spent $30,000 to $40,000 to secure passage of the bill.[309]

Early in the contest the administration announced that no further appointments would be made until the vote on the Kansas bill took place. It

302. Johannsen, *Stephen A. Douglas,* 622.
303. Nevins, *Emergence of Lincoln,* 1:238.
304. Johannsen, *Stephen A. Douglas,* 627.
305. "Lecompton in Southern Illinois," *Chicago Tribune,* January 12, 1858, 2.
306. Nevins, *Emergence of Lincoln,* 1:258–59.
307. Summers, *Plundering Generation,* 253–54.
308. Nevins, *Emergence of Lincoln,* 1:297.
309. Covode Committee Report, 148.

then brought federal officeholders to Washington and had them lobby legislators directly.[310] This was a particularly disturbing development, for reasons indicated by the president's graphic warning to Congressman Horace
F. Clark of New York: it would be "impossible" to obtain re-election if the
"federal patronage in his district was arrayed against him." Why? Because
when turned out en masse, federal officeholders were numerous enough to
take over virtually any nominating convention. Hence the conversion of
Congressman Dan Sickles of New York, who was told that a vote against
Lecompton would cost an ally in the local surveyor's office his job.[311] Eager to strip Douglas of influence in his home state, the administration fired
scores of officeholders in Illinois, including the state mail agent, the Chicago postmaster, and the federal marshal.[312] In Pennsylvania the president won
an endorsement of Lecompton from the legislature and in turn the votes of
Representatives William Dewart and Wilson Reilly.[313] (When federal officeholders took over the state convention again the following year and passed
resolutions endorsing the administration's Kansas policies, anti-Lecompton
Democrats withdrew and held their own "Democratic states' rights" convention.)[314] Indiana also helped. In January 1858 Jesse Bright's machine extracted
an endorsement of the Buchanan administration's Kansas policies from the
state Democratic convention, despite bitter resistance.[315]

Strangely, most of the attempts to influence local nominating conventions occurred after the defeat of the Lecompton bill. This may have stemmed
from an old Jacksonian's desire to emphasize the importance of party "regularity"; it may also have arisen out of a thirst for vengeance. In New York,
the September 1858 state Democratic Softshell convention—replete with
federal officeholders—passed resolutions applauding the administration for
resolving the dispute in Kansas.[316] With Buchanan's approval, Senator John
Slidell of Louisiana undertook an operation in Illinois aimed at denying
Stephen Douglas re-election to the U.S. Senate. Postal agent Charles Lieb
traveled the state to interrogate postmasters regarding their feelings toward
the senator.[317] By the end of the summer, postmasters in Rockford, Bloom-

310. Nichols, *Disruption of American Democracy,* 171.
311. "Influences behind the Lecompton Bill," *New York Times,* July 22, 1858, 1.
312. Summers, *Plundering Generation,* 253.
313. Nevins, *Emergence of Lincoln,* 1:293.
314. Coleman, *Disruption of the Pennsylvania Democracy,* 114, 118.
315. "Great Row in Indiana—The Little Giant Floored," *Chicago Tribune,* January 11, 1858, 1.
316. "The Platforms," *New York Weekly Tribune,* September 25, 1858, 4.
317. Johannsen, *Stephen A. Douglas,* 622.

ington, Peoria, Belleville, Galesburg, and countless smaller towns lost their posts.[318] Much of the administration's activity centered around Isaac Cook, whom the president appointed the state's top postal agent. Cook sent out word to the state's postmasters that he expected them to win election as delegates to the state Democratic convention. "If you cannot come to the convention as a delegate, which I trust you will be able to, you must at all events make your appearance there, as we intend to organize the national Democratic Party, and it behooves the friends of the administration to be on hand with their armor on." Writing to a newspaper editor regarding the convention, Cook casually dangled a postmastership: "I . . . shall expect much to see you at Springfield, Illinois on the twenty-first when more will be done in relation to the postmasters and offices than at any other time, as I shall have an opportunity of then seeing most of the friends of the administration who are applying for positions."[319]

Douglas won the nomination; the administration remained undeterred. In Illinois and other northern states, the administration set up its own candidates in the general elections, backed them with legions of party workers on the federal payroll, and attempted to sabotage the campaigns of regularly nominated Democratic candidates who had voted against Lecompton. In doing so, it replaced one party creed that had stood since the 1820s—respect for party nominations—with a more ominous one: all party members must heed the line set at the top, even when it meant disaster. The madness began in May 1858, when the *Washington Union* announced that the administration viewed Douglas as an outcast.[320] Administration Democrats ("Danites") in Illinois held their own convention and nominated a slate of candidates for the state legislature. Federal employees in the state had their salaries assessed for the support of Danites. With the postmasters sending anti-Douglas newspapers to Illinois voters and the *Washington Union* attacking the senator as an abolitionist, it was clear that he faced a long, arduous struggle.

It was about to get worse. As a hero to antislavery elements pleased with his stand on Lecompton, Douglas occupied unfamiliar ground. Just four years before, northerners had burned him in effigy in reaction to the Kansas-Nebraska Act. Even in Chicago, Douglas was hissed into submission by a hostile crowd upon his return home in September 1854. Yet he had

318. Nevins, *Emergence of Lincoln*, 1:371–72.
319. Quoted in Johannsen, *Stephen A. Douglas*, 623.
320. Nevins, *Emergence of Lincoln*, 1:348–51.

come within a hair of the presidential nomination in 1856, and until recently Democrats of all sections considered Douglas the obvious choice in 1860. The defeat of Lecompton turned many in the South against him and in the process badly damaged his presidential prospects. Still, Douglas had no choice but to oppose the bill. Although Illinois had been a Democratic state for thirty years, a recent deluge of northeasterners had begun to change its outlook. These "Yankees" bitterly opposed the extension of slavery in the territories. Douglas's opponent in the 1858 Senate race, Abraham Lincoln, typified the evolving nature of the Illinois electorate. A wealthy if unpretentious lawyer, Lincoln had not enjoyed much of a political career before 1858. He served in the legislature during the 1830s and won a single term in the U.S. House of Representatives as a Whig in 1846. Beginning around the time of the fight over the Kansas-Nebraska bill, Lincoln emerged as a skilled and sinewy critic of the further extension of slavery. He succeeded in attacking the institution in purely moral terms—something rare outside the far north at that time—by pointing to the antislavery rhetoric of the Founding Fathers.[321] (The practice of treating the Founders as antislavery in outlook was common among Republicans, as they spent a great deal of time fighting off charges of extremism during the 1850s.)[322]

Illinois Republicans nominated Lincoln to run for the U.S. Senate in 1858. The candidate's knowledge of slavery-related issues proved critical, as Douglas had loosened his own version of strict construction to the point that the Republicans would not be able to hold his feet to the fire on economic issues such as river and harbor bills. Moreover, his rejection of Lecompton meant that the only issue on which Republicans could attack Douglas was the Kansas-Nebraska Act—now four years old. Republicans, on the other hand, needed a candidate who could demonstrate the incompatibility of Douglas's cherished doctrine of popular sovereignty and the Supreme Court's ruling in *Dred Scott.* At first it did not appear that Lincoln would be up to the task. In a June 16 speech kicking off his campaign, he spoke in apocalyptic terms that left him susceptible to charges of extremism. "A house divided against itself cannot stand. I believe this government cannot endure permanently half slave and half free. I do not expect the Union to

---

321. Ibid., 340–41.
322. On one occasion, Charles Sumner spoke at length regarding what he saw as George Washington's abolitionist tendencies. *Congressional Globe,* 33d Cong., 1st sess., April 24, 1854, Appendix, 23:267.

be dissolved—I do not expect the house to fall—but I expect it will cease to be divided. It will become all one thing, or all the other." Did that mean abolition? Not quite. "Either the opponents of slavery will arrest the further spread of it, and place it where the public mind shall rest in the belief that it is in the course of ultimate extinction; or its advocates will push forward till it shall become lawful in all states, old as well as new, north as well as south." Lincoln went on to torment his listeners with the possibility that the Supreme Court would hold unconstitutional state laws banning slavery.[323] One historian has called this last assertion "absurd."[324] That may have been true; yet, as the *Lemmon* case indicated, there were those who believed that the Constitution provided a right to travel with one's slaves throughout the whole of the Union. The real defect in the speech was the assertion that the country could not remain half slave and half free. Many viewed it as a thinly veiled call for federal abolition of slavery within the states.

On his way home from Washington during the summer of 1858, Douglas found his reception far different from that of 1854. His supporters met him at Michigan City, Indiana, with a brass band. Upon arriving in Chicago, the senator criticized Lincoln's "house divided" remark—surely it was possible for different practices to prevail in various parts of the Union.[325] Lincoln answered Douglas in a July speech in Chicago by aligning himself with the Founders. He pointed to the Northwest Ordinance and the Constitution's authorization of a ban on the slave trade. These acts served as "a clear indication that the Framers of the Constitution intended and expected the ultimate extinction of that institution." Perhaps aware of the controversy generated by his "house divided" remarks, Lincoln insisted that he had no desire to effect immediate abolition: "I believe there is no right, and ought to be no inclination in the people of the free states to enter into the slave states, and interfere with the question of slavery at all." Lincoln went on to acknowledge that, if elected, he would seek to prohibit slavery in the territories despite *Dred Scott*. As he saw it, unless he removed the slave Dred Scott from his master, he could not be held to have violated that ruling. The Supreme Court "had no right to lay down a rule to govern a coordinate branch of the government, the members of which had sworn to support the Constitution."[326]

323. *Works of Lincoln*, 1:240, 244.   324. Nevins, *Emergence of Lincoln*, 1:362.
325. Ibid., 352, 364–65.   326. *Works of Lincoln*, 1:253–56.

Near the end of the summer, Lincoln suggested a series of debates, and Douglas agreed. The first, on August 21 at Ottawa, Illinois, saw Douglas attack Lincoln and the Republicans as abolitionists. Lincoln responded by claiming once again that the Founders shared his determination to limit slavery's spread. He used *Dred Scott* to go on the offensive, warning that the Supreme Court was about to discover a right to carry slaves through all parts of the Union. In support of this assertion, he cited the November 1857 *Washington Union* that suggested that state emancipation laws might violate the privileges and immunities clause. The candidates next debated at Freeport, near the Wisconsin state line. After Lincoln answered a series of questions asked of him by Senator Douglas (he accepted the Fugitive Slave Act and would vote to admit slave states if their residents manifested a desire to establish slavery), he put his own query to the senator. Was there, he asked, any means by which the territorial legislatures could prohibit slavery without violating the *Dred Scott* decision? Douglas thought there was. Slavery, he announced, "cannot exist a day" without "local police regulations" that can only be established by the legislatures. Thus, "if the people [of a territory who] are opposed to slavery . . . elect representatives" who refuse to enact such laws, they will "effectually prevent the introduction of it in their midst."[327] With what became known as his "Freeport Doctrine," Douglas appeared to have eviscerated *Dred Scott*. Northern Democrats had long struggled with the decision; at first they brushed it off by dismissing Taney's comments regarding the territorial legislatures as mere dictum and therefore not binding. For those with national ambitions this approach was wholly inadequate— disavowal of a Supreme Court decision protecting slavery did not win one friends in the South. Douglas therefore had to find a way to both accept the decision and preserve the approach to the territories question that remained the central tenet of the Democratic Party in the north: popular sovereignty. The "Freeport Doctrine" appeared to provide the answer. Despite Douglas's intentions, it still gave offense in the South. The Supreme Court recognized a right to carry slaves into the territories, and the man who expected to receive the Democratic nomination in 1860 was busy explaining to northerners how they could undermine that right.

Two weeks later, at Jonesboro, it was Douglas who went on the offensive. Lincoln's "house divided" rhetoric would, he warned, cause "warfare between

327. Ibid., 291–98, 315.

north and south." Why could not the Republicans leave slavery where "our fathers placed it?" You and not we, Lincoln answered, disturbed the Missouri Compromise with the Kansas-Nebraska Act. The Republican nominee then returned to Douglas's Freeport Doctrine. Regulations, he insisted, need not be in place for a slaveholder to settle in the territories—the institution entered the country without the help of statutes. Besides, territorial courts were likely to apply the legal maxim "there is no wrong without a remedy" and protect slave owners who suffered losses. At Galesburg, on October 7, the candidates again clashed over the Supreme Court. Lincoln had made a habit of citing Andrew Jackson's bank veto in support of the proposition that the high Court's opinions were not binding on the other branches; therefore Congress need not accept *Dred Scott* as a limitation upon its powers. Douglas perceived a difference between the two cases. "Because General Jackson would not do a thing which he had a right to do, but did not deem expedient or proper, Mr. Lincoln is going to justify himself in doing that which he has no right to do." A week later Douglas again complained of Republicans' lack of respect for the Supreme Court, insisting that its opinions were the "law of the land" and "binding on every good citizen." He devoted most of his ammunition to Lincoln's "house divided" rhetoric and insisted that despite his opponent's vows to the contrary, the Republican lawyer intended to eradicate slavery throughout the Union. "How is he going to bring it about? Why, he will agitate; he will induce the north to agitate until the south shall be worried out, and forced to abolish slavery."[328]

In the end, Douglas's gambit paid off: by gutting *Dred Scott* and thereby preserving popular sovereignty, he held off his challenger. The victory came at a great cost: the permanent loss of the South. Many southerners dated their refusal to support Douglas in 1860 not from Lecompton but from the time he told northerners how they could undermine the rights of slaveholders. Unfortunately, the campaign did the same for Lincoln. With his "house divided" speech and talk of putting slavery back where it would be destined for "ultimate extinction," he made it difficult for southerners to resist the idea that he would attack slavery in their own region. In a way, Lincoln had been right; as he pointed out, the Founders had been antislavery, at least in theory. That the matter was now in dispute indicated that the South had changed, while the rest of the nation held to its original course.

328. Ibid., 342, 347, 358, 455, 473, 471.

THE FEDERAL MACHINE

The 1858–59 midterm elections took place in a climate of corruption. In Brooklyn the naval yard hired twenty-seven hundred men just before the election and fired them immediately after it. The Philadelphia naval yard also saw an oddly timed jump in hiring.[329] The results began trickling in during October. They revealed that for the second time in four years, the party of Jefferson and Jackson had sustained a once-in-a-lifetime whipping. In Pennsylvania the ranks of administration Democrats dropped from fifteen to two (out of twenty-five seats). Of the two Buchanan Democrats who survived, Congressman Thomas Florence probably did so only because of the votes of temporary hires at the Philadelphia naval yard.[330] The casualties included Representative J. Glancy Jones, a friend of Buchanan's and chairman of the Committee on Ways and Means. Even the president was moved to describe his party's defeat as "so great that it is almost absurd."[331]

The slaughter in Pennsylvania may have had more to do with the Tariff of 1857, which lowered rates on iron, than with Lecompton. Yet similar results in other, less protection-sensitive states made clear that the administration's overreaching in Kansas was primarily responsible for the slaughter. New Hampshire—long the most Democratic state in the upper North—went Republican in the spring. Ohio gave exactly one of its twenty-two seats in the House to administration Democrats. Republicans also did well in normally Democratic Iowa. New Jersey—widely viewed as a key state in 1860—returned five Republicans and three Douglas (popular sovereignty) Democrats to the House. Illinois elected five Republicans and four Douglas Democrats. Supporters of Stephen Douglas won a narrow majority of seats in the Illinois legislature, thus ensuring his re-election to the U.S. Senate. If Republicans had received a few thousand additional votes, Lincoln would have had administration Danites to thank for his victory.[332] Nowhere was the carnage worse than in New York, where the administration won only four of thirty-three seats available—all of them in New York City. Empire State Democrats Horace Clark and John Haskin voted against Lecompton in the House; for their trouble they had to battle candidates funded by the administration (both won). Although half the states would not hold their elections for the thirty-sixth Congress until 1859, it was clear by the end of

---

329. Summers, *Plundering Generation*, 255.   330. Nevins, *Emergence of Lincoln*, 1:400.
331. Quoted in ibid., 1:400.   332. Ibid., 1:396–98.

1858 that the Democratic Party had lost the House, as the number of admin-istration Democrats in the North dropped to just nineteen, from a high of ninety-three in 1854.[333]

Many were struck by the methods employed in the campaign. The *New York Times* blamed the Democrats' loss on "the attempt of the administration to load the machinery of party with the gross weight of an overgrown fed-eral patronage."[334] The belief that the president's allies had triggered the del-uge of corruption was so widespread that Buchanan felt compelled to issue a letter criticizing the practice of vote buying.[335] Other ominous developments occurred as well. Lincoln had not been the only Republican whose rhetoric touched a nerve. William Seward—the leading candidate for the 1860 Repub-lican presidential nomination—warned on September 25 of an "irrepressible conflict" between two systems of labor. Like Lincoln, he thought the country must eventually become "either a slaveowning nation or entirely a free-labor nation." Northern moderates attacked the message as needlessly provocative; southerners concluded that abolition had finally overtaken the North.[336]

When the thirty-fifth Congress met for its final session, slavery did not, for once, dominate the agenda. Instead, debate focused on an intercontinen-tal railroad, tariff revision, Oregon, and the purchase of Cuba—long sought by proslavery elements. Northern legislators posed a greater threat to the ad-mission of Oregon than their southern counterparts. They took offense at the proposed state constitution, which prohibited blacks from entering the state. Those already there could not vote, enter into contracts, or sue. At least one lawmaker believed these limitations would violate the privileges and im-munities clause. Many Republicans questioned whether Oregon ought to come in before Kansas when it had only half its population. Some credited the special treatment accorded Oregon to the fact that it promised to add another state to the ranks of the "Democracy" (the Democratic Party). Talk also turned to fears of centralization. Federal spending increased sharply dur-ing the 1850s. Annual appropriations went from $48 million to $80 million in seven years. One lawmaker pointed out that federal spending had grown from one dollar for every citizen in 1830 to three dollars in 1858.[337] A burst-

333. Potter, *Impending Crisis*, 326.

334. "The Lesson of the Elections," *New York Times*, November 4, 1858, 4.

335. *Works of Buchanan*, 10:23–24.

336. Nevins, *Emergence of Lincoln*, 1:409 (Buchanan quotation), 412.

337. See speech of Nehemiah Abbott of Maine of February 21, 1859, *Congressional Globe*, 35th Cong., 2d sess., Appendix, 28.2:190–93.

ing treasury helped give rise to several powerful factions and lobbies. They found that cooperation from Congress in the form of private acts, patents, land grants, tariffs, and subsidies (such as those that went to steamship lines) could be indispensable. Americans heard rumors of a band of congressmen who conspired to stall passage of bills aiding private interests until they were properly compensated. The *New York Times* was moved to warn that corruption was "infecting every department of our government."[338] It was as if the capital was nothing more than a giant trough. Many recoiled at the centralizing effects of the congressional lottery. Senator Andrew Johnson of Tennessee observed that "all parts of the nation look up to the federal government for contracts. . . . they look up here for jobs; they look up here for cases of speculation and fraud; and the government furnishes the means for them; while your states . . . are sinking into mere petty corporations . . . mere satellites of an inferior character, revolving around the great central power here at Washington."[339]

The increase in federal spending arose in part out the navy's transition from sail to steam. Some pointed to the inflation produced by California gold as well. That did not, however, explain the sharp rise in the ranks of those employed in the executive branch. Certainly the nation's terrific growth played a role; the population increased from 23 million to 30 million during the 1850s. Congressman A. H. Cragin detected another cause. He warned that the "patronage of the executive" had been "vastly augmented for the purpose of giving greater facility to the party in power." There was, he continued, "an army of federal office-holders" who "cover the land like the frogs of Egypt."[340] The naval yards in particular drew the attention of lawmakers. In early 1859 a House committee investigated the role played by the yards in the recent election. While the majority report was tentative, a minority report drafted by John Sherman of Ohio revealed that a whole new layer had been added to the federal political machine. More than ten thousand men had been employed in the naval yards at the time of the 1857 fall elections. Fewer than seven thousand toiled in them in the spring of 1858. The variation may have stemmed from the fact that navigation remained a seasonal affair. The hearings made clear that employment at the yards corresponded with political as well as meteorological activity. The pay-

338. "Our Public Peril," *New York Times,* April 19, 1860, 4.
339. *Congressional Globe,* 35th Cong., 2d sess., January 25, 1859, 28.1:583.
340. See ibid., Appendix, 221–23, 176.

roll at the Brooklyn yard peaked in early November—when the New York state elections occurred—while Philadelphia's topped out in mid-October, at the time of Pennsylvania's elections.[341] By one estimate, the Brooklyn yard hired four times as many men as it actually needed. Witnesses testified that members of Congress pressured yard officials to bring in additional men on the eve of elections—an easy enough task, as itinerant laborers in the big cities were constantly knocking at the doors of these facilities. The new hires were sent out to the polls on behalf of such congressmen as Dan Sickles of New York.[342] Twenty-seven hundred men were said to have been hired at the Brooklyn naval yard in order to assist Congressman William Maclay.[343]

The most stunning aspect of the investigation was its revelation of pervasive executive branch meddling in county and state nominating conventions. The naval yards report explained in graphic detail why the president could warn Democratic members of Congress that he had the power to keep them from being renominated. Bernard Donnelly, a painter at the Brooklyn naval yard, testified that he had attended a Democratic convention in Jamaica, New York, along with other yard employees in order to secure the nomination of Congressman John A. Searing. They did so at the behest of their boss, the yard's master painter. Undoubtedly a newcomer to American politics, Mr. Donnelly appeared to be less than impressed with the behavior of his co-workers at the convention. "They acted in a noisy manner about the place; seemed to take a deep interest in having Mr. Searing re-nominated, and opposed all those who were inclined to go for some other candidate. They were rather abusive in their manner." Donnelly also recalled a warning his boss had issued: only Searing men were wanted at the yard. John Vandervoot, a master laborer at the Brooklyn naval yard, admitted to being one of the shepherds. Of the hundred or so men who worked under him, he took twenty-five to a primary meeting in New York City, where delegates to the state Democratic convention in Syracuse were selected. As Vandervoot recalled, no one was very particular about attending only those meetings that took place in his own district.[344]

It was not until 1860 that the full extent to which the federal executive branch had been converted into a national political machine became known. Shortly after the House of Representatives finally organized itself in February (southerners sat on their hands for two months rather than cooperate

341. *Navy Yards Report*, 1:73.
343. Richards, *Slave Power*, 210.
342. *Navy Yards Report*, 4:130–32, 76, 72.
344. *Navy Yards Report*, 4:49, 51, 304, 307.

in the election of a Republican Speaker), the majority established a committee chaired by Pennsylvania's "Honest John" Covode. The committee was charged with investigating every last allegation of abuse of power by the Buchanan administration. The question of whether members of Congress had been bribed in connection with Lecompton was the main object of the inquiry. Lingering rumors of fraud in the 1856 and 1858 elections also received attention.[345] The resulting investigation was the first to receive extensive coverage in the national press. At times it appeared to be something of a witch hunt, and to some degree it was. The hearings were timed to coincide with the Democratic national convention at Charleston in April, and the Covode Committee released its report in June, just before the Republican convention in Chicago. Republican Party operatives distributed thousands of abridged versions of the report that fall.[346] The committee uncovered a variety of excesses. An employee of the Philadelphia customhouse recalled handing out two thousand naturalization blanks in Pennsylvania's state elections of 1856 and that, overall, six thousand blanks had been distributed—easily exceeding the Democratic margin. Thomas McDonough, another Philadelphia customhouse employee, testified that "committees of naturalization" were set up by the party in each of the city's wards to distribute naturalization papers to cooperative immigrants. More recently, the customhouses had adapted that favorite of the naval yards—Election Day hiring. Augustus Schell, collector of the Port of New York, acknowledged that the customhouse hired men just before the 1858 elections and discharged them immediately afterward.[347]

The star witness of the hearings was printer Cornelius Wendell, an erstwhile Republican whose brand-new plant enabled him to secure almost all of the lucrative printing contracts available in Washington. He used his profits to subsidize Buchanan newspapers in the North. Wendell's testimony before the Covode Committee revealed that he also served as treasurer for the first national political machine. In the 1858 campaign he contributed funds to eight Democratic candidates in Pennsylvania, New Jersey, and other critical states. Between 1854 and 1858 he spent more than $100,000 on elections in the North. During the Lecompton struggle, the printer spent between $30,000 and $40,000 lobbying members of Congress. Wendell admitted that he expected to be compensated for his efforts in the form of "a

345. The resolution describing the committee's assignment may be found in *Congressional Globe,* 36th Cong., 1st sess., March 29, 1860, 29.4:1437.

346. Summers, *Plundering Generation,* 273.

347. Covode Committee Report, 388–93, 477.

continuation of the work from government." M. P. Bean, the assistant clerk in the House, accepted $5,000 from Wendell, who made it clear that the money was to be used for the purpose of getting as many representatives as possible to vote for the English bill. Rumor had it that both Lawrence W. Hall and S. S. Cox (Ohio congressmen) had sold their votes. According to one witness, Cox claimed that the president had assured him that places were available for his friends in the Interior Department. Perhaps the most damaging news was Wendell's admission that he discussed his expenditures with the president.[348]

If Wendell was the star witness, Lecompton was the investigation's primary scandal. The Covode hearings made clear what everyone had suspected all along—the Lecompton constitution's unique provisions concerning slavery had been devised with the assistance of administration officials. H. L. Martin, a land office clerk, recalled an 1858 meeting with Interior Secretary Jacob Thompson that took place on the eve of Martin's departure for Kansas. Thompson admitted that popular ratification was necessary, yet he thought a supposedly antislavery constitution might be written so that it protected the rights of slaveholders. Thompson suggested a clause providing that all slave owners already in Kansas as well as their descendants could not be divested of their slaves. Martin later testified that upon arriving in Kansas, he became deeply involved in drafting the Lecompton constitution. The charter protected the rights of slave owners in the very manner that had been suggested by Thompson.

As the hearings began, Washington was intrigued by a rumor of a July 1857 letter from the president to Governor Walker in which Buchanan reaffirmed his support for submission of Lecompton in its entirety to a popular vote. When a clerk testified to the letter's existence, Attorney General Jeremiah Black publicly berated him outside the hearing, only to have Walker produce it on the eve of the Democratic convention in late April. Even that was not the worst of it for poor Mr. Black. David Webster, a Philadelphia lawyer, testified on May 25 regarding the attorney general's attempts to bribe John Forney, at one time Buchanan's personal editor. Following a split with the president, Forney joined Free Soil ranks as editor of the staunchly independent and popular *Philadelphia Press.* He bitterly opposed Lecompton. Aware of his growing influence, the administration sought to have Forney publish an article calling on Free Soil Democrats to acquiesce in the pro-

348. Ibid., 459, 148, 191, 124–25, 279, 466.

posed constitution. The plan failed when Forney rejected an offer of mone-
tary compensation as well as consulates in Russia and Great Britain. Forney
himself testified regarding the episode on June 11. Cornelius Wendell recalled
that the president "was desirous to have Mr. Forney go abroad." The committee uncovered other attempts to manipulate the press. Matthew Johnson, the former editor of the *Washington Union,* testified about discussions
he had with Democratic operative M. P. Bean. With the encouragement of
Senator Fitch of Indiana, Bean proposed to go home to Ohio in order to
purchase Republican newspapers and "change their tone" on Lecompton.[349]

The Covode Committee's investigation also provided further evidence
of the penchant of federal officials for using civil servants to influence state
nominating conventions. Francis McCormick testified that while he had
been employed at the Philadelphia customhouse, the collector had requested
that he use his influence to secure the nomination of a favorite in the 1858
state elections. When McCormick insisted on supporting another candidate, he was removed. Andrew Brumaker, a laborer at the Philadelphia customhouse, recalled that the collector had fired employees whose only failing
was an inability to secure the election of Buchanan delegates to the Democratic state convention. Perhaps the most damaging testimony was that of
Patrick Lafferty, a former carpenter at the Philadelphia naval yard. On one
occasion he visited the national capital and the executive mansion; unfortunately, the visit occurred shortly after Lafferty had refused to carry out the
collector's wishes regarding elections for the city's executive committee. The
president complained that Lafferty "kept him in hot water all the time" and
would have to be removed.[350]

The committee report was blistering. It decried the "open employment
of money" in connection with the Lecompton bill; the attempts of federal officers to "control the sentiments of the people in their primary political movements"; the "utterly disproportionate" amounts of money "squan-
dered upon a profligate press devoted to the interest of the administration";
and the involvement of customhouse officials in naturalization frauds.[351] A
charge leveled by the *New York Times* on the eve of the hearings—that the
president "sought ward politicians, men who could control primary meetings
and pack a convention successfully"—had received ample confirmation.[352]

349. Ibid., 158–59, 163–67, 97–99, 112–13, 222, 297, 311, 150.
350. Ibid., 360–61, 365–66, 371.          351. Ibid., 6, 9, 19, 26–27.
352. "In the Right Direction," *New York Times,* March 6, 1860, 4.

Republicans used the report to portray Buchanan as the head of a national political machine. Representative C. L. Beale of New York spoke of men "residing in each state, exerting their official influence in that state, but owing fealty to the federal center alone—men who control state conventions and election precincts by violence, whose salaries are assessed by the central power for corruption funds."[353]

The Covode Committee uncovered, as one historian put it, "the most devastating proof of government abuse of power since the founding of the Republic."[354] Even if it was true, as a biographer of Buchanan claimed, that the practices uncovered were "common to every administration since the days of Andrew Jackson," the fact remains that they progressed furthest under his watch.[355] Buchanan applied these tactics, after all, to a party system that had become dangerously dependent on the federal civil service for patronage. In doing so, he centralized power in the American political system to a degree that would have been unimaginable in 1787.

### THE ELECTION OF 1860

By the spring of 1859 the country had returned to an almost normal state. Kansas was no longer a subject of dispute. Despite losing the battle over Lecompton, southern Democrats could point to *Dred Scott* and claim victory in the long war over the power of Congress to ban slavery in the territories (although the Freeport Doctrine continued to irritate some). In the spring 1859 state elections, Whig or "opposition" movements in the South did well at the expense of Democratic "fire-eaters." Unfortunately, bad weather was coming in—from Kansas, of all places.

John Brown had already earned national fame as the ringleader of the Pottawatomie Massacre, when, in response to the "sack of Lawrence," Brown and his cohorts pulled five Kansas residents from their cabins on the night of May 25, 1856, and hacked them to death. Although he was among the most wanted men in America, Brown moved freely about the North during the late 1850s.[356] He therefore had the time to finance and prepare for his next mission—an invasion of the South itself, with the goal of fomenting a

353. *Congressional Globe,* 36th Cong., 1st sess., June 12, 1860, Appendix, 29:428.
354. Summers, *Plundering Generation,* 258.
355. Klein, *President James Buchanan,* 339.
356. Allan Nevins, *The Emergence of Lincoln,* vol. 2, *Prologue to the Civil War, 1859–1861* (New York: Charles Scribner's Sons, 1951), 26.

general insurrection among the slaves. On a peaceful night in October 1859, Brown began his crusade by occupying an empty federal armory at Harper's Ferry, Virginia. Once the building was secured, a contingent left the main force to capture a nearby planter and free his slaves. Meanwhile, Brown and his men stopped a train and killed a porter before returning to the armory. By the middle of the following morning, local residents had pinned down the invasion force with rifle fire. Brown and his cohorts retreated to an engine house within the armory. Shortly thereafter, U.S. troops stormed the building and captured the assailants; they were turned over to Virginia authorities, who charged them with treason.

Incompetent and insane people lose themselves in causes just as sane ones do; the tragedy of John Brown was that so many sane people believed in him—and in the possibility of inciting a slave insurrection.[357] Some of New England's most prominent citizens provided money for what they thought would be an invasion of the lower Appalachians.[358] Following Brown's hanging in December 1859, bells tolled across the Northeast in memory of a man many had come to view as a martyr for freedom. In the South, where fears of slave insurrections had become epidemic (despite the fact that none had occurred in thirty years), many residents concluded that northerners intended to liberate their slaves by force. The fears and anxieties of the past returned; it was as if the Unionist sentiment that flowered in the South during the past year had never been born. The Mississippi legislature responded to Brown's raid by declaring that election of a president unwilling to protect slave property would lead to concerted action on the part of the southern states.[359] It also elected an open disunionist, John J. Pettus, governor. Southern voters elsewhere took up the cause as well, sending a number of extremists to the thirty-sixth Congress.

When the last of the returns came in during the fall of 1859, it became clear that while the Republicans had won more seats in the House than the Democrats, they still lacked a majority. American Party representatives from the upper South held the balance of power. A long and draining battle over the speakership ensued when Congress met that December. Southern legislators made it clear that they would be more than happy to see the government cease operating rather then acquiesce in the election of Republican

357. Potter, *Impending Crisis*, 372–73.
358. McPherson, *Battle Cry of Freedom*, 204.
359. Potter, *Impending Crisis*, 384.

John Sherman as Speaker. Talk of secession was widespread, and members of Congress came to the Capitol armed. After more than fifty ballots, the House settled upon William Pennington of New Jersey, in early February. Debate revolved around slavery-related issues. Northerners were told that they must go along with the reopening of the slave trade. Fearful that territorial legislatures would not protect the institution in the West, a handful of southerners demanded that Congress enact a slave code for the territories. The *Charleston News* held that "if the Constitution confers upon slavery the right to go into the territories . . . then it also imposes the duty of protecting that right, and this cannot be done without positive proslavery legislation, and a federal slave code for the territories." The *Richmond Enquirer* agreed.[360]

The movement picked up steam in late 1859, in part because the legislatures in the Kansas and Nebraska territories both passed legislation that purported to prohibit slavery. In his annual message, Buchanan hinted at his support for a slave code.[361] Two months later, in February 1860, Mississippi senator Jeff Davis pushed the issue into the congressional spotlight. He offered a series of resolutions in the Senate, one of which declared that "it is the duty of the federal government there [in the territories] to afford for [slavery], as for other species of property, needful protection; and if experience should at any time prove that the judiciary does not possess power to insure adequate protection, it will then become the duty of Congress to supply such deficiency." Was legislation really necessary? Senator Albert G. Brown, Davis's fellow Mississippian, thought so—every territory but New Mexico, he pointed out, had taken steps to ban slavery.[362] In fact, both Utah and New Mexico—the only two territories far enough south to be suitable for slavery—had enacted their own slave codes for the purpose of protecting the institution. New Mexico did so in large part because of administration pressure.[363] Senator Fitch of Indiana thought that slave owners in the territories could rely on the federal judiciary. Yes, he admitted, Nebraska and Kansas had passed laws banning slavery, but those measures had not been tested in federal court. John Crittenden agreed—not a single case had occurred in which a slaveholder had been stripped of his property through the acts of a

360. *Charleston News* and *Richmond Enquirer* quoted in the *New York Weekly Tribune*, September 25, 1858, 2.

361. Richardson, *Messages and Papers of the Presidents*, 5:554 (December 19, 1859).

362. *Congressional Globe*, 36th Cong., 1st sess., February 1860, 29.1:658, 1002.

363. Fehrenbacher, *Slaveholding Republic*, 293.

territorial legislature.[364] Oddly, no one bothered to propose a bill that would establish a slave code, and therein lies the secret to the whole episode. Davis's proposal had nothing to do with the actual state of the territories and everything to do with the upcoming presidential campaign. He offered the resolutions in order to sabotage Stephen Douglas's bid for the Democratic nomination, by imposing a price for southern support that the senator could not possibly meet. Radicals moved to exploit the opportunity provided by Davis; they began spreading the view that a slave code alone could prevent secession. Alabama Democrats, who had already selected their delegates to the national convention, instructed them to withdraw if the convention did not approve a plank endorsing a slave code.[365]

Thus far no American presidential candidate had commenced his campaign under more difficult circumstances than Stephen Douglas did in the summer of 1859. Radical southerners, administration officials, and Buchanan Democrats in the North all hated him, in part because of his role in the defeat of Lecompton and in part because of his vaunted Freeport Doctrine. Douglas had been expelled from the leadership of his party when his fellow Democrats in the Senate removed him from his post as chairman of the Committee on Territories. His former allies goaded him repeatedly— rumors abounded that John Slidell of Louisiana had tried to force him into a duel and that Senator Fitch of Indiana nearly succeeded in doing so.[366] For a time, Douglas retained a bodyguard. His caution may well have been justified; later that fall, a proslavery Californian, David S. Terry, former chief justice of the state supreme court, shot and killed Free Soil senator David S. Broderick in a duel. Douglas announced his candidacy in a June 1859 letter in which he expressed his opposition to a federal slave code, the notion that the Constitution bestowed a right to carry slaves into the territories, and reopening the slave trade.[367]

The race for the Democratic nomination followed a predictable course. The northern wing of the "Democracy" returned to the Douglas bandwagon after his stand against Lecompton. Southern Democrats supported Vice President John C. Breckinridge, a thirty-nine-year-old Kentuckian. (Buchanan chose not to seek a second term.) It was apparent that Douglas would

364. *Congressional Globe*, 36th Cong., 1st sess., March 6, 1860, 29.1:1007 (Fitch), and May 24, 1860, 29.3:2341 (Crittenden).

365. Nevins, *Emergence of Lincoln*, 2:225.        366. Ibid., 1:452.

367. Johannsen, *Stephen A. Douglas*, 704.

have a majority of delegates going into the convention. The Illinois senator came into the contest with the mindset of a candidate who would not be bargained into submission. He had stepped aside in 1852 and 1856; he would not do so in 1860. The administration thus faced long odds when it decided to use its influence to secure the nomination for Breckinridge. Although success was never really within its reach, its skillful deployment of federal patronage enabled the administration to create a great deal of mischief. This had much to do with the state of the northern Democratic Party itself. Although anti-Lecompton or Douglas Democrats still prospered throughout the North, regular party organizations had atrophied severely. Consequently they became very susceptible to manipulation by administration officials, who continued to manage the federal civil service with an eye toward controlling state party machinery.[368]

New England Democratic organizations had weakened more than those of any other region; they also proved most willing to follow the administration's script. Americans witnessed the spectacle of party editors in the most antislavery region of the country coming out for Breckinridge as early as 1859.[369] The administration sought to gain control of the state delegations that the northeastern states would send to the Democratic convention.[370] It had only limited success in Massachusetts.[371] The administration fared better in New Jersey, where time-tested tactics such as the packing of primary meetings enabled it to secure the election of cooperative delegates.[372] Buchanan forces won tentative control of the Pennsylvania delegation, though only after the president stopped the Philadelphia collector from giving in to complaints that the delegate selection process had been rigged.[373] In a key loss, Jesse Bright was unable to secure Indiana for Breckinridge. Federal officeholders led by Senators Fitch and Bright fought hard to gain control of the Democratic convention that met in Indianapolis in January, but in the end they came up short.[374] After Michigan's regular Democratic convention endorsed Douglas, a group of administration Democrats—mostly federal officeholders—held their own state convention and endorsed Breckinridge.[375]

368. Potter, *Impending Crisis*, 393.
369. Summers, "Dough in the Hands of the Doughfaces," 86.
370. Johannsen, *Stephen A. Douglas*, 746.
371. Klein, *President James Buchanan*, 341.
372. Gillette, *Jersey Blue*, 82.
373. Nichols, *Disruption of American Democracy*, 340.
374. Nevins, *Emergence of Lincoln*, 2:201.
375. Formisano, *Birth of Mass Political Parties*, 283–84.

The president and his allies also attempted to impose their will in Douglas's home state. Federal workers in Illinois had their salaries assessed for the *Chicago Herald* (the local administration sheet), and Douglas complained that his mail was being opened by Buchanan men at the post office.[376] The dedication of state Democrats to their senator proved too strong, and Buchanan's forces had to settle for another Danite convention and their own Democratic slate.

The administration had more success out west. Doughface senator Joe Lane and a squadron of executive branch officers won control of Oregon's delegation.[377] Buchanan forces also took California.[378] The South did not have to be bought to oppose Douglas, though Senator Pierre Soule claimed that federal offices had purchased Louisiana for Breckinridge. Douglas men in other southern states also thought that nominating conventions had been rigged by extremists and pro-administration men.[379] And then there was New York. The Democracy of the Empire State, despite its long antislavery tradition, held to an equally ancient custom and split in half in 1860, one part supporting Douglas and the other the administration. The latter held its convention in January 1860 and selected a pro-Breckinridge delegation headed by New York City mayor Fernando Wood.

The Democratic national convention met in Charleston, South Carolina, in mid-April 1860. The meeting was top-heavy with public employees; out of twenty-five hundred delegates, Douglas supporters counted more than five hundred federal civil servants.[380] The gathering was probably doomed from the start, as delegates from seven southern states threatened to withdraw if the platform did not include a plank endorsing a territorial slave code. Caleb Cushing served as convention chairman. Since leaving office, Pierce's attorney general had fought for the repeal of Massachusetts' personal liberty law (it provided procedural safeguards for persons accused of being fugitive slaves). Cushing had also embraced annexation of Cuba and Mexico. More recently he had concluded that it was the duty as well as the right of the South to secede if it did not receive adequate reassurances from the North.[381] Under Cushing's guidance, the convention flirted with the notion of seating administration delegations from Illinois and New York until regularly elect-

376. Johannsen, *Stephen A. Douglas*, 703.     377. Nevins, *Emergence of Lincoln*, 2:284.
378. Klein, *President James Buchanan*, 341.     379. Nevins, *Emergence of Lincoln*, 2:210.
380. Elbert B. Smith, *The Presidency of James Buchanan* (Lawrence: University Press of Kansas, 1975), 106.
381. Nevins, *Emergence of Lincoln*, 2:207, 205.

ed delegates from the Northwest threatened to leave if it did so. Douglas supporters won that battle and gained a second victory when the convention allowed delegates to vote as they wished when selecting a nominee (instead of requiring that each state delegation vote as a unit). The handful of Douglas supporters in southern delegations were thus free to vote for him. Not all went well for the Illinois senator. The platform committee approved a plank endorsing a slave code by a vote of seventeen states to sixteen (Oregon and California voted with the fifteen slave state delegations).[382] A minority platform avoided the slave code issue. Instead it acknowledged continuing disagreement "over the institution of slavery within the territories."[383] Douglas men resolved to have the convention adopt the minority platform.

On April 27 William L. Yancey of South Carolina took the floor. He declared that acceptance by the South of popular sovereignty would mean that it had consented to the loss of constitutional rights. George E. Pough of Ohio in turn warned southerners that the demand for a slave code amounted to an insistence that the North accept slavery and its extension as good for the country. Perhaps sensing overconfidence on the part of his brethren, built by years of winning these battles, Pough cautioned them: "Gentlemen of the south, you mistake us! We will not do it!"[384] Shortly thereafter, the convention approved the minority platform on slavery in the territories—thereby turning aside demands for endorsement of a slave code. The head of the Alabama delegation promptly rose from his seat and informed Chairman Cushing that the delegates from his state were leaving in accordance with the instructions of his state's Democratic convention of the previous January. They proceeded to walk out, along with delegates from seven other states—far more than had been expected by Douglas forces. Without the quorum necessary to nominate a candidate, the convention sputtered helplessly before adjourning in early May.

Democrats tried again in mid-June, this time in Baltimore. Despite administration attempts to seat alternative state delegations, Douglas forces again won control. When the majority voted to admit only some of those who had walked out in Charleston, southerners withdrew. The remaining delegates voted to go forward with the selection process, and Douglas won the nomination. The convention closed by adopting the party's 1856 resolu-

382. Johannsen, *Stephen A. Douglas*, 750.
383. Quoted in Nichols, *Disruption of American Democracy*, 301.
384. Quoted in Nevins, *Emergence of Lincoln*, 2:217.

tions concerning slavery in the territories, albeit with a new provision expressing the hope that the Supreme Court might give northern Democrats something more reasonable to work with in the future.[385] Shortly thereafter, southern Democrats met in their own convention and nominated John C. Breckinridge for president and Senator Joseph Lane of Oregon for vice president.

For more than three years following the election of 1856, William Seward enjoyed frontrunner status for the 1860 Republican presidential nomination. Almost from the moment he lost to Douglas, Abraham Lincoln set out to obtain that prize for himself. He traveled throughout the North, focusing on the same themes he had emphasized during the 1858 campaign. Lincoln assured listeners that Republicans only wished to limit slavery to its present area. In a possible reference to the *Lemmon* case, he repeatedly warned (at least sixteen times, according to one count) that the Supreme Court was about to extend slavery into the North itself.[386] As for the territories question, Lincoln defended the Republican position—that a ban fell within the authority of Congress—by pointing to the Founders. In a February 1860 speech at New York City's Cooper Union, he pointed out that of thirty-nine delegates to the Constitutional Convention, twenty-one had served in Congress at the time that it prohibited slavery in the Northwest Territory. Therefore he did not accept the notion that Congress lacked the power to prohibit slavery in the territories.[387] The New York press, already leery of Seward, applauded the speech. Many feared that nomination of the senator would cost the Republicans the advantage on the corruption issue they had gained from the Covode Committee hearings.[388]

Seward gave what was in effect his first campaign speech on February 29, 1860. Echoing the Republican platform of 1856, the New York senator spoke of the party's determination to save the territories from both polygamy and slavery. After making his customary concession to moderation—Congress lacked authority to interfere with slavery in the states—Seward nevertheless went on to predict that there would soon be as many Republicans in the South as in the North (no idle threat given the region's ten thousand post

385. The "restrictions imposed upon the territorial governments by the Constitution, as the same has been, or shall hereafter be, finally determined by the Supreme Court of the United States, should be respected by all good citizens." McKee, *National Conventions and Platforms*, 63.

386. Finkleman, *Imperfect Union*, 318.

387. *Works of Lincoln*, 1:603.

388. McPherson, *Battle Cry of Freedom*, 217.

offices). Seward closed by declaring that all persons of "generous and chari-
table natures" would concede that John Brown and his associates "acted on
earnest though fatally erroneous convictions."[389] Between his compliments
for John Brown and memories of his "irrepressible conflict" speech of 1858,
Seward burdened himself with the weight of extremism as well as corruption. (Although he himself was above reproach, the senator's allies in Albany
had recently given away New York City railroad franchises for almost nothing.)[390] While Republicans agreed with Seward on many points, the party
had a formidable task ahead if it was to win the executive branch in 1860. As
most observers had already conceded California and Oregon to the Democrats, Republicans would have to take Pennsylvania, New Jersey, and either
Indiana or Illinois, as well as every other northern state in order to win.[391]
The contest would be decided in states that were not Republican—Pennsylvania did not even have a statewide Republican organization. Lincoln came
from Illinois and thus held out the promise of winning that critical state.
His perceived moderation in comparison to Seward helped as well. This was
somewhat unfair; he too had implied that slavery must eventually be terminated throughout the United States. Lincoln, however, did not make the
mistake of praising John Brown.

As late as the spring of 1860, observers did not view Lincoln as a leading candidate for the Republican nomination. Newspapers instead focused
on Salmon Chase of Ohio, Edward Bates of Missouri, Simon Cameron of
Pennsylvania, and Seward. The situation changed somewhat with the nomination of Lincoln by the Illinois state Republican convention on May 8; the
*Chicago Tribune's* endorsement also helped. The baggage of the other candidates also enhanced Lincoln's prospects. Chase was widely viewed as even
more of an extremist than Seward—he believed that the due process clause
of the Fifth Amendment *prohibited* slavery in the territories. Cameron's
hopes fell apart over rumors of corruption that far exceeded Seward's difficulties. Edward Bates's background as a former slave owner stunted what
might otherwise have been a formidable candidacy. Lincoln received an in-
valuable boost from the decision to hold the Republican national convention in Chicago. His managers used their control of the floor to separate
delegates from key states and those of New York, who were said to have

389. *Congressional Globe*, 36th Cong., 1st sess., February 29, 1860, 29.2:910–15.
390. Summers, *Plundering Generation*, 267.
391. McPherson, *Battle Cry of Freedom*, 216.

brought bundles of cash with which to purchase the nomination for Seward. They also packed the gallery with Lincoln partisans. The convention met at the Wigwam on Lake Street in May 1860. When Seward failed to obtain the nomination on the first ballot, the rush began. With ten thousand spectators pouring forth unsolicited advice from the gallery, New England delegates broke from Seward on the third ballot. Lincoln then received votes from Ohio and surpassed the number of votes necessary for the nomination. The convention aided its candidate by dropping the belligerent language of the 1856 platform and replacing it with a modest program that merely stated the party's opposition to the extension of slavery, though it implied that the due process clause barred Congress from giving "legal existence" to slavery in the territories.[392]

No election in American history has ever been decided by one issue, and the contest of 1860 held to this rule. Republicans added a plank to their platform for every possible constituency. Two attacked the administration (for Lecompton and corruption); others promised a transcontinental railroad, protective tariffs, and improvements to rivers and harbors (for the "accommodation and security of an existing commerce"). Still another plank promised a homestead act and attacked the idea that recipients of free land were nothing more than "paupers or suppliants for public bounty."[393] The Republican embrace of programs aimed at voters' pocketbooks was no accident. Although most members of the party were former Whigs and thus disposed by nature to loosen the federal purse strings, there was more to their platform than ideology. Party leaders realized that a campaign built on moral abstractions alone could not win. As Horace Greeley, publisher of the *New York Tribune*, put it, the country "will only swallow a little antislavery in a great deal of sweetening. An antislavery man per se cannot be elected; but a tariff, river-and-harbor, pacific railroad, free-homestead man may succeed although he is anti-slavery.... I aim to have as good a candidate as the majority will elect."[394] Republican speakers around the country followed the script. In the Northwest they spoke of homesteads; in the East, of tariffs; a Pacific railroad was discussed in the West, and promises of river and harbor appropriations were heard near the Great Lakes. Not since the days of Henry Clay had federal largesse played such a prominent role in national

392. Quoted in McKee, *National Conventions and Platforms*, 114.
393. Ibid., 114–15.
394. Quoted in Potter, *Impending Crisis*, 420.

politics. Republican Party leaders saw to it that the message reached voters. While in 1856 their fund-raising had lagged, in 1860 Republicans amassed enough cash to flood the North with literature. The residents of one Illinois county alone received more than six thousand documents before July 1.[395]

By and large, labor resisted Republican enticements such as higher tariffs and supported Stephen Douglas. So did the scores of Democratic newspapers in the North that had lost their places at the federal trough during the intraparty wars of the past four years. The region's politicians also supported Douglas; Tammany Hall gave him an enormous parade in New York City.[396] Douglas then lit out across the country in one of the first stump campaigns in American history. At Norfolk in August Douglas courageously answered two queries in the only way a Jacksonian Democrat could: Lincoln's election would not justify secession, and in the event of such a thing, the president must react just as Jackson had in 1832—with the threat of force.[397] The South—or least the proslavery men who professed to speak for it—reacted with outrage. John C. Breckinridge undoubtedly took heart, as the speech sealed Douglas's fate in that region. The vice president's prospects were not great under any circumstances; in order to win he would have to carry the whole of the South, California, Oregon, Illinois, Pennsylvania, and either Indiana or New Jersey. That task was complicated not only by the presence of Douglas but also by the Constitutional Union party, a loose amalgamation of former Whigs that nominated John Bell of Tennessee for president and Edward Everett of Massachusetts for vice president. Breckinridge obtained Buchanan's endorsement in July; while that was of little consequence to voters, it did mean that the executive branch's army of civil servants would labor on his behalf. Federal census workers, marshals, and a formidable fleet of publicly fed newspapers provided a skeleton organization for Breckinridge in the North. Democratic machines in California and Oregon gave assistance as well.[398]

Despite Douglas's intensity, he was unable to engage Lincoln in anything resembling a public debate. The Republican candidate took the advice of his managers and said nothing, even when southerners taunted him as an extremist who would abolish slavery in the states. Democrats attacked Lincoln

---

395. Nevins, *Emergence of Lincoln*, 2:301–2.
396. Nichols, *Disruption of American Democracy*, 340.
397. Johannsen, *Stephen A. Douglas*, 788–89.
398. Nichols, *Disruption of American Democracy*, 336–37.

on every possible front. They warned that he would follow Seward's suggestion and seek legislation adjusting the federal judicial circuits—thereby causing the transfer of seats on the Supreme Court from the South to the North.
Democrats also predicted that a Republican administration would fill federal offices in the South with antislavery men. The administration sheet, the
Washington, D.C., *Constitution,* warned that Lincoln would cover the South
with abolitionist postmasters.[399] Howell Cobb predicted that a Republican
administration would use federal places in the South to organize a band of
"apologists" who would assist it in its "insidious warfare" on southerners.[400]
Cobb knew from experience how a skilled deployment of patronage could affect the internal affairs of a state. As Buchanan's treasury secretary and coun-
selor, he observed the political operations of an administration that spent
four years exploiting federal patronage to harass Free Soil Democrats in their
own states. It was no coincidence that many of the most strident secessionists were the same men who, as Democratic Party leaders, had intruded in
the affairs of northern state political organizations. They knew well the havoc
that could be wreaked. Federally subsidized newspapers could spread the antislavery message in the South. Executive branch employees could stage their
own nominating conventions and sustain a party even where it lacked popular support.

As fall neared, all eyes turned to the state elections under way in the
North. In September the Republicans easily won contests in Vermont and
Maine. In October the Republicans carried Pennsylvania by thirty-two
thousand votes and Indiana by ten thousand. Acknowledging the inevitable,
Douglas headed south to preach against secession. He need not have bothered; a section-wide scare over rumors of slave insurrections had turned the
region into an armed camp by the time of the presidential election. Militias
assembled, and two persons were hanged on suspicion of inciting the slaves
to revolt.[401] The verdict surprised no one. Lincoln obtained at least a plurality
in every northern state, thus winning the section's 180 electoral votes and the
presidency (he received clear majorities in all of these states except California, Oregon, and New Jersey). Breckinridge won the lower South, John Bell

399. Nevins, *Emergence of Lincoln,* 2:280, 290 (September 21, 1860).
400. Ulrich B. Phillips, ed., *The Correspondence of Robert Toombs, Alexander H. Stephens and
Howell Cobb,* 2 vols. (Washington, D.C.: Annual Report of the American Historical Association, 1911, 1913), 2:514.
401. Nevins, *Emergence of Lincoln,* 2:311.

took the border states, and Douglas was left with only Missouri. Yet the verdict was less clear than it first appeared. Lincoln won Indiana with the support of only 51 percent of the voters; in his own Illinois he garnered just over 50 percent. He failed to obtain 40 percent of the national vote—350,000 fewer votes than the combined total of Douglas and Breckinridge. There were other weak links in Lincoln's victory as well. It was of course sectional, as his name did not even appear on the ballot in most southern states. Lincoln also did poorly in the urban North. Of the section's eleven largest cities, he managed to obtain a majority in only four. German and Irish Catholics proved particularly unsympathetic to Republican overtures.[402] Democrats appeared to be on their way to winning back the House of Representatives.

Perhaps the most interesting aspect of the election of 1860 was that it may not have turned on slavery at all. Economic issues such as tariffs and homesteads played a critical role in key states.[403] While votes had been purchased with bribes in 1856, in 1860 they were obtained with promises of federal policies designed to enrich the voter. Yet only the tactics of 1856 were viewed as a threat to public virtue; those of 1860 were celebrated for promoting national development. Southerners looked at Republican enticements and wondered if the sort of realignment Democrats had feared since 1840 had taken place. With the lure of the tariff, homesteads, and improvements to rivers and harbors, the forces of centralization had just prevailed in a purely sectional election. There was no reason to think the appeal of these policies would decline in the future. Tariffs in particular promised to win thousands of votes in the urban North. For southerners, permanent minority status and confiscatory taxes seemed to beckon.

Even at that late date, there was still a market for moderation in the South. Breckinridge won only 45 percent of the southern vote—the rest had gone to either Douglas or John Bell. Following the election, some of the South's leaders began cooling their heels. Alexander Stephens of Georgia called on his section to drop its demand for a slave code and embrace the old Democratic doctrine of nonintervention in the territories.[404] The governors of Louisiana, North Carolina, and Georgia all declared that a Republican victory alone did not justify secession. Other factors mitigated against compromise. Hard feelings over the Brown raid continued to fester, particularly after it became known that one of the most wanted men in the country

402. Potter, *Impending Crisis*, 443.          403. Ibid., 430.
404. Johannsen, *Stephen A. Douglas*, 764.

had spent two years in the North openly raising money for his raid. Much of the elite of Boston insisted on making a martyr of the man following his execution (Henry David Thoreau called him an "angel of light").[405] Republicans also participated in the beatification of Brown—to the point that the party was widely identified with him in the South.

Many southerners feared that Republicans did not respect the limits imposed upon the federal government by the Constitution. Would they attempt to attack slavery in the South itself despite their protests to the contrary? Lincoln and Seward had struggled to overcome this perception; they failed to do so, at least as of November 1860. Rather than immediate abolition, southerners anticipated a policy of harassment that would involve everything from abolitionist postmasters to unsympathetic federal judges. Thus the warning of Virginia senator James Mason regarding the intentions of Republicans: "I do not mean by any immediate blow, by any present law; but it is their purpose, having obtained possession of the federal power, to use that power in every form to bring that social condition [slavery] to a close."[406]

Southerners also feared that it would be only matter of time before Republicans and their Free Soil allies in the Democratic Party enacted legislation prohibiting slavery throughout the territories. Robert Toombs of Georgia spoke of this concern in the Senate in January 1861. Casting the whole dispute in terms of property rights ("We demand of the common government to use its granted powers to protect our property as well as yours"), he proceeded to name the South's price: the right to emigrate to the territories with their slaves, punishment of those who stole slave property, northern cooperation with respect to fugitive to slaves, and a federal law punishing those who abetted invasions of other states.[407] There was also the issue of Congress's powers of taxation and appropriation. As J. H. Hammond of South Carolina put it in the Senate in early 1858, "what guarantee have we, when you have this government in your possession, in all its departments . . . that you will not plunder us with tariffs; that you will not bankrupt us with internal improvements and bounties on your exports?"[408]

---

405. Quoted in Nevins, *Emergence of Lincoln*, 2:98.
406. *Congressional Globe*, 36th Cong., 2d sess., December 1860, 30.1:35.
407. Ibid., 268–69. Jefferson Davis blamed secession on prohibition of slavery in the territories, the Republicans' disavowal of *Dred Scott*, and the election of a "sectional president." Jefferson Davis, *The Rise and Fall of the Confederate Government*, 2 vols. (New York: Thomas Yoseloff, 1888; reprint, New York: Sagamore Press, 1958), 1:83–85. In June 1862 Congress banned slavery in the territories. 12 *Stats at Large* 432 (June 19, 1862).
408. *Congressional Globe*, 35th Cong., 1st sess., March 4, 1858, Appendix, 27:70.

Southerners became even more disenchanted when they learned that proslavery forces had lost control of the Senate. The North now enjoyed a 36-30 majority, and with the departure of doughface senators such as William Gwyn (California) and G. N. Fitch (Indiana), Democratic control would depend on, of all people, Stephen Douglas. The admission of more states would only increase Republican influence. The South's last real check on federal power was gone. Northern Democrats might help hold the House (at least until 1863), but what good was that when they refused to go along with that most fundamental southern principle—a constitutional right to take slaves into the territories? And then there was the matter of the federal judiciary. How long would it be before Lincoln put some creative abolitionist like Salmon P. Chase on the Supreme Court? Southerners expected Republican-appointed judges to uphold bans on slavery enacted by territorial legislatures. They anticipated that *Dred Scott* would be ignored or reversed. Some feared that state laws barring free blacks from southern cities and states might be held invalid as impermissible regulations of commerce.

Nothing filled southerners with more fear than the prospect of Republican control of federal offices. "It is not hostile legislation we have most to fear," wrote one essayist, but "the insidious influence of the executive department, through its thousands of functionaries, sewing discord, insubordination and insecurity throughout the south."[409] The post offices proved to be a source of particular concern. Since the late 1830s postmasters had made a practice of quietly removing abolitionist tracts from the mail. With Lincoln's election, southerners feared that Republican postmasters would distribute antislavery materials in every southern town. Cassius Clay believed that through the effective use of patronage, Republicans could "revolutionize the slave states . . . in two administrations."[410] The *Charleston Mercury* hinted at the fear that may have really driven secessionists when it warned that the executive branch would use federal offices to split slaveholders and nonslaveholders in the South by offering jobs to the latter. "The thousands in every county, who look up to power, and make gain out of the future, will come out in support of the abolition government. . . . They will organize; and from being a Union party . . . they will become, like the government they

409. Quoted in Michael P. Johnson, *Toward a Patriarchal Republic: The Secession of Georgia* (Baton Rouge: Louisiana State University Press, 1977), 43.
410. Quoted in Eric S. Foner, *Free Soil, Free Labor, Free Men: The Ideology of the Republican Party before the Civil War* (New York: Oxford University Press, 1971), 123 (see also 314).

support, Abolitionists. The contest for slavery will no longer be one between the north and the south. It will be in the south, between the people of the south."[411] As one historian noted, secessionists were reluctant to make this argument out loud—although it was, in his view, the strongest argument they had—because it required publicly questioning southerners' allegiance to slavery.[412]

The profoundly fragile nature of slavery as a social institution greatly exacerbated southern fears of the possible effects of Republican activity in the South. Slavery had already retreated from those areas of Maryland and Delaware where its inefficiencies turned the eyes of men toward alternative means of obtaining wealth. Its negative effect on economic development was apparent to anyone who had traveled in both the North and the South. A conspiracy of silence had to be maintained throughout the entire region if the institution was to be maintained. Thus the fear of antislavery postmasters and newspapers: by merely speaking the truth about the inefficiency of slavery, they would undermine it and the power of the planter class in their respective states as well.

When southerners expressed concern over the capacity of federal officers to create trouble in the South, they won little sympathy from their opponents. Republicans newspapers did not help matters when they began to take a distinctly Jacksonian view of the party press; one editor declared that the "government may legitimately use its patronage and influence to encourage the growth of principals congenial with its own."[413] In a December 1860 letter, the president-elect insisted that he would not allow political considerations to affect his appointments.[414] On another occasion Lincoln predicted that the adhesive of office would hold the Union together: "were it believed that vacant places could be had at the North Pole, the road there would be lined with dead Virginians."[415]

Roads would be lined soon enough. Although talk of adjustment filled the air in late 1860, the fact that Congress did not meet until mid-December proved fatal. Recalling their failed effort to convene a sectional convention in 1850, southern radicals proceeded state by state. South Carolina went first;

411. *Charleston Mercury* of October 11, 1860, quoted in Johnson, *Toward a Patriarchal Republic*, 44.

412. See Johnson, *Toward a Patriarchal Republic*, 44–45.

413. Quoted in Foner, *Free Soil, Free Labor, Free Men*, 122.

414. *Works of Lincoln*, 4:151–52.

415. Quoted in Potter, *Impending Crisis*, 432.

it held elections for a state convention in mid-November and before Christmas had seceded from the Union. As members of Congress finally began trickling into Washington, the outgoing president greeted them with a rather hollow annual message. He denied that a state could secede and claimed that the federal government had no legal authority to take action if it did.[416] The first assertion was correct; the second was not. The difficulty of ratification undermines the claim that the states believed they were entering into a voluntary association. Did the Antifederalists labor furiously to prevent the formation of a league from which the states could withdraw at any time? They did not. Buchanan's plea of helplessness was less compelling—the use of force to prevent secession received express authorization from the Constitution, which empowered Congress to "suppress insurrections."[417]

When Congress convened in early December, each house turned to the secession crisis. A Senate committee of thirteen, headed by John Crittenden, proposed a constitutional amendment that purported to permanently ban federal interference with slavery in the states. The committee also suggested measures to reestablish the Missouri Compromise line, requiring compensation for slave owners when northern states prevented the recapture of fugitives, and an amendment barring emancipation in the capital without the consent of Virginia and Maryland. The committee rejected its own resolutions by a vote of 7-6. (Jeff Davis and Robert Toombs of Georgia voted with five Republican senators against the proposals.) In the House, a committee of thirty-three devised similar measures. Most were discarded, but both houses of Congress passed a constitutional amendment that purported to ban future amendments prohibiting slavery. It did not receive consideration from the states.[418]

Secession moved forward in early 1861. Conventions in Florida, Georgia, Alabama, Mississippi, Louisiana, and Texas all passed secession resolutions before February 1. In the upper South, the voters of Virginia, Kentucky, and Tennessee elected unionist majorities to their state conventions. As one historian pointed out, the unionist sentiment that remained in these

416. Richardson, *Messages and Papers of the Presidents*, 7:3163–67.

417. See Article I, Section 8. For analysis of the legality of both secession and the use of force to defeat the rebellion, see David P. Currie, *The Constitution in Congress: Descent into the Maelstrom, 1829–1861* (Chicago: University of Chicago Press, 2005), 230–43.

418. For the proposed measures, see *Congressional Globe*, 36th Cong., 2d sess., December 18, 1860, 30.1:114. For the text of the amendment, see 12 *Stats at Large* 251. None of the legislatures ratified the amendment.

states was conditional—it would last only as long as the federal government allowed the lower South to depart unmolested.[419] Congress went about its business, and after legislators from the seven seceding states left, that business was largely Republican. A new tariff with higher rates went through in March. Congress passed bills organizing the territories of Nevada, Colorado, and Dakota. Stephen Douglas pointed out that these acts said nothing about slavery and claimed that the Republicans were not firebrands after all, but by then it did not matter.[420] That spring southerners shelled Fort Sumter in the Charleston, South Carolina, harbor when the federal government refused to evacuate it. The new president responded by calling for seventy-five thousand troops to put down the rebellion. Virginia, Tennessee, North Carolina, and Arkansas promptly seceded from the Union. They joined a confederation that had already been formed by the states of the lower South. The Confederate States of America adopted a constitution that closely resembled that of the United States, with the government's powers subject to a variety of important restrictions.[421]

In leaving the Union, radical southerners believed they had no choice. As the *Montgomery Advertiser* explained, "Henceforth the [federal] government, with all its patronage and power, will be in the hands of the enemies of the Southern States." It predicted that abolitionists would use federal offices to rule the South; emancipation and possibly even race war, such as that which occurred in Haiti, would follow.[422] As the Augusta (Georgia) *Constitutionalist* put it, the federal government would soon "pass into the hands of that sworn enemy, and . . . African slavery, though panoplied by the federal Constitution, is doomed to a war of extinction. All the powers of a government which has so long sheltered it will be turned to its destruction. The only hope for its preservation, therefore, is out of the Union."[423] The hunter had become the hunted, and with his own weapons, to boot.

---

419. McPherson, *Battle Cry of Freedom*, 255.

420. See 12 *Stats at Large* 172 (February 28, 1861) (Colorado); ibid., 209 (March 2, 1861) (Nevada).

421. The Confederate constitution did not have a general welfare clause; it banned internal improvements except for navigational aids and river and harbor appropriations. A tariff power was granted, but the Confederate Congress was expressly banned from using it to "promote or foster any branch of industry." It also barred the president from removing lower-level executive branch employees without cause. The judiciary was weakened. See Emory, *Confederate Nation*, 307–22.

422. *Montgomery Advertiser*, November 10, 1860, quoted in the *New York Daily Tribune*, November 15, 1860, 7.

423. Quoted in Potter, *Impending Crisis*, 448.

# Conclusion

For seventy-two years the American experiment in constitutional government enjoyed enormous success. A handful of communities along the seaboard burgeoned into an industrial and agricultural colossus, well on its way to first place among nations. The Constitution and the government it established played a critical role in this process by ensuring the sanctity of contracts, clearing the stage of restrictions on trade, and encouraging innovation and entrepreneurship with patents, copyrights, trade routes, and the protection of capital. Adam Smith's description of the conditions that enabled Great Britain to prosper during the eighteenth century applied equally to antebellum America: "a general liberty of trade . . . the liberty of exporting, duty free, almost all sorts of goods which are the produce of domestic industry to almost any foreign country . . . the unbounded liberty of transporting them from any one part of our own country to any other . . . but above all, the equal and impartial administration of justice . . . which by securing to every man the fruits of his own industry, gives the greatest and most effectual encouragement to every sort of industry."[1] The American confederation derived much of its success from creating a duty-free area of enterprise larger than Britain or any other free nation on earth.[2]

The experiment began to unravel when its framework was forced to serve ends beyond its original purposes and stand as the government of a nation, at least in the territories. Americans moved beyond their original agreement in purchasing foreign territory and then found that they could not agree how to govern it. Fractures appeared when one side in this dispute refused to accept the prospect of losing the contest. The Supreme Court played a critical role in turning a disagreement over governance into cause for dissolving the Union. By converting what had been a dispute over the merits of legislation into an assault upon a constitutional "right," the Supreme Court invited southerners to turn a political loss into a breach of the constitutional contract and a cause for dissolution.

1. Adam Smith, *The Wealth of Nations* (London, 1776; New York: Knopf, 1991), 546.
2. Johnson, *History of the American People*, 531–32.

Debate over the causes of the Civil War has lasted, at the time of this writing, almost a century and a half. Even at the beginning of the twenty-first century, Americans subscribed to competing explanations for secession; a dwindling group continues to cite the growth of federal power as the cause, while others point to friction over slavery. The age of the dispute has done little to aid the claims of the former, which were dismissed almost as soon as they were offered. The future of slavery was the primary cause of the trepidation that led southerners to leave the Union. The secession resolutions of the states, comments of southern newspapers, and transcripts of congressional debates are replete with the conviction that a Republican-controlled national government would threaten the institution in the South itself.

Despite its longevity, this disagreement rests upon a fallacy. Secession was a product of both centralization and friction over slavery. The two worked together in bringing about the fracture of the Union. Slavery was the end to be protected, and maintenance of the limits on federal power was the means. A half-century of fractious disputes over the growing powers of the federal government ignited a small but stubborn fire of mistrust and contempt. The dispute over slavery turned what had been a smoldering coal into a conflagration. Southerners seceded out of fear for the future of slavery under a Republican-controlled federal government because of the increased potency of that government. The patronage available within the executive branch alone made the notion of risking the future under a Republican administration intolerable for many. Centralization also worsened sectional strife by raising the specter in southern minds of a Republican Party maintaining in perpetuity its hold on national power through the embrace of programs that appealed to the pecuniary interests of voters, i.e., tariffs, land grants, and river and harbor subsidies. That secession ultimately proved a mistake even from the perspective of radical southerners—it resulted in a war that laid waste to their region, the destruction of the Confederacy, and the abolition of slavery—cannot alter the fact that it was based upon a sincere calculation about the future of slavery under a northern-controlled national government.

Neither the folly of secession nor the tragedy of the Civil War and its six hundred thousand deaths supports the conclusion that the growth of federal power in antebellum America was a negative development. The Louisiana Purchase occurred only because Congress expanded its powers by construction. While the state ratifying conventions may not have known they were granting an unlimited power to purchase land, who could doubt that the purchase of Louisiana—as well as of Texas and the Mexican cession—provided benefits of incalculable value to the United States? If original intent is the standard by which expansions of federal authority are to be measured, then the statutes enacted by Congress under its commerce clause–based police power also qualify as examples of federal jurisdiction growing by construction beyond the national government's original assignment. Most if not all federally funded internal improvements also fell into this category. The obvious utility of these endeavors weakens the temptation to regret the growth of federal power. So does the fact that centralization achieved emancipation of the slaves (albeit indirectly) decades before this would have occurred without secession and war. That the growth of federal power proved a positive force overall does not lessen the significance of its destructive aspects, which revealed propensities within the federal system that remain evident a century and a half after secession. Only knowledge of these past malfunctions will enable us to ensure that our federal system serves the ends for which it was designed.

Despite the fact that the antebellum era saw the jurisdiction and influence of the federal government expand sharply, the period may still be properly designated an "age of strict construction." Early excesses in congressional appropriations were followed by a more restrained approach, and the novel method of interpretation implicit in acts such as the assumption of state debts fell out of favor almost as soon as it was offered. Yet if strict construction remained the dominant method of constitutional interpretation during the antebellum period, it did so in the face of resistance. On occasion, advocates of a broader approach to the Constitution succeeded. These forces developed interpretations of the commerce, territories, and bankruptcy clauses that aided the passage of distribution and bankruptcy acts, internal improvement subsidies, commercial regulations, and land grants that would have surprised, if not necessarily displeased, the ratifiers. By the 1850s original intent was under enormous pressure. Strict constructionists were unable to keep majorities in both houses of Congress from passing bills addressing subjects not found in the Constitution, such as education and the poor. While the dam maintained by originalists remained intact in 1861, it had developed a multitude of leaks.

The limits on federal authority saw erosion within the courts as well as in Congress. Both institutions possessed the right to determine the limits of their own jurisdiction, subject to correction by the states if they exceeded their rightful authority. The federal judiciary, like Congress, mastered the art of expanding its sphere without fatally offending those who could check it—the Eleventh Amendment being the lone exception to the success of the judges in that endeavor. Like their brethren in the legislative branch, members of the judiciary embraced interpretations devoid of any relationship with original intent in order to give novel readings to the clauses of the Constitution, thereby expanding their own authority. The *Dartmouth College* case and its progeny represent the most tangible and destructive example of this practice. In assuming the power to invalidate all state laws that impaired the value of corporate charters, the Supreme Court severely impaired the ability of the states to regulate their own corporations. With its commerce clause jurisprudence, the Court threatened to withdraw from the states the right to enact even "police legislation."

The first grievance listed in the Declaration of Independence was the Crown's penchant for invalidating the acts of colonial assemblies. The Supreme Court's excesses also struck at the right of Americans to govern themselves, at least if one views the power to enact laws as essential to the exercise of that right. Over a period of centuries the English-speaking peoples developed and refined representative institutions that advanced civilization by imposing the rule of law upon what had previously been a bleak existence for all but the strong. The Americans introduced to this process a judiciary armed with the power to invalidate laws passed by elected assemblies. This innovation proved a success when judges invalidated legislation that actually violated one of the constitutions governing the legislatures and Congress. When judges reached beyond their authority to invalidate critical laws even when they violated no constitution, they reintroduced arbitrary rule at the expense of representative government.

This is not to say that the Supreme Court lacked strict constructionists during the antebellum period; on the contrary, most of the justices aspired to adhere to the understanding of the Constitution evident in 1787–88. This group turned back efforts to invalidate all state laws regulating interstate and foreign commerce; it also limited the damage wrought by the *Dartmouth College* doctrine with its refusal to give a broad reading to the powers bestowed by corporate charters. It did not stop the judiciary's gradual assumption of a veto power over state laws affecting corporations and, to a lesser extent, commerce. John C. Calhoun's lament that strict construction was not "worth a farthing" seemed to apply with particular force to the judiciary, for the simple reason that jurists such as John Marshall and Joseph Story refused to embrace that method of interpretation.

The most destructive aspect of centralization during the antebellum period was the federal spoils system. It played a critical role in pushing secession forward during the winter of 1860–61. Even the refusal of Republicans to acquiesce in a right to carry slaves into the territories paled in comparison with the prospect of antislavery postmasters and newspapers in the South itself. (In seceding, southern states effectively renounced their claims to the territories.) Southern politicians raced to complete the process of secession before Lincoln's inauguration because they feared the power that antislavery federal officeholders could wield in their own states.

While the problem of patronage has nothing to do with constitutional construction, it played a critical role in advancing the growth of federal power, as it brought the reality of an overgrown and uncontrolled government home to every American. To be surveyed by a collector or postmaster in the exercise of one's right as a citizen to assemble; to have that right trampled by intruding legions of land office or customhouse workers; to find one's local newspaper riddled with the half-truths of administration editors; to see executive branch favorites prevail in the political arena over citizens of only local reputation—was to cede a portion of the right of self-government. By 1861 federal influence had penetrated into every corner of America to corrupt and warp its political life, from primary meetings on Long Island, to the newspapers of New Orleans, to the post offices that dotted the prairies. Just as the influence of the British Crown expanded in silence to undermine a Parliament that by law appeared supreme during the eighteenth century, executive branch jobs and contracts concentrated power in Washington during the nineteenth century, even as politicians and editors championed the rights of the states. Strict construction may have fought its competitors to a draw during the antebellum period, but the use of offices to control political activity in towns throughout America ensured that an age of constitutional conservatism was also one of political centralization.

# Selected Bibliography

Adams, John. *The Works of John Adams.* Edited by Charles Francis Adams. 10 vols. Boston, 1850–56.

Ames, Herman V., ed. *State Documents on Federal Relations.* Philadelphia, 1906.

Bailyn, Bernard, ed. *The Debate on the Constitution: Federalist and Antifederalist Speeches, Articles, and Letters during the Struggle over Ratification.* 2 vols. New York: Literary Classics of the United States, 1993.

———. *The Ideological Origins of the American Revolution.* Cambridge: Harvard University Press, 1967.

Baker, Jean H. *Affairs of Party: The Political Culture of Northern Democrats in the Mid-Nineteenth Century.* Ithaca: Cornell University Press, 1983.

———. *The Politics of Continuity: Maryland Politics from 1858 to 1870.* Baltimore: Johns Hopkins University Press, 1973.

Benton, Thomas Hart. *Thirty Years' View: A History of the American Government for Thirty Years, from 1820 to 1850.* 2 vols. New York: Appleton & Co., 1864.

Berger, Mark L. *The Revolution in the New York State Party Systems.* Port Washington, N.Y.: Kennikat Press, 1973.

Bergeron, Paul. *The Presidency of James K. Polk.* Lawrence: University Press of Kansas, 1987.

Bridges, Amy. *A City in the Republic: Antebellum New York and the Origins of Machine Politics.* Ithaca: Cornell University Press, 1984.

Calhoun, John C. *The Papers of John C. Calhoun.* Edited by Clyde N. Wilson. 28 vols. Columbia: University of South Carolina Press, 1959–2003.

Cole, Donald B. *Jacksonian Democracy in New Hampshire, 1800–1851.* Cambridge: Harvard University Press, 1970.

———. *Martin Van Buren and the American Political System.* Princeton: Princeton University Press, 1984.

———. *The Presidency of Andrew Jackson.* Lawrence: University Press of Kansas, 1993.

Coleman, John F. *The Disruption of the Pennsylvania Democracy, 1848–1860.* Harrisburg: Pennsylvania Historical and Museum Commission, 1975.

Commager, Henry Steele, and Samuel Eliot Morison. *The Growth of the American Republic.* 5th ed. New York: Oxford University Press, 1962.

Commager, Henry Steele, William Leuchtenberg, and Samuel Eliot Morison. *The Growth of the American Republic.* 6th ed. New York: Oxford University Press, 1968.

Cornell, Saul. *The Other Founders: Anti-Federalism and the Dissenting Tradition in America, 1788–1828.* Chapel Hill: University of North Carolina Press, 1999.

Cunningham, Noble E., Jr. *The Jeffersonian Republicans in Power: Party Operations, 1801–1809.* Chapel Hill: University of North Carolina Press, 1963.

Currie, David P. *The Constitution in Congress: Democrats and Whigs, 1829–1861.* Chicago: University of Chicago Press, 2005.

———. *The Constitution in Congress: Descent into the Maelstrom, 1829–1861.* Chicago: University of Chicago Press, 2005.

————. *The Constitution in Congress: The Federalist Period, 1789–1801*. Chicago: University of Chicago Press, 1997.

————. *The Constitution in Congress: The Jeffersonians, 1801–1829*. Chicago: University of Chicago Press, 2001.

————. *The Constitution in the Supreme Court: The First Hundred Years, 1789–1888*. Chicago: University of Chicago Press, 1985.

Dangerfield, George. *The Awakening of American Nationalism*. New York: Harper & Row, 1965.

————. *The Era of Good Feelings*. New York: Harcourt, Brace & World, 1952.

Elkins, Stanley, and Eric McKitrick. *The Age of Federalism*. New York: Oxford University Press, 1993.

Elliot, Jonathon, ed. *The Debates in the Several State Conventions on the Adoption of the Federal Constitution*. 5 vols. New York, 1836. Reprint, New York: Burt Franklin, 1968.

Ellis, Richard E. *The Union at Risk: Jacksonian Democracy, States' Rights and the Nullification Crisis*. New York: Oxford University Press, 1987.

Farrand, Max, ed. *The Records of the Federal Convention of 1787*. 4 vols. New Haven: Yale University Press, 1966.

Fehrenbacher, Don E. *The Dred Scott Case: Its Significance in American Law and Politics*. New York: Oxford University Press, 1978.

————. *The Slaveholding Republic*. Completed and edited by Ward M. McAfee. New York: Oxford University Press, 2001.

Filler, Louis. *The Crusade against Slavery, 1830–1860*. New York: Harper & Brothers, 1960.

Finkleman, Paul. *An Imperfect Union: Slavery, Federalism, and Comity*. Chapel Hill: University of North Carolina Press, 1981.

Fish, Carl. *Civil Service and the Patronage*. New York: Russell & Russell, 1963.

Formisano, Ronald P. *The Birth of Mass Political Parties: Michigan, 1827–1861*. Princeton: Princeton University Press, 1971.

————. *The Transformation of Political Culture: Massachusetts Parties, 1790s–1840s*. New York: Oxford University Press, 1983.

Gillette, William. *Jersey Blue: Civil War Politics in New Jersey, 1854–65*. New Brunswick: Rutgers University Press, 1995.

Haines, Charles Grove. *The Role of the Supreme Court in American Government and Politics, 1789–1835*. Berkeley and Los Angeles: University of California Press, 1944. Reprint, New York: Da Capo Press, 1973.

Haines, Charles Grove, and Foster Sherwood. *The Role of the Supreme Court in American Government and Politics, 1835–1864*. Berkeley and Los Angeles: University of California Press, 1957.

Hamilton, Alexander. *The Papers of Alexander Hamilton*. Edited by Harold C. Syrett and Jacob E. Cooke. 27 vols. New York: Columbia University Press, 1961.

Hargreaves, Mary W. M. *The Presidency of John Quincy Adams*. Lawrence: University Press of Kansas, 1985.

Holt, Michael F. *The Rise and Fall of the American Whig Party: Jacksonian Politics and the Onset of the Civil War*. New York: Oxford University Press, 1999.

Jefferson, Thomas. *Writings of Thomas Jefferson*. Edited by Paul Leicester Ford. 10 vols. New York: G. P. Putnam's Sons, 1892–1899.

Jensen, Merrill. *The Articles of Confederation: An Interpretation of the Social-Constitutional History of the American Revolution, 1774–1781*. Madison: University of Wisconsin Press, 1970.

Johannsen, Robert W. *Stephen A. Douglas*. New York: Oxford University Press, 1973.

Johnson, Paul. *A History of the American People*. New York: HarperCollins, 1998.

Ketcham, Ralph, ed. *The Antifederalist Papers and the Constitutional Convention Debates.* New York: Penguin Books, 1986.

Klein, Philip Shriver. *President James Buchanan.* University Park: Pennsylvania State University Press, 1962.

Levy, Leonard. *Original Intent and the Framers' Constitution: The Debate over Original Intent.* New York: Macmillan, 1988.

Lincoln, Abraham. *Abraham Lincoln: His Complete Works.* Edited by John G. Nicolay and John Hay. 12 vols. New York: Century Co., 1907.

Madison, James. *The Writings of James Madison.* Edited by Gaillard Hunt. 9 vols. New York: G. P. Putnam's Sons/Knickerbocker Press, 1908.

Main, Jackson Turner. *The Antifederalists: Critics of the Constitution, 1781–1788.* Chapel Hill: University of North Carolina Press, 1961.

Malone, Dumas. *Jefferson the President: First Term, 1801–1805.* Boston: Little, Brown, 1970.

———. *Jefferson the President: Second Term, 1805–1809.* Boston: Little, Brown, 1974.

Martis, Kenneth C. *The Historical Atlas of Parties in the United States Congress, 1789–1989.* New York: Macmillan, 1989.

McCormick, Richard P. *The Second American Party System: Party Formation in the Jacksonian Era.* Chapel Hill: University of North Carolina Press, 1966.

McCoy, Drew R. *The Elusive Republic: Political Economy in Jeffersonian America.* Chapel Hill: University of North Carolina Press, 1980.

McDonald, Forrest. *States' Rights and the Union: Imperium in Imperio, 1776–1876.* Lawrence: University Press of Kansas, 2000.

McKee, Thomas Hudson. *The National Conventions and Platforms of All Political Parties, 1789–1905.* Baltimore: Friedenwald Co., 1906. Reprint, New York: Da Capo Press, 1971.

McPherson, James M. *Battle Cry of Freedom: The Civil War Era.* New York: Oxford University Press, 1988.

———. *Ordeal by Fire.* Vol. 1, *The Coming of the Civil War.* New York: McGraw-Hill, 1981.

Miller, John C. *The Federalist Era.* New York: Harper & Row, 1960.

Morris, Richard B. *The Forging of the Union, 1787–1789.* New York: Harper & Row, 1987.

Morrison, Chaplain W. *Democratic Politics and Sectionalism: The Wilmot Proviso Controversy.* Chapel Hill: University of North Carolina Press, 1967.

Nevins, Allan. *The Emergence of Lincoln.* Vol. 1, *Douglas, Buchanan, and Party Chaos, 1857–1859.* New York: Charles Scribner's Sons, 1950.

———. *The Emergence of Lincoln.* Vol. 2, *Prologue to the Civil War, 1859–1861.* New York: Charles Scribner's Sons, 1951.

———. *Ordeal of the Union.* Vol. 1, *Fruits of Manifest Destiny, 1847–1852.* New York: Charles Scribner's Sons, 1947.

———. *Ordeal of the Union.* Vol. 2, *A House Dividing, 1852–1857.* New York: Charles Scribner's Sons, 1949.

Nichols, Roy Franklin. *The Disruption of American Democracy.* New York: Macmillan, 1948.

Peterson, Merrill D. *The Great Triumvirate: Webster, Clay and Calhoun.* New York: Oxford University Press, 1987.

———. *The Jefferson Image in the American Mind.* New York: Oxford University Press, 1959.

Peterson, Norma Lois. *The Presidencies of William Henry Harrison and John Tyler.* Lawrence: University Press of Kansas, 1989.

Poore, Ben Perley. *Reminiscences of Sixty Years in the National Metropolis.* 2 vols. Philadelphia: Hubbard Brothers, 1886.

Potter, David M. *The Impending Crisis, 1848–1861.* New York: Harper & Row, 1976.

Rayback, Joseph G. *Free Soil: The Election of 1848.* Lexington: University Press of Kentucky, 1970.

Presser, Stephen B. *The Original Misunderstanding: The English, the Americans and the Dialectic of Federalist Jurisprudence.* Charlotte, N.C.: Carolina Academic Press, 1991.

Prince, Carl. *The Federalists and the Origins of the U.S. Civil Service.* New York: New York University Press, 1977.

———. *New Jersey's Jeffersonian Republicans: The Genesis of an Early Party Machine, 1789–1817.* Chapel Hill: University of North Carolina Press, 1964.

Rayback, Joseph G. *Free Soil: The Election of 1848.* Lexington: University Press of Kentucky, 1970.

Remini, Robert V. *Henry Clay: Statesman for the Union.* New York: W. W. Norton, 1991.

———. *Martin Van Buren and the Making of the Democratic Party.* New York: Columbia University Press, 1959.

Richardson, James D., ed. *A Compilation of the Messages and Papers of the Presidents, 1789–1897.* 10 vols. Washington, D.C.: U.S. Government Printing Office, 1896–1899.

Rossiter, Clinton, ed. *The Federalist Papers.* New York: Penguin Books, 1961.

———. *Seventeen Eighty-Seven: The Grand Convention.* New York: Macmillan, 1966.

Rutland, Robert A. *Ordeal of the Constitution: The Antifederalists and the Ratification Struggle of 1787–88.* Norman: University of Oklahoma Press, 1966.

———. *The Presidency of James Madison.* Lawrence: University Press of Kansas, 1990.

Schlesinger, Arthur M. "The State Rights Fetish." In *The Causes of the Civil War,* ed. Kenneth M. Stampp, 3d ed., 66–70. New York: Simon & Schuster, 1991.

Schlesinger, Arthur M., Jr. *The Age of Jackson.* Boston: Little, Brown, 1953.

Sellers, Charles. *The Market Revolution: Jacksonian America, 1815–1846.* New York: Oxford University Press, 1991.

Sharp, James Roger. *American Politics in the Early Republic: The New Nation in Crisis.* New Haven: Yale University Press, 1993.

Smith, Culver H. *The Press, Politics, and Patronage: The American Government's Use of Newspapers, 1789–1875.* Athens: University of Georgia Press, 1977.

Smith, Jean Edward. *John Marshall: Definer of a Nation.* New York: Henry Holt & Co., 1996.

Stampp, Kenneth, *America in 1857: A Nation on the Brink.* New York: Oxford University Press, 1990.

———, ed. *The Causes of the Civil War.* 1959. Reprint, New York: Simon & Schuster, 1991.

*Statutes at Large of the United States of America, 1789–1873.* 17 vols. Boston: Little, Brown, 1845–74.

Storing, Herbert J., ed. *The Complete Anti-Federalist.* 9 vols. Chicago: University of Chicago Press, 1981.

Story, Joseph. *Commentaries on the Constitution of the United States.* 2 vols. 4th ed. Boston: Little, Brown, 1873.

Summers, Mark W. "Dough in the Hands of the Doughfaces? James Buchanan and the Untameable Press." In *James Buchanan and the Political Crisis of the 1850s,* ed. Michael J. Birkner, 68–87. Annbury, N.J.: Associated University Press, 1996.

———. *The Plundering Generation: Corruption and the Crisis of the Union, 1849–1861.* New York: Oxford University Press, 1987.

Taylor, John. *Construction Construed and Constitutions Vindicated.* Richmond: Shepherd & Pollard, 1820.

———. *New Views of the Constitution of the United States.* Washington, D.C., 1823.

U.S. Congress. *Annals of the Congress of the United States, 1789–1824.* 42 vols. Washington, D.C.: Gales & Seaton, 1834–56.

———. *Register of Debates.* 14 vols. Washington, D.C.: Gales & Seaton, 1825–37.

Van Deusen, Glyndon G. *The Jacksonian Era.* New York: Harper, 1959.

Warren, Charles. *The Supreme Court in United States History.* 2 vols. Boston: Little, Brown, 1926.

White, Leonard D. *The Federalists: A Study in Administrative History.* New York: Macmillan, 1956.

———. *The Jacksonians: A Study in Administrative History, 1829–1861.* New York: Macmillan, 1954.

———. *The Jeffersonians: A Study in Administrative History, 1801–1829.* New York: Macmillan, 1956.

Williams, David C. *David C. Broderick: A Political Portrait.* San Marino, Calif.: Huntington Library, 1969.

Wood, Gordon S. *The Creation of the American Republic, 1776–1787.* Chapel Hill: University of North Carolina Press, 1969.

Wright, Benjamin Fletcher, Jr. *The Contract Clause of the Constitution.* Cambridge: Harvard University Press, 1938. Reprint, Westport, Conn.: Greenwood Press, 1982.

# Index

CPSIA information can be obtained at www.ICGtesting.com
Printed in the USA
BVOW05s2004280514

354686BV00001B/3/P